D1756781

Tradition and Innovation in French Garden Art

Penn Studies in Landscape
Architecture

John Dixon Hunt, Series Editor

This series is dedicated to the study and promotion of a wide variety of approaches to landscape architecture, with special emphasis on connections between theory and practice. It includes monographs on key topics in history and theory, descriptions of projects by both established and rising designers, translations of major foreign-language texts, anthologies of theoretical and historical writings on classic issues, and critical writing by members of the profession of landscape architecture.

Tradition and Innovation in French Garden Art

Chapters of a New History

Edited by
JOHN DIXON HUNT and MICHEL CONAN
With the assistance of Claire Goldstein

PENN

University of Pennsylvania Press

Philadelphia

Publication of this volume was supported by the Dean,
Graduate School of Fine Arts, University of
Pennsylvania.

10 9 8 7 6 5 4 3 2 1

Published by
University of Pennsylvania Press
Philadelphia, Pennsylvania 19104-4011

Library of Congress Cataloging-in-Publication Data

Tradition and innovation in French garden art :
    chapters of a new history / edited by John Dixon Hunt
    and Michel Conan ; with the assistance of
    Claire Goldstein.
        p. cm. — (Penn studies in landscape architecture)
    Papers from a symposium held at the University of
Pennsylvania.
    Includes bibliographical references.
    ISBN 0-8122-3634-3 (cloth : alk. paper)
    1. Gardens, French—History—17th century—
Congresses.   2. Gardens, French—History—18th
century—Congresses.   3. Gardens—France—
History—17th century—Congresses.   4. Gardens—
France—History—18th century—Congresses.
5. Landscape architecture—Netherlands—History—
17th century—Congresses.   6. Landscape
architecture—Netherlands—History—18th century—
Congresses.   I. Hunt, John Dixon.   II. Conan, Michel.
III. Goldstein, Claire.   IV. Series.
SB457.65 .T725 2002
712'.0944'09033—dc21

Contents

Preface

JOHN DIXON HUNT

In the absence of any modern history of French garden art and landscape architecture, this volume offers twelve chapters toward such an extended and up-to-date history. Their authors review some of the most interesting and innovative moments of French garden history in studies that trace a story from what is habitually taken as the golden age of French garden art in the late seventeenth century up to the immediate present, when a renaissance of French design theory and practice is clearly visible.

Why we lack any efficient and plausible narrative of the *longue durée* of French garden art may be explained in part by the concentration of so much energetic and enthusiastic research and writing upon the period dominated by André Le Nôtre. The dominance of this particular episode has meant that the larger story has been neglected; in particular, the quite remarkable and distinctively French episode of "natural," picturesque, or "English" gardening has never attracted the same attention and expertise as the earlier. But another explanation involves the difficulty of our deciding what shape to give to a full-scale narrative of French design once the "climax" of Le Nôtre has passed: how is a coherent story line to be found for the various interventions that followed that glorious moment in French garden art? For if Le Nôtre truly represented the high point of French garden art, as many in France have been encouraged to think, then its subsequent rejection or "decline" would demand far less serious attention. Yet even a superficial glance at the wealth of garden theory and practice during the late eighteenth and early nine-

teenth centuries, which is reviewed in this volume by Michel Baridon, David Hays, Yves Luginbühl, Joseph Disponzio, and Michel Conan, must call into question the conventional neglect of post–Le Nôtrean work.

While this volume deliberately seeks to draw into the spotlight French garden design outside the seventeenth century, it still does not propose a seamless or even a continuous narrative; above all, it does not subscribe to a history of progress and improvement that seems to be required of garden narratives. Rather, it seizes other opportunities by asking each author to focus upon a significant moment without needing to conform to some holistic narrative of progression. We allow ourselves to read the different moments of garden art in relation to a whole cluster of cultural concerns, which change with the time and place of the garden discussed; overall, this has meant invoking town planning, engineering, optics, scientific and philosophic movements, bourgeois ethics, foreign imports, vernacular workings of the land, the rise of professional landscape practice, even the modernist refusal to recognize the garden itself as the prime site of intervention in the landscape. That contextual emphasis in its turn is based upon the shared assumption that our chapters will transgress disciplinary boundaries: granted that the "garden" itself is a discipline, it has proved constantly necessary to extend our enquiries into a range of social histories and into the history of the representation of nature. The offer, then, of chapters for a fresh history identifies a series of milestones by which the evolution of French garden art may begin to be measured; each milestone succeeds the other in a rhythm and with a logic that is local and contingent.

Le Nôtre clearly retains his fundamental place in this story: most familiarly, in Hamilton Hazlehurst's invocation of new archival material from Dampierre for his continuing analysis of optical effects in Le Nostre's work (Hazlehurst retains the original spelling of the architect's name). But in Chandra Mukerji's essay, extending her work in *Territorial Ambitions and the Gardens of Versailles* (1997), and in Elizabeth Hyde's innovative examination of the flower culture of Louis XIV, we see Le Nôtre situated in a much more extensive field of ideas and practices, with gardens as a prime expression of political and cultural forces. If Le Nôtre has now to be positioned vis-à-vis both military engineering and horticultural technology, his work only gains in richness and scope, and his garden work assumes a more nuanced place within an intricate material culture and a complex national agenda.

The chapters that address garden practice and theory after the seventeenth century have less conventional assumptions to work with (or against). As Michel Baridon's opening paragraph forcibly reminds us, the final decades of the *ancien régime* saw an astonishing explosion of new garden work, work which five contributors to this volume explore in different ways. Here our contributions must attend most to innovations in French garden art, but some surprising continuities lurk beneath the surface—not least transformations in the private experience of gardens from the old world of Le Nôtrean design, where Hazlehurst strikingly draws out the individual visitor's responses to spatial forms, to the bourgeois culture for which Gabriel Thouin was writing. Nor are these continuities only diachronic: one general theme that emerges, unscripted and undirected, but with considerable force, from all these essays is the intersection at every period of French garden theory and practice of the public and private, of the then and

now (whenever "now" is taken to be), of professional and amateur, of garden art *tout pur* and the larger landscape of agriculture and forestry, of city and country, and (not least) of aesthetics and politics. These will be, we think, the issues for new narratives of the French garden that will build upon our discussions; just as we have extended the thinking of previous historians in the field, so we hope that our new chapters will stimulate fresh explorations of an important history.

We end this collection with the reflections of a contemporary practitioner. Bernard Lassus takes the French word *histoire* in its double sense of history and story. *Histoires* as stories, scenarios for contemporary garden visiting, cannot evade their own position in the *histoire* or narrative of French garden history extending over several centuries and in different cultural situations. The current practitioner has always to confront the twin demands on his own work of tradition and innovation, of convention and continuity, on the one hand, and of new departures and fresh formulations, on the other. But in a country which has both an impressive record of garden making as well as an equally radical reputation for artistic invention, today's designer has even more responsibility than his predecessors for tomorrow's gardens and their visitors.

All the chapters here collected were first delivered as talks at a symposium organized at the University of Pennsylvania under the joint sponsorship of the Graduate School of Fine Arts, the French Institute for Culture and Technology, and the Morris Arboretum of the university. Since then the papers have been exhaustively revised (and in two cases translated), a process that frustrates expectations of a speedy access to the symposium's deliberations but which in fact transforms the original papers into valuable proposals for further historical discussion and enquiry. Support for this publication is warmly acknowledged from Dean Gary Hack of Penn's Graduate School of Fine Arts and from the Department of Landscape Architecture and Regional Planning.

1. The Cultivation of a King, or the Flower Gardens of Louis XIV

ELIZABETH HYDE

In his portrait of the French court at the end of the seventeenth century, the duc de Saint-Simon assessed the contributions and career of André Le Nôtre on the occasion of the gardener's death. In touting the architectural genius of Le Nôtre, Saint-Simon claimed that the gardener dismissed the importance of the parterre in the French garden: "He said of parterres, that they are only for nursemaids who, unable to leave their children, promenade in [the parterres] with their eyes and admire them from the third floor."[1] Le Nôtre's purported slight against the parterre is hardly surprising. After all, the parterre was merely a building block in the larger architectural scheme of his creations. But it would be a mistake to interpret Saint-Simon's words as evidence that parterres and the plants with which they were constructed were in any way unimportant or insignificant in the royal gardens of Louis XIV.

Historians of Versailles have made known a few scattered accounts of floral excesses committed by Louis XIV. The planting plan for the border or *plate-bande* of the Trianon gardens, for example, with its requisite 96,000 plants,[2] and Saint-Simon's account of the king and his courtiers being driven from the Trianon gardens because the air there was so heavily scented by jasmine and tuberose blossoms[3] have become familiar enough that they have ceased to amaze. But the study of royal financial records and archival documents concerning the king's gardens confirms that, whether or not Le Nôtre approved of the parterres that held them, plants, and specifically flowering plants, were more plentiful and more important to Louis XIV's gardens and the king's iconographical program than has been assumed. Indeed, they were deemed so vital that flowers were subjected to the same Colbertian mercantilistic treatment as the king's "artisans of glory" (to borrow Orest Ranum's elegant phrase)[4] devoted to the production of medals, tapestries, and paintings.

In the late sixteenth century, many new varieties of flowers were imported into western Europe. They immediately captured the attention of erudite and wealthy men for whom the collection of interesting historical artifacts, coins, medals, books, paintings, and natural history phenomena had become a favorite pastime. These "curious florists," as they called themselves, amassed collections of flowering plants which they displayed in their gardens, waxed poetic about in their flower gardening manuals, and traded with their peers. Some collectors coveted a particular species and set about acquiring different varieties of that flower; others attempted to obtain specimens of as many different species as possible. Fashion dictated a fairly limited number of worthy flowers called "florists' flowers"; tulips, anemones, ranunculi, auriculas, narcissi, iris, carnations, and hyacinths, as well as particularly fragrant flowers such as jasmines and tuberoses were those deemed most desirable. These flowers became the focal point for collectors and for the flower parterre. Planted in the garden, they demonstrated that the master of the house was not only conscious of the latest trends, but also wealthy enough to afford such blossoms, and sufficiently curious about Nature and the art of improving it to acquire and cultivate them.

Flowers conferred all of these qualities on Louis XIV and his gardens, too, although in the capable hands of the king's ministers and gardeners, such flowers became anything but rare in the royal flower beds. Through flower purchases recorded in royal account books, it is possible to discern some idea of the large scale of floriculture undertaken by the king's gardeners. Flower purchases for Versailles began as soon as the gardens began to be used for staging the fêtes of 1664 and 1668. In 1668, for example, such purchases were first recorded in the *Comptes des bâtiments* when 400 Spanish jasmines ("jasmins d'Espagne") were sold to the king, along with 420 carnations and 12,000 tulip bulbs intended for the Tuileries gardens.[5] Floral expenditure accelerated into the 1670s, especially with the expansion of the royal gardens at Versailles and the construction of the *Trianon de porcelain*, which was celebrated especially for its fragrant flowers. In 1670, for example, 545 jasmines and tuberoses and 7,560 jonquils were purchased.[6] In 1672, 2,000 more jonquils and 10,000 tuberoses were added,[7] and 6,400 tuberoses and 7,000 narcissi were purchased for the royal gardens in 1674 and 1675.[8]

Flower purchases continued at such a pace until they dramatically increased in the mid-1680s, most likely because of the enlargement of the Trianon gardens and the subsequent construction of Marly. In 1686 alone, for example, the king reimbursed gardeners for more than 165,000 flowers (table 1).[9] Purchases in the following year were almost as impressive. In 1687, more than 96,500 flowering bulbs and plants were acquired (table 2).[10] Much of the floral expenditures in the 1680s were intended for the newly expanded gardens at the Trianon palace. But by 1690, similar numbers of flowers were purchased to furnish the royal gardens at Marly. To fill the parterres at Marly, more than 163,900 flowers and 144 cases of tulips[11] were purchased in 1690 (table 3).[12]

The massive expenditure for flowers intended for the gardens at Trianon and Marly in the 1680s and 1690s suggests that the majority of flowers to be found in the gardens of Versailles were indeed planted in the parterres of Trianon and Marly. Indeed, between 1668 and 1710, for almost 30 percent of the total number of flowers purchased for

the royal gardens, royal accounts identified the gardens at Trianon as the destination of the specimens purchased. Twenty-four percent were intended for Marly.[13] But, according to the accounting records, flowers were included in other royal gardens as well, among them Choisy, Clagny, Fontainebleau, the Orangery at Versailles, the pépinière du Roule, the Jardin des Plantes, the Tuileries, and Saint-Cyr. Flowers were also occasionally incorporated into various *bosquets* in the main park of the Versailles gardens. In 1690, for example, 600 hepaticas and 750 primroses were planted in the *salle du conseil*, to which were added 100 auriculas in 1691 and various flowering bulbs in 1692.[14] And the *salle du bal* was filled with 100 double *giroflées*, 300 double *oeillets*, and 2,150 double white juliennes in 1691.[15] Thus while flowers at Versailles were heavily concentrated at the Trianon and Marly, the larger park of Versailles and parterres at other royal palaces were hardly devoid of flowers.

The large numbers of flowers planted in the royal gardens were matched by the large number of species represented in them (table 4). The lengthy list of flowering plants and shrubs included in the royal gardens included all of the prominent and fashionable "florists' flowers"—the tulips, anemones, crown imperials, hyacinths, irises, carnations, ranunculi, and auriculas highly desired by collectors. But the royal parterres were also furnished in a

Table 1. Sampling of Flower Purchases in 1686

Assorted flowering bulbs	105,850
Cyclamen	4,000
Double jonquils	10,050
Hyacinths	9,313
Jonquils	1,200
Orange lilies	2,000
Primulas	2,000
Ranunculi	18,850
Tuberoses	1,765
Tulips	10,000

Table 2. Sampling of Flower Purchases in 1687

Auriculas	1,000
Crocuses	13,900
Double carnations	2,350
Double juliennes	1,180
Double veroniques	6,700
Fritillaries	1,800
Hyacinths	30,650
Irises	7,100
Marguerites	7,850
Narcissi	20,000
Primulas	3,975

Table 3. Flowers Purchased for Marly in 1690

Double violet juliennes	300
Double orange hyacinths	1,604
Irises	1,075
Narcissi	148,850
Oculus Christi	3,650
Single orange hyacinths	1,300
Spanish carnations	1,100
Tulips	144 cases
Valerians	1,100

Table 4. Flowering Plants and Bulbs Purchased for Royal Gardens

Anemones, single	Hepaticas, double	Pansies
Anemones, double	Honeysuckle	Pasque flowers, single
Auriculas	Hyacinths, single	
Bellflowers	Hyacinths, double	Pasque flowers, double
Cornflowers	Irises	
Crocuses	Jasmines	Peonies
Crown imperials	Jonquils, single	Primulas
Cyclamens	Jonquils, double	Ranunculi
Eglantines	Lilacs	Roses
Everlastings	Lilies	Snowdrops
Feverfew	Marguerites	Sweet rockets
Girofleés, single	Narcissi, single	Tuberoses
Girofleés, double	Narcissi, double	Tulips
Hellebores	*Oculus Christi*	Valerian
Hepaticas, single	*Oeillets*	Veroniques

diversity of flowering species extending beyond the "florists' flowers." Thus while the king's collection of flowers easily conformed to the dictates of fashion, the variety of plants included demonstrates a desire to keep the royal parterres filled with blossoms even when the predominantly spring-flowering bulbs had finished blooming.

The list also demonstrates Louis XIV's partiality to fragrant flowers. Great numbers of tuberoses, jasmines, and narcissi, all celebrated for their perfume, were planted in the Trianon gardens. A small pavilion known as the "cabinet des parfums" was constructed in the gardens in 1671 in which courtiers could take respite from the sun and, more importantly, experience the fragrances emitted by the king's flowers, perhaps to be convinced of the king's power by the overwhelming scents.[16] The Parisian journal *Mercure Galant*, founded by Jean Donneau de Visé, described for its readers the 1686 visit of the ambassador of Siam to Versailles. While there, according to the report, the ambassador and his entourage toured the Trianon gardens and the cabinet des parfums, which "pleased them extremely, because they love strong odors, & they admire the manner of perfuming with flowers."[17] That the ambassador, who hailed from the exotic

and legendarily floral and fragrant lands to the East, was impressed by the French king's flowers was seen as a high compliment indeed.

Particularly rare florists' flowers were acquired for the king's private gardens (fig. 1). The king's private parterre in the expanded gardens of the Trianon de Marbre, accessible only through the apartments of the king and Madame de Maintenon, was described by Le Nôtre himself as a "private garden, which is always full of flowers that are changed every season in the pots, and one sees neither dead leaves nor shrubs that are not in flower."[18] The author of *Les Curiositez de Paris, de Versailles, de Marly, de Vincennes, de S. Cloud, et des environs* described it as a place "filled with the rarest and most beautiful flowers in all seasons, [which] persuades winter not to approach."[19] For this special garden, anemones, double wallflowers, cyclamens, and 26,290 hyacinths, some of which were described as "very rare," were purchased in 1688 and 1689.[20] A special planting of rare flowers was similarly attempted at Marly. In 1700, flower gardener Jean Loitron was charged with the "maintenance, planting, and cultivation of rare and other flowers in the new garden of Marly," while 1,500 livres were expended to acquire "rare flower bulbs."[21] Although the garden languished in poor growing conditions,[22] an additional 2,000 livres were spent annually on the Marly collection between 1703 and 1706 for other flowers specifically designated as "rare."[23]

The sheer number of flowers incorporated into the royal gardens suggests that flowers were important to the conception of the gardens; their importance is further demonstrated by the degree to which the king's ministers and gardeners went to acquire the flowers needed to fill his gardens. The British traveler Martin Lister concluded his description of Marly writing, "I could not refrain from saying to the Duke of Villeroi, who was pleased to accompany me much in this walk, that surely all the gardens of France had contributed to furnish this profusion of flowers."[24] His compliment was, in fact, based in truth. The provision of flowers for Marly and, indeed, all of the royal gardens required not only great amounts of money to acquire specimens from all over the country and the world, but also the organization of flower cultivation on a grand scale. The flowers favored by the king and his gardeners for use in the royal gardens were expensive and not easily found in the numbers needed to furnish the lushly planted parterres. It was thus necessary for Louis XIV and Colbert both to seek flowers from wherever they were available and to

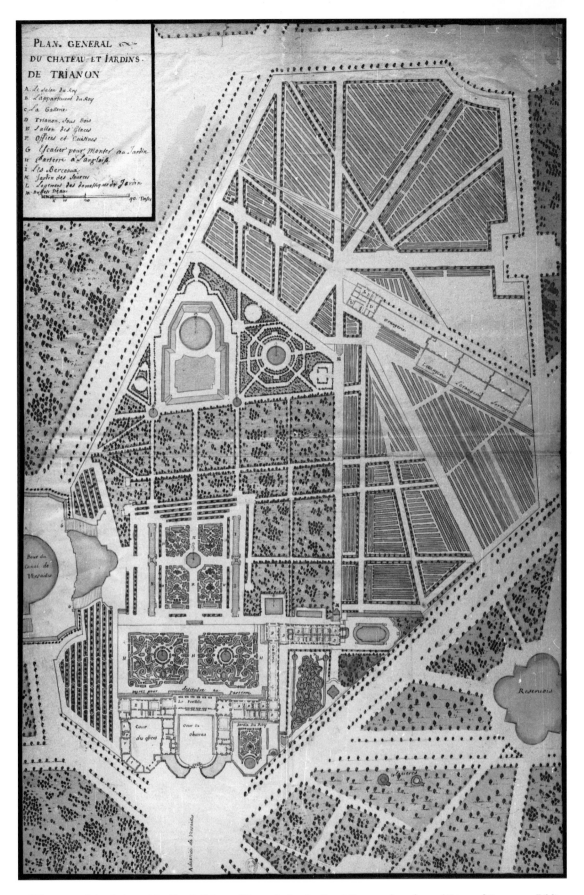

1. "Plan general du chateau et jardins de Trianon [General plan for the château and gardens of Trianon]," ca. 1700. Bibliothèque Nationale de France, cliché H 186631.

set about creating a supply structure to assure that the king's gardens would be kept in blossom at all times.

Flowers for the royal gardens were acquired from numerous *fleuristes*, gardeners, and traders in Paris and all over France. In 1670, for example, a member of the Trumel family of gardeners was reimbursed for flowers purchased in Toulon, Lyon, and Marseille,[25] while Isaac Blandin bought for the royal gardens 7,560 jonquils from Caen in northern France.[26] In the same year, orange trees, jasmines, and tuberoses were brought from Lyon to the pépinière du Roule.[27] During the following years, orange trees for the Trianon were acquired in Orléans, while additional oranges for the royal gardens were found in Berny.[28] Octavian Henry bought 10,000 tuberoses from Avignon.[29] In 1685, cyclamens and lilies were gathered in Dauphiné, Auvergne, and Savoye by Pierre Trutry for the Trianon,[30] while M. Chauvelin, the intendant of Picardy and Artois, forwarded hepaticas, cornflowers ("jassées"), pansies, and bellflowers to the king in 1687.[31] From Normandy, 16,300 ranunculi and 50 double anemones were imported in 1688.[32]

The king was also interested in gathering botanically interesting and rare flowers for his collection. For that purpose he dispatched his *fleuristes* and *curieux* farther afield, armed with the king's purse, to search for specimens. In 1673, a Sieur Subleau, *trésorier général des galères*, was reimbursed for money spent "to purchase books, flowers, and other curiosities from the Levant for the service of His Majesty."[33] Subleau was again paid in 1675 for the purchase of flowers and animals.[34] American specimens were sought for the collections in the more botanically inclined Jardin du Roi in Paris. A "bill for a box of plants and seeds for the garden of the king" sent on board the ship *La Marie* from Guadaloupe to the Marquis de Villacerf (the *surintendant*) in 1698 listed twenty-five different plants including white and red lilies, musque, and acacia.[35] Native French specimens were also sought for the king's gardens. Pierre Truitté was paid in 1689 for "flowering plants that he was going to search for on the mountains of Dauphiné and Piedmont for the garden at Trianon."[36]

This complex network of acquisition was not enough, however, to keep the royal gardens full. To compensate for its shortcomings and significant expense, the king and his first minister set in place, in typical Colbertian fashion, a system of nurseries that became the largest suppliers of flowers, flowering shrubs, and trees to the royal gardens. Louis XIV's first step came in 1669 with the enlargement and unification of a series of small nurseries (*pépinières*) in Paris known as the pépinière du Roule. Located in the faubourg Saint-Honoré where Claude Mollet, gardener to both Henri IV and Louis XIII, and Claude's son André had established their own nurseries and gardens,[37] the royal nursery became an impressive garden in its own right. Martin Lister reported:

At my return to Paris, I was shewn the pipiniere [*sic*], or royal nursery of plants in the Fauxbourgh St. Honoire, by M. Morley, who is master of it, and one of the ushers of the king's bed-chamber. . . . This ground, inclosed with high walls, is extremely large, as it ought to be for the supply of the king's gardens; several acres were planted with pines, cypresses, &c. and there were vast beds of bulbous roots and the like. I found but little difficulty in crediting his assertation, that in the space of four years, he had sent to Marli, eighteen millions of tulips and other bulbous flowers. He also told me that in furnishing the Trianon (a peculiar house of pleasure) with its parterres, . . . with flowerpots every fourteen days during the season, required not less than thirty-two [thousand] pots from this nursery.[38]

Lister's account of the *pépinière* illustrates the immensity of this horticultural operation. The gardeners of the *pépinière* gathered seeds, bulbs, and young trees from sources all over France and even abroad.[39] Once bulbs could support flowers, or the fruit trees bear fruit, they were dispatched to the numerous royal gardens including Versailles, the Trianon, Marly, Clagny, the Tuileries, and Fontainebleau.

By the eighteenth century, the *pépinière* had become so successful that it even entertained requests for shrubs, flowering trees, and flowers from nobility residing in and around Paris, although most requests were refused as the royal gardens took priority over all the others.[40] Yet in supplying plant material for the primary royal gardens, the nursery system was so effective that additional (though smaller) royal nurseries were constructed behind the Trianon de Marbre and at Marly. By 1705, a four-story structure called the Château neuf de Trianon was erected in the expanded nursery plots at the Trianon. The size of the building, together with the distribution of its space, illustrates the sophistication of the Trianon nursery operation. Two adjoining rooms on each of the four floors were given over to the "Inspecteur des Bastiments," but the majority of the building served the gardens. The basement level was dominated by a large orangery, although it is not apparent from

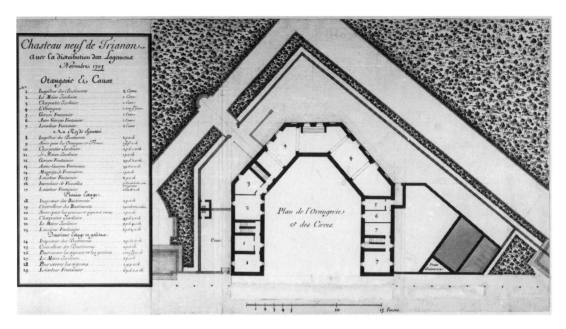

2. "Plan de l'Orangerie et des Caves [Plan of the Orangery and Cellars]," 1705. Bibliothèque Nationale de France, cliché H 186658.

the plan how the plants received light (fig. 2). On the rez de chausée could be found a spacious *serre*, or greenhouse, for orange trees and flowers. The first floor, too, contained a heated room, this one specially for seeds and rare bulbs (fig. 3). Most of the top floor consisted of a *serre*, complete with skylights, to keep seeds and bulbs warm and dry, to force flowers out of season, and to winter over exotic or delicate flowers (fig. 4).

The most enterprising innovation of Jean-Baptiste Colbert and Louis XIV, however, was the purchase in 1681 and 1682 of a piece of land in Toulon on the French Mediterranean coast, for 11,540 livres[41] for the purpose of "raising flowering bulbs for furnishing every year the gardens of the royal household."[42] During the reign of Louis XIV, Toulon served as an important royal naval base. The royal presence meant that communications networks and personal connections between the king's administration and Toulon were already in place, which, together with the city's proximity to southern (and therefore climatically milder) flower-growing markets, made it an ideal location for a royal acquisition center. In addition, royal gardeners in the south of France could more effectively gather the tuberoses, jasmines, narcissi, and hyacinths that were usually acquired from southern sources. The garden in Toulon would thus serve the king by purchasing small bulbs and seeds and raising them to maturity, at which time they would be shipped to royal gardens in Paris and at Versailles. Another 8,192 livres was spent on the construction of the garden, walls to enclose it, sheds to hold supplies, and a house for the gardener.[43] An original plan of the garden indicates that the house was built at the head of the garden (fig. 5). On either side of the axis were three large square plots, each quartered and filled with parallel rows for planting. Gardening sheds were placed at the corners of the garden at the top near the house.[44]

In September 1683, De Vauvré, the *intendant de la marine* in Toulon, established projections for the number of bulbs he anticipated being able to send to the royal gardens (fig. 6). De Vauvré estimated that 65,000 bulbs could be provided for Trianon, Clagny, the Orangery at Versailles, the Tuileries, St. Germain, and the pépinière du Roule.[45] Among them were 30,000 tuberoses, 20,000 *narcisses de Constantinople*, 13,000 hyacinths, and 2,000 jonquils. In addition, De Vauvré expected that 800 livres would be needed for the day laborers to prepare the ground, plant the bulbs, and cultivate them; 400 livres for the inspector appointed to oversee the plantations and the packing of the bulbs for shipment; 300 livres for the wages of a gardener who would be sent from Paris; and 700 livres to pay for the packing and transport of the bulbs from Toulon to Lyon.[46]

The gardeners at Toulon initially had to acquire the immature bulbs and seeds that they hoped to

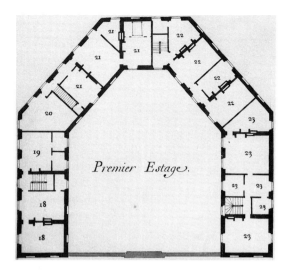

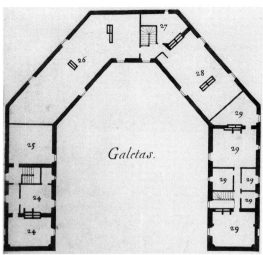

3. "Premier Estage [First Floor]," 1705. Bibliothèque Nationale de France, cliché H 186660.

4. "Galetas [Attics]," 1705. Bibliothèque Nationale de France, cliché H 186661.

increase for shipment to the royal gardens. For this they turned to local merchants and importers. An expense report from 1688 reveals that in that year 69 livres 10 sols were paid to Sieur Jean Michel, a French merchant living in Tunis, for 6,000 narcissi. The gardeners also reimbursed "various private citizens" for bulbs they had supplied. A man named Aubert and identified only as the "Consul de la Nation françoise" was reimbursed for 1,000 tuberoses and 6,000 Roman hyacinth bulbs.[47] Thus by taking advantage of the geographical location of Toulon, the king was able to buy flowers directly and more cheaply from southern sources.

As early as 1688, bulbs were indeed being packed and shipped from Toulon to Lyon. André Hermitte, a muledriver, was employed repeatedly during the 1680s and 1690s to transport cases of bulbs to Lyon, where they were handed over to Monsieur Du Bois, the "commissaire des guerres," who sent the bulbs on to Paris.[48] By 1691, the Toulon garden was shipping thousands of mature bulbs north to Paris from where they were distributed among several royal gardens, but especially to Trianon, the Tuileries, the pépinière du Roule, the Orangery at Versailles, and Fontainebleau.

Royal gardeners in Paris and at Versailles kept a close watch over the operations of the Toulon garden and expressed great concern for the quality of the bulbs that were being sent. In August 1693, for example, an accounting of the bulbs received at the Trianon was made in which the gardener noted that of the 5,500 *narcisses de Constantinople* received, 3,100 were too small to bear flowers that year,

as were a significant portion, maintained the gardener, of the totus albus, hyacinths, and jonquils.[49] A similar list was drawn up for the bulbs sent to the pépinière du Roule.[50] A royal gardener named Jacques Robert dispatched a letter on 12 August 1693 to Toulon, informing De Vauvré that the gardener in charge of raising the bulbs in Toulon was no longer to send those that could not bear flowers. Robert wrote that, in the future, cases of immature bulbs would be neither paid for nor counted.[51]

A more formal letter followed on 7 September 1693 from the *surintendant* (by this time Edouard Colbert, the Marquis de Villacerf) to De Vauvré in Toulon. The *surintendant* wrote, "I am obliged to inform you, Monsieur, that of the narcissus, Roman hyacinth, and jonquil bulbs amounting in all to 21,000, which were sent from Toulon last July 10, there are a great number of them that did not bear [flowers] because they are only *cayeux* which will not flower."[52] Colbert continued, imploring De Vauvré to be sure that the Toulon gardener complied with his request, as the cost of transporting the immature bulbs to Paris was greater than their value. As a final warning, he reminded De Vauvré, "By the establishment of this garden according to the memorandum that you sent to Monsieur de Louvois [on] 15 September 1683[,] you [agreed to] furnish every year 65,000 bulbs, [while] you furnished this year only 24,000 including 3,000 tuberoses, and the expense of the garden is the same [as originally projected]."[53]

Despite the complaints about the immature bulbs, the arrangement between the Toulon gar-

5. "Plan du Jardin du Roy a Toulon [Plan of the Garden of the King in Toulon]," ca. 1683. Centre historique des Archives nationales à Paris, O¹2124¹.

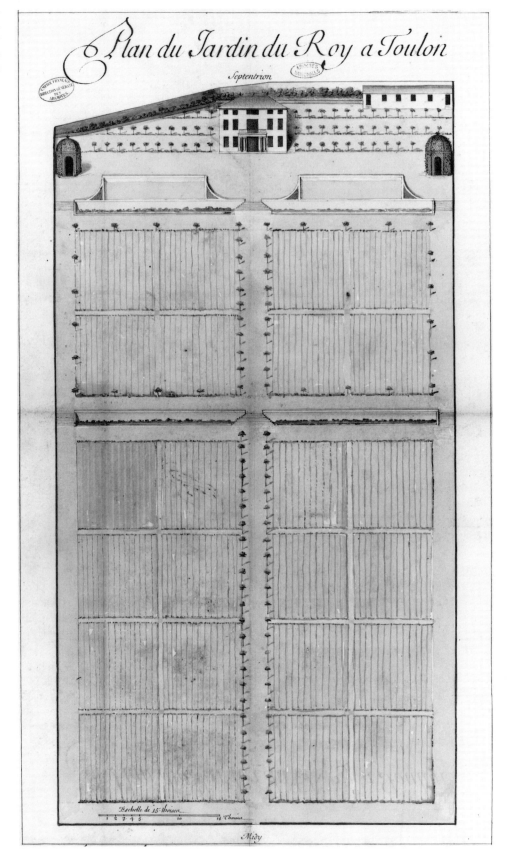

Toulon

Distribution des Oignons

de fleurs qui doivent estre fournir chaque année de la
Pepiniere de Toulon pour les Jardins des maisons Royalles
et letemps auquel Il les faut envoyer

Noms des maisons Royalles	Oignons de Thubereuse a envoyer au mois de feurier ou au premier de mars	Oignons de Narcisses de Constantinople a envoyer le premier Juillet	Oignons de Hyacinthe a envoyer le premier Juillet	Oignons de hyacinthe Delnin a envoyer le 1er juillet	Oignons de Jonquille a Envoyer le premier Juillet	Total des Oignons
Pour Trianon	8000	6000	4000			18000
Pour Clagny	8000	6000	1500			15500
Pour L'Orangerie deversailles	2000	2000	1500			5500
Pour les Tuileries	3000	2000	2000			7000
Pour St Germain et Duval	3000					3000
Pour Le Roule	4000	4000	3000	1000	2000	6000
Pour Envoyer ou il sera ordonné	2000					2000
Total	30000	20000	12000	1000	2000	65000

fait a Toulon le 15e Septembre 1683

6. "Distribution des oignons de fleurs qui doivent estre fournir chaque année de la Pepiniere de Toulon pour les Jardins des maisons Royalles [Distribution of the flowering bulbs which should be furnished each year from the Nursery of Toulon for the Gardens of the Royal Households]," 1683. Centre historique des Archives nationales à Paris, O[1]2102[1] cotte 4.

den and the royal gardeners endured, and the garden continued to supply flowering bulbs for the royal gardens to the apparent satisfaction of the king's gardeners. The contract with Toulon was renewed in 1697 and again in 1701.[54] The operation of the royal flower nursery in Toulon, then, demonstrates both the importance of flowers to the king's garden, and the inability of the French commercial flower market to meet the king's floral demands. That Colbert turned his mercantilistic principles of managing the national economy to the king's flower beds emphasizes how important flowers were deemed for the glorification of his patron.

Although the Toulon garden's bulbs were by their very nature ephemeral in comparison to the tapestries of Gobelin or the medals struck in the king's honor, the role played by flowers in celebrating Louis XIV's reign was central to the evocation of the notion that the age of Louis XIV was a Golden Age in French, even European, history. Flowers, as the very symbols of springtime, fertility, and the promise of abundance, suggested prosperity. Flowers had notably figured in the classical descriptions of the Golden Age. Ovid described the idyllic Golden Age in his *Metamorphoses* as "a season of everlasting spring, when peaceful zephyrs, with their warm breath, caressed the flowers that sprang up without having been planted."[55] And Virgil's prophetic "Fourth Eclogue" described the coming of a flower-filled second Golden Age. Addressing the child born to usher in the age, he wrote: "But for thee, child, the Earth untilled, as her first pretty gifts,/ Shall put forth straying ivy and foxglove everywhere,/ and arum lilies mingled with smiling acanthus flowers./ . . . Of themselves/ from the ground whereon thou liest shall spring flowers for their delight."[56] Seventeenth-century French engraved allegories of the four ages of civilization prominently featured flowers in representations of the Golden Age. Michel de Marolles, for example, depicted it as a young woman tending a beehive wearing a garland and crown of flowers. The accompanying caption explained, "[D]uring the Golden Age, the age dear to heaven,/ Flora is eternally crowned with roses."[57] Similarly, Nicolas Bonnart depicted flowers in his engraving of the Golden Age (fig. 7). The caption explained, "We represent [the Golden Age] under the emblem of a pretty and young girl simply dressed, caressing a lamb on which she has placed a garland of flowers."[58]

Louis XIV was hardly the only monarch to represent his reign as a Golden Age. The symbolism re-

lated to the Golden Age had been fully exploited in the panegyric literature dedicated to Elizabeth I in England, who had herself been represented as Flora, among other deities.[59] But, unlike earlier monarchs, Louis XIV had the floricultural capabilities to demonstrate the truth of his claim, to create in his gardens evidence of the Golden Age. His miraculous birth in 1638 had been celebrated as the fulfillment of Virgil's prophecy,[60] and as an adult king, his gardens were filled with the floral signs of eternal springtime. His gardens were a living garland crowning his rule. Surviving planting plans of the royal gardens, in addition to offering rare and intriguing information on seventeenth-century floriculture, support the notion that gardens were intended to impart the idea of that eternal springtime of the Golden Age. The Trianon plan for a *plate-bande* includes rows of tulips alternating with hyacinths and white narcissi; between the rows were planted series of perennials including juliennes, veroniques, sweet williams, orange hyacinths, cornflowers, pasque flowers, Spanish *oeillets*, and *violettes de mer* (fig. 8). The center row of the border garden, as Mark Laird has demonstrated,[61] was planted with a single row of taller perennials in series including feverfew, bellflowers, wallflowers (or tall carnations), white lilies, and valerian. The flowering bulbs of course bloomed in the spring, and the perennials not until later; the planting plan therefore illustrated what the garden would have looked like throughout the growing season.

A *plate-bande* for the gardens at Marly was designed according to a similar principle (figs. 9, 10). The "Memorandum on perennials, annuals, and flowering bulbs appropriate for furnishing the small side of the long avenue of the Royal Garden of Marly" includes instructions for keeping the garden in flower "in all seasons."[62] According to the plan, the border of the Marly garden was planted in alternating rows of flowering bulbs, annuals, and perennials. The bulbs were to be planted in a twelve-bulb sequence that included six different floral species of varying colors which the gardener expected to bloom in March, April, and May. The sequence called for a yellow narcissus, a pink and yellow tulip, a white narcissus, a blue or white hyacinth, a double white narcissus, a tulip, a narcissus, a pink and yellow tulip, a white narcissus, another blue or white hyacinth, a double white narcissus, and a tulip. Between the rows of flowering bulbs were sequences of annuals and perennials that, according to the accompanying notes, would bloom from April through November, and in some years, wrote the gardener, "to Christmas."[63] The variety

7. Nicolas Bonnart, "L'Aage d'or [Golden Age]." Bibliothèque Nationale de France, cliché C 1958.

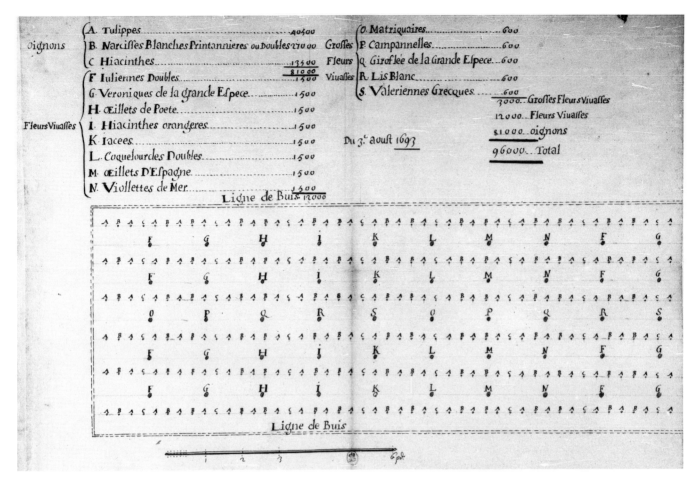

8. Planting plan for the Trianon garden, 1693. Bibliothèque Nationale de France, cliché B 11189.

of species included in the border was greater than in the Trianon border. Here the flowers were arranged in series of three, the only species common to each series being statice. The series included such groupings as purple *giroflée*, bicolor pansies, or auriculas, "basillique minor," and statice. White everlastings, pansies, white amaranth, double marguerites, silver *souci*, camomile, and single anemones were all incorporated into the garden. The plan demonstrates that the king's flower gardens were coordinated so that they would flower during the entire growing season and beyond. While we would not expect that the king's flower beds would have been empty at any time of the year, the planting plans reveal that the floral displays *were conceived* as continually flowering gardens—a living display of perpetual springtime.

The floral plantings in the king's gardens, carefully orchestrated to suggest that Louis was the harbinger of eternal prosperity, were fully exploited for their symbolic value. As early as 1661, Louis XIV had performed the role of eternal Spring in Jean-Baptiste Lully's *Ballet des saisons*. The young king danced to verses from the libretto by Isaac de Benserade that celebrated the springtime ushered in with his reign:

> The young vigor of Spring
> > Dissipated bad times,
> > All the mutinous and strange winds
> > Who amid thick fog
> > Caused great tempests
> > Have been banished forever,
> And in the air is a profound peace.
> > This season who strongly pleases
> > Sends to the cold northern climates
> > Winter who surrenders to war,
> > And produces for our posterity
> > In the most noble place on the Earth
> > The great and immortal Flower
> > Who spreads his odor over all of
> > Europe.[64]

Memoire des plantes vivac[es]
plantes annuell[es]
et oignons de fleurs propre[s]
a garnir Les petit costier[s]
Le long des allée du Jardin
roialle de marly

premierement

1 — Narsis Nonpareille Jaune		givoflee printanier violet	pensee velout[e]
2 — Tuliper Postur Cle Rouge Jaune		1 2 3 4 5 6 7 8 9 10 11 12	
3 — Narsis claz printanie		Musle de lion rouge	Statisee
4 — Jasint bleu ou blancs		quoquelavia claz	oreille dourse
5 — Narsis claz double		Basiliquee Mimov	Statisee
6 — tuliper printanier bordea		Immortelle blanc	pensee
7 — Narsis nonpareillet Siboo		givoflee rouge	Statisee
8 — Postur Cle blanch et Rouge		Musipula claz	Buflalmon Jaune
9 — Narsis claz printanie	Buflalmon Jaune	belle samine rouge	Statisee
10 — Jasint bleu ou blancs	Statisee	amavoule blanc	pensee
11 — Narsu claz doubl	pensee	Immortelle goidelin	Statisee
12 — tuliper printanier	Statisee	givofle printanier violet	Mignardise
	Mignardise	tovaspy minov claz	Statisee
	Statisee	Marguerit double	pensee
	pensee	tovaspy violet	Statisee
	Statisee	tiguenieu rouge	Crreson dinde
	Crreson dinde	pensee minov	Statisee
	Statisee	Intevinon claz	pensee
	pensee	tovaspy maiov claz	Statisee
	Statisee	souly argentee	Camomille
	Camomille	Onemonne simple	Statisee

9. "Memoire des plantes vivaces, plantes annuelles, et oignons des fleurs propres a garnir les petit costiere le long des allées du Jardin Roialles de Marly [Memorandum on perennials, annuals, and flowering bulbs appropriate for furnishing the small side of the long avenue of the Royal Garden of Marly]," ca. 1700. Centre historique des Archives nationales à Paris, O¹2102¹ cotte 4, page 1.

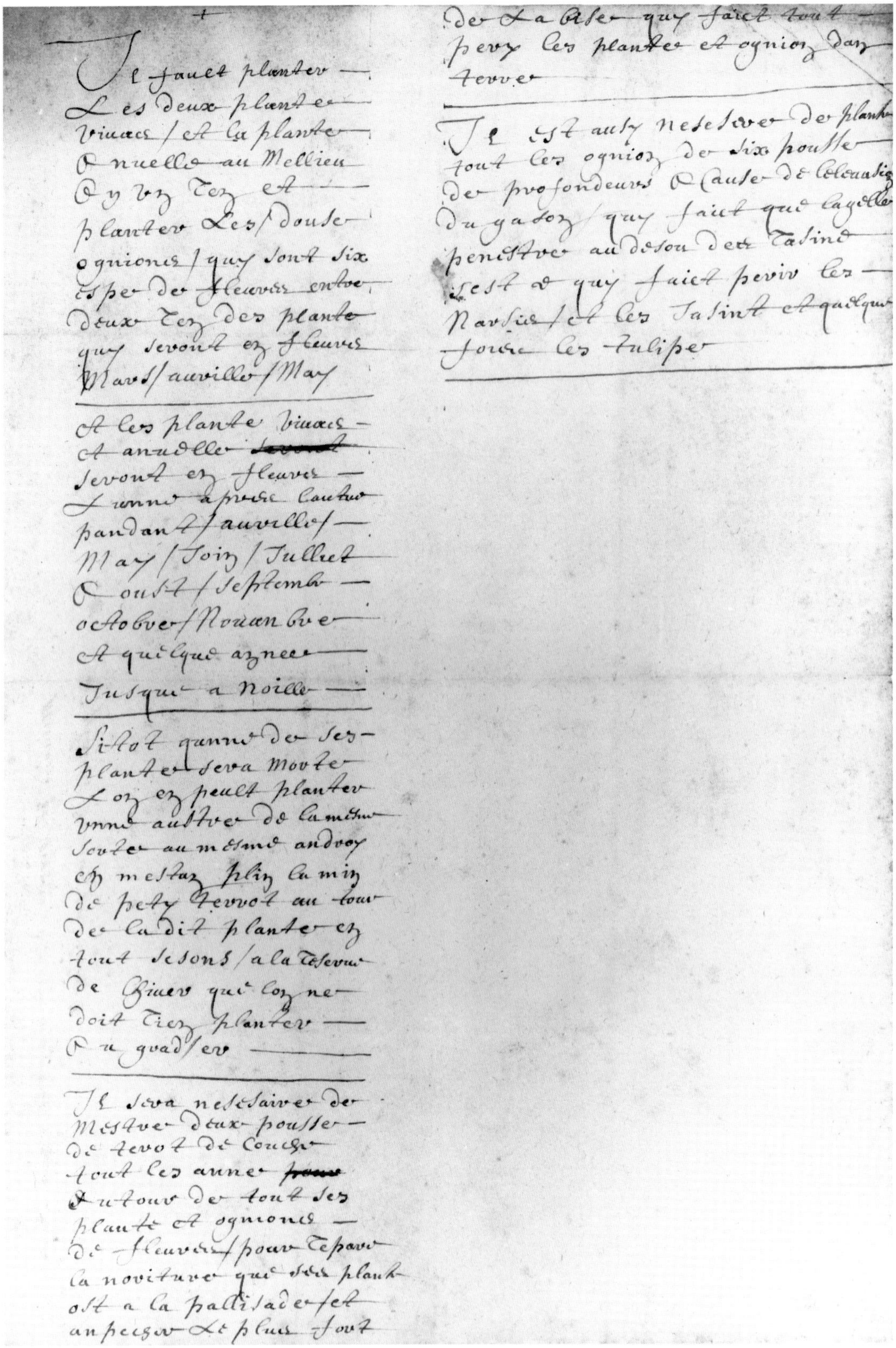

Il fault planter —
Les deux plantes
viuaces / Et la plante
annuelle au Mellieu
Oy un Ter et
planter Les douze
ognions / quy sont six
especes de fleures entre
Deux Ter des plantes
quy seront en fleures
Mars / auuril / May

Et les plantes viuaces
et annuelles [strikethrough]
seront en fleures —
d'vnne apres l'autre
pandant / auuril /
May / Join / Jullet
d'oust / septembre —
octobre / Nouanbre —
Et quelque annee
Jusque a Noille —

Sitot qanne des ses
plantes sera Morte
L'on en peult planter
vnne austre de la mesme
Sorte au mesme androy
en mestan plein la min
de petÿ Terrot au tour
de ladit plante en
tout sesons / a la reserue
de l'hiuer quil l'on ne
doit Ter planter —
ou grad / ser —

Il sera nesesaire de
Mestre deux pousse
de terrot de couche
tout les anne —
autour de tout ses
plantes et ognions —
de fleures / pour réparer
la nouriture que des plante
ost a la pallisade / et
an peuser le plus tout

der La Pese quy faict tout
peuy les plantes et ognion dan
terre

Il est aussy nesesaire de planter
tout les ognion de six pousse
de profondeur d Cause de la coulation
du gadon / quy faict que la gelle
penestre au deson des racine
[?]est o quy faict periv les
Narsie / et les racine et quelque
foue les tulipe

---

10. "Memoire des plantes vivaces, plantes annuelles, et oignons des fleurs propres a garnir les petit costiere le long des allées du Jardin Roialles de Marly [Memorandum on perennials, annuals, and flowering bulbs appropriate for furnishing the small side of the long avenue of the Royal Garden of Marly]," ca. 1700. Centre historique des Archives nationales à Paris, O[1] 2102[1] cotte 4, page 2.

Benserade therefore not only drew upon the theme of eternal springtime, but also on the symbolism of an individual flower, the everlasting, to suggest the peace and prosperity of Louis XIV's rule.

Flowers were similarly featured in the grand fêtes staged by the king in 1664, 1668, and 1674, each of which took full advantage of their setting in the gardens of Versailles. The 1664 *Plaisirs de l'île enchantée*, for example, staged ostensibly in honor of Louis XIV's queen, Marie-Thérèse, though widely known to have been a celebration of the love the king professed at the time for his new mistress, Louise de la Vallière, opened with a procession in which Apollo was escorted by the Four Ages. The Golden Age, according to the official account of the fête, wore gilded armor that "was also covered in diverse flowers which made one of the principal ornaments of this happy age."[65]

Fresh flowers were heavily used to decorate the gardens in the 1668 and 1674 fêtes. In 1668, royal flower gardener Michel Le Bouteux was paid 900 livres for the "festoons, bouquets, and floral ornaments that he furnished for the decoration of the [*bosquets*] of the feast, ball, and *collation*.[66] According to André Félibien's official account of the spectacle, the *bosquet de l'Etoile* was decorated for the collation with vases "remplie de fleurs," while baskets and flowers decorated the theater constructed for the performance of Molière's *George Dandin*. For the supper served in the bassin de Flore, seventy-four porcelain vases were filled with diverse flowers above which hung numerous festoons constructed of flowers. Floral festoons, too, decorated the *salle de bal*.[67]

Flowers similarly adorned the *bosquets* of the Versailles gardens during the 1674 fête held in honor of the king's victories in the Franche-Comté. Arranged in porcelain pots and vases, or woven into garlands and festoons, flowers ornamented the salle du Conseil and the theater constructed in the cour de marbre for the performance of the "tragédie lyrique" entitled *Alceste, ou Le triomphe d'Alcide* (music by Jean-Baptiste Lully, libretto by Philippe Quinault).[68] And on the second day of the 1674 fête, the courtiers in attendance were treated to a concert at the Trianon palace, where, wrote Félibien in the official description of the event, "one always finds springtime," and "one always sees there special beauties and the air one breathes there is perfumed with the most fragrant flowers."[69] The flower gardens of the Trianon were supplemented with porcelain vases filled with flowers, while large floral festoons were hung from the porticoes. In staging his triumphant celebration of 1674, the king

took advantage of the flower-filled setting of the Trianon gardens. Further, his panegyrist Félibien specifically referred to the Trianon as a place where flowers always blossomed, where eternal springtime reigned.

The showcasing of Louis XIV's power and floricultural wealth was further incorporated into the ballets and operas staged in his honor. In the 1669 *Balet Royal de Flore*, another collaboration between Lully and Benserade, the goddess Flora danced with Louis XIV who portrayed Apollo, while Jupiter and Destiny proclaimed the royal function of flowers:

> You have two brilliant jobs;
> You crown love on the beautiful complexion of Flora;
> > And on the brow of the most
> > powerful of Kings,
> > Who is followed by Victory,
> > You crown Glory.[70]

In the 1671 "tragédie en musique" *Psyché*, it was Flora who summoned Venus to the earth to bring peace and love.[71]

In the 1676 "tragédie en musique" *Atys*, another Quinault and Lully collaboration, the goddess Flora was featured in the prologue in which Time questioned why Flora defied Time and provided flowers year round for the king, an obvious reference to the king's spectacular ever-blossoming flower gardens. It was necessary, Flora explained, to bring floral pleasure to the king in winter because in the spring he would return to the glory of war.[72]

In 1689 the newly enlarged Trianon palace actually served as a setting for the performance of Michel-Richard Delalande's ballet *Le Palais de Flore*, staged to celebrate the glorious return of the dauphin from battle. According to the text, the ballet was set in "The Palace of Flora and eternal Springtime, which until now have [existed] only in the imagination of Poets, [but which] are [now] veritably found here." The text continued:

The Theater of Trianon knows no more superb decoration than the Trianon itself. The splendor of the marbles and the beauties of the architecture first attach the sight on this grand façade called the peristyle; and the pleasure is intensified by the openings of the arcades; between several rows of columns, one discovers these fountains, these gardens, and these parterres always filled with all sorts of flowers. One cannot remember that it is the middle of winter, or one believes that one has been transported sud-

POVR LA PIETÉ,

DANS LA PIECE DE L'ELEMENT DE LA TERRE:

Vn Girasol, auec ce Mot, COELESTES SEQVITVR
MOTVS, pour dire que *Sa Majesté* se conduit par les mou-
uemens du Ciel en toutes ses actions, ainsi que le Girasol suit
le mouuement du Soleil qu'il regarde toûjours.

Malgré l'Element qui m'enserre,
Et la Loy du Destin, qui m'attache à la Terre,
Dans le plus haut des Cieux sont mes tendres amours.
Du Diuin Autheur de ma vie,
I'ay toûjours la trace suiuie,
Et la suiuray toûjours.

PERRAVLT.

11. "Pour la pieté, dans la piece de l'element de la terre. Un Girasol . . . [For piety, in the element of earth. A Sunflower . . .]" in *Tapisseries du roy, ou sont representez les quatre elemens et les quatre saisons avec les devises qui les accompagnent et leur explication* (Paris: Sebastien Mabre-Cramoisy, 1679). Princeton University, Marquand Library of Art and
Archaeology, Department of Rare Books and Special Collections, PUL.

POVR LE PRINTEMPS,

DANS LA PIECE DE LA SAISON DV PRINTEMPS.

Des Fleurs printanieres dans vn Parterre, qui ont pour Ame ce Mot, TERRÆ AMOR ET DECVS; pour fignifier que fi la Terre aime les Fleurs, comme fes premieres productions, & celles qui font fon plus bel ornement, Sa Majefté n'eft pas moins l'amour & l'ornement de toute la Terre.

Si lors que la Terre fe pare
De ce prefent des Cieux fi charmant & fi rare,
Elle l'aime fi tendrement;
N'eft-il pas jufte qu'on la voye
En faire fes plaifirs, fon amour, & fa joye,
Comme elle en fait fon ornement?

PERRAVLT.

12. "Pour le printemps, dans la piece de la saison du printimps. Des Fleurs printanieres dans un Parterre. . . . [For spring, in the piece of the season of spring. Spring flowers in a parterre. . . .]," in *Tapisseries du roy, ou sont representez les quatre elemens et les quatre saisons avec les devises qui les accompagnent et leur explication* (Paris: Sebastien Mabre-Cramoisy, 1679). Princeton University, Marquand Library of Art and Archaeology, Department of Rare Books and Special Collections, PUL.

denly to another climate, when one sees the delicious objects which denote so agreeably the abode of Flora.[73]

The "eternal Springtime which had existed only in the imagination of the Poets" was a clear reference to the perpetual springtime of the Golden Age described by Ovid and Virgil. In the ballet, Flora, who was portrayed by Mademoiselle de Blois, the king's daughter by his mistress Madame de Montespan, summoned the flowers of the Trianon garden to join her in honoring the victorious dauphin. A nymph and zephyr issued her command:

> At the sight of Flora
> You hasten to blossom.
> Come in your pretty hands,
> Fragrant harvest,
> Smiling riches,
> Roses, jasmines,
> Anemones, amaranths,
> Kind flowers come to adorn
> The victorious head that she wants to crown.[74]

The ballet dancers representing flowers honoring the dauphin were merely personifications of the flowers growing in the Trianon gardens that honored the king and his son by their very presence. By 1688 the Trianon was itself duplicated as an appropriately sumptuous setting for the 1688 performance of the opera *Zephire et Flore* by Du Boullay. The prologue took place in a stage that, according to the text, "represents the new Trianon palace with its gardens."[75]

The symbolism of individual flowers was also exploited by the king's iconographers. In 1668, for example, Jacques Bailly, accompanied by members of the king's "petite académie," or the Académie des Inscriptions et Belles-Lettres, designed a series of devices that were incorporated into tapestries woven for the king at Gobelins. Organized around themes of the four elements and the four seasons, the tapestry designs included several floral devices. Bailly's designs, in addition to being incorporated into the proposed tapestries, were also engraved and published in a lavish format in 1679.[76] The sunflower, a part of the representation of the element "earth," symbolized, as the accompanying verses explained, the king's piety, demonstrated by his willingness to follow the movements of the heavens (fig. 11).[77] The rose, incorporated into the image of spring, demonstrated Louis XIV's powerful combination of grace and good looks with military might.[78] And the snowdrop, incorporated into the representation of winter, explained

that "Those who can speak of the glory of His Majesty [know] that all the obstacles cannot prevent him from shining and that he flourishes in the middle of difficulty."[79] Finally, the king was compared to a parterre filled with spring flowers (fig. 12). The parterre, explained the flowers, were the earth's premiere production, "its most beautiful ornament," just as "His Majesty is no less the love and ornament of all the earth."[80]

The flowers in Louis XIV's gardens not only allowed him to exploit their symbolism as Bailly had done for the tapestry designs, but they also allowed him to claim that his was indeed a Golden Age, that he was the prophesied Augustan leader guiding his realm into an unending period of prosperity. Scholars have suggested, based on their readings of ballet and opera *livrets*, that the Trianon and its gardens were expressions of an eternal springtime believed to have been ushered in by Louis XIV.[81] Knowledge of the extent to which the king, his ministers, and his gardeners went to make sure that his gardens were flower filled suggests that expressions of the king's reign as a Golden Age through flowers were deliberate and important. For it was the perpetual presence of flowers in the king's gardens, which then became fodder for the king's iconographers, that allowed him to demonstrate that the Golden Age, the eternal springtime, had truly arrived. Despite Le Nôtre's opinion of parterres, the role they played in glorifying the king was considerable, for in allowing the king to demonstrate literally the prosperity and fertility of his reign, he could lay claim to the Golden Age and equate his powers with the deities of antiquity. As a panegyrist of Louis XIV exclaimed in 1688 in his *Histoire de Louis le Grande contenüe dans les rapports qui se trouvent entres ses actions, & les qualités, & vertus des Fleurs, & des Plants*, "When one wants to speak of . . . beautiful gardens, in the future one will no longer name those of [the goddess] Flora[,] but the gardens of LOUIS LE GRAND."[82]

Notes

1. Louis de Rouvroy, duc de Saint-Simon, *Mémoires. Additions au Journal de Dangeau*, ed. Yves Coirault, vol. 1 (Paris: Gallimard, 1983), 739. "Il disait des parterres," wrote Saint-Simon, "qu'ils n'étaient que pour les nourrices qui, ne pouvant quitter leurs enfants, s'y promenaient des yeux et les admiraient du second étage."

2. "Manière de planter les fleurs," Bibliothèque Nationale de France (hereafter B.N.), Cabinet des Estampes, Va 78g f.t.2.

3. Quoted in Pierre-André Lablaude, *The Gardens of Ver-*

sailles, preface by Jean-Pierre Babelon (London: Zwemmer, 1995), 104. Saint-Simon writes, "All of the compartments in each of the parterres were changed every day, and I have seen the king and the entire court driven out of the garden, although it is vast and built in terraces overlooking the Canal, because the scent of the tuberose hung so heavy in the air."

4. Orest Ranum, *Artisans of Glory: Writers and Historical Thought in Seventeenth-Century France* (Chapel Hill: University of North Carolina Press, 1980).

5. Jules Guiffrey, *Comptes des bâtiments du roi sous le règne de Louis XIV*, 5 vols. (Paris: Imprimerie Nationale, 1881–1901), 1: 247–48.

6. Guiffrey, *Comptes des bâtiments*, 1: 394, 477–78.

7. Ibid., 1: 620, 669.

8. Ibid., 1: 804, 835, 876.

9. Ibid., 2: 1019, 1025–27.

10. Ibid., 2: 1214, 1216, 1217.

11. The number of bulbs per case was not indicated.

12. Ibid., 3: 447, 450.

13. According to my analysis of the entries in Guiffrey's *Comptes des bâtiments*, approximately 30 percent of entries for flower purchases were for the Trianon gardens, 24 percent for Marly, 5 percent for the pépinière du Roule, 1.5 percent for Clagny, and only 4.15 percent for Versailles. Approximately 30 percent, however, were designated for "les jardins des Maison Royales," a category that likely includes not only the gardens of Versailles, but also each of the gardens singled out above. Of the money spent on the purchase of flowers for the royal gardens, 52 percent went for flowers for the "jardins des maison royales," 23.2 percent for the Trianon gardens, 13.8 percent for Marly, and 2.6 percent for Versailles. See Guiffrey, *Comptes des bâtiments*, vols. 1–5.

14. Guiffrey, *Comptes des bâtiments*, 3: 447, 590, 739.

15. Ibid., 3: 591.

16. Floral scents gained popularity over stronger animal-based scents at the court of Louis XIV. Scholars investigating the role of scent and perfumes in history assert that flower-based perfumes became more popular in the eighteenth century when, as Alain Corbin argues, the French rejected animal scents in favor of floral fragrances. See Alain Corbin, *The Foul and the Fragrant: Odor and the French Social Imagination*, trans. by Miriam L. Kochan, Roy Porter, and Christopher Prendergast (Cambridge, Mass.: Harvard University Press, 1986), chap. 4, "Redefining the Intolerable," and chap. 5, "The New Calculus of Olfactory Pleasure." Flower-based scents, however, were popular in the late seventeenth century when guidebooks appear instructing people on the concoction of floral perfumes, oils, powders, and pomades. See, for example, Simon Barbe, *Le Parfumeur François, qui enseigne toutes les manieres de tirer les odeurs des fleurs; & à faire toutes sortes de compositions de parfums. Avec le secret de purger le tabac en poudre; & le parfumeur de toutes sorts d'odeurs. Pour le divertissement de la noblesse, l'utilité des personnes religieuses & necessaire aux baigneurs & perruquieurs* (Lyon: Thomas Amaulry, 1693).

17. *Mercure Galant*, November 1686, 115–17. The *Mercure Galant* reported that "Le Cabinet des Parfums leur plût extrémement, car ils aiment forts les odeurs, & ils admirerent la maniere de parfumer avec des fleurs."

18. André Le Nôtre, "Description du Grand Trianon en 1694, par André Le Nostre," in R[agnar] Josephson, *Revue de l'histoire de Versailles et de Seine-et-Oise* (1927): 20. Le Nôtre described the parterre as a "jardin particulier quy est toutjours [sic] plein de fleurs que l'on change touts les saisons dans des pots et jamais on ne void de feuille morte ny arbrisseaux quy ne soit en fleurs."

19. *Les Curiositez de Paris, de Versailles, de Marly, de Vincennes, de S. Cloud, et des environs. Avec les adresses pour trouve facilement ou ce qu'ils renferment d'agréable & d'utile. Ouvrage enrichi d'un grand nombre de figures* (Paris: Saugrain, 1716), 349. The author wrote, "ce beau lieu, qui est rempli de fleurs des plus rares & des plus belles dans toutes des saisons, persuade qui l'hyver n'en sçauroit approcher." Authorship of this book is disputed; it is sometimes attributed to G. L. Le Rouge, but Le Rouge was active later in the eighteenth century.

20. Guiffrey, *Comptes des bâtiments*, 3: 124, 311, 739.

21. Ibid., 4: 656. Loitron was charged with "l'entretien, plant et culture des fleurs rares et autres du nouveau jardin de Marly."

22. Woodbridge, *Princely Gardens: The Origins and Development of the French Formal Style* (New York: Rizzoli, 1986), 234.

23. Guiffrey, *Comptes des bâtiments*, 4: 997, 1105, 1215, 5: 75.

24. Martin Lister, *An Account of Paris, at the Close of the Seventeeth [sic] Century: Relating to the Buildings of that City, its Libraries, Gardens, Natural and Artificial Curiosities, the Manners and Customs of the People, Their Arts, Manufactures, & c.* (London: Black, Young & Young, 1823), 180.

25. Guiffrey, *Comptes des bâtiments*, 1: 470. The Trumel in question was most likely Antoine Trumel who had served as the flower gardener at Vaux-le-Vicomte for Nicolas Fouquet and who had been given the responsibility in 1670 for organizing the pépinière du Roule. For more on the Trumels, see Woodbridge, *Princely Gardens*, 225–28.

26. Guiffrey, *Comptes des bâtiments*, 1: 477–78.

27. Ibid., 1: 473.

28. Ibid., 1: 540, 835.

29. Ibid., 1: 669.

30. Ibid., 2: 1019.

31. Ibid., 2: 1030, 1213.

32. Ibid., 3: 134.

33. Ibid., 1: 683. Subleau was reimbursed for money spent "pour achat de livres, fleurs et autres curiositez de Levant pour le service de S.M."

34. Ibid., 1: 735.

35. Archives Nationales de France (hereafter A.N.), Maison du Roi O¹2101¹ cotte 4. The document was titled "Facture d'une boëte de plantes et grains pour le jardin du Roy."

36. Guiffrey, *Comptes des bâtiments*, 3: 311. Truitté was paid for "plantes de fleurs qu'il va chercher sur les montagnes de Dauphiné et Piedmont pour le jardin de Trianon."

37. Aubert Aubert de Petit Thouars, *Notice historique sur la pépinière du roi au Roule; faisant suite à un discours sur l'enseignement de la botanique, prononcé dans cet etablissement, le 24 mai 1824* (Paris: Gueffier, 1825), 1.

38. Lister, *An Account of Paris*, 187–89.

39. A. N., Maison du Roi O¹2102¹ cotte 7. For example, in 1684 a Sieur Cotereau presented to Ballon, a royal gardener in charge of the nursery, a statement of the flowers he could provide for the royal gardens. In the document, an exceptionally rich source because of the detail with which Cotereau described different species, Cotereau

filled seven pages with numbers of plants required or requested by the royal gardeners together with the prices quoted by Cotereau. For the Trianon, Cotereau promised he could produce 100 double white anemones, 100 double white ranunculi, 100 double white ranunculi flecked with pink and violet, 100 blue and yellow aromatic ranunculi, 1,000 ranunculi "du bagadet dont la fleur est plus grande que les autres," and 1,000 ranunculi "géant de Rome de pareilles grosseur panaché." Cotereau claimed to be able to obtain "couteront" and "pastout bleüe" from Flanders and Holland, and white hyacinths, Roman hyacinths, double white hyacinths, tuberoses, single jonquils, and double narcissi, all from Provence. Among the variety of other plants listed are many others including narcissi "du Japon couleur de chair," narcissi "du Japon couleur de feu," narcissi "[c]alices rouge jaunes odorant," iris, purple fritillaries, white fritillaries, black striped fritillaries, daylilies in yellow, red, and violet, martagons, crown imperials, yellow cyclamen, blue cyclamen "de bonne odeur," white dogtooth violets, red hellebores, hepaticas, everlastings, pinks, and citrus trees.

40. A.N., Maison du Roi O^{1}2103 and O^{1}2104.

41. A.N., Maison du Roi O^{1}2124^1 cotte 3.

42. A.N., Maison du Roi O^{1}2124^1 cotte 1. The Toulon garden was purchased to "elevér oignons de fleurs qu'il faut fournir tous les ans pour les jardins des Maisons Royalles."

43. A. N., Maison du Roi O^{1}2124^1 cotte 3.

44. A. N., Maison du Roi O^{1}2124^1 cotte 1 and O^{1}1905 no. 3.

45. A. N., Maison du Roi O^{1}2102^1 cotte 4.

46. A. N., Maison du Roi O^{1}2124^1.

47. A. N., Maison du Roi O^{1}2124^1.

48. A. N., Maison du Roi O^{1}2102^1 cotte 4.

49. A. N., Maison du Roi O^{1}2102^1 cotte 4.

50. A. N., Maison du Roi O^{1}2102^1 cotte 4.

51. A. N., Maison du Roi O^{1}2124^1 cotte 2.

52. A. N., Maison du Roi O^{1}21241^1 cotte 2. Colbert wrote, "Je suis obligé M. de vous informer que des oignons de Narcisse de constantinople, de totus albus, d'hyacintes romaines et des jonquilles montant les tous à 21 miliers qui ont esté envoyer de Toulon le 10 juillet dernier, il y en a la plus grande partie qui ne porterant point parceque ce ne sont que des cayeux qui ne pouront fleurir. . . . Je vous supplie d'obliger le jardinier du jardin de Toulon à ne donner que des oignons portans, parcequ'autre qu'ils ne servent à rien, la voiture côute au Roy et il tant mieux en avoir moins et qu'ils soient bons."

53. A. N., Maison du Roi O^{1}2124^1 cotte 2. He reminded De Vauvré, "Par l'establissement de ce jardin suivant le memoire que vous envoyastes [*sic*] à M. de Louvois le 15 septembre 1683. L'on fournissoit tous les ans 65,000 oignons l'on n'en a fournir cette année que 24,000 y compris 3,000 tubereuses, et la dépense du jardin est egale."

54. A. N., Maison du Roi O^{1}2124^1.

55. Ovid, *Metamorphoses*, trans. Mary Innes (London: Penguin Classics, 1955), 32.

56. Publius Virgilius Maro, *The Eclogues and the Georgics*, trans. R. C. Trevelyan (Cambridge: Cambridge University Press, 194X), 14, lines 18–23.

57. Michel de Marolles, "L'Siècle d'or," B. N., Cabinet des Estampes, Oa 46. The caption reads, "DURANT le Siecle d'or, Siecle chery du Ciel, Flore eternellement se couronnoit de roses."

58. N[icolas] Bonnart, "L'Aage d'or," B. N., Cabinet des Estampes, Oa 58 pet. fol., c 1958. The caption reads, "Nous est represente soubs l'Embleme d'une belle, et jeune fille simplement vetüe, carressant un mouton a qui elle met une guirlande de fleurs, et joüant avec un enfant pour marquer l'innocence des moeurs de ce siècle, la ruche d'abeilles represente la douceur, et l'union; l'olivier est le simbole de la paix qui regnoit alors."

59. See Frances A. Yates, *Astraea: The Imperial Theme in the Sixteenth Century* (London: ARK Paperbacks, 1985).

60. According to Jean-Pierre Néraudau, "In 1638, in order to celebrate the birth of Louis XIV, it was from the Fourth Eclogue of Virgil that Campanella borrowed his prophetic tone, for want of finding in Ovid the same verses of a providential infant, and even so the mythological themes which illustrated the power of Louis XIV came almost exclusively from the *Metamorphoses*." ["En 1638, pour célébrer le naissance de Louis XIV, c'est à la quatrième églogue de Virgile que Campanella emprunte ses accents prophétiques, faute de trouver chez Ovide le même envers un enfant providential, et pourtant les thèmes mythologiques qui illustreront le pouvoir de Louis XIV vienne presque exclusivement des *Métamorphoses*."] Néraudau, "La présance d'Ovide aux XVIe et XVIIe siècle ou la survie du prince de poésie," in *La Littérature et ses avatars: Discrédits, déformations et réhabilitations dans l'histoire de la littérature*, ed. Yvonne Bellenger (Paris: Klincksieck, 1991), 15.

61. Mark Laird, *The Formal Garden: Traditions of Art and Nature* (London: Thames and Hudson, 1992), 43–44; and Mark Laird, "Ornamental Planting and Horticulture in English Pleasure Grounds, 1700–1830," in *Garden History: Issues, Approaches, Methods*, ed. John Dixon Hunt (Washington, D.C.: Dumbarton Oaks, 1992), 243–77. Laird provides an intriguing watercolor interpretation of what the flower border might have looked like.

62. A. N., Maison du roi O^{1}2102^1. The "Memoire des plantes vivaces, plantes annuelles et oignons de fleurs propres a garnir les petit costiere le long des allé du Jardin Roialle de Marly" includes instructions for keeping the garden in flower "en tout sesons."

63. "Memoire," ibid., 2.

64. Isaac de Benserade, *Ballet des saisons. Dansé à Fontainebleau par sa Majesté le 23 juillet 1661* (Paris: Robert Ballard, 1661), 18. "La jeune vigeur de Printemps/ A dissipé le mauvais temps,/ Tous ces vents mutins & fantasques/ Qui parmy des broüillards épais/ Causoient de se grandes bourasques/ On esté bannis pour jamais,/ Et dans l'air il a mis un profonde Paix./ Cette Saison qui plaist si fort/ L'envoye aux froids climats du Nort/ L'Hyver qui vous livroit la guerre/ Et produit pour nostre bonheur/ Au plus noble endroit de la Terre/ La grande & l'immortelle fleur/ Qui par toute l'Europe épandra son odeur."

65. *Les Plaisirs de l'île enchantée* (Paris: Robert Ballard, 1664), repr. in Molière, *Oeuvres complètes*, vol. 1 (Paris: Gallimard, 1971), 757. The Golden Age wore gilded armor that "était encore paré des divers fleurs qui faisaient un des principaux ornements de cet heureux âge."

66. Guiffrey, *Comptes des bâtiments*, 1: 305. Michel Le Bouteux was paid for the "festons, bouquets et ornemens de fleurs qu'il a fourni pour la décoration des salles du festin du bal et de la collation."

67. André Félibien, *Relation de la fête de Versailles du dix-huit juillet mille six cent soixante-huit. Les Divertissements de*

Versailles donné par le roi à toute sa cour au retour de la conquête de la Franche Comté en l'année mille six cent soixantequatorze (1668, 1674), ed. Martin Meade (n. p.: Éditions Dédale, Maisonneuve et Larose, 1994), 36–37, 44, 66, 76, 78.

68. Félibien *Relations*, 111–21.

69. Ibid., 117–19.

70. Isaac de Benserade, *Balet Royal de Flore. Dansé par Sa Majesté en 1669* (n.p., n.d.). Jupiter and Destiny sang, "Vous avez deux brillans emplois;/ Vous couronnez l'amour sur le beau teint de Flore:/ Et sur le front de plus puissant des Rois,/ Qui traîne après lui la Victoire,/ Vous couronnez la Gloire."

71. *Psyché, tragedie en musique*, in *Recueil des opera, des ballets, et des plus belles piéces en musique, qui ont été représentées devant sa Majesté Tres-Chrétienne. Dernière edition*, 2 vols. (Amsterdam: Abraham Wolfgang, 1690), 1: 28.

72. Philippe Quinault, *Atys*, in *Recueil des opera*, 1: 240. Flora and Time sang, "Les plaisirs à ses yeux ont beau se présenter,/ Si-tôt qu'il voit Bellone, il quitte tout pour elle;/ Rien ne peut l'arrêter/ Quand la Gloire l'apelle."

73. Michel-Richard Delalande, *Le Palais de Flore dansé à Trianon devant Sa Majesté le 5 janvier 1689*, in *Recueil des sujets paroles d'une partie des ballets, dansez devant sa Majesté* (Paris: Christophe Ballard, 1709), 7. "Le Palais de Flore & le Printemps eternel qui jusques à present n'avoient esté que dans l'imagination des Poëtes, se trouvent veritablement icy. Le Theatre de Trianon ne sçauroit avoir de plus superbe decoration que Trianon mesme. L'éclat des Marbres, & les beautez de l'Architecture attachent d'abord la veüe sur cette grande façade appellée le Peristile; & le plaisir redouble lorsque par les ouvertures de ses Arcades, entre plusieurs rangs de riches Colonnes, on découvre ces Fontaines, ces Jardins, & ces Parterres toujours remplis de toutes sortes de fleurs. On ne se souvient plus qu'on est au milieu de l'Hiver, ou bien l'on croit avoir esté transporté tout d'un coup en d'autres Climats, quand on voit ces delicieux objets qui marquent si agreablement la demeure de Flore."

74. Delalande, *Le Palais de Flore*, 14. "A l'aspect de Flore/ Hastez-vous d'éclore./ Venez en ses belles mains,/ Moissons odorantes,/ Richesses riantes,/ Roses, Jasmines,/ Anemones, Amarantes./ Aimables fleurs venez orner/ Le front victorieux qu'elle veut couronner."

75. Michel du Boullay, *Zephire et Flore*. Opéra, in *Recueil des opera*, 2: 368. The prologue took place in a theater that "représente le nouveau Palais de Trianon, avec ses Jardins."

76. *Tapisseries du roy, ou sont representez les quatres elemens et les quatre saisons avec les devises qui les accompagnent et leur explication* (Paris: Sebastien Mabre-Cramoisy, 1679).

77. Jacques Bailly, *Devises pour les tapisseries du roi*, manuscript (1668); ed. Marieanne Grivel and Marc Fumaroli (Paris: Herscher, 1988), 19.

78. Ibid., 28.

79. Ibid., 40. The manuscript explained, "Ce qui peut se dire de la gloire de sa Majesté que tous les obstacles ne peuvent empescher d'eclatter, & que fleurit au milieu de difficultez."

80. Ibid., 26. The device of the border of spring flowers was included "pour signifier que . . . la terre aime les Fleurs comme ses premiers productions & celles qui font son plus bel ornement." The caption continued, "Sa Majesté n'est pas moins l'Amour & l'ornement de toute la terre."

81. For Jean-Pierre Néraudau, the Trianon was the king's expression of his reign as one of "eternal springtime," and mythological references promised perpetual abundance and fertility in the kingdom of the Sun King. Louis Marin gives greater consideration to the king's power in the creation of the Trianon and the king's mastery of the seasons, suggesting that the Trianon was a place where the king could work and display his most powerful magic. That magic, explains Marin like Néraudau, was used in the creation of perpetual springtime. See Néraudau, *L'Olympe du Roi Soleil: Mythologie et idéologie royal au Grand Siècle* (Paris: Société des Belles-Lettres, 1986), 249–53, and Louis Marin, *Portrait of the King*, trans. Martha M. Houle, foreword by Tom Conley (Minneapolis: University of Minnesota Press, 1988), 193–95.

82. Jean Donneau de Visé, *Histoire de Louis le Grand contenüe dans les rapports qui se trouvent entres ses actions, & les qualités, & vertus des Fleurs, & des Plants* (1688), B.N., ms. français 6995. "Quand on voudra parler de quelques beaux jardins, on ne nommera plus à l'avenir ceux de Flore; mais les jardins de LOUIS LE GRAND."

2. Engineering and French Formal Gardens in the Reign of Louis XIV

CHANDRA MUKERJI

Louis XIV was not a modest man, so it is no surprise that he had ambitions to make France the cultural and political center of all Europe.[1] The problem was to amplify his power so it could be felt well beyond his own court. The social solution to this problem was organizational: to fashion in his name a state bureaucracy that would make his will felt in all corners of France and make his reign a matter of concern for those beyond France's borders. The military solution was material: to carve out part of the European continent and mark it as French, using fortresses to claim the land and demonstrate the French state's capacity to control and expand its territory. The cultural one was more conceptual: to declare France the New Rome, heir to the ancient empire but distinctly Catholic, replacing Italy as the touchstone for both the Great Tradition and its elaboration in the service of Catholicism. The cultural project seemed to be a matter of ideology, requiring the kind of political publicity-making that Peter Burke has identified with the reign. But Burke has shown that this campaign was in many ways a failure, while the reign was not.[2]

Did this mean that the cultural project failed, but the political one survived in spite of it? Since France became the source of the dominant forms of European taste during much of the late seventeenth and early eighteenth centuries, leading fashion and design while also capturing classicism and making it French, this argument seems absurd. If anything, the political power of the regime was less sure than its cultural domination.[3] But the power of French culture was located less in words than in material forms. The cultural ambitions of the king and his court—the claim to leadership of the Great Tradition—took material and social demonstrations to make them believable, which the propaganda of the period was not. Only works and not words could effectively link the three worlds of action—social, military, and cultural—into a single form, amplifying the power of the regime and making the claim to empire seem somehow natural or inevitable. As a crucial site for this kind of cultural demonstration, the gardens of Versailles took on surprising significance. Louis XIV lavished disproportionate attention on them and developed itineraries for governing their use as a means of political education of visitors to the court.[4]

The cultural analyst Jean-Pierre Néraudau has argued that, as Paris was reconfigured to become the New Rome for the French empire, the château and gardens at Versailles were reworked to mark them as the palace of the sun, as described by Ovid.[5] Along with this program of symbol building, other reminders of the Roman heritage were embedded into the land of France. The landscape with its highly engineered surface, topped with triumphal arches and friezes of ancient helmets, arrows, and spears, implied a continuity between the military might of Rome and that of the current regime.[6] The orderly garden spaces demonstrated a desire for lawlike order reminiscent of Rome, and the vast and complex water system was engineered in part using Roman techniques and was ostentatiously constructed (to some degree) by soldiers, following the Roman practice of building public works to keep up the army's physical discipline during times of peace.[7] In this way, France was claimed to be the new Rome for its military prowess as much as for its cultural acumen.

The display of military engineering made particular sense for France as a way of claiming a classical heritage. Ancient Rome had, after all, an extraordinary bent toward reconfiguring the landscape for strategic advantage, making engineering a significant part of the classical traditions being explored in the period. Ancient Rome had also extended into France, leaving behind enduring roadways, aqueducts, baths, and remains of coliseums. There was little of the statuary that was so plentiful and revered in Italy and to the east. This meant that ancient Rome was a living presence in France, but mostly where it had altered the French landscape in ways that remained intact over centuries. This material heritage at once made Roman culture seem deeply entwined with the French, while it also provided a tempting model of how to build an empire and make it endure.[8]

Part of the claim to be the New Rome was an ambition to make contemporary France historically monumental enough to capture the imagination of future generations. In Madame de Scudéry's *Promenade*,[9] much of the discussion taking place in the gardens of Versailles revolved around the greatness of princes, and whether works or words were better means of conveying their achievements to future generations. And while André Félibien wrote as propagandist for the king and court, he often suggested that embellishing nature with art in gardens was a particularly apt way of celebrating a great leader.[10] As the past was opened up to analysis by French thinkers and artists, the future seemed more pressing and more manipulable.[11] One response was to write propaganda. But even the writers of the period felt that engineering could importantly stabilize the landscape both politically and culturally. The route to French greatness, then, was not hard to trace. France needed to eclipse Italy in military engineering as well as art to make France the New Rome, and the court needed to demonstrate this new cultural authority in a way that would make it convincing. The gardens of Versailles were a convenient venue for this.

I have argued elsewhere[12] that the terracing patterns used in French formal gardens were derived from military engineering, particularly the tradition of fortress design from Roman sources. This was not simply a matter of borrowing engineering technique, as Thierry Mariage has suggested,[13] but also a matter of purpose. Both gardens and fortresses of the period used elevations to control vision, giving garden topography in France a function not to be confused (as it often is in the literature) with the problem of transferring Italian gardening forms to the flat French landscape.[14] Fortress engineering was indeed a way to provide topographical complexity for strategic advantage in flat landscapes. Most French fortresses were built in the northeastern corner of France and were designed to give French soldiers elevations from which to view and control their enemies while keeping attackers from seeing clearly how to stage an assault.[15] The complex layers of walls and ditches of bastion systems made visibility and invisibility a strategic resource. French gardens that repeated these structures might have seemed to be seeking to restore the kind of topographical complexity that came naturally to the Italian hillside gardens, but they were actually deploying military techniques of land control (fig. 1). The result was an illusion of openness in gardens that played well against the alternately subtle and surprising dips in the landscape, giving them the illusory qualities that Hamilton Hazlehurst describes so precisely.[16]

The military structure of seventeenth-century garden topography is surprisingly easy to recognize, once it is pointed out.[17] Less readily identifiable are the military significance of the design of the *petit parc* and the engineering of water systems, both of which furthered France's representation as a well-measured and culturally dominant land worthy to be the New Rome. The *bosquets* of the *petit parc* constituted a landscape like those commonly represented in military maps, presenting a terrain that was alternately a soldier's dream and nightmare. The water system at Versailles was built with military labor in a manner aping Roman practice, and was designed with technologies that improved upon those from the classical era, suggesting that France was now ready to move Europe beyond the wisdom of the ancients. As the valley at Versailles was made more and more breathtaking and orderly, using these culturally loaded means, French claims to empire were made to emerge (apparently naturally) from the land itself.

THE GROWTH OF MILITARY ENGINEERING IN FRANCE

Military engineering became a particularly important issue in France during the sixteenth and seven-

1. Terrace over the Orangery at Versailles. Photo by Becky Cohen.

teenth centuries because of a problem that plagued all parts of Europe. Towns that had planned their security around an encircling system of tall, thin stone walls found themselves defenseless in the face of cannon, particularly when used with metal cannonballs. These walls fell like piles of blocks whenever they were pierced near the ground. By sloping defensive walls and backfilling them with dirt, towns could make bastions that could withstand the attacks; cannonballs would not go through a great mound of dirt and would roll down the sloped facing.[18] But building such structures meant redesigning the defenses so the new walls, now sloped and less tall, were not easily scaled by attackers. To solve these problems, Italian military engineers turned to fortress designs based on a classical model: the ideal city tradition.[19] Ideal cities with their star-shaped patterns of defenses made direct assaults by enemies more difficult. Soldiers approaching the fortifications were always

visible from at least one direction, and soldiers were easily hit while trying to scale the walls. Military engineers now concentrated on approaching fortified towns by building ditches and piercing the defenses by tunneling under them. Sieges became a matter of digging passageways and building mounds of dirt to protect soldiers (fig. 2). Warfare was won less by wounding enemies than engineering the landscape to favor the objectives of one army over the other.[20]

There is an interesting parallel between this movement in the military design of spaces and the design of gardens in early modern Europe. At the beginning of the Renaissance, Italian gardens were built with thin stone walls around them, defining an interior Eden assumed to be safe and ideal. But during the period when Italian military engineers were involved in rebuilding so many urban defenses, Italian gardens developed with mounds and terraces. The shift did not stand out as an inten-

192

2. Ditches used for a siege. Allain Manesson-Mallet, *Les Travaux de Mars*, 1696. Bibliothèque Nationale de France.

tional introduction of military engineering to Italian garden design, since the Edenic feel of even the grand parks was retained. Most mannerist gardens kept a visibly important exterior wall, only articulating a more systematic relation between house and garden. The centrality of the residence in these gardens has led historians to treat mannerist parks as power-centered. But even though military engineering techniques may have furthered this design shift in Italian gardens, the kind of power at stake was still presented as either more personal or spiritual than a matter of strategic ability.[21]

This changed, however, after sixteenth-century Italian military engineers and gardeners brought their traditions to France. The connections between military design and noble daily life were more on the surface of French culture. Many of those who brought Italian design to Italy, such as Leonardo da Vinci and Sebastiano Serlio, already combined interests in the arts, sciences, and warfare.[22] But in France they found themselves mixing war and art in new ways: designing gardens inside fortified residences, designing defenses for tender plants against the cold, and teaching the French skills in land measurement for engineering as well as aesthetic discipline.

The French were perhaps more overtly concerned about military engineering in their homes and in their garden art because they were so vulnerable along their borders. With the growth of the Hapsburg Empire, France became encircled by enemies. During this period of religious unrest and monarchical instability, France was even weak enough to tempt its enemies. So the French worked surprisingly hard on rebuilding the fortifications around border cities to prepare them for attacks using cannon and thus discourage enemies from invading. Much of this work had to be done with local money, even when it was in short supply, because the royal treasury was none too full itself. But this alone could not solve the problem of keeping France from incursions because local authorities were in no position to know the latest innovations in military engineering and bastion design. This led to the establishment in France of the engineers of the king (many of whom were Italian), who were itinerant experts on fortification and were sent to the aid of local authorities with the will to build up their defenses but no way to do it.[23]

During the seventeenth century, Italian military engineers transformed the French border regions with their work. These fortification experts only drew the plans, which then had to be realized by local architects and builders. This meant that the French slowly gained experience in battlement design, at the level of both conceptual and practical knowledge. This training in military design affected French architects and aligned their work with military engineering from the ancients.[24] In the reign of Henry IV, the duc de Sully was instrumental in promoting the work of some French military engineers who gained a fine reputation in the period, including Jacques Androuet Du Cerceau, Salomon de Brosse, and Jean de Beins. These men and a handful of others used Italian techniques to good effect, beginning to transfer expertise in land control from Italy to France.[25]

In roughly the same period, French gardeners were comparably applying Italian precedents and developing their own techniques of garden design. Under the influence of Olivier de Serres, some explored the economic advantages of market-oriented gardening and rational land use. Following Jacques Boyceau,[26] some became more intellectual about their practices, studying classical architecture to improve garden design and embedding ideas from the new science into their representations of the natural world.

The consequence of these two shifts—in military engineering and garden design—was that the techniques of land control in France reached a high enough level to allow their social and political uses to be more carefully examined and pursued. Serres's name was buried (along with memories of the French Protestant politics he helped to shape), but not the tradition of political *aménagement* itself. *Aménagement* was simply emptied of its commercial premises (Protestant taint) and translated into garden engineering (the military world of nobles) —another type of rational land management and one more easily tied to the Great Tradition. In this context and with the rise to power of Louis XIV, military engineering based on Roman precedent took on new importance and hence visibility in French formal gardens.[27]

By the time the young Louis XIV came to power, military engineers in France were already surprisingly well trained in cartography and siege tactics, ready to take him successfully to war. At the same time, French gardeners were well positioned to use military engineering and land management techniques to design a new and distinctive type of French garden with a more overtly political sensibility.

French gardens increased dramatically in size during the seventeenth century, claiming the landscape in a forceful way as they became more clearly territorial and less personal, and their center of gravity moved away from the house into the countryside. The military engineering employed in these sites, used to build up terraces and cut out canals, had Italian roots but was not celebrated as such. Statuary, garden layout, fountain design, and the design of parterres all had marked debts to Italian precedents. But the topographical features of the landscape seemed mute about their origins. This helped to naturalize the military of aspects the gardens, including the use of warlike symbolism, territorial markers, and signs of victory. France was presented as inevitably capable of dominating its territory using precisely the kinds of strengths that had characterized Rome.

THE MILITARY LANDSCAPE IN FRANCE

The parallels between French gardening and military engineering, their common debt to Italian readings of Roman forms, and their reappropriation in France may suggest how French gardening began to explore and develop its roots in military design, but it does not show clearly where there was a confluence of design features used for both dominating the countryside *and* setting out a pleasure garden. The grading patterns based on battlement wall systems that were used in French gardens certainly became an important site for this, but there were additional places in gardens, particularly those at Versailles, where references to military engineering were elaborated. Many of the *bosquets* at this seat of the French court reproduced in miniature elements of the landscape and built environment of concern to the military and routinely represented in the cartography of the period. The canal, *isle royale, marais, encelade,* and *bosquet des domes* all represented elements of nature that plagued soldiers and required serious attention for the development of military strategies: rivers, ponds, swamps, mires, and waterfalls. At the same time, the *salle de bal, orangerie,* terrace, *jardin potager, salle des festins,* the early *parterre d'eau,* and the *obélisque* fountain all displayed structures used by soldiers in France for military advantage: sloped and backfilled walls, underground passages, battlement structures, fortress forms, moats, and ditches. Making better sense of these connections and the resulting gardening patterns requires returning to the history of military engineering in France, this time with greater attention to the uses of cartography.

Military engineers from Italy brought to France not only fortification techniques, but also the sophisticated Italian cartographic practices that were used to plan and defend against sieges. French military surveyors adopted their methods with enthusiasm and produced massive numbers of city plans detailing defenses.[28] They also acquired the necessary topographical intelligence to plan troop movements and to identify places needing new walls or citadels (fig. 3). The Italians may have taught them the cartographic skills they used, but the French seem to have taken these practices more to heart. As the Englishman Ellis Veryard put it when he visited France:

> I am inform'd, by such persons as pretend to know the Affairs of *France*, that this King spends more Money on Intelligence than all the *European* Princes besides, which proves extreamly Beneficial in time of War, and in support of a Government in time of Peace. . . . They never besiege a Town but their Engineers have been privately at work in the place for a considerable time beforehand, viewing the Fortifications, taking all the necessary Heighths and Distances, finding out the Magazines, the quantity of the Stores, the strength of the Garrison, sounding the Depth of the Ditches, and the like; so that they rarely fail of accomplishing their Designs.[29]

New books on geometry published in the period also taught noblemen soldiers how to measure the trajectory of cannon fire, using triangulation, and how to measure distances from a target.[30] Thus military cartography in France became a powerful, if commonplace, tool of power.

Jean-Baptiste Colbert, working in the name of Louis XIV, stimulated the growth of two other fields of French mapmaking: academic cartography and civil surveying. These were stylistically distinct from both each other's and the maps of military cartographers. The styles of work were clearly tailored to the different purposes of maps and yielded identifiable imagery for each of these social worlds.

For the gentlemen of the Académie, cartographic measurement was supposed to use a grid of latitude and longitude to locate the results of accurate ground-based surveys in a mathematically precise frame (fig. 4).[31] If the military surveyors became specialists in topographical details and local inventories, the men of the academy developed the opposite skills. They treated the countryside as either a planar surface or (for topographical studies) a cross section of land drawn on a plane. Their two-dimensional images avoided rather than documented most of the details of the local landscape.

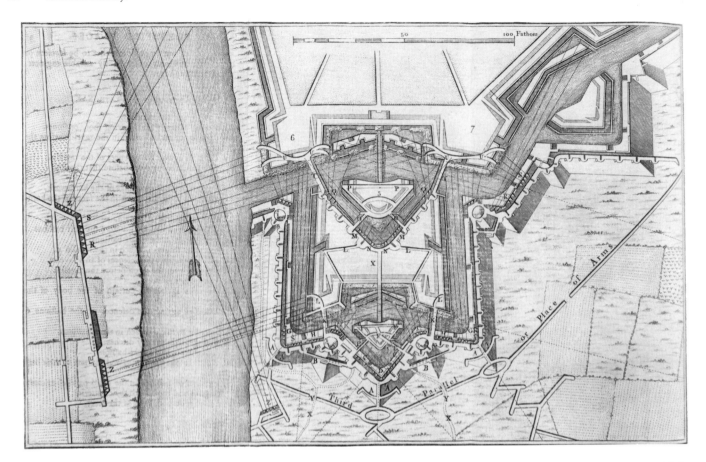

3. Cannon lines of fire in fortress design. John Muller, *The Attack and Defense of Fortified Places*, 1991. University of California, Santa Barbara.

The other group of cartographers developed under Colbert's tutelage were civil surveyors,[32] particularly the forestry workers contracted to document French forests and to help Colbert manage timber reserves.[33] The results were occasionally sophisticated surveys but usually simple plot plans marked with information about the location of large trees and waterways that might conduct timber to mills or shipyards (fig. 5). There was no technical or strategic frame for these images. The plot plans were more inventories of natural resources than maps tracing power relations. They tended to represent land parcels as flat (like academy surveys), but like military maps, they focused on local features.[34]

In contrast to the forestry and academy mapmaking, French military cartography had a distinct character, paying greater attention to elevations, transportation, and local differences among sites than other forms of mapmaking. Army maps took stock of waterways and forests, although not with the same measured detail as the forestry surveys. Most of all they depicted the interplay of barriers and open spaces—those vital topographical features that encouraged or inhibited movement through the landscape (fig. 6). Fortresses, city wall systems, and the most imposing natural barriers, such as crags, rivers, and rock faces, appeared the most consistently in military maps. But frequently, too, they contained information about the streams, swamps, and other waterways that interrupted transport. At the same time, they showed the roads and canals built to carry people and things unimpeded through the countryside. They also often marked the bridges, mountain passes, and trails that provided means of circumventing the problems of a complex terrain and gave troops the ability to move strategically. In sum, they recorded local problems and possibilities for territorial domination—themes with powerful salience for a political center like Versailles.

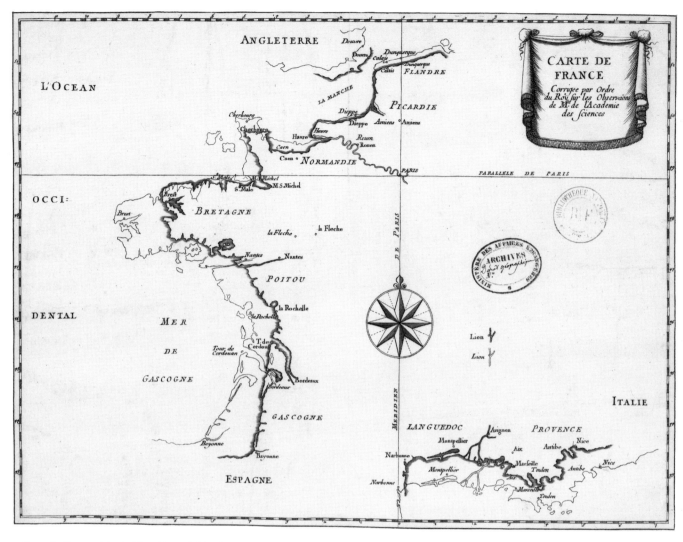

4. Carte de France. Ms. de l'Académie. Bibliothèque Nationale de France.

FRENCH FORMAL GARDENING AS A MAPPING PROCESS

The *petit parc* at Versailles certainly looked like a map, not only on paper but from the terrace and windows of the château. It had a drawn quality, but described natural features (fig. 7). Still, the park did not look at all like a map of French territory, like the one being worked out by the Académie. It was also not an academic map highlighting the measured relations among spaces at the expense of local differences in the landscape. The *bosquets* may have been related to one another in measured proportions, but each had a distinct way of joining sculpture, water, plantings, and walkways. The park was also certainly not like a forestry map with large land parcels and occasional clumps of

interesting trees. It was full of waterworks, statues, buildings, and walkways. Passing through the forest rooms was like moving through a tree-filled countryside that was dotted with habitations and clearings: isolated local landscapes with characterizing landmarks. This was the kind of countryside familiar to military cartographers.

Such attention to a military view of the countryside might seem odd and unlikely in the king's pleasure garden, but in this period a great park did not simply stand for sensual delight and leisurely study.[35] The hunting park was traditionally a place to practice the arts of war, a site for training gentlemen in cavalry skills and engendering blood lust. That is why it is unsurprising that Corneille used the garden as a symbol of courage and virility, pitted against a pale and deso-

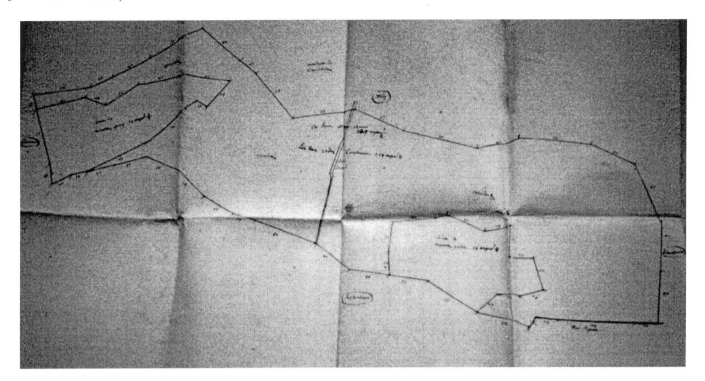

5. Forest plan. Louis de Froidour. Regional Archives, Toulouse.

late yearning for peace that was equated with a desert:

> Arise at this sight, fountains, flowers, woods
> Drive out this detritus, the baneful images [of a
>   war-ravaged landscape]
> And form gardens, such as with four words
> The great art of Medée gave rise to at Colchis.[36]

The *petit parc* was anything but a desert; it was jammed with lush trees, profuse waterworks, and massive artworks—symbols and demonstrations of human accomplishment. It was explicitly filled, too, with signs of virility, from the explosive fountains to triumphal arches and multiple statues of Hercules with his club in hand and the skin of a wild beast slung over his back. The *bosquets* also highlighted features of the landscape of greatest concern to the army. They were topographically complex, patterned with barriers and passageways: walls, trees, hedges, and trellises, on the one hand, and walkways, stairs, and ramps, on the other. The different areas of *petit parc* were punctuated with waterworks that alternately impeded movement and facilitated it, and they played on the changing visibility and invisibility of garden features. They presented a space likely to appeal to those with

military experience or aspirations, like the nobles who frequented the gardens.

The formal structure of the *bosquets* within the *petit parc*, rather than obscuring or overlaying the military references in the landscape (as in Italian gardens), seemed to help reveal patterns in their variations. The *bosquets* farthest from the château were crossed by walkways quite unlike those typical of Italian Renaissance and Mannerist gardens. They were not set out in a regular geometrical pattern. Instead, they were laid out like the lines of sight used by surveyors to measure the land with economically few calculations. This oblique reference to cartographic practice pointed to a technical connection between garden design and military mapmaking. It also pointed to an important tool of power. As James C. Scott has argued, using roads and canals to cut into land areas, particularly wilderness and forests, was a technique of population and territorial control already central to this regime. It was as appealing to Colbert as it was to military cartographers. No wonder this capacity for power was highlighted in the park.[37]

The *bosquets* located one rank closer to the château at Versailles were organized quite differently; they used conventional geometrical patterns like Italian Mannerist gardens, but they were nonethe-

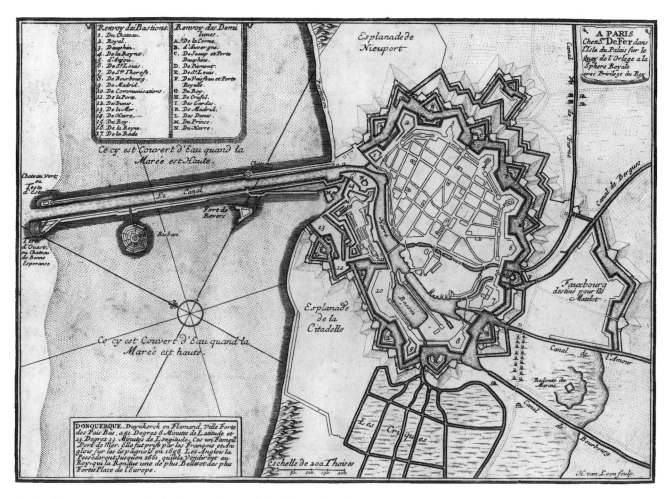

6. Plan of Donquerque. Nicolas de Fer, *Introduction à la fortification*, [1705?]. University of California, Berkeley.

less designed—significantly—with the simple geometrical figures that Nicolas de Fer touted as appropriate for building fortresses.[38] The pentagon (employed in the *bosquet de l'Etoile*) was among the most favored fortress forms. The equally important octagon was not represented here; instead the *bosquet de la girandole* and *bosquet Dauphin* were both set out in the same general form: the square within a square. This pattern suggested an eight-pointed figure but foregrounded the square itself, which was still the fundamental geometrical basis for many fortress designs. This group of *bosquets* pointed toward the geometry of military engineering—the use of measured figures for defenses that would both order and dominate the landscape.

Finally, the *bosquets* at the back of the château engaged the problem of grading, managing the differences in elevation between the terrace and the rest of the park. They took up the decorative and

symbolic possibilities of fortress walls, sloping hillsides, both great and small grades, and the resulting terraces and problems of access. To the north and west, great walls were built to hold up the hillside and form barriers between the château and the countryside beyond. These "defenses" were punctured, in turn, by ramps, steps, and passageways that allowed visitors the pleasure of ascending to the heights of the garden—the level of the king and his court—where they could survey the town, the nearby plateaus, and the royal hunting forests. The terrace itself was made flat and open like the terraces on battlements designed for surveying the land below. Finally, the series of levels and slopes to the north of the château provided a playful miniature version of the land-control patterns used more dramatically at the other two sides of the terrace.

Thus the layout of the *petit parc* seemed designed to highlight aspects of the natural and built en-

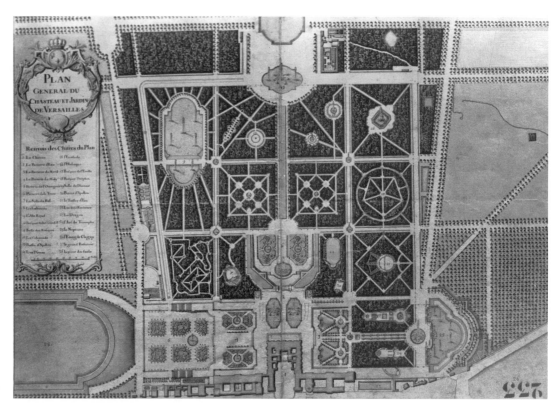

7. *Plan Generale de Petit Parc de Versailles*. Girard. Archives Nationale.

vironment intrinsic to the cartographic sensibility developed in France by the military. This space sometimes drew attention to topography and elevation; at other times it presented models of fortress design; and at still others it referred to the survey geometry around which military engineers concocted their strategies for waging war. Hence the garden was not only engineered using military models, but also obliquely referred to this in its overall design.

If the structured relations in the plan of the *petit parc* could not speak for themselves about the debts to military engineering in formal garden design, then the symbolic content of the park helped to make the connections. The attention to barriers and passageways at the heart of military mapmaking (and fortress engineering for that matter) also provided the design focus for the park at Versailles. The canal itself, of course, was the most dramatic and effective barrier in the royal gardens, as was apparent to anyone wanting to cross the park on foot. But arrayed with miniature ships for carrying nobles from one part of the landscape to another, it could also be a passageway. In this regard, it mimicked rivers and canals, which for the military were often a mixed blessing. Sometimes a river was a

vital conduit for ships, troops, and supplies. Other times it was a line of defense that inhibited further movement. The French army designed a wide array of temporary bridges to try to reduce the impediments of rivers, while they also dredged harbors and rivers to make them more efficient carriers of military supplies. When Nicolas Tassin went to chart the northern coastline of France, he paid particular attention to the rivers, sandbars, drainage ditches, and the like which shaped travel through this region.[39]

The *marais* and *encelade* also pointed to another concern of military cartographers: the swamps and mires that could be even more debilitating than rivers since they offered no easy passage and could not be spanned with a temporary bridge. The *marais* at Versailles may have been treated as a silly amusement designed by the king's mistress, but it had a pride of place in his itineraries that goes beyond sentimentality. It was a site that showed a kind of transcendence of and pleasure in one of the most frustrating environments encountered by soldiers (fig. 8). Even the statue of the *encelade*, that great giant struggling to free himself from the earth, depicted this figure in the *bosquet* at Versailles as falling into something like a bog or quicksand in which

8. *The Encelade.* G. Marsy. Photo by Becky Cohen.

his efforts to move only dragged him deeper into the earth. The moral of the story told by the fountain might have been about the dangers of trying to rise above one's station, but the message was conveyed through a soldier's nightmare.

The *isle royale*, on the other hand, was the utopian counter to this dystopia. A great lake was constructed with a grassy bridge through its center. This levee was the sort of land bridge used in many French fortresses at their entrance because it could comfortably span a moat, but it also could easily be destroyed to frustrate an enemy. Similar levees built in swampy regions of France, particularly along drainage canals, were also useful in helping transport soldiers and supplies. The military sometimes built them when they did work to control rivers and reclaim land around them, and they recorded the results of their efforts in early military maps. At Versailles this form was interestingly employed and naturalized in the *isle royale*.

If some *bosquets* at Versailles represented supposedly natural forms that interrupted and provided passage through the terrain, others presented characteristics of the built environment cultivated by military engineers. The *salle de bal* was an open amphitheater built with walls backfilled with dirt,

and it was cut into steps—miniature terraces—that, on one side, provided seats for an audience and, on the other side, created an elaborate cascade. This space clearly had Roman references, and like its Roman counterparts, used grading, stone walls, and visibility as its design elements (like a fortress), but it reversed the principles of battlements. It turned inward, facilitating visibility rather than inhibiting sight, and it contained walls designed to be easily scaled. Symbolically, the *salle de bal* seemed to take the viewer underground, too, rather than up into a mountainous fortress. The space itself was snuggled against the side of the terrace, and the cascade was covered with rocks and seashells—riches from beneath the sea and under the earth, not from the mountains. The reversals made the space seem very intimate and exotic, and a distinct contrast to the massive, imposing, and intimidating terraces hovering above.

The terrace, particularly viewed from below at the southwest corner, appeared almost as a fortress structure in itself. The hundred steps running up to it were made so far above the ground level that anyone or anything on the terrace was invisible to those located at the foot of the stairs. Standing on the terrace itself, in contrast, gave visitors great vistas in three directions: toward the town (to the north), the *parterre du Midi* and *lac d'eau des Suisses* (to the south), and the central *allée* (to the west). These three vistas suggested three forms of domination: of the local environs, of a distant region of France (the Midi), and of France as a whole, vast territory.

Tunnels were also a vital part of military engineering that showed up under the terraces at Versailles. The Orangery, dug into the hillside to house tender plants in the winter, looked very much like an oversized wine cellar, but so did the permanent tunnels built in fortresses in France—structures that were even called "caves." Behind the Orangery, under the terrace, there were smaller, but similarly designed tunnels for the water system. The fountains at this site could not be supplied with water from the main pump and reservoir system because the terrace was the highest point in the garden. A set of underground cisterns, built like vast tunnels, was constructed underneath the *parterre d'eau* for its water supply.[40] This would seem to have little relation to military engineering or claims to be the New Rome, but it was at this time that vast tunnels began to be placed under fortress walls for moving troops unseen by the enemy. This work was an outgrowth of the tunneling used to pierce fortress walls during sieges, but, being more permanent, it was not constructed with wooden supports; rather, it used stone arches of the sort used in Roman waterworks.[41] This military technology might not have been advertised in the gardens, but it was part of what indebted this fortresslike area of the park to military engineering.

Oddly enough, the *jardin potager* was the space at Versailles more overtly tied to military architecture.[42] It was shaped like a miniature fortress with a set of ramparts along which the king and his retinue could walk and survey the fruit trees growing at their feet. The stone walls for these ramparts had tunnels through them, the purpose of which is not clear, but the source of which is evident from the discussion above. The fortress wall system worked well for raising tender fruits and vegetables because the plants in the *potager* were warmed by solar heat captured in the stone walls. Where glass screens were set in front of trees planted against south-facing walls, the result was an effective sort of greenhouse. The *potager* may not have looked like the market gardens that produced so much of France's fruits and vegetables, but it worked as an effective means for forcing plants to produce earlier and more luscious fruits and vegetables for the royal table. It enclosed its bounty in an architecture that echoed the military ambitions of the king.

Fortress footprints also often found their way into fountain designs at Versailles. On top of the terrace and in front of the château, there were a series of *parterres d'eau*, an early version of which was made up of a reflecting pool with a flat stone surface in the middle (large enough to walk on) shaped in the pattern of a traditional fortress footprint. Similar patterns were used in the design of the *salle des festins*, the *salle de conseil*, and the *obélisque* fountain that replaced the *salle de conseil*. The *salle des festins*, like the *parterre d'eau*, provided means for visitors to enter the fortress area, but the *obélisque* did not. It was made up of a moatlike pool around a stone fortress shape with another pool in its center containing the fountain itself. For all the variations, these reminders of French military engineering were simple and visible enough to connect French gardening with the regime's military ambitions, the army's technical skills, and the state's territorial control.

WATERWORKS FOR A NEW ROME

The French military was showcased in these ways at the gardens of Versailles, but the ties between French military capacities and the claim to be the New Rome were not clearly made. The engineering of the ancients may have shaped the patterns of fortress design that entered the gardens, but they were not marked to make this an important aesthetic or political statement. This meant that the territorial control in the gardens might have demonstrated the political ambitions and resources of France, showing the state to be a military force to be reckoned with in Europe, but it was not enough to make France seem the natural descendant of the Roman Empire. Ancient Rome built great cities and monuments, not just an army (fig. 9). Versailles needed to be splendid in some way that tied it to Rome, surpassed Italy, and showed enough innovation to suggest that France held the keys to Europe's future.

In this context, the water system gained increasing attention from the king, his ministers, surveyors, scientists, entrepreneurs, and fountainers. The wisdom of the ancients about waterworks was known to be enormous;[43] the king and court also knew that the Romans used soldiers to build elements of their water supplies, disciplining their military men while creating monuments to Rome.[44] If the fountains at Versailles were made glorious enough to provide clear evidence that the French could similarly construct waterworks as grand as

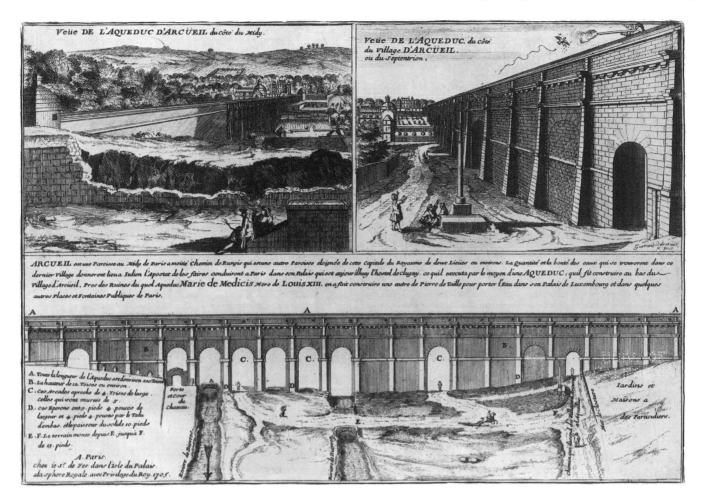

9. Roman aqueduct. Nicolas de Fer, *L'Atlas Curieux*, 1705. University of California, Berkeley.

those in ancient Rome, then the gardens would visibly (and gracefully) confirm France's readiness to take on both the political and cultural leadership of Europe.

To make such a system, however, French engineers had to be able to use Roman technology and develop it for the glory of France; this was not easy. There were many technical and logistical failures along the way; the Loire, for example, could not be tapped for its waters in spite of plans for that to be done.[45] Many innovations did not have the desired effect; the attempts to use local groundwater never did yield an adequate supply even as more pumps and reservoirs were added to the system. If France was supposed to be the natural descendant of the Roman Empire, it was supposed to achieve its technical and military greatness with ease, not stumble around ineffectively looking for water. But the waterworks never seemed to work easily at Versailles, much to the frustration of Louis XIV and Colbert.

Not only was water itself a problem, but so were the stories told about its paucity or unwanted abundance at Versailles.[46] Provocatively, the stories underscored the assumption in the period that something fundamental about France's politics and culture could be read into (or from) the engineering of a water system. It is hard to know when tales about the water system were first crafted, and how much currency they had at the time, but there was evidence of them in the writings of contemporaries. The search for water at Versailles was early on turned into a kind of morality play—sometimes a battle between the Ancients and the Moderns, sometimes a story of the cruel ineptitude of absolutism, and sometimes a tale of the military arriving to save the day. Certainly, the success of the Machine de Marly suggested that machine-building (a modern technology) could be more effective for hydraulic systems than Roman engineering.[47] On the other hand, news of the large number of deaths of soldiers working on the aqueduct at Maintenon led to the circulation of stories about the king's vanity and the destructiveness of absolutism. In one fashion or another, all these stories addressed the question of France's greatness and located the answer not in the words written about the king, court, and country, but the actions of French engineers and their effects—good and bad—on the countryside and people of France.[48]

Stories aside, the effectiveness of French efforts to reappropriate the military heritage of the Romans depended not on a moral balance, but rather on the application of multiple streams of French cartography and engineering to the practical problems of territorial management. Even when the results were attributed to the military (and the Roman inheritance in France of military engineering), it was the confluence of these different traditions that made the search for water succeed—both in supplying Versailles and realizing the political goals of the project. To see this, we need to look at the engineering of the most successful source for Versailles: the dams, reservoirs, and canals of the Satory plateau.

Abbé Picard from the Académie, not a military man, was the one who first suggested tapping this plateau more systematically to create an adequate water supply for the gardens. Even while the main source for Versailles was being developed around Clagny and the north side of the garden, the water of the Bièvre and surrounding areas had been tapped for the south side of the park. Abbé Picard had been involved in this early work, doing the elevation studies necessary for building a modest system of *estangs* on this side of the garden. He learned at the time that much of this region was higher than the main park, and that reservoirs in this area could be more effective than anticipated in capturing water. The *estang de Renard* and the improved *estang de Val* were a significant, if not grand, success.[49]

Picard realized much more was still possible, but did not immediately suggest this solution, as he was being called upon to assess more exciting and dramatic proposals for diverting river water to the king's park. These projects also required him to make elevation studies of the region, including possible routes for bringing water from the Eure River to Versailles. This idea at first seemed absurd, since the river at the point nearest to the park was actually lower than the garden. However, he located a site farther up the Eure but not too far from Versailles where the river rushed downstream from a substantially higher elevation. This finding suggested that one could tap the river at the higher elevation and bring the supplies to Versailles through a system of channels and pumps. The logical route downhill, however, kept the water on the side of the Eure that was farther away from Versailles. This led to the proposal for an aqueduct at Maintenon that could channel the flow across the river again, carrying it to the park. The aqueduct proved a miserable failure, but the aspirations for this project led scientists, entrepreneurs, and cartographers to think more about the region south of the park (fig. 10).[50]

Another proposal suggested bringing water from the Loire River to Versailles. The engineer Pierre-Paul Riquet, who had successfully planned and initiated construction of the Canal du Midi, brought this plan to Colbert, who had it assessed by Abbé Picard. Picard was apparently contemptuous of Riquet's surveying instruments and found the results of his elevations faulty. The water source was not only lower than the valley of the garden, but would have had to be brought over the Satory plateau with its daunting mountains. Picard surveyed the area to see if there was indeed any conceivable route to Versailles. While he did not find one, he did note gorges on the Satory plateau where runoff could be captured to provide a larger water supply for Versailles.[51]

French scientists and engineers knew from the ancients that narrow mountain passes could be dammed when they were dry, creating earthen bowls that would fill with water after a rain. A set of reservoirs built this way on the same plateau could then be linked and connected to the water system in place south of Versailles. Even parts of the incomplete Eure canal system could be employed for the project, taking advantage of the work already completed. If soldiers could construct the dams, and link them to this earlier military work, they would create a system that would seem (at least on the surface) a triumph of military engineering in the Roman style, a great monument to the regime, and a fine piece of land management.[52]

By the time this project was realized, Picard had died, but another academician, Philippe de La Hire, had taken his place. The Marquis de Louvois was now in charge of the project, too, since Colbert had also died. The longtime minister of war was finally placed officially in charge of royal building projects—an apt enough assignment in the New Rome. When Louvois asked Vauban to assess the work, it seemed that scientific surveying was finally to be put in the service of military engineering to yield an appropriately glorious and effective water system for Versailles.[53]

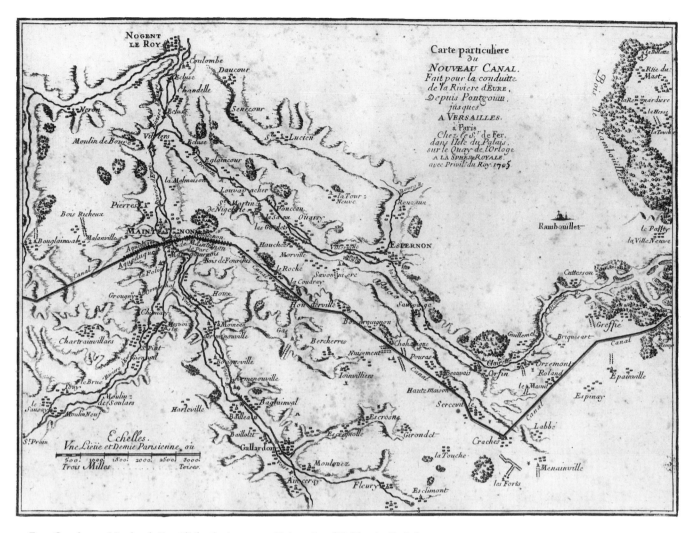

10. Eure Canal map. Nicolas de Fer, *L'Atlas Curieux*, 1705. University of California, Berkeley.

But it also took civil engineering to bring the water system to fruition. It was the work of less-celebrated engineers and untouted moderns, as well as the traditions of the Romans, the labors of military engineers, and the surveys of scholar-scientists, that made this work possible. Military engineers, even those schooled in the work of the ancients and fine survey techniques, men who could measure elevations very precisely and build structures that could endure through most conditions of war, could not have done the work alone. They were not as skilled as academicians like Picard or La Hire in comparing elevations over the kinds of distances required for the water system at Versailles, and they did not normally build structures over such immense stretches of terrain. Even the academicians could not complete the project on their own with just their mathematical skills and abstract knowledge of the ancients. Someone had to construct the conduits for the water, spanning valleys and cutting through hillsides; this required some practical as well as articulated engineering skills cultivated primarily by the civil engineers who built the French road system. Conducting water to the gardens was more like road building than fortress construction, requiring only a narrow pathway for the conduits and a smooth downslope for most of the journey. An occasional pump could push water up a small hill, but good engineering was meant to minimize this. A pump could break or the windmill powering a pump could simply stop when the winds slowed. This was acceptable for a while, since a reservoir or holding tank could keep supplies available in the short run. But in the long run, it was best—and the king wanted the best—to create a smooth surface for uninterrupted trans-

11. Routes des Postes du Royaume de France. Nicolas de Fer, *Atlas ou Recüeil des cartes geographiques*. University of California, Berkeley.

port of water to Versailles. The civil engineers had the necessary skills for that job.[54]

Entrepreneurs were hired to construct the water supply system, and they brought civil engineers to the project. This paralleled the arrangement typically used in building major roads in France. Local entrepreneurs were authorized by the state and funded by local authorities to lay out the roads and bridges for their regions (fig. 11). They created ribbons of control in the complex landscape—

just what was needed for carrying water through a series of reservoirs to Versailles.[55]

The use of civil engineers for this work made sense, once the decision had been made not to use closed pipes through the valleys. The knowledge of hydraulics in the period was advanced enough that engineers knew water would rise to its own level. In a closed pipe, the water sent into a valley would resurface on the other side as long as the far bank was at a lower elevation than the near one. The problem was that pipes broke easily. If this water system was to be a monument to France, it had to be as stable as possible. So this kind of piping was avoided, and instead the pathways for the water were constructed like the best roadways. Many small bridges were built across gullies, and ditches and tunnels were dug through hills.[56]

The result certainly looked like the work of military engineers. Roads had been constructed by Roman soldiers, as were the aqueducts and conduits for Roman water systems. But this is not how the French allocated their engineering projects. Although military engineers were certainly skilled at building roads and bridges around fortresses, and devised passages through complex terrains where post roads were not laid out, they were not France's primary road builders. It was not that the army could not build the water transport system from Satory; this kind of work was just not the specialty of military engineers. The truth was that these soldiers did much of their engineering under conditions of war in which temporary structures made more sense than permanent ones.[57] They made wooden bridges to span a small river quickly. They launched sieges using tunnels shored up with wood that would deteriorate over time. When the battle was over, the structures were not needed. Army engineers were in some ways ill-equipped to build monuments other than fortresses or something like them.

This did not mean that military engineers had nothing to contribute to the Satory water system. They built the dams for the water supply. These earthen constructions resembled the battlements and levees for fortresses that were so central to military life. They were also part of the heritage of military engineering derived from the ancients that was well known to the French military. In the end, soldiers did indeed help build a great water system for Versailles and made a very dramatic and visible contribution to the Satory project. The system itself was clearly modeled on the engineering of the ancients, and could easily, if not entirely appropriately, be celebrated as a triumph of French military engineering. Still, the role of the military in the project was surprisingly modest. It was only during the late stages of the project that Vauban made a few recommendations about expanding the system to make it more effective. Still, he did not make any fundamental design innovations. But talk about Vauban's success at Satory, even if mostly fictional, provided a way to celebrate both France's leading engineer and French military engineering.[58]

The water system at Versailles helped make the gardens stunning and demonstrated the submission of this element of nature to the will of the monarch. The beauty of the result, particularly when the fountains spewed from sculpture with a decidedly classical form, seemed to align France and Rome aesthetically as well as technically. The fact that soldiers had indeed worked to build this monument made it easy to tell stories about natural abilities, military prowess, and cultural inheritance. The naming of the *lac d'eau des Suisses* after the Swiss Guard highlighted the role of soldiers in constructing the water system for Versailles—even those who stayed inside the park's walls. The fact that the water system itself was a marvel that used all the techniques of ancient Rome, combined with French innovations, suggested that the mantle of power and cultural hegemony had already passed to the New Rome of Louis XIV. As Néraudau suggested, the value of Versailles as a political site lay not simply in the conscious and adept deployment of mythology, but the creation of a basis for believing it—the demonstration of efficacy at a monumental level.[59]

Notes

1. Chandra Mukerji, *Territorial Ambitions and the Gardens of Versailles* (Cambridge: Cambridge University Press, 1997), chap. 1.

2. Peter Burke, *The Fabrication of Louis XIV* (New Haven: Yale University Press, 1992).

3. Mukerji, *Territorial Ambitions*; Jean-Marie Apostolidès, *Le Roi-Machine: Spectacle et politique au temps de Louis XIV* (Paris: Editions de Minuit, 1981); Louis Marin, *Des pouvoirs de l'image* (Paris: Editions de Seuil, 1993); Louis Marin, *Portrait du Roi* (Paris: Editions de Minuit, 1981); Chandra Mukerji, *From Graven Images: Patterns of Modern Materialism* (New York: Columbia University Press, 1982), chap 5.

4. Christopher Thacker, "La manière de montrer les jardins de Versailles," *Garden History* 1 (1972): 49–69.

5. J. P. Néraudau, *L'Olympe du Roi Soleil* (Paris: Société des Belles-Lettres, 1986), 234–37.

6. Monique Mosser and Georges Teyssot, *The Architecture of Western Gardens* (Cambridge, Mass.: MIT Press, 1991).

7. L. A. Barbet, *Les Grandes Eaux de Versailles: Installations Méchaniques et Estangs Artificiels, Descriptions des Fontaines et de leurs Origines* (Paris: H. Dunod et E. Pinat, 1907).

8. Does this explain the popularity of the translation of Vitruvius in France? See Antoine Picon, *Claude Perrault ou la curiosité d'un classique* (Paris: Picard Editeur, 1989).

9. Madeleine de Scudéry, *La Promenade de Versailles* (Geneva: Slatkine Reprints, [1669] 1979).

10. André Félibien, *Description de la Grotte de Versailles*

(Paris: Chez Sébastien Mabre-Cramoisy, 1672); André Félibien, *Relation de la Feste de Versailles du 18e Juillet 1668* (Paris: Pierre le Petit), and Bibliothèque Nationale (hereafter B.N.), Lb37. 360.

11. Part of the arguments about Ancients and Moderns focused on science and technology as the source of the strength of moderns: Charles Perrault, *Parallèle des Anciens and des Modernes* (Geneva: Slatkine Reprints, [1692] 1979). The French could see the material heritage of Rome and the possibility of its improvement. This is part of the idea behind Perrault's colonnade. See Picon, *Claude Perrault*.

12. Mukerji, *Territorial Ambitions*, 39.

13. Thierry Mariage, *L'Univers de Le Nôtre* (Brussels: Pierre Mardaga,1990), 42–45, 51–53; trans. Graham Larkin (Philadelphia: University of Pennsylvania Press, 1999).

14. See, for example, Derek Clifford, *A History of Garden Design* (New York: Praeger, 1963); see also Christopher Thacker, *The History of Gardens* (Berkeley: University of California Press, 1979); and F. Hamilton Hazlehurst, *Gardens of Illusion* (Nashville: Vanderbilt University Press, 1980).

15. Bernard Pujo, *Vauban* (Paris: Albin Michel, 1991), chap. 6; Michel Parent and Jacques Verroust, *Vauban* (Paris: Editions Jacques Fréal, 1971), 129–32, 147–61, 200–206; Alfred Rebelliau, *Vauban* (Paris: Fayard, 1962), 49–51, 312–13; Jacques Dollar, *Vauban à Luxembourg, place forte de l'Europe (1684–97)* (Luxembourg: RLT Edition, 1983); Nelly G. d'Albissin, *Genèse de la frontière franco-belge: Les variations des limites septentrionales de la France de 1659 à 1789* (Paris: Editions A. & J. Picard, 1970), chap. 2; Mukerji, *Territorial Ambitions*, 55–56. For a description of how border towns were used to control trade as well as troop movements, see Ellis Veryard, *An Account of Divers Choice Remarks as well as Geographical, Historical, political, Mathematical and Moral; Taken in a Journey through the Low Countries, France, Italy, and Part of Spain with the Isles of Sicilly and Malta* (London: S. Smith and B. Walford, 1701), 61.

16. Hazlehurst, *Gardens of Illusion*; see also his essay in this volume. By comparing the profile of a wall system from Allain Mallet's *Travaux de Mars* to the elevations in Le Nôtre's first garden at Vaux-le-Vicomte, we can see more clearly how garden topography resembled the complex of walls and ditches used in the fortresses of the period. The main portion of the garden was structured like an extended version of the level area commonly found in the center of bastion walls, and some of the shapes were not transferred to the garden, but the whole complex of levels and ditches were startlingly similar. See Allain Manesson Mallet, *Les Travaux de Mars ou l'Art de la Guerre* (Amsterdam: Jan et Gillis Janson à Waesbergue, 1684).

17. Mukerji, *Territorial Ambitions*, chap. 2.

18. Carlo Cipolla, *Guns, Sails and Empires: Technological Innovation and the Early Phases of European Expansion, 1400–1700* (New York: Minerva Books, 1965), chap. 1.

19. Helen Roseneau, *The Ideal City: Its Architectural Evolution* (Boston: Boston Book and Art Shop, 1959); A. E. J. Morris, *History of Urban Form* (London: George Godwin, 1979).

20. Cipolla, *Guns*, chap. 1; Pierre Rocolle, *2000 ans de fortification française*, vol. 1 (Limoges and Paris: Charles-Lavauzelle, 1973), 175–212; Sébastien Le Prestre Vauban, *De l'attaque et de la défense des places* (The Hague: Chez Pierre de Hondt, 1736); John A. Lynn, *Giant of the Grand Siècle* (Cambridge: Cambridge University Press, 1997), 547–93.

21. Mukerji, *Territorial Ambitions*, 24.

22. Anne Blanchard, *Histoire Militaire de la France* (Paris: Presses Universitaires de la France, 1992), 48–49; see Sebastiano Serlio, *Sebastiano Serlio on Architecture*, vol. 1, trans. V. Hart and P. Hicks (New Haven: Yale University Press, 1996), xiii–xiv.

23. Blanchard, *Histoire Militaire*, 47–49.

24. Ibid., 42–43, 48–49, 53–54.

25. Ibid., 50–55. For examples of some of this work, see *Livre d'architecture, de Jacques Androuet, du Cerceau, auquel sont contenues diverses ordonnances de plants et éleuations de bastiment pour seigneurs, gentilshommes, & autres qui voudront bastir aux champs; mesmes en aucuns d'iceux sont desseignez les basses courts . . . aussi les jardinages et vergiers* (Paris: J. Androuet du Cerceau, 1615); *Le premier [-second] volume des plus excellents bastiments de France auquel sont designez les plans de quinze bastiments, & de leur contenu . . . , par Jacques Androuet du Cerceau* (Paris: J. Androuet du Cerceau, 1607), 2 vols. in 1. For descriptions of the work of de Beins and de Brosse, see François de Dainville, *Le Dauphiné et ses confins vus par l'ingénieur d'Henri IV Jean de Beins* (Geneva: Droz; Paris: Minard, 1968); Jacques Pannier, *Un architecte français au commencement du XVIIe siècle, Salomon de Brosse* (Paris: Librairie centrale d'art et d'architecture, 1911).

26. Mukerji, *Territorial Ambitions*, 41–42, 45; Mariage, *Le Nôtre*, 43.

27. Mukerji, Territorial Ambitions, 152–69. For a discussion of this tradition, see also C. Mukerji, "The Properties of Properties," forthcoming in *Bourgeois Influences on Garden Art*, ed. Michel Conan (Washington, D.C.: Dumbarton Oaks).

28. John Marino, "Administrative Mapping in the Italian States," in *Monarchs, Ministers, and Maps*, ed. David Buisseret (Chicago: University of Chicago Press, 1992), 5–25; Rocolle, *Fortification*, 195–230; Blanchard, *Histoire Militaire*, 112–13, 402–8; Mukerji, *Territorial Ambitions*.

29. Veryard, *Account*, 105.

30. Mukerji, *Territorial Ambitions*, 42; Sébastian Le Clerc, *Practique de la geometrie sur le papier and sur le terrain* (Paris: Chez Thomas Jolly, 1669). These only became visible (if ever) when some pieces began to be copied or reproduced in print in sheets or atlases. (The reuse of cartographic images in new volumes resembled the patterns in science publishing in the period as described by Adrian Johns, *The Nature of the Book* [Chicago: University of Chicago Press, 1998].) The book that Nicolas de Fer assembled for the military education of the dauphin, *Introduction à la Fortification*, was an interesting use of this genre of maps; it was a compilation of images, mostly of cities with strategic interest, and drawn by different mapmakers: Nicolas de Fer, *Introduction à la Fortification dedié à Monseigneur le duc de Bourgogne* (Paris: Chez l'auteur dans l'Isle du Palais sur le Quay de l'Orloge à la Sphere Royale, avec priv. du Roy, n.d.). There were other political needs and uses for mapmaking in early seventeenth-century France. Maps of the postal routes made the road system more visible and easier to improve through the engineering of bridges and other land improvements. These maps obviously also had use for planning troop movements, but they were published rather than kept secret like most

military maps. These published works were meant mostly to make visible the resources of the kingdom such as its road system. In a slightly different vein, Nicolas Sanson made many ecclesiastical maps, using techniques familiar to general political maps. He was employed by the church when state funds were hard to come by, and he made these maps of church lands which were in part political maps (areas of influence) and partly the church equivalent of estate maps, showing the location of various church holdings. Coastal maps and plans of harbors were also important to the military. As early as the 1630s, Christophe Tassin mapped the coastal regions of northern France, partially to make these remote corners of France more recognizable to his patron, Richelieu, but partially also to make a military inventory of the strengths and weaknesses of the borders of the kingdom. In the same period, Jean de Beins began pioneering work on mountain passes in the Alps. Together these works constituted a very detailed, if not technically systematic, body of work about the outlying regions and natural boundaries of the French countryside. See Buisseret, *Monarchs*, chap. 4, esp. 109, 114, 115.

31. Jacques Cassini, *De La Grandeur et de la Figure de la Terre. Suite des Mémoires de l'Académie Royale des Sciences, Année MDCCXVIII* (Paris: Imprimerie Royale, 1720); John Noble Wilford, *The Mapmakers* (New York: Vintage, 1981), chap. 8; Joseph Konvitz, *Cartography in France, 1660–1848* (Chicago: University of Chicago Press, 1987), esp. chap. 1; Monique Pelletier, *La Carte de Cassini* (Paris: Presse de l'Ecole des Ponts et Chaussées, 1990), chap. 2; Wilford, chap. 8; Jean-Paul Duranthon, *La Carte de France* (Paris: Solar, 1978).

32. M. Devèze, *Une admirable réforme administrative: La grande réformation des forêts royales sous Colbert (1662–1680)*, Annales de L'Ecole Nationale des Eaux et Forêts et de la Station de Recherches et Expériences (Nancy: Ecole Nationale des Eaux et Forêts, 1962), pt 1, chaps. 2–3; Paul W. Bamford, *Forests and French Sea Power, 1660–1789* (Toronto: University of Toronto Press, 1956), 14–19. André Corvol, *L'homme et l'arbre sous l'Ancien régime* (Paris: Economica, 1984), chap. 1, argues that the problems of the forest were not remedied by the forest management system put in place by Colbert because it was designed on the basis of insufficient knowledge of the forests and what they needed to grow.

33. For an exhaustive description of what the new foresters did in each forest, see Devèze, pt. 2; Bamford, *Forests and French Sea Power*, 18–20. For an example of the fines levied on the local elite in one area, see Devèze, *Réforme*, 114–15. Corvol, *L'homme et l'arbre*, 17–28, argues that the surveys were not as well executed as many others writing on this subject have suggested. Devèze (ibid., esp. 76–77) is particularly insistent that these reforms were more important for the revenues they raised and the economic rationality they aspired to than their espoused military purposes.

34. See Roger Kain and Elizabeth Baigent, *The Cadastral Map in the Service of the State* (Chicago: University of Chicago Press, 1992), 210–12.

35. See this theme in the words of La Fontaine, quoted in Néraudau, *L'Olympe du Roi Soleil*, 160:

Il veut sur le théâtre ainsi qu'à la campagne
La foule qui le suit, l'éclat qui l'accompagne:

Grand en tout, il veut mettre en tout la grandeur . . .
Ses divertissements resentent tous la guerre:
Ses concerts d'instruments ont le buit du tonnere,
Et ses concerts de voix ressemblent aux éclats
Qu'en un jour de combat font les cris des coldtas.
Les danseurs, par leur nombre, éblouissent la vue,
Et le battl paraît exercise, revue,
Jeu des gladiateurs, et tel qu'au champ de Mars
En leurs jours de triomphe en donnaient les Césars.

36.   Naissez à cet aspect, fontaines, fleurs, bocages,
Chassez de ces débris les funestes images,
Et formez des jardins tels qu'avec quatre mots
Le grand art de Médée en fit naître à Colchos.

From the prologue of Corneille, *La Conquête de la toison d'or*; see Corneille, *Oeuvres complètes*, preface by E. Lebègue, ed. A. Stegmann (London: Macmillan, 1963), 596. This passage is followed by a detailed description of the garden that should be set up for the upcoming scene, underscoring the centrality of the garden and its lushness to this piece.

37. James C. Scott, *Seeing Like a State* (New Haven: Yale University Press, 1998).

38. De Fer, *Introduction à la Fortification*.

39. Nicolas Tassin, *Les plans et profils de tovtes les principales villes et lievs considerables de France . . .* (Paris: S. Cramoisy, 1638); Buisseret, *Monarchs*, 109, 114, 115.

40. Barbet, *Versailles*, 38–39.

41. See John Muller, *The Attack and Defense of Fortified Places. In Three Parts* (London: T. & J. Egerton, 1791), esp. pls. IX and XI. See also M. Belidor, *Les sciences des ingenieurs dans la conduite des travaux de fortificationet d'architecture civile* (Paris: Claude Jombert, 1729).

42. Mukerji, *Territorial Ambitions*, chap. 3.

43. The significance of water engineering to the Romans was an issue of particular concern to those interested in building canals in this period. We can see what Roman plans concerned them in Pierre Salies, "De l'Isthme gaulois au Canal Royal des Deux Mers," in *Le Canal du Midi: Grands moments et grands sites*, ed. Jean-Denis Bergasse (Cessenon: J. D. Bergasse, 1982), 57–61. There was also widespread interest in Virtuvius' writings, which included a large section on hydraulics. See, for example, Pollio Vitruvius, *Architecture, ou Art de bien bastir, de Marc Vitruve Pollion; romain antique mis de latin en francoys, par Ian Martin* (Paris, J. Gazeau, 1547); *Abregé des Dix livres d'architecture de Vitruve* (Paris: J. B. Coignard, 1674); *Architecture generale de Vitruve: reduite en abregé, par M. Perrault de l'Academie des sciences a Paris. Derniere ed., enrichie de figures en cuivre* (Amsterdam: Aux dépens des Huguetan, et se vend chez George Gallet, 1681). And the Académie was rife with proposals when the issue of Versailles's water system was under discussion. See Seymour L. Chapin, "Science in the Reign of Louis XIV," in *The Reign of Louis XIV*, ed. Paul Sonnino (Atlantic Highlands, N.J. and London: Humanities Press International, 1990), 186–87.

44. This is mentioned by Vauban as a model for French soldiers. See Lynn, *Giant of the Grand Siècle*, pt. 4.

45. Barbet, *Versailles*, 52–53. It is interesting to note that the aqueduc d'Arcueil was restored to use by Thomas Francine, from the same family as François and Pierre Francine, who built most of the fountains and much of the local water system at Versailles for Louis XIV. The com-

bined interest in ancient hydraulic engineering and fountains was realized in both generations. Thomas' brother Alexandre was fountainer at Fontainebleau. See Belidor, *Les sciences des ingenieurs*, 48–54.

46. Néraudau points out that the waterworks at Versailles were such cultural icons that there was even music written in their honor, such as Delalande's *Fontaines de Versailles* (1683) and Philidor's *Canal du Parc* (1687).

47. John Locke, in his travels to France, exalted Louis XIV for having brought the greatest achievements in the arts of building and science: "the very *Muses* of the fabulous *Helicon* seem to have remov'd to settle on the banks of the *Seyne*, and *France* now vies in all particulars with the most famous of the ancients, whether *Roman* or *Greeks*." *Locke's Travels in France*, ed. I. Lough (New York: Garland, 1984), 4:626. How does Locke reach this conclusion? From going to Versailles, and particularly from viewing the water system. "All the fabulous stories of the ancients, at the sight of these become credible, and we scarce believe our own eyes amidst so many wonderful things as fill so great a tract of land" (4:627). He goes on to describe in detail the Machine de Marly and the system of pumps, pipes, cisterns, and reservoirs that take the river water to the gardens of Versailles and Marly (4:630). Although Locke can become ironic about the praise heaped on the monarch by his followers and propagandists, he is deeply impressed by the technical accomplishments and aesthetic achievements of the gardens.

Veryard is not so sanguine about the place. "The most considerable [of the royal residences] is *Versailles*, where the King usually resides, and did its Situation answer the Magnificence and Beauty of the Architecture, nothing of this nature could exceed it. I could not but admire that so much Money should be spent in beautifying a Bogg, for such is the Ground all round it, which was formerly unhealthy, till the Waters were in some measure drain'd," *Accounts*, 67. All of Veryard's ambivalence about the king is voiced here: the sense of awe at his accomplishments; a kind of moral disapproval about a king known as a manipulator; and a gnawing anxiety about French power as both marvelous and dangerous. But again Veryard is won over by the waterworks, both the fountains and the massive water system supplying them (ibid., 68).

Northleigh is more overtly disgusted by the French: "I have rendered [the Latin verses] into *English* according to the pompous Ostentation of the *French*" (quoted in John Longh, *France Observed in the Seventeenth Century by British Travelers* [Boston: Oriel Press, 1984], 16–17). But he is still impressed by the Versailles water system and the military discipline that makes French soldiers so powerful (ibid., 71, 123). He is more worried and confused than impressed by the king's popularity: "his Subjects there, tho they pay for it, are so affected with the fame of his Victories, that they leave all to him and his Glory unconcern'd for peace or their own prosperity; nay, some of their Politicians think War as necessary among them and their Troops, as the Romans did among their Legions to keep their Arms from Rust, and the Men from Rebellion" (ibid., 108). In the end, his disgust prevails in his assessment of the French nation and its king: "For as Victorious as he is, he will hardly reach the true Character of a Caesar" (ibid., 123). Despite all the claims to being the New Rome, the successes of the army, and the great engineering feats, France falls short for this observer.

48. For the propaganda campaign of the reign, see Burke, *Louis XIV*. For the association of the water system at Versailles with France's leadership of Europe and the Great Tradition, see Néraudau, *L'Olympe du Roi Soleil*, 238–39. Néraudau (ibid., 238) quotes Combes: "L'italie doint céder présentement à la France le prix et la couronne qu'ell a remportée jusques aujord'hui sur toues les nations du monde, en ce qui regarde l'excellence d l'architecture, la beauté dela sculpture, la magnificence de la peinture, l'art du jardinage, la structure des fontaines and l'invention des aqueducts. Versailles sel suffit pout assurer à jamais à la France la gloire qu'elle a à présent de surpasser tous les autres royaumes dans la science des bâtiments. Aussi est-elle redevable de cetter hate estime à la grandeur et à la magnificence de Louis le Grand, son invincible monarque." For celebrations of Vauban and his work at Versailles, see, for example, Jean-Marie Pérouse de Montclose, *Versailles*, trans. J. Goodman (New York: Abbeville Press, 1991), 34. For an interesting juxtaposition of military engineering and hydraulic engineering, see the use of fountains from Paris in the border of an almanach entitled "Louis XIV et son gouvernement." The border is mostly composed of military forms: triumphal arches, the arsenal, and Les Invalides. This image suggests that the water system was indeed in this period included in the monuments to France's military power. See almanach no.23 in Maxime Préaud, *Les effets du soleil: Almanachs du règne de Louis XIV* (Paris: Réunion des Musées Nationaux, 1995), 78–79. Crump also suggests literary connections between water and classical culture in this period. She says Urfé's obsession with water and reflection in his writings was due to his generation's interest in Horace. See Phyllis Crump, *Nature in the Age of Louis XIV* (London: Routledge, 1928), 129. The association of waterworks with engineering—even classical engineering—was not left outside the walls of the garden either, as Crump (ibid., 46–50) suggests in the discussion of grottoes and their importance to garden art in the sixteenth and seventeenth centuries. For a discussion of the water system at Versailles itself and the role of the water system in demonstrating the greatness of a monarch in peace as well as war, see Madeleine de Scudéry, *La Promenade de Versailles*, 78–83. See also Mme. de Lafayette, *Mémoire de la Cour de France*, 106–7, cited in Hélène Himelfarb, " 'Palais' et 'chateaux' chez les Mémorialistes," in *Dix-huitième siècle*, 30, nos. 1–2 (June 1978): 92–93. An odd mixture of classical references and celebratory language is to be found in a poem by Cassan, *The Nymphe de Chanceaux ou l'arrivée de la Seine au Château de Marly* (Paris: Antoine Chrestion, 1699), 1–16. A nymph from the river Seine is picked up by the Machine de Marly and is forced up into the aqueducts. She is reassured by Apollo and arrives at Marly, which she finds so beautiful she falls asleep. Louis XIV wakes, finding the nymph in the garden along with the first of the Seine water, and asks her to make it her home. For archival material on the water system, see particularly VA 64–65.

There are many histories of the water system at Versailles that reproduce some of the variations in the meaning of the system during the period of its development. For example, André Corvisier in his book, *Louvois* (Paris: Fayard, 1983), 388–92, looks at the water system as an opportunity for Louvois to try out a new kind of power, using his role in the military and his new appointment as superintendent of buildings after the death of Colbert, to make engineering miracles finally solve the problem of water for Versailles. He ends the story with the failure of the Eure River project, but certainly situates this project as a failure of military engineering in the Roman style. See also Chapin, "Science," 186–87, for the Académie's role in helping to build the water system, once Louvois replaced Colbert. For a celebration of Vauban that includes the water system, but minimizes the failure of the Eure project in order to show that Vauban was as skilled a civil engineer as a military one, see Paul Bondois, *Deux ingénieurs au siècle du Louis XIV: Vauban et Riquet* (Paris: Librairie Picard, n.d.), 43–46.

For a history of the water system that oddly ignores the failure of the Eure project, see Albert Mousset, *Les Francines* (Paris: Editions Auguste Picard, 1930), esp. 73–93. Mousset surprisingly omits any serious mention of the Satory part of the water system. The early work on the Bièvre is mentioned, and the author gestures toward later improvements in this region as though it had no consequence. The story of the Eure project, on the other hand and equally oddly, is told in a celebratory fashion without mention of the technical failures and many deaths of soldiers camped by the Eure to do this work. By Mousset's account in this book, it would be easy to infer that all was going well at Maintenon when the soldiers were called off to war. The author also ends up celebrating the Machine de Marly as the great success story of Versailles's water system, mentioning in passing that the resulting Seine river water was mostly used to supply Marly. The author leaves in question what supplies were indeed getting to Versailles if Marly was taking up the bulk of the water being elevated by the machine. But getting the water sources straight seems less important to the author than arguing that the French were particularly good at hydraulic engineering in this period. While this may have been true of the main subjects of the story, the Francine family, it was hardly the case for French engineers in general. There was much interest and improvement in hydraulics in this period, but there was also some questionable work done. The early machine at Buc was not a showpiece of engineering. The famous Machine de Marly was a very leaky machine built by a man not schooled in hydraulics per se. So this story told by Mousset seems odd. But it is true that the Francine brothers seemed to have been very creative, learned, and experienced engineers. In Paris they oversaw the rebuilding of Roman water works as well as the construction of new machines to satisfy the Parisian population's need for

water. They repeatedly argued in good *aménagement* tradition that the well-being of the people and the power of France depended upon a good water supply. Importantly for this analysis, they also helped to produce many of the parallels between the water systems in Paris and at Versailles. Pierre and François Francine helped to develop both. Pierre in Paris continued work that François had started before being called by the king to the seat of the French court. These two hydraulic engineers not only helped revive in France the use of Roman engineering for waterworks, but also stimulated experimentation with new machines. They were learned moderns, making the success of the water system at Versailles a victory for modern French culture, while also helping to draw parallels between French engineering and that of the ancients. Fenelon was particularly critical of the pursuit of glory through works in his fictional commentary on the reign, Telemachus. See François de Fenelon, *Telemachus, son of Ulysses*, trans. P. Riley (Cambridge: Cambridge University Press, 1994), for example, 68–70, 110–11, 156–57, 181, 196–97. For Fenelon's position among critics of the regime, see Paul Sonnino, "Intellectual History of the Reign," in Sonnino, *Louis XIV*, 201–4.

49. Barbet, *Versailles*, 39–51.

50. Ibid., 74–81.

51. Ibid., 52–54; Marie-Joelle Paris, *Versailles: Le Grand Aqueduc de Buc ou de la manière de conduire les eaux au parc* (Buc: Office municipal des associations de Buc, 1986), 26–28. Abbé Picard, "Relation de plusieurs Nivellemens faits par order de sa Majesté," in *Traité du Nivellement* (Paris: Chez Estienne Michallet, 1684), 140–75.

52. Paris, *Versailles*, 13–19.

53. Barbet, *Versailles*, 61–75.

54. Paris, *Versailles*, 47–58. John Evelyn commented on the high quality of French roads compared to English ones, and Louis Coulon noted that French roads were better than their German counterparts in the period. See Crump, *Nature in the Age of Louis XIV*, 59.

55. Paris, *Versailles*, 47–58.

56. Ibid.

57. Belidor, *Les sciences*.

58. Maxime Préoud, *Les effets du soleil: Almanachs du règne de Louis XIV* (Paris: Réunion des Musées Nationaux, 1995), B.N. See the image of the ministers surrounded by fountains in Paris to see the symbolic importance of this water system in the propaganda of the period.

59. Néraudau, *L'Olympe du Roi Soleil*, 237.

3. Jules Hardouin Mansart and André Le Nostre at Dampierre

F. HAMILTON HAZLEHURST

Aside from the formality and grandeur of scale always considered to be the basic ingredients of the seventeenth-century garden, other aspects were fundamental in the practice of landscape architecture during this period. With this in mind, the discussion that follows focuses on the innovative methods and philosophy in general lying behind garden practice of the seventeenth century which sparked appreciation and understanding in the eyes of the beholder then as it does today.

The gardens of the time are marked by an all-pervasive sense of order and restraint, balance and equilibrium; all of the parts are carefully related to one another and to the whole. Inevitably, the garden is subordinate to the architecture it is calculated to embellish, and thus the building is the chief actor on stage. There exists, however, a constant interplay between the architecture and its surroundings either when a structure is seen from afar or when the landscape is viewed from the structure itself.

In his gardening practice, André Le Nostre embraces the notion that there must be diversity in the midst of congruity. When designing broad expanses of terrain, there are naturally large areas of intervening spaces between salient features in the gardens. These features, when observed from varying vantage points, come together visually in different but ever-compatible combinations. As a consequence, there is frequently an interplay between near and distant motifs in the gardens as they relate to the building. Always, there is a reason for creating features large and small in the design; nothing is ever left to chance.

For the rational French mind desirous of being intellectually in control of the environment, Le Nostre, using geometry as a unifying factor, created a context for a building that breathed a spirit of total harmony. Contributing to the sense of perfect balance was the vital ingredient of visual measurability promoted by the calculated placement in the landscape of such features as stairs, sculptures, pools, and fountains. These served to define the spaces and the intervals that lay between them. In addition, Le Nostre introduced the visitor to his gardens to an intellectual game that served to quicken his sensibilities to visual perception. This was accomplished by means of optical gymnastics that at once deceived the eye while providing simultaneously certain "surprises" which delighted the beholder upon discovering them. This discovery was made possible only by actually walking through the garden, thereby experiencing the multifarious relationships existing therein.

Once having grasped the subtleties of Le Nostre's approach, the optical interplay of features within the design is recognized as the energizing ingredient that brings a landscape plan to life in a very provocative way. Once attuned to the gardener's method, the visitor to a given site seeks and finds an endless variety of visual tricks—the leaven of what might otherwise be perceived as too formal a landscape.

The optical tricks and subtleties in Le Nostre's

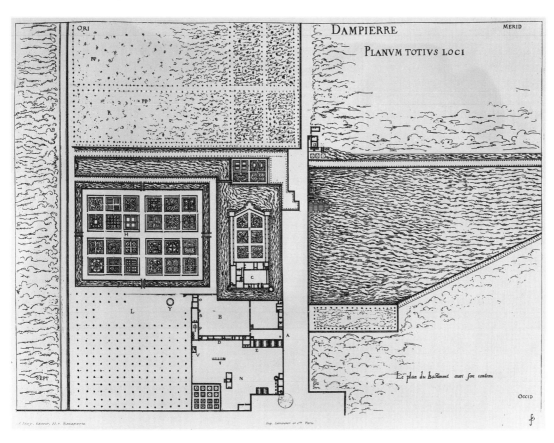

1. Jacques Androuet Du Cerceau, Dampierre. *Les plus excellants bastiments de France*, 1575.

garden designs are of fundamental importance to an appreciation and understanding of the gardens under Louis XIV. They form the basis for all of Le Nostre's gardens, some of the most important of which were done in collaboration with Jules Hardouin Mansart, for example, Versailles, Grand Trianon, Meudon, St.-Cyr, and Chantilly. To this list must be added the Château de Dampierre in the valley of the Chevreuse, a project that the architect and landscape architect undertook together, the result of which was a singularly brilliant scheme that brought monumental grandeur to the château and perfect visual harmony to a particularly challenging site. Work there spanned most of the decade of the 1680s, that is, from at least 1680 to 1688.

The Dampierre property was already well known, however, as an important château had been erected on the site in the mid-sixteenth century. Built by Jean Duval, treasurer of François I, it was soon acquired by Cardinal Charles de Lorrraine in whose family it remained until Claude de Lorraine, duc de Chevreuse, willed it to his wife, Marie de Rohan; her first husband had been the connétable de Luynes. She, in turn, gave the château to Louis-

Charles d'Albret, duc de Luynes, son of her first marriage. Soon thereafter, he in turn transferred the title of the estate to his son, Charles-Honoré d'Albret (1646–1712). It was this duc de Luynes who married Jean-Baptiste Colbert's eldest daughter, Jeanne Marie. Colbert, Louis XIV's minister, undoubtedly encouraged his new son-in-law, and offered him financial advice, to build a new château at Dampierre worthy of his exalted station.

Fortunately, we know the appearance of the Jean Duval/Cardinal de Lorraine château and garden, thanks to the engravings of Jacques Androuet Du Cerceau which appeared in his 1575 publication *Les plus excellants bastiments de France* (figs. 1, 2). The château is shown surrounded by a water-filled moat. Extending outward to the south of the building, an extensive garden is enclosed by covered galleries. The garden's outer limits are marked by two-story pavilions placed at the corners of this symmetrically designed area.

To the east of the château, a sizable rectangle is presented as an island garden by virtue of the fact that it is surrounded by water; biaxial access to it is provided by bridges. The Du Cerceau delinea-

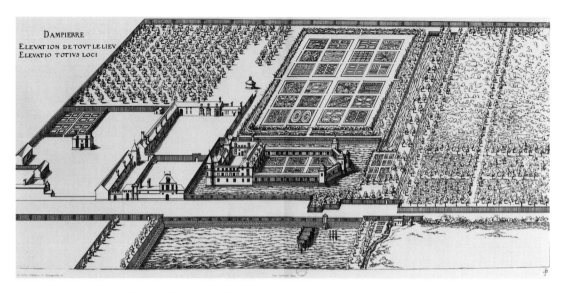

2. Jacques Androuet Du Cerceau, Dampierre. *Les plus excellants bastiments de France*, 1575.

tions describe the island's wealth of decoration in the form of parterres of infinite variety of pattern.

The other major feature in this sixteenth-century garden is the large *étang* or pond located west of the château. Unfortunately, Du Cerceau does not describe its full extent, although we do know that, as early as the middle of the seventeenth century, there was an island toward its outer limits which was graced with five pavilions. Despite the fact that the Duval/Lorraine château and its adjacent garden suggest symmetry when viewed in the plan, the elevations reveal an architecture of a highly irregular order (fig. 3). The principal façade is embellished by round corner towers connected to one another by a hodgepodge of architectural forms. There is no central axis bisecting the structure. The central entrance portal is, in fact, placed to one side, and access to it is from a side road rather than on axis with the building. Finally, the plan indicates a series of enclosed spaces with no overall design that would harmoniously link the building with its surroundings.

It was essentially the Dampierre of the sixteenth-century Du Cerceau depictions that Charles-Honoré d'Albret de Luynes, duc de Chevreuse, inherited and, in all probability with the encouragement of Colbert, determined to rebuild. Though the property was willed to him by his father, it was not until 1679 and the death of his grandmother, the venerable Marie de Rohan, that the title to the estate was actually passed on to the young duke. Hence it seems unlikely that any designs, projected or otherwise, would have been undertaken before

that date. More likely as a date for the initiation of the vast new reconstruction program is the early fall of 1680, as it was then that André Le Nostre returned from his sojourn in Italy which had started in late January or early February of that year. Surely the architect and landscape gardener would have collaborated from the very beginning of the project. It is certain that as early as 1683 work was well under way. This is borne out by construction expenditures recorded in the château's archive for that year and for six years following. In addition, there is a letter from J. H. Mansart to the Grand Condé at Chantilly, dated 25 February 1683, which describes his presence at Dampierre: "Je les aures envoyé plutost, n'était, que j'ay esté oblige d'aler à Dampierre che[z] Monsieur le Duc de Chevreause, Monsieur Colbert l'ayant soueté." Not only does the document place Mansart at Dampierre on that date, but it also indicates the direct involvement of Colbert in the building proceedings. It is of interest to remark, too, that Mansart and Le Nostre were working simultaneously at Chantilly, Mansart on plans for the orangery and Le Nostre on the monumental staircase, the Grand Degré.

If one accepts the premise that the design for the "new" Dampierre did not get under way until Le Nostre's return from Italy, then the latter part of 1680, 1681, and 1682 may be viewed as the years of preparation for the formidable undertaking. Substantiating this premise, two highly significant plans have surfaced from the Dampierre archives. These illustrate the project in the very process of evolution, making them invaluable as

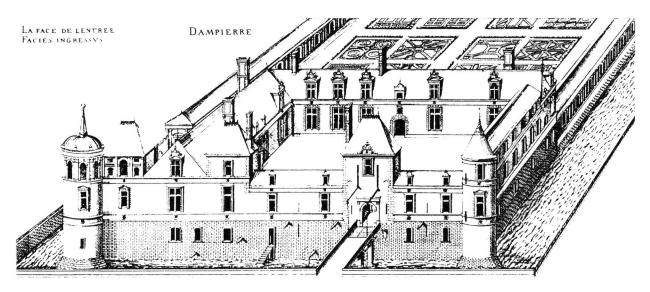

LA FACE DE LENTREE
FACIES INGRESSVS   DAMPIERRE

3. Jacques Androuet Du Cerceau, Dampierre. *Les plus excellants bastiments de France*, 1575.

documents describing the several stages in the development of the château as well as important sources for providing insight into the working methods of the architect and landscape designer together.

Before considering these two plans, it should be pointed out that the general layout of the reconstructed Dampierre follows the traditional axial scheme established earlier in the seventeenth century and illustrated by certain homogeneous designs such as those of Jacques LeMercier's Château de Richelieu and François Mansart's Château de Balleroy and Maison-Lafitte. Axial planning became a formula adopted by Louis le Vau and Le Nostre at Vaux-le-Vicomte and, of course, at Versailles, perhaps the best known of the château and garden complexes. Thus the earlier of the two Dampierre plans (fig. 4), henceforth referred to as Plan A, reveals the traditional axial arrangement, a straight line bisecting the château before continuing across the terrain to infinity. With this design, the château is now harmoniously linked to its surroundings.

The entrance side of Dampierre reminds us of Colbert's Sceaux and Versailles in the distribution of its parts—the entrance portal with symmetrically placed guardhouses, the series of forecourts ever diminishing in size until the *cour d'honneur*, like the Cour du Marbre at Versailles, is reached. The sense of regularity and the massing of the architectural components comprising the design also recall Versailles. Even the brick and yellow limestone find their counterpart in the materials used on

the entrance side of the palace of the Sun King. So Mansart, who knew Versailles so well, was surely motivated, whether consciously or not, by his own and others' work there.

There are a number of elements described on Plan A that command our attention. As indicated on this plan, to the east of the château the sixteenth-century garden island has been retained, but instead of a multiplicity of parts, as recorded in the many small parterres on Du Cerceau's engraving, the island's embellishments are now reduced to four garden plots formed by paths intersecting one another at an octagonal basin. The essential simplicity of the design assures a sense of monumental scale seen lacking in the earlier arrangement. And now, beyond the garden island is another generously scaled plot, known as La Presqu'île after the fact that it is surrounded by water on two sides only. In its center is a sizable quatrefoil basin, the irregular contours of which are repeated in the surrounding turfed areas. In addition to this central basin with its four water jets, eight small circular fountains underscore the outer limits of La Presqu'île.

To the immediate south and beyond the so-called canal extending the length of the water island and La Presqu'île is a prominent feature in the shape of an amphitheatre with a *rond point* beyond it from which radiate ten *allées*. These extend outward through the forested terrain to terminate in additional garden features, the most impressive of which is a large circular basin with a single water jet, located near the eastern border of the garden.

For Le Nostre, the most challenging area to com-

4. Dampierre, Plan A. Archives of the château.

mand his attention was that along the central axis which extended outward from the garden façade of the château. Plan A records a possible solution and probably the initial one proposed by the landscape designer. Immediately in front of the château is a single embroidered parterre, embellished by five pools—four round and one octagonal—and each with its individual water jet. This arrangement is in a sense both embroidered parterre and *parterre d'eau*. It is significant to note that the notion of a water parterre had long been in the mind of Le Nostre, as is witnessed in efforts to enhance the esplanade in front of the garden façade at Versailles. There, as early as 1674, a large pool in the shape of a cloverleaf was proposed as a proper enhancement; the idea was clearly a reality by 1680, since it appears with great clarity in an Israel Silvestre engraving of 1682. In other words, the proposed treatment at Dampierre is, at the very least, akin to the Versailles solution.

Beyond the parterre as recorded on Plan A, and

ever on axis, is a large pool octagonal in form. Its southern margin is marked by a grotto that seems to have been inspired by Le Nostre's earlier efforts at Vaux-le-Vicomte and Fontainebleau. Above the grotto, the landscape gardener introduced three basins—two of quatrefoil shape and one circular —and provided each with single water jets. The space is surrounded by a *vertugadin*, a turfed greensward laid out on a slope of crescent form. From the middle of this semicircular area, forming the outer limit of the *vertugadin*, the central allée plunges into the distant reaches of the forest. In the Plan A drawing, this allée narrows appreciably, thereby dramatically increasing the sense of distance when viewed from the château.

As mentioned earlier, the sixteenth-century Du Cerceau plan does not describe the terminal element of the *étang*, namely, the island with its five pavilions. Although depicted on both Plans A and B (figs. 4, 5), this attractive feature is not the invention of either Le Nostre or Mansart, since the island and

5. Dampierre, Plan B. Archives of the château.

its embellishments are recorded as being present on the site at least as early as 1661 when Anne of Austria visited Dampierre.

Plan B, surely by the same unidentified hand as Plan A, is clearly of later date and, in fact, shows the château and its surroundings as they were largely realized. Certain modifications have been made to features already cited on Plan A. The general axial lines, however, are identical, and such features as the water island, La Presqu'île, the *étang* with its pavilions, and the amphitheater in front of the *vertugadin* remain the same.

New features on Plan B are of special interest. To the left of the château on the entrance side, there are now a number of garden plots of varying geometric shape; these are traversed by numerous radiating and circular paths. Most illuminating on Plan B are the landscape elements extending outward from the château's garden façade. The vestigial "water parterre" of Plan A has been suppressed and replaced by two identical, symmetrically placed, quatrefoil-shaped parterres, each graced with two circular basins both with single water jets. In addi-

tion, the southern margin of the octagonal basin sees the elimination of the "grotto," which is now replaced by a rather low but continuous cascade some fifty-four feet wide (fig. 6). Beyond, at the higher level, the disposition of parts of Plan B is the same described on Plan A. The forms of the basin here—round and quatrefoil—together with similar shapes marking the central parterre, assure a pleasing visual harmony between the two areas, a harmony that was found lacking in the projected scheme on Plan A.

A comparison of Plans A and B shows that Le Nostre modified the position of certain of the allées traversing the terrain. Most obvious in Plan B is the landscape architect's elaboration of the garden design in those sectors extending outward into the far reaches of the property. The prolonged central axis, only hinted at on Plan A, is now fully delineated and is enriched by a number of intricately shaped *bosquets* carved out of the heavily forested surroundings; even here, regularity and symmetry prevail.

Plans A and B, though invaluable as documents

6. Dampierre, cascade.

that reveal the principal features of both building and landscape design, cannot convey the nature of the terrain. This can be understood only by visiting the actual site. The Château de Dampierre is located in a valley through which courses the small Yvette River, the important source for the *étang*, moat, and other garden features. There is a steeply rising hill on the north or entrance side of the building complex, and a long, gently rising slope forms the southern axis.

Let us undertake a visit to the château, initially restricting our observations to the visual effects encountered along the principal axis which so precisely bisects the building (fig. 7). The entrance pavilions recall those of Chantilly, Sceaux, and St.-Cloud. These are followed by a series of three forecourts of diminishing size separated from one another by balustrades. The rather severe and massive entrance façade of brick and yellow limestone (fig. 8) reveals that the round towers of the older building have been retained, but now there is an all-pervasive symmetry that includes advancing arcaded wings to the sides. The central block, or *corps de logis*, surrounded by a water-filled moat (invisible from afar) (fig. 9), consists of projecting corner pavilions, which, through several setbacks, join the central pavilion made prominent by superim-

posed classical orders, surmounted by a triangular pediment and a mansard roof. The strong horizontal linkage of brick stringcourses in the façade is consistent except for the pedimented central pavilion; there the linkage is broken by the classical orders. Mansart, in a somewhat unorthodox manner, places the Corinthian order over Doric (instead of Ionic over Doric). By placing the entablature and the bases of the orders on different levels from the brick stringcourses to the sides, Mansart ingeniously creates the impression that the central pavilion projects forward in a markedly three-dimensional fashion. As a result, the orders appear to be virtually freestanding, lending a powerful sense of mass to the center of the building. In reality, the central pavilion is quite flat in contrast to the projecting masses of the corner pavilions to either side.

The terrain opposite the entrance (figs. 10, 11) is marked by a fairly precipitous slope that is divided at regular intervals into six superimposed terraces. At the base of the incline is a large watering trough formed of straight and sinuous contours (fig. 12). The shape of this area reverses the undulating contours of the terraces above.

Let us take a walk to the top of this hill. In the process, we shall encounter a series of visual impres-

7. Dampierre, entrance façade.

8. Dampierre, entrance façade, *corps de logis*.

9. Dampierre, water moat.

sions, all carefully calculated by Le Nostre. Looking back at the château at ground level (fig. 13), nothing is visible beyond the building, and the advancing arcaded wings are partially concealed. Upon ascending paths to the sides of the terraced slope, we find that a return to the center of each terrace provides a subtly different visual impression of the château as it relates to its surroundings. A view of the building from the first terrace (fig. 14) records compatible shapes in the mansard roofs of the château and those of the entrance pavilions. The château and entrance pavilions "come together" in this view to suggest a single ensemble, and, in truth, the gatehouses visually become wings of the building instead of the actual arcaded wings, which from this vantage point have completely disappeared. The lower edge of the roofs of the entrance pavil-

ions lines up perfectly with the brick stringcourse marking the division of the first and second stories of the château. And breaks in the mansard roofs of the pavilions line up with the breaks in the mansard elements of the château. From the first terrace the distant allée on the far side of the château would appear for the first time; it would seem to be designed on a vertical plane.

The present gateway (fig. 15) dates from the mid-eighteenth century in the time of Louis XV. It lacks the simple monumentality of scale present in the château. Its ornate floral motifs and overall delicacy are very different from the original gateway as described on Plan A (fig. 16). This was to be a heavy masonry portal whose weightiness and monumentality would permeate the entire architectural complex. With Mansart's gateway, there would have

10. Dampierre, view from château to entrance pavilion.

11. Dampierre, watering trough and terraces.

12. Dampierre, water trough.

13. Dampierre, gateway and entrance façade.

14. Dampierre, view from first terrace.

been, no doubt, a pleasing interplay between the contoured balustrade of the watering trough and the undulating curves of the portal. And, and in turn, it is likely that the forms of the portal would have interacted with the components in the central pavilion of the château.

When the château is viewed from the third terrace (fig. 17), the watering trough area assumes less importance. Now the wings come into view and become involved in the total design, which includes entrance pavilions, central block, and the symmetrical wings. Again, breaks in the mansard roofs of the entrance pavilions line up with the brick stringcourses between the first and second stories of the château and with the cornices of the side wings. The width of the distant allée is visually similar to the width of the central pavilion of the entrance façade; this suggests that the allée was to read as a vertical "spire" that would affix itself to the château. Thickly planted hornbeam hedges would have concealed the stuccoed walls at the sides of the outermost forecourt, and, as a result, would have afforded an interesting interplay of colors—the green of the hornbeam contrasting with the brick and yellow limestone of the building.

Though the fourth and fifth terraces provide additional visual impressions, let us move directly to the sixth terrace, or summit (figs. 18, 19). From this spot, the allée in the distance is now joined by a semicircular form that rests upon the center of the building to create the effect of a dome with spire (an idea that Le Nostre and Mansart would later perfect at the Château de Pontchartrain [1692]).

Halfway up the allée atop the hill (fig. 20), the château appears at once to be far below, yet at the same time one has the impression of its being fairly close by—indeed, it appears to be right at the end of the tree-lined allée, the intervening space being totally obscured. It is an interesting visual effect and reflects the kind of game that Le Nostre delights in playing in many of his garden schemes. The distant greensward continues to embrace the entire roofline of the *corps de logis*, and from here the château, so far as can be observed, is accompanied by one-story wings; the turfed terraces, the watering trough, the entrance pavilions, and the arcaded components of the wings have disappeared.

Finally, when the château is viewed from the end of the axis (fig. 21), it reads as a well-proportioned, perfectly symmetrical one-story structure, and from this point it appears diminutive in scale and, indeed, looks like a small but elegant pavilion. From this spot, it seems apparent why Mansart elected to use the Corinthian over the Doric order

15. Dampierre, eighteenth-century entrance gateway.

16. Dampierre, original gateway design.

17. Dampierre, view from third terrace.

18. Dampierre, view from sixth terrace.

19. Dampierre, view from sixth terrace.

20. Dampierre, view from top of hill.

21. Dampierre, view from end of axis.

22. Dampierre, garden façade.

23. Dampierre, garden façade, *corps de logis*.

rather than the traditional Ionic over Doric. Ionic, the order of grace and elegance, would have been found wanting in projecting any sense of richness and strength when viewed from this considerable distance; by contrast, the intricate, grandly scaled Corinthian order would visually "carry" satisfactorily from a distance.

What we have observed on the entrance side of Dampierre is merely a prelude to the optical gymnastics awaiting the visitor to the garden side of the château. In seventeenth-century château and garden planning, there is generally an interest in axes viewed from both directions, and in this regard Dampierre is no exception. Today, as we have seen, a view southward from the garden façade of the château indicates the presence of a single parterre (see fig. 6), followed by an octagonal pool with cascade, a greensward and amphitheater, and an allée striking off into the distance. Thus we see an obvious simplification of the garden's components compared with those described in both Plans A and B.

The château façade has, however, retained its appearance as designed by Mansart (fig. 22). It is grander, more monumental in scale than the entrance façade. The architecture gives the impression of balance and symmetry; it appears to be comprised of a central block and two seemingly identical wings set back and extending broadly outward (they are, in reality, not symmetrical). The wing to the west is contemporary with Mansart's building, but the one to the east dates largely to the sixteenth-century complex. There is, however, an overall sense of balance and harmony, and, importantly, the general disposition strongly reminds one of Mansart's garden façade at Versailles with its advancing central block and two attendant wings. The *corps de logis* (fig. 23) is a majestic three-story structure with prominent dormers. The façade is centralized by a projecting pavilion, a variant of the central pavilion on the entrance façade. Five bays wide, its three middle bays are embellished with classical orders—again a variation in treatment of the entrance façade. Instead of being constructed primarily of brick and limestone, the central pavilion is largely of stone; its weightiness enhanced by the monumentally scaled staircase of the same material. The importance of this central pavilion is further underscored by the presence of a stone balustrade and urns along its roofline and by the presence of its own mansard roof. Clearly the central part of the *corps de logis* was to be considered as a single architectural entity. Again, as on the entrance façade, there is no horizontal linkage in the brick stringcourse between the floors as they re-

24. Dampierre, garden façade and moat.

late to the central unit with its classical orders of Corinthian over Doric. Once more, Mansart's treatment is designed to make the center of the façade appear to project forward, optically speaking. And so it does, and to such a degree that it comes as a surprise to find that the center of the façade is quite flat (fig. 24). A view from the side also reveals the presence of the water-filled moat. Again, as on the entrance façade, it is virtually hidden from view when the château is seen from a short distance away. From afar, the moat is visible only at the corners of the *corps de logis* as it retreats back to the arches of the wings. And from this distant view, the arches appear to be attached to the central block which, in reality, is not the case.

The central allée, which had read as a strongly vertical element when seen from the steeply ter-raced area on the entrance side of the château, now reads as a gently rising slope of relatively short extent (fig. 25). Actually, only a small part of this avenue is visible as this undeviatingly straight allée extends more than a kilometer before terminating in a broad plateau. Let us venture to the summit in order to reconstruct the diversity of optical impressions the visitor would encounter upon descending this axis. Today the trees along the allée have grown to such a degree that an unencumbered view of the axis is virtually impossible to attain. Only in wintertime, when the trees are divested of their foliage, would the vista be visible. However, reconstruction of the changing optical impressions present along the axis is made possible by using contour maps of the terrain (figs. 26, 27). From the top of the slope, the château would

25. Dampierre, central allée.

not have been visible. Instead, from the summit one would have had an uninterrupted vista terminating in the farthest reaches of the landscape in the greensward of the distant rising hill. Only on progressing down the axis would the château come into view and then only by degrees. When first seen (fig. 28), only the central pavilion of the *corps de logis* would appear—its actual width and height being obscured by the breadth of the allée and the subtly changing degrees of slope. Here the central pavilion reads as a single-storied structure, surmounted by a green "dome" formed by the turfed hill on the far side of the building. From this point onward, the visitor would encounter a series of rapidly changing visual impressions that would alter his perception of the château as it related to its surroundings. Upon advancing forward (fig. 29), the central pavilion would become two-storied, retaining its "dome," while its width would remain the same. Farther down the allée (fig. 30), the two stories would be joined by a solid stone foundation comprised of a monumental staircase; in this view, the actual width of the *corps de logis* would continue to be concealed, the limited sighting of the château resulting from the enclosing trees. Progressing farther, the château would begin to expand laterally to expose the width and height of the central block (fig. 31). This lateral expansion would continue until the arched "wings" became a part of the central block. Finally, on emerging from the tree-lined allée (fig. 32), the full extent of the château would be bared to view, including the Versailles-like wings. In this progression forward, then, we have moved from an impression of a diminutive structure to the realization of a monumentally scaled architectural scheme.

The last major feature to be considered is Le Nostre's modification of the *étang* appearing on the Du Cerceau plan (see figs. 1, 26). His changes required massive expenditures and considerable hard labor for those involved in executing its contours. The modifications made appear to have been born primarily of the desire to create precise visual effects. With the new angling of the pond on its southern flank and with a slight change on its straight northern margin, the island with its pavilions would have been the perfect point of focus when viewed from the side of the château. In addition, as a result of a subtle increase in the diameter of the *étang* as it retreated into the distance, the island and its pavilions would have seemed closer to the château than they actually were. Conversely, the château when viewed from the island would have appeared farther away. To go a step further, owing to the new

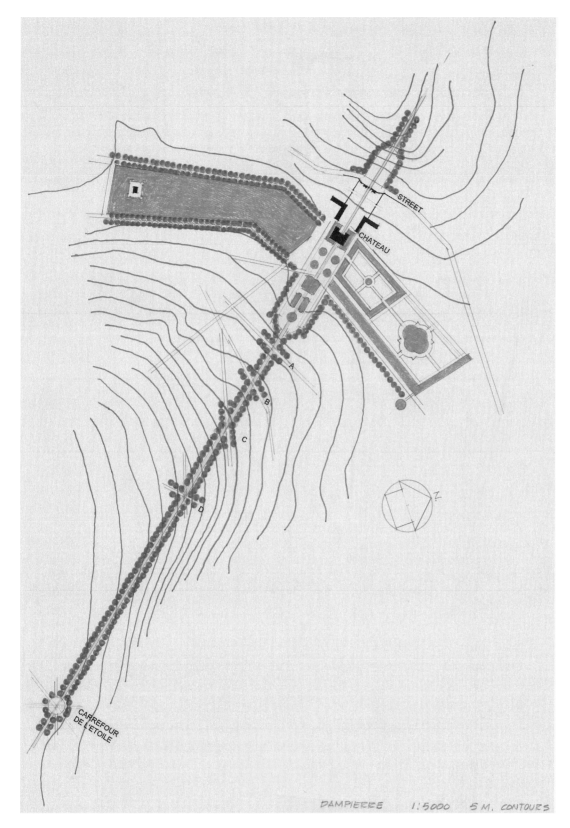

STREET

CHATEAU

A

B

C

D

Z

CARREFOUR
DE L'ETOILE

DAMPIERRE   1:5000   5 M. CONTOURS

26. Dampierre, plan. Drawing by P. H. Holt III.

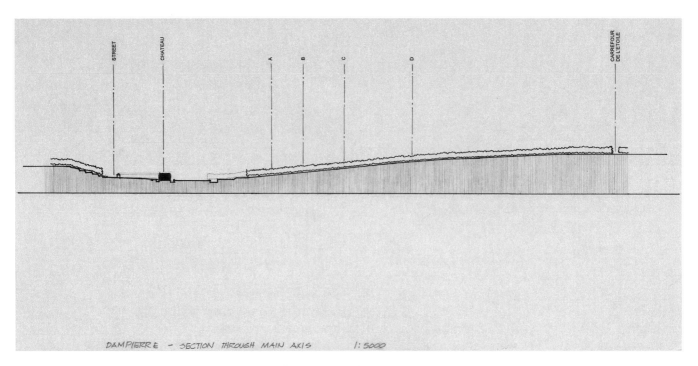

DAMPIERRE - SECTION THROUGH MAIN AXIS   1:5000

27. Dampierre, cross section of plan. Drawing by P. H. Holt III.

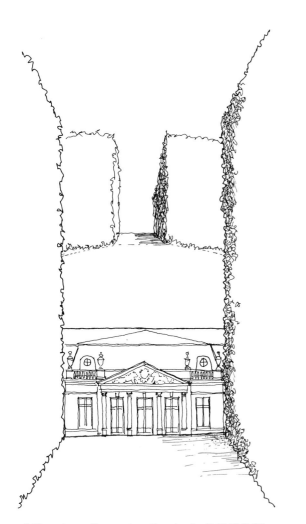

28. Dampierre, distant view. Drawing by P. H. Holt III.

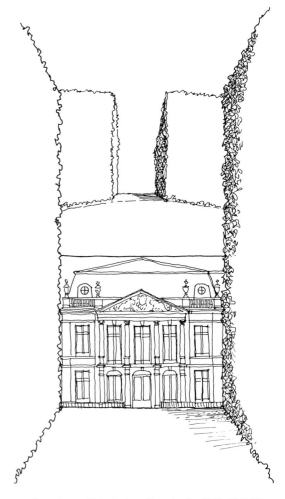

29. Dampierre, distant view. Drawing by P. H. Holt III.

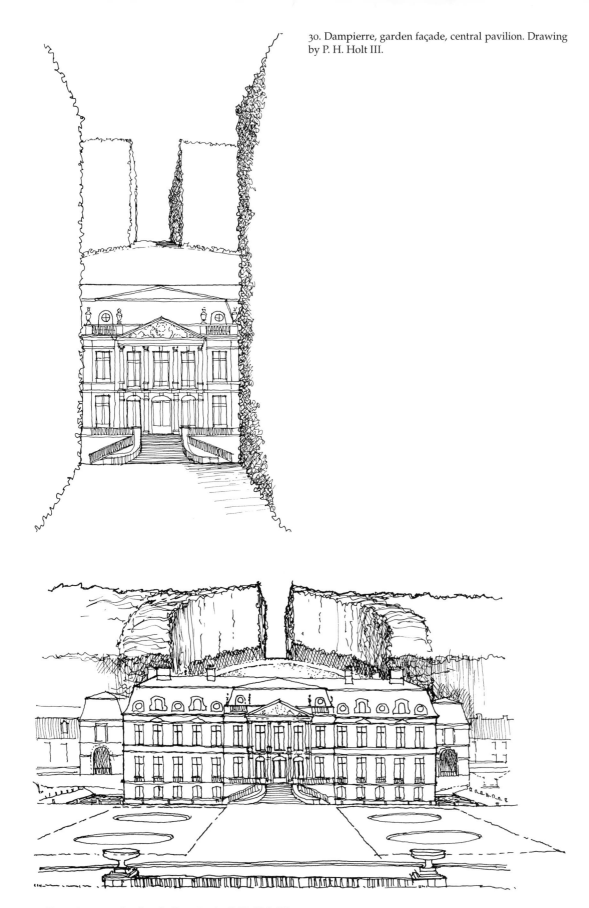

30. Dampierre, garden façade, central pavilion. Drawing by P. H. Holt III.

31. Dampierre, garden façade. Drawing by P. H. Holt III.

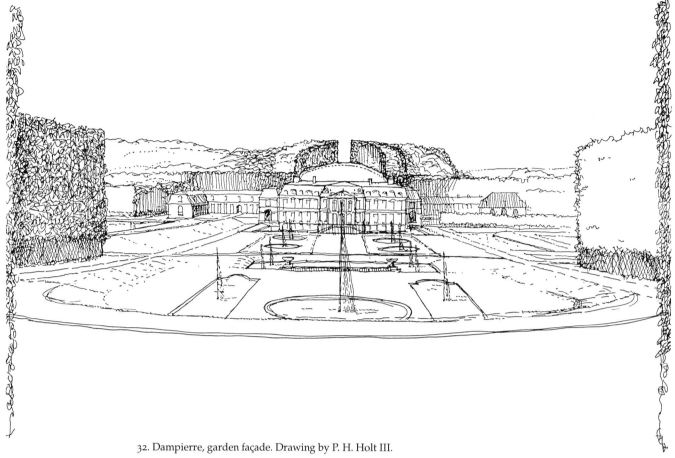

32. Dampierre, garden façade. Drawing by P. H. Holt III.

33. Dampierre, garden façade seen from an angle.

angle on the southern flank of the *étang*, that part of the pond would have been concealed when the château was viewed from the island.

At the very angle that forms the two axes on this south margin of the *étang*, there was, until recently, a stone bench, surely placed there by Le Nostre. From that specific vantage point, one would see the château at an angle (fig. 33); the three-storied garden façade would have read as a two-storied structure, as the basement story would have been obscured by a raised terrace that embraced the western flank of the building. Yet most important in all these modifications is the singular fact that the relation of all the parts to one another and to the whole would have remained in perfect visual harmony.

At Dampierre, André Le Nostre once again emerges as the master manipulator of the natural landscape. It is through his subtle visual effects that both harmony and diversity became integral to the seventeenth-century French garden. Comprehension of these visual dynamics demands that the visitor become wholly familiar with the individual site. Equally important, architect and landscape designer must be considered as one entity; basically, they are inseparable. Without their constant, concentrated interaction, the unique achievements of the period would never have been realized.

ACKNOWLEDGMENTS

It is with profound gratitude that I acknowledge the kindness of the Duc and Duchesse de Luynes. I am particularly indebted to the helpful hand extended by the duke's sister, Princesse Inez Murat. In addition, Thomas de Luynes, the family archivist, graciously made available original plans of the Château de Dampierre and its gardens. And clearly, I owe a lasting debt to Philetus H. Holt, AIA, for his meticulous and wonderfully informative drawings that serve to make intelligible the ideas set forth in this essay.

4. Making Breathing Room

Public Gardens and City Planning in Eighteenth-Century France

RICHARD CLEARY

"Public promenades are among the most important embellishments [of a city]," Louis de Mondran, an *amateur* of architecture, wrote, in 1754, "because they contribute to the health of its inhabitants. It is appropriate and necessary for large cities . . . to have many beautiful promenades."[1] Mondran was not alone in holding such views in mid-eighteenth-century France. Many others, including members of the intellectual elite, governmental administrators, architects, and military engineers, professed similar interest in the creation of public green space. Through their effort cities and towns across the country boasted newly laid out promenades and public gardens. This chapter examines three aspects of this phenomenon: the promenade as buffer between town and country, the emergence of public gardens, and the role of promenades and gardens as components in urban master planning.

THE PROMENADE AS BUFFER BETWEEN TOWN AND COUNTRY

The history of promenades in France is well established in outline, but in-depth studies of individual sites are rare.[2] Promenades, or *promenoirs* as the more elaborate versions sometimes were known, were places designed for recreational walks and carriage drives. They became distinctive features of French cities and towns in the seventeenth century.

An early example of a pedestrian promenade was the Mail de l'Arsenal in Paris (fig. 1), a proprietary venture nominally headed by one Loys Boutard, a member of the guard stationed at the Arsenal on the Right Bank of the Seine near the Bastille.[3] In 1604 the crown authorized him to lay out a pitch for the newly popular game of pall mall, which, on low-lying land between the wall of the Arsenal and the river, involved hitting a wooden ball with a mallet through an iron hoop. The Mail consisted of a long, narrow playing surface enclosed by low fences and bordered by trees, a parallel tree-lined walk along the Seine for spectators, and a structure for storage and equipment rental. During the course of the century, similar *mails* were established throughout France in cities and towns, as well as on private estates. In urban areas, they typically occupied land of marginal value, such as the flood-prone embankment along the Seine or the edges of fortifications. The sport lost much of its appeal in the eighteenth century, but the grounds remained popular settings for walks and often were preserved as public promenades.

In 1616, a decade after the establishment of the Mail de l'Arsenal, Maria de' Medici commissioned a far grander promenade along the Seine on the west side of Paris.[4] The Cours la Reine (fig. 2) was fifteen hundred meters long and more than forty meters wide, lined with shade trees, and divided into separate lanes for pedestrians and carriages. Admission was at the discretion of the crown, which favored aristocratic visitors. In contrast, money bought ac-

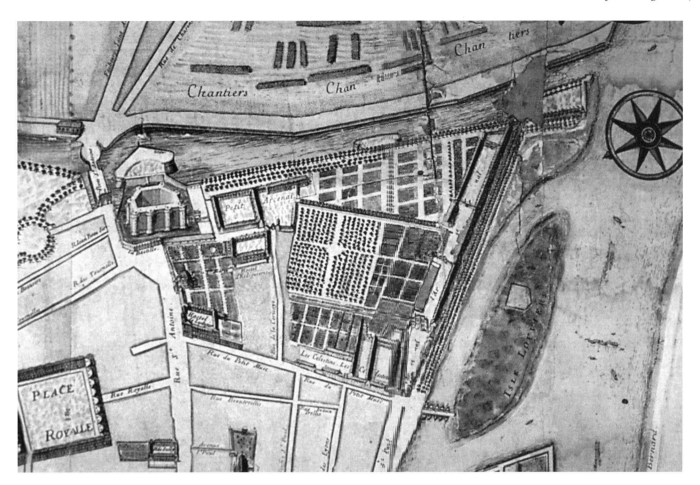

1. Paris, map by François Blondel and Pierre Bullet, 1675–76, detail showing the Right Bank south of the Bastille. The tree-lined Jeu de Mail occupies the sliver of land between the Arsenal and Seine.

cess to the Mail de l'Arsenal, which was enjoyed by a broader spectrum of aristocratic and bourgeois society.

Although their use and clientele differed, the two promenades mark the introduction of a new type of landscape in Paris. Previously, sport had been conducted on undeveloped land, such as the Pré aux Clercs on the Left Bank, while excursions into the countryside on foot or by carriage utilized public thoroughfares.[5] The Mail and the Cours, however, provided specially designed and clearly demarcated settings for these activities.

The number of promenades increased rapidly in the late seventeenth and eighteenth centuries owing to a fortuitous convergence of interests and opportunities. These included the sustained fashion for social walking and carriage drives among the aristocracy and the bourgeoisie, the aesthetic and political desire of administrators to bring order to both the appearance of the city and the behavior

of its residents, and belief in the creation of public green spaces as a matter of public health.[6]

In most instances new promenades were built on the outskirts of cities, often atop or in place of obsolete fortifications. This was the case in Paris where in the early 1670s the crown began replacing the city's fortifications with a ring of tree-lined promenades, known initially as the Cours des Remparts and later as the Boulevard (fig. 3). Like the construction of the Cours la Reine, this ambitious, long-term undertaking required much excavation and fill, provisions for drainage, and the planting of a forest of shade trees. The elevated carriage road and flanking sidewalks offered a prospect from which citizens could survey city and countryside and served as a boundary marking the city limits. Although the broad roadway potentially could speed the flow of traffic around the perimeter of Paris, the crown attempted to restrict commercial vehicles to narrower roads along the base of the rampart.

2. Paris, Cours la Reine. Engraving by Aveline, late seventeenth century. Bibliothèque Nationale de France, Cabinet des Estampes, Ed 63 Folio.

The boulevards were an amenity that heightened the appeal of speculative real estate developments adjacent to them. For example, the planning of the Place Louis-le-Grand (now the Place Vendôme) in the late 1680s included links to the boulevards as well as to the internal street system, so that the carriages of the owners of the newly built townhouses could promenade without first encountering the traffic delays common in the older neighborhoods of the Marais and the Palais Royal.[7]

Seventy years later, circulation along the boulevards remained a factor in the planning of the Place Louis XV (now the Place de la Concorde).[8] By locating the *place* on the undeveloped Esplanade between the Tuileries gardens and the Champs-Elysées, the crown sought to both improve the awkward junction where the northern boulevard met the Champs d'Elysées and the Cours la Reine and to establish a river crossing to connect with the southern boulevard (fig. 4). Ange-Jacques Gabriel's design solved this problem and provided an elegant setting for Edme Bouchardon's statue of Louis XV. By combining a *place royale* with the city's promenades, however, he fused two architectural types formerly viewed as distinct. A *place royale* was an

urban form made up of hard surfaces: buildings and pavement. A promenade, on the other hand, was suburban and green. Neither one nor the other, the Place Louis XV drew negative reactions from critics such as Marc-Antoine Laugier: "The new Place Louis XV will be after all a grand and beautiful thing, but one can call it a *place* only in the most casual sense. It is not one of the city's crossroads. It doesn't even have the appearance of being within the walls. Surrounded by gardens and groves of trees, it simply presents the image of an embellished esplanade in the midst of a charming landscape."[9]

Laugier's simultaneous appreciation of the quality of the space and concern for its typological identity reflect his effort to define the elements of urban form and to generate guidelines for their use. The rate of urban development and innovation, however, outpaced categorization by theorists and regulation by government administrators.

Although the crown had hoped to contain the growth of Paris within the ring of boulevards, it succumbed to pressure from well-connected aristocratic and bourgeois speculators looking beyond city limits. By the mid-eighteenth century, stretches

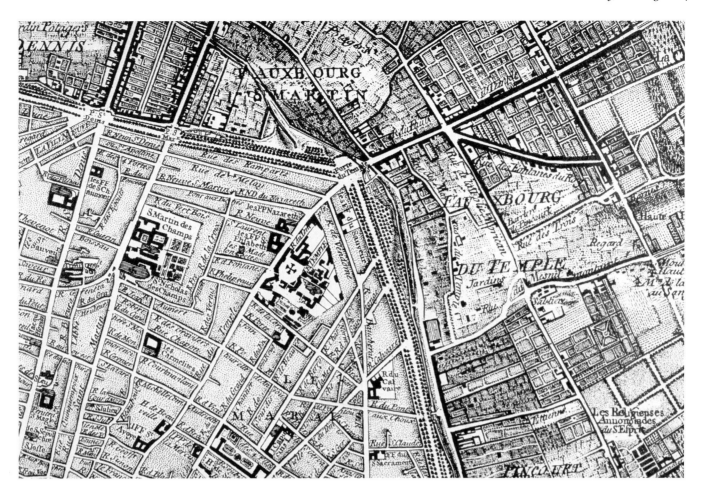

3. Paris, map by John Roscque, 1754, detail showing the northeastern portion of the city. The Cours des Remparts, or Boulevard, follows the line of the old fortifications.

of the northern boulevards were lined on both sides by residential and commercial buildings. Instead of delimiting the city's edge, the boulevards were becoming interior streets. Broad and tree-lined, they retained features of external promenades, but the adjacent buildings closed previous vistas of the countryside and the city center and changed the predominant scenographic character from panoramic to middle-distance views. Moreover, *promeneurs* now could do more than walk, ride, or people-watch as they made their way along the boulevards. Theaters, cafés, and other entertainments clamored for their attention and money, and people from a variety of social classes now rubbed shoulders, not always happily.[10]

The incremental stages of this unplanned transformation merit sustained investigation. Among the underutilized sources for such a history are the building permits issued by the Bureau des Marchands. As Jean-Louis Harouel has shown, these

documents include details such as specifications for the color of private fences (green in 1769), the building of sidewalks, and the introduction of street lighting that indicate how building owners and civil authorities first sought to protect the image of the boulevards as buffers between city and suburb and then gradually reinforced their character as city streets.[11]

At the end of the ancien régime, Parisian authorities had an opportunity to consider a different approach to handling growth along the city's perimeter. The wall of the Fermiers Généraux, authorized in 1784, was intended to improve the collection of taxes on goods entering the city and the governance of the outermost quarters, which were reputed havens for smugglers. Besides the eleven-foot-high wall, the architect, Claude-Nicolas Ledoux, designed the *barrières*, or toll stations, and a peripheral boulevard.[12] He also planned to replace the free-wheeling, popular *guinguettes*, which offered cut-

4. Paris, Place Louis XV (now Place de la Concorde), designed by Ange-Jacques Gabriel, begun 1754. Painting by Alexandre-Jean Noel, ca. 1779, Musée Carnavalet, Paris, P1206; ©Photothèque des Musées de la Ville de Paris. The Cours la Reine is at the left, the Tuileries garden is at the right, and the entrance to the Boulevard is reached by the rue Royale between the two buildings in the background.

rate wine just outside the city limits, with eight state-run taverns, which promised a disciplined architecture if not a well-behaved clientele. Set in parklike landscapes and linked by the tree-lined boulevard, the taverns would have formed a necklace of green space around the city. As we have seen with the Mail de l'Arsenal and the Cours la Reine, Ledoux's scheme would have created a carefully designed setting for activities that previously had been conducted in less structured circumstances.

THE PUBLIC GARDEN

The classic suburban promenade was intended as a place for exercise and stately procession. Its linear, regular layout encouraged movement, and although benches often were provided along the walking lanes, there was little in the way of sculp-

ture, decorative plantings, ponds, or fountains to arrest the eye and encourage prolonged examination. Such features were to be found in the private gardens of the crown, the church, and the urban elite, which offered the privileged classes outdoor settings for intimate activities such as reading, contemplation, or private conversations. The general public, however, was not as fortunate.

On occasion, some private gardens were open to members of the public. In Paris, the degree of public access to the royal garden of the Tuileries palace was an ongoing topic of discussion during the late seventeenth and eighteenth centuries (fig. 5). For example, as work on André Le Nôtre's redesign of the garden neared completion in the late 1670s, Jean-Baptiste Colbert planned to deny access on the grounds that the general public would damage the new plantings; Charles Perrault took credit for convincing the minister otherwise. In his *Mé-*

5. Paris, Tuileries garden. Drawing by Gabriel Saint-Aubin, 1760. Bibliothèque Nationale de France, Cabinet des Estampes, Ef 35a Reserve.

moires he recalled explaining to Colbert how people respected the garden to such an extent that even the women and children of the petite bourgeoisie would not even touch the flowers, much less attempt to pick them. He went on to tell of the many reasons people visited the garden. "There are those recovering from illness who come for the fresh air; others come to speak of business, marriage, and all those subjects more easily discussed in a garden than in a church."[13] During the eighteenth century, the Tuileries often was described as a public garden, but admission remained at the pleasure of the crown, which generally limited access to "people of quality" through such devices as dress codes.

A variety of settings for walking and sitting beckoned those who passed inspection (fig. 6).[14] An elevated promenade along the Seine offered prospects of the river and the garden. Inside the western entrance, an octagonal basin bounded by ramps, high terraces, and a wall of trees was the focal point of a large, open space much frequented by visitors. More privacy could be found in the center of the garden among the many *bosquets*, parterres, and groves of trees secluded from the sights and sounds of the city.

Public gardens controlled by local jurisdictions were not an invention of the eighteenth century but proliferated then in number and variety.[15] By mid-century they were increasingly regarded as an essential feature of well-appointed cities. In 1746, for example, the royal intendant responsible for Bordeaux, the Marquis de Tourny, prodded the municipal government into petitioning the crown for permission to acquire land outside the city limits for a public garden. The petition stated, "our city now only lacks a public garden, where persons of both sexes might walk freely," and noted, "the exercise of the promenade, so necessary to maintain good health, also distracts one from engaging in less innocent amusements."[16] In addition to citing public health and morality, Tourny and the city officials justified their proposal in terms of its benefits to business. "In a commercial town," Tourny wrote, "it should be regarded as essential, or at least extremely useful, for commerce that there be a garden where merchants, who must meet together frequently, may conduct business. It is in some respects a second exchange, an evening market."[17]

The crown approved Tourny's proposal, and the Jardin Public was laid out on a scale that dwarfed the gardens of the city's private residences and recalled the Tuileries garden as a figure within the overall city plan (fig. 7). Like the Tuileries garden, it was composed of *bosquets* and parterres symmetrically disposed around a central axis and featured a tree-lined promenade overlooking the Garonne River. This classic scheme would remain the model for public gardens to the end of the eighteenth cen-

6. Paris, Tuileries garden. Drawing by Israel Silvestre, late seventeenth century. Louvre, Cabinet des Dessins, 33012; Réunion des Musées Nationaux.

tury. Michel Vernes has pointed out that as late as 1802 the landscape theorist Jean-Marie Morel advocated regular plans for public gardens in his *Théorie des jardins* (second edition) as being more conducive to social interaction than picturesque plans, which favored solitude.[18]

With the proliferation of public gardens came greater variety of garden types. Botanical gardens inspired by older examples, such as the Jardins du Roi (known today as the Jardins des Plantes) in Paris and Montpellier, brought the pleasures of the aristocratic *cabinets* of natural science to the bourgeoisie. Another appropriation of an aristocratic model was the planning of public gardens attached to city halls in the manner of *hôtels particuliers*. Such was the case in Pierre Contant d'Ivry's project of 1748 for a new city hall in Paris on the Left Bank of the Seine opposite the Grande Galerie of the Louvre.[19] Contant prepared the design in response to the city's decision to build a *place royale* honoring Louis XV. He located the *place* with its statue of the monarch as a forecourt to the city hall, behind which he included an enclosed garden consisting of a central allée terminated by a round basin, flanking parterres, and two outer allées lined by shade trees (fig. 8).

The site was not a *tabula rasa*. Buildings belonging to the Augustine and Theatine orders, aristocratic hôtels, and other residences, which would have to be purchased and demolished, occupied it. Furthermore, the city hall and garden would have blocked direct access to the Quai Malaquais from the rue des Saints-Pères, an arterial street. These were formidable obstacles to overcome, but Contant apparently believed that the expense and inconvenience would reward the city with a much more impressive symbol of its authority than its medieval seat on the Place de Grève. The new building's proximity to the Louvre would have underscored the close ties between city and crown and contributed to the monumental character that architects and officials had sought for the area since Henri IV had built the Grande Galerie of the Louvre at the beginning of the seventeenth century.

Contant's scheme aggrandized municipal authority by reinterpreting aristocratic building types at palatial scale. By the time of the French Revolution, other designers explored ways of creating more explicitly didactic public gardens. In 1791, for example, an entrepreneur, Pierre-François Palloy, proposed a National Garden adjacent to the Place de la Bastille that was to have trees shaped to sug-

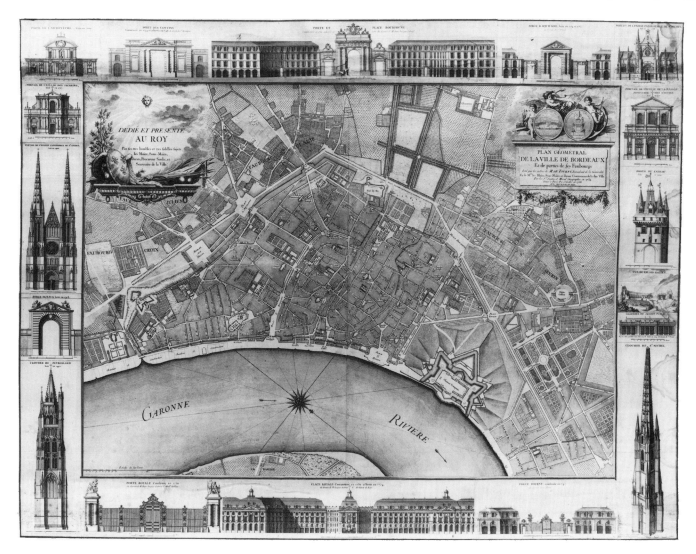

7. Bordeaux, plan engraved by J. Lattré, 1755. Archives Nationales, N II Gironde 1; Centre Historique des Archives Nationales Atelier de Photographie. The Jardin Public is at the right and adjacent to the Château Trompette.

gest the towers and walls of the demolished symbol of tyranny.[20]

PROMENADES AND PUBLIC GARDENS IN URBAN MASTER PLANS

From the middle decades of the eighteenth century, officials and designers in many French cities included public green space as an integral component of master plans for urban development. Like the Marquis de Tourny in Bordeaux, they often made the case that the planning of promenades and public parks was a matter of utility as well as beautification. An outstanding example of such thinking was Louis de Mondran's propos-

als of 1752–54 for the embellishment of Toulouse (fig. 9).[21] Mondran was neither an architect nor an administrator but an *amateur* and respected supporter of the arts in Toulouse. Mondran's scheme was partly implemented, and its signature feature, the Grand Rond, a large, verdant oval outside the city wall, remains prominent in the city's plan. Radiating from the Grand Rond, and conveniently adjacent to the quarter favored by the city's elite, were promenades offering appropriately elegant and well-defined vantage points for observing city and countryside. Mondran also intended them as an armature for new residential quarters consisting of low, mostly one-story houses surrounded by greenery, which were not realized. He noted that the considerable length of the promenades was nec-

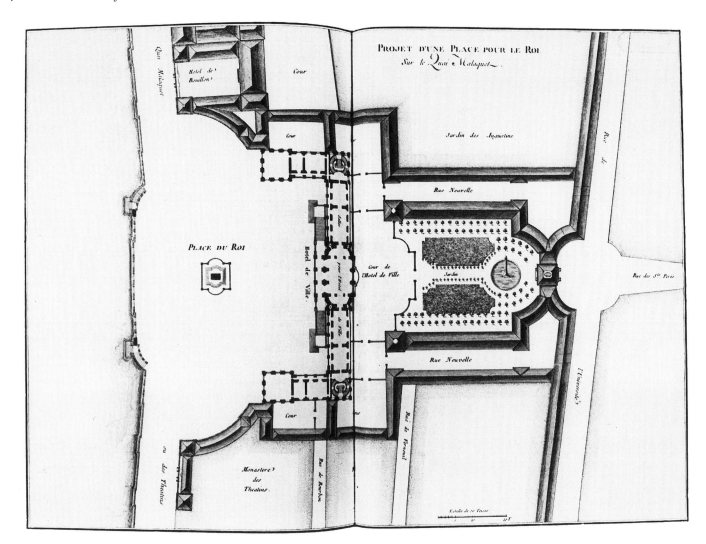

8. Paris, project for the Place Louis XV on the Quai Malaquais, Pierre Contant d'Ivry, ca. 1748. Pierre Patte, *Monumens érigés en France à la gloire de Louis XV*, 1765; Avery Architectural and Fine Arts Library, Columbia University in the City of New York.

essary to allow for the long walks most beneficial for good health and argued that the entire enterprise would stimulate the economy of Toulouse and help to make the city a more competitive commercial center.

Mondran's master plan also included four public gardens. The present Jardin Royal located between the city wall and the Grand Rond was the largest of these and the only one to be realized. Like the Tuileries garden and the Jardin Public in Bordeaux, it was to have had both outward-looking prospects and internally focused settings. For the former Mondran planned a perimeter terrace shaded by linden trees and equipped with stone benches, and for the latter he arranged six shaded *boulingrins* on either side of a central allée. Within the city wall,

Mondran planned two connected gardens behind the Capitole, the city hall. One was to have been attached to the Capitole in the manner of Contant d'Ivry's project for the Paris city hall. The other was to have been a botanical garden. In addition to the gardens evidently intended for the city's more affluent citizens, Mondran proposed a fourth garden and adjoining promenade in the vicinity of the Hôspital de la Grave that were to have provided access to healthy air for the poor and infirm, safely removed from the elite. Such explicit attention to the less fortunate members of the city's population was rare in the eighteenth century.

At the same time Mondran was promoting his vision for Toulouse, the architect Antoine-Mathieu Le Carpentier was engaged in equally ambitious

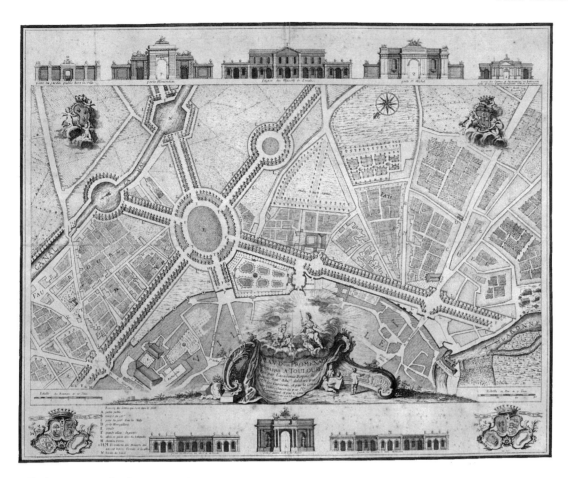

9. Toulouse, project for the Promenade de l'Ovale, Louis de Mondran, 1752. Engraving by Baour, Musée Paul-Dupuy, Toulouse, inv. no. 2003. The Jardin Public, labeled "A" is located between the Ovale (the Grand Rond) and the city wall.

planning for Rouen.[22] In 1749, the municipal government had commissioned him to evaluate the condition of the city hall. Informed by the projects of Contant d'Ivry and others for the Place Louis XV in Paris, he proposed to replace the old building with a palatial structure on a new site at the head of a *place royale* (fig. 10). Aligned axially behind the new city hall was to have been a large Jardin de Ville composed of a principal allée, flanking *parterres*, a circular fountain, and ranges of trees along the sides. Although the overall plan was conventional, the garden departed from the aristocratic townhouse model in the openness of its visual and physical connections to the surrounding neighborhood. At the end adjacent to the city hall, a cross street was to replace the terrace that typically makes the transition from garden to building. The far end was to border an octagonal *place* separated only by a fence. Midway along each side was to have been another cross street that may have allowed traffic to traverse the garden.

In 1758, Le Carpentier published his project in a book in which he explained his vision of the city hall as something more than the seat of government. "The communal house (*maison commune*) of the citizens," he wrote, "must be able to receive the Muses who cultivate their talents and contribute to their pleasures."[23] To this end he planned a concert hall and meeting rooms for the local academy of science, letters, and art in addition to the rooms required for municipal governance. Across the *place*, he proposed building a theater. Thus the city hall was to have been the hub of a civic center, and one can imagine its garden populated by the enlightened recipients of the Muses' favors.

Le Carpentier incorporated the city hall and public garden in a master plan that he proposed for the improvement and expansion of Rouen. The garden and its cross street would have marked the border between the old town and a new quarter that was to have extended to the Hôtel Dieu (the municipal hospital), which had recently been installed

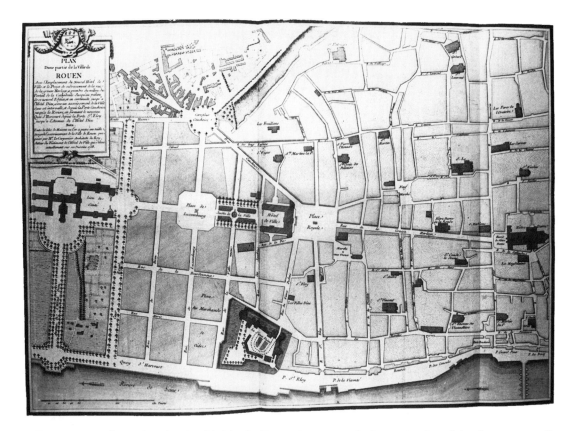

10. Rouen, master plan project, Antoine-Mathieu Le Carpentier, ca. 1757. Le Carpentier, *Recueil des plans, coupes et élévations du nouvel hôtel de ville de Rouen*, 1758; Avery Architectural and Fine Arts Library, Columbia University in the City of New York. The new quarter between the proposed *hôtel de ville* and the hospital is indicated by darker shading.

in the former hospital for plague victims outside the old city walls. In addition to defining the new quarter, an important objective of the plan was improving circulation throughout the city. To this end he treated the movement of traffic as choreography that would, he wrote, "multiply [the city's monuments] and link them, providing the most advantageous points of view possible and creating a chain that visitors might naturally follow." He added, "It will draw from the locale all the advantages that art might borrow."[24]

His approach to planning as art inspired by, but improving upon, nature—in this case the existing urban landscape—recalls the language of Abbé Laugier, who five years earlier, in 1753, had offered this advice on town planning in his *Essai sur l'architecture*: "One must look at a town as a forest. The streets of the one are the roads of the other; both must be cut through in the same way. The essential beauty of a park consists in the great number of roads, their width and their alignment. This, however, is not sufficient: it needs a Le Nôtre to design the plan for it, someone who applies taste and

intelligence so that there is at one and the same time order and fantasy, symmetry and variety."[25]

Le Carpentier's plan for Rouen is a textbook example of how a mid-eighteenth-century architect might achieve Laugier's call for order and variety in the transformation of a city. Le Carpentier proposed widening and straightening the rue de la Grande Horloge, the city's main street, and planned views of the cathedral and the new city hall as dramatic focal points. *Places* of different shapes (rectangles, circles, octagons), public gardens behind city hall and the Vieux Palais, and a grand *cours* alongside the Hôtel Dieu offered citizens access to fresh, healthy air and a pleasing contrast to the rows of buildings lining the streets.

Arguably, the most spectacular instance of designing public green space as part of a master plan for urban expansion occurred in Nîmes.[26] The success of the local textile industry in the eighteenth century generated wealth and a steady increase in population. Housing, however, was in short supply, and increased demand by residents and industry strained the city's primary source

11. Nîmes, master plan project, Jacques-Philippe Mareschal, published 1774. Collection Musée du Vieux Nîmes, 1557.

of water, the ancient springs at the base of Mont-Cavalier outside the city walls to the west.

Following a drought in 1719, governmental officials began exploring ways of improving the collection and distribution of water. This engineering problem rapidly expanded in scope as the designers assigned to the task realized that they had an opportunity to integrate the planning of the water supply with an expansion of the city beyond its walls. The presence of ancient Roman ruins around the springs offered an incentive to think of beautification as well as utility.

In 1744 the crown assigned responsibility for the expanded scope of work to the provincial director of fortifications, Jacques-Philippe Mareschal. He addressed the water supply problem by enlarging the collection basin at the spring and building a new canal to conduct the water to the heart of the city (fig. 11). Along the canal, he planned a promenade that intersected with a broad tree-lined boulevard, the present Avenue Jean Jaurès, which formed the spine of the new district that more than doubled the area of the city. The far end of the boulevard intersected with a long *jeu de mail*.

The focal point of the entire development was

the ancient spring, which Mareschal transformed into the Jardin de la Fontaine (fig. 12). He valued the Roman remains and integrated them into his design by retaining portions of their plan and incorporating ancient stone into new construction. His work was not an archaeological restoration but an effort to provide Nîmes with a living link to its ancient origins. Similar attitudes can be seen in contemporary urban development schemes in other French cities including Lyon and Reims.[27]

Mareschal divided the garden into five zones. The first consisted of the approaches from the old city to the east and the new district to the south, which were lined with trees and small pavilions. Gates separate the approaches from the next three zones forming the garden proper. The garden zones include an island formed by the water-supply canal, the spring surrounded by the major Roman remains, and terraces ascending the south of Mont-Cavalier. The fifth and final zone was a terrace to the west that contained an obelisk dedicated to the city's prosperity under the beneficent rule of Louis XV.

Of these features, the hillside terraces were only partially realized, and the picturesque path and

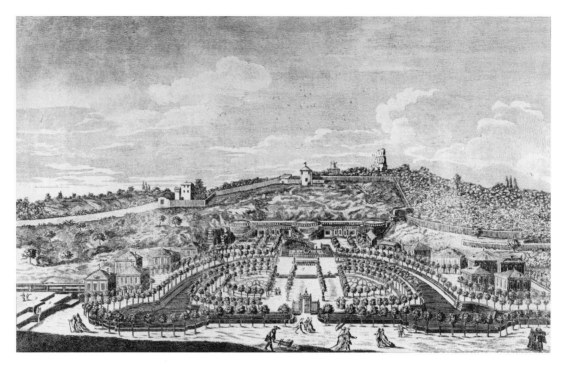

12. Nîmes, Jardin de la Fontaine. Engraving, 1808, Collection Musée du Vieux Nîmes. The spring and ancient ruins are in the middle ground beneath the hillside terraces. The water supply canal flows around the island and off right to the city center. At left is the terrace, no longer extant, which had an obelisk honoring Louis XV.

plantings that we see today were established later in 1819. The pavilions and the western terrace were demolished in 1871 to accommodate the construction of the present Avenue Franklin Roosevelt. These are major changes, but enough of Mareschal's scheme survives for visitors to appreciate the range of possibilities that he created for movement and observation at various scales and distances.

Utility and embellishment were the twin beacons guiding urban design in the mid-eighteenth century. The examples of Toulouse, Rouen, and Nîmes illustrate how designers utilized promenades and public gardens to meet both objectives. It is noteworthy that, although the political will to plan and realize these projects typically issued from officers of the crown, the design process itself was not centralized. The professional status of designers varied widely. For example, Mondran was an *amateur*, Le Carpentier is known primarily as an architect of Parisian residences, and Mareschal was a military engineer. None belonged to the Bâtiments du Roi, the royal building service, and only Le Carpentier was a member of the Académie Royale d'Architecture. Nevertheless, they shared a remarkably coherent sense of purpose and employed a common design vocabulary informed less by theoretical writings, which were few at mid-century, than by awareness of the emerging conventions of contemporary practice, which they creatively adapted to the unique circumstances of their cities.

Notes

1. Louis de Mondran, *Projet pour le commerce et pour les embelissemens de Toulouse lu dans une séance de l'Académie Royale de Peinture, Sculpture et Architecture, par un des Membres de cette Académie* (Toulouse: Chez M. J.-H. Guillemette, 1754), 10; quoted in Georges Costa, "Louis de Mondran, économiste et urbaniste (1699–1792)," *La Vie Urbaine* n.s. 1 (1955): 52–53.

2. See Pierre Lavedan, *Histoire de l'urbanisme: Renaissance et Temps modernes* (Paris: Henri Laurens, 1941), 447–52; Mark Girouard, *Cities and People: A Social and Architectural History* (New Haven: Yale University Press, 1985), 166–67, 174–79, 186–98; Daniel Rabreau, "Urban Walks in France in the Seventeenth and Eighteenth Centuries," in *The Architecture of Western Gardens: A Design History from the Renaissance to the Present Day*, ed. Monique Mosser and Georges Teyssot (Cambridge, Mass: MIT Press, 1991), 305–16.

3. Marcel Poëte, *La promenade à Paris au XVIIe siècle* (Paris: Armand Colin, 1913), 136–42.

4. Ibid., 109–35.

5. Poëte (ibid., 1–27) discusses the uses of open space in seventeenth-century Paris.

6. For the fashion for social walking, see Rabreau, "Urban Walks"; for urban design and public administration, see Richard Cleary, *The Place Royale and Urban Design in the Ancien Régime* (New York: Cambridge University Press, 1999); Jean-Louis Harouel, *L'embellissement des villes: L'urbanisme français au XVIIIe siècle* (Paris: Picard, 1993); and Antoine Picon, *French Architects and Engineers in the Age of the Enlightenment*, trans. Martin Thon (New York: Cambridge University Press, 1992); for public health issues, see Richard Etlin, "L'air dans l'urbanisme des Lumières," *Dix-huitième siècle* 9 (1977): 123–34.

7. Cleary, *Place Royale*, 49.

8. Ibid., 97–102, 239–41.

9. Marc-Antoine Laugier, *Observations sur l'architecture* (The Hague, 1765), 172.

10. See Robert Isherwood, *Farce and Fantasy: Popular Entertainment in Eighteenth-Century Paris* (New York: Oxford University Press, 1986).

11. Harouel, *L'embellissement des villes*, 42–44.

12. Anthony Vidler, *Claude-Nicolas Ledoux: Architecture and Social Reform at the End of the Ancien Régime* (Cambridge, Mass.: MIT Press, 1990), 208–50.

13. Charles Perrault, *Mémoires de ma vie*, quoted in Délégation à l'Action Artistique de la Ville de Paris, *Le Louvre et son quartier*, exhibition catalogue (Paris: Mairie Annexe du 1er Arrondissement, 1982), 72. The question of public access to gardens in eighteenth-century Paris is examined by Jean-Louis Harouel, "Caliban hors du jardin: Le droit d'accès au jardin public parisien à la fin de l'Ancien Régime," in *Histoire du droit social: Mélanges en hommage à Jean Imbert*, ed. Jean-Louis Harouel (Paris: Presses Universitaires de France, 1989), 295–300.

14. F. Hamilton Hazlehurst, *Gardens of Illusion: The Genius of André Le Nostre* (Nashville: Vanderbilt University Press, 1980), 167–85.

15. *Monuments historiques* has devoted two themed issues to the subject of public gardens. The first, on "Jardins de Paris," 142 (Dec.–Jan. 1986), includes Michel Vernes, "Genèse et avatars du jardin public," 4–10; and Henri Bresler, "Il faut qu'un jardin soit ouvert ou fermé," 17–23. The second, "Jardins des provinces," 143 (Feb.–March 1986), includes Violaine Lanselle, "Inventaire des jardins publics," 97–115, which provides short entries organized by province and city. See also *Jardins en France, 1760–1820: Pays d'illusion, Terre d'expériences*, exhibition catalogue (Paris: Caisse Nationale des Monuments Historiques et des Sites, 1977), 150–68.

16. Letter from the *maire* and *jurats* of Bordeaux to the Marquis d'Argenson, 2 July 1746. Archives municipales de Bordeaux, BB (Registre de correspondance, 1740–50); published in *Archives historiques du département de la Gironde* 38 (Paris: Picard; Bordeaux: Feret, 1903), 291.

17. Letter from the Marquis de Tourny to the Marquis d'Argenson, 2 July 1746. Archives départementales de la Gironde, c. 1185; published in *Archives historiques du département de la Gironde*, 293.

18. See Vernes, "Genèse et avatars," 7.

19. Cleary, *Place Royale*, 217–18.

20. James A. Leith, *Space and Revolution: Projects for Monuments, Squares, and Public Buildings in France, 1789–1799* (Montreal: McGill-Queen's University Press, 1991), 75–77.

21. Costa, "Louis de Mondran"; Robert A. Schneider, *Public Life in Toulouse, 1463–1789: From Municipal Republic to Cosmopolitan City* (Ithaca, N.Y.: Cornell University Press, 1989), 344–52.

22. Cleary, *Place Royale*, 261–65.

23. Matthieu Le Carpentier, *Recueil des plans, coupes et élévations du nouvel hôtel de ville de Rouen, dont la construction a été commencée en Mai 1757, avec les Plans d'un accroissement et autres ouvrages projettés pour cette Ville* (Paris: Charles-Antoine Jombert, 1758), 8.

24. Ibid.

25. Marc-Antoine Laugier, *An Essay on Architecture* (1753), trans. Wolfgang and Anni Herrmann (Los Angeles: Hennessey & Ingalls, 1977), 128.

26. The most accessible publication on the Jardin de la Fontaine and the expansion of Nîmes is the brief book by Victor Lasalle, *La Fontaine de Nîmes de l'antiquité à nos jours* (Paris: Cadran, 1967). The fundamental scholarly study of the administrative environment is the unpublished thesis by Lucien Solanet, "Rôles des autorités administratives dans l'urbanisme et le développement artistique du Bas-Languedoc aux XVIIe et XVIIIe siècles" (thèse de droit, Montpellier, 1953). Passing references to this work appear in Harouel, *L'embellissement des villes*. For the economic and social context, see Line Teisseyre-Sallmann, "Urbanisme et société: L'exemple de Nîmes aux XVIIe et XVIIIe siècles," *Annales: Economies, sociétés, civilisations* 35.5 (1980): 965–86. For Mareschal, see Anne Blanchard, *Les ingénieurs du "roy" de Louis XIV à Louis XVI: Etude du Corps des Fortifications* (Montpellier: Université Paul-Valéry [Montpellier III], 1979), 446–50.

27. At Lyon, the Place Louis-le-Grand (Place Bellecour) was developed at the beginning of the eighteenth century with the knowledge that ancient Roman monuments had existed nearby. At Reims, the Place Louis XV and related improvements planned in the 1750s alluded to the city's history as Roman Durocotorum. See Cleary, *Place Royale*, chap. 6.

5. The Tree

Rural Tradition and Landscape Innovation in the Eighteenth Century

YVES LUGINBÜHL

The expansion of a study of tradition and innovation in garden art into the domain of landscaping and land use originated in an attempt to put into both a sociological and a historical perspective the models that structure thought about nature and in particular about its aesthetic, symbolic, and phenomenological dimensions; this essay also seeks to define the garden as a field of social representations of nature and of rural societies during the transition from the Classical to the Romantic era. The object that forms the basis of this study is considered to be essentially natural, the tree. But it has become as well a social construct and an object shaped both by the practices of rural European societies and by garden designers.

The tree, in fact, provides a means of comprehending both the evolution of garden art over the course of the eighteenth century and the ties established between agrarian practices, learned thought in the peasant classes, and the representations of nature constructed by the French elite during the transition from absolute monarchy to the Republic.

This study analyzes first the shapes that European, particularly French, agrarian practices gave to the tree, keeping in mind the social context to which they belong. Second, the production of these tree forms will be placed in the context of the passage from the ancien régime to the Republic, demonstrating how learned thought on the tree was profoundly modified by this political and philosophical transition. Returning to the subject of the garden, the final section illuminates the conse-

quences that this evolution of thought on the tree had upon garden art.

THE SHAPES OF TREES IN RURAL AREAS: AN EXPRESSION OF SOCIAL RELATIONS IN THE CLASSICAL FEUDAL SYSTEM

For several centuries, at least from the tenth to the eighteenth century, but in all likelihood even before this period, the tree was exploited as a natural resource by the European peasant classes for several purposes (construction, firewood, leaves for animal feed) and given a particular form, empirically but precisely designed to fill these functions effectively. This does not mean, however, that trees were used only for utilitarian purposes; they also carried symbolic and aesthetic value, most often tied to religious beliefs or to local social history. But this is not the main subject of my analysis.

The main interest lies in the modes of social organization, a knowledge of which history will provide an understanding of these distinctive shapes, capable of shocking the uninitiated, especially the urban populations "discovering" certain parts of the countryside. The social organization of feudalism rested, in effect, upon the subordination of vassals to the lord, and upon the assumption of a system of rules regulating the use of natural resources, to which each person, as a member of the community, had to conform. These rules, the rights of use, established the rhythm of social life, but at the same time implied the practices which had given such unusual shapes to the trees, resulting from the regularity of size intended to insure the survival of the social group through a negotiated division of natural resources (fig. 1). This type of law, incidentally, was not a strictly French invention; it was practiced in both Eastern and Western Europe, because it was a corollary of the most widespread modes of social organization in the whole of Europe. It concerned the resources taken not only from vegetation, but from all that nature had to offer to societies: minerals, water, and so on.

These forms were divided among the production of wood for construction, firewood, and greenery for animal feed, at a time when the forest did not have the same appearance that it now has; it had been greatly reduced as a result of ill-timed usage by peasants, by feudal lords (for the construction of their châteaus), and by blacksmith-artisans (for metalworking). Different territories produced very dissimilar types of trimming, which gave the trees a very strange appearance, compared with the image that we have constructed of the tree, according to which it raises its branches in a somewhat architectural fashion. These types could be called *têtard*, the most common shape in Europe, or *têteau*, a type specific to the Berry region of France; but certain local peasant societies invented a whole system of different trimming shapes corresponding to the various distinctive functions. This was the case in Brittany, where one could find oak *ragosses* or *ragoles*[1] and chestnut *tassées*,[2] destined to provide firewood or greenery for the animals, and *coupelles*,[3] with straight, shooting boles, reserved for construction (figs. 2, 3). These unusual treatments of trees were closely linked to the relations between proprietors and farmers, which were crystallized into the rules of the feudal social system. These rules had to be respected by both the former and latter groups in their treatment of natural resources, including trees.

The methods of treatment or management of trees help us to understand the shapes better. The social objective of a *têtard* tree was to furnish firewood or building wood, and its trimming was regulated by a very precise schedule, due to social constraints. The branches, chopped down on a regular basis, were to go to farmers, the trunk to the proprietor; this rule was strictly followed. Trimming was a collective effort, a chore shared by community members, which strengthened the solidarity of farmers, often poor peasants who bitterly fought over the least valuable part of the tree, while the trunk, which provided the wood used to construct building frameworks and furniture, went to the proprietor, an emancipated laborer, or the lord. This rule assumed that the farmer, whose job was to maintain the land and its vegetation, had also to keep track of the renewal of young trees, without necessarily planting new ones, but by assuring the growth of trees developed from spontaneous seeding.[4] He also needed to keep the property lines precisely delineated and the markers in good shape. There could be no exceptions made to these rules, and violations were severely punished; certainly, there were numerous attempts to bypass the regulations, as the rigidity of the constraints tempted farmers to get round common practices. Still, this code remained in use until the twentieth century, and even today, in certain regions, reference is made in legal disputes to these regulations still in effect in the local chambers of agriculture.

The connection between these regulations and the shapes given to trees by the peasants is not apparent at first glance; however, it follows a remarkably strict rationale. Trimming was calculated so that the cutting of branches could be completed in the fastest possible manner, following a precise organizational method that gathered the farmers together in the following groups: the young men climbed the trees and cut the branches with a single stroke of an axe, working from top to bottom, without cutting the trunk; the older men, on the ground, watched the trimmers work and chopped the branches into equal logs. As for the women, the young bundled the thin branches, which would be used to light fires, and the older women prepared a meal and an alcoholic drink, the "flippe,"[5] which they brought at midday to encourage the trimmers in their work.

This type of duty was an occasion for the farmers to build upon the feelings of solidarity that tied them to one another, feelings that were really no more than an expression of their common battle against the proprietors. It was a sort of festival, lost today, as the strong ties it encouraged were loosened by profound changes in European rural societies. In any case, this method of organization implied that the trees would take a particular shape, which varied by region and which apparently took into account both the particular relations between negotiators and the climatic and pedological variability of the land, and determined how often trees would be trimmed. For example, in one area where the climate was warmer and more humid, trimming would take place every four years, whereas in a nearby area with a cooler, drier micro-

1. *Riches Heures du Duc de Berry, le mois de juin*, ca. 1440. Musée Condé de Chantilly.

2. Trimmed trees in Brittany: *ragosses* and *coupelles*. Photo by Y. Luginbühl.

climate, it was done only every seven years. Consultation of local regulations allows us to verify that, within a given region, this timetable could vary widely, corresponding to local ecological or social conditions, which were recorded empirically in the rights of use.

These shapes were, therefore, a cultural expression of nature, developed in negotiations between social forces and, over the long term, through precise observations of plant growth and of the trees' reactions to trimming; it was necessary to insure the perenniality of these Breton *ragosses*, with their gnarled trunks, in order to prolong as much as possible the availability of firewood and foliage. This practice did not in any way adversely affect the life of the tree, as some have argued, either on aesthetic grounds or by claiming that repeated trimming led to the trees' premature death. Some *ragosses* are quite old, as old as the *coupelles* that more closely correspond to the image of the beautiful tree held by the majority of the population today. Still, the tortuous or gnarled silhouette of *ragosses* and *têtards* was, from the eighteenth century on, the target of agronomists and educated foresters, but also of aesthetes who sought to impose a different representation of the tree, one that conformed to a new

philosophy of nature and of society that was developing at that time.

THE SHAPE OF THE TREE IN A NEW WAY OF THINKING OF NATURE AND SOCIETY

The passage from absolute monarchy to a republican regime, which corresponds to the political determination to put an end to feudal practices and to take preliminary steps toward democracy, was accompanied by a radical transformation of the representation of trees, manifested in literature as well as in the domains both of agricultural and forest economy and of garden art. Several factors come into play in this transformation, of which the most important will be discussed.

Obviously, the economic factor is important, and it would be used substantially in the argument of foresters who, since the sixteenth century, had tried to impose a new forest culture. The corps of forest guards was instituted by François I, and since that time the French government had never stopped working to reinforce the capacity of the kingdom's forests to provide wood for the con-

3. Trimmed trees in Brittany: recently trimmed *ragosses*. Photo by Y. Luginbühl.

struction of warships and merchantmen. However, the forest, which was most often within the system of communal lands, was regularly exploited by the peasants, and the trees that grew there hardly resembled those that the royal technicians wished to see grown; after all, the tree that would produce wood for shipbuilding was that grown for timber, with a straight, slender trunk, not the tree altered by pruning. Starting in the sixteenth century, the conflict between peasants and foresters brought to light these two opposing images of the tree, which is still deep-rooted in some regions, reaching its peak in the nineteenth century with bloody confrontations in which the rural populations were accused of lacking in culture and of being incapable of understanding the general interest, that is, the interest of the state.

The Colbert ordinance of 1669, which established the forest properties of the crown, did not question the rights of communal use in existing forests, because Jean-Baptiste Colbert knew that in that case he would be attacking a bastion that could provoke popular revolt. It was not until the Revolution and the law of 1791 permitting the privatization of common lands that the French government began officially to suppress what had fundamentally marked the functioning of the feudal system.[6]

This brings us to the second factor that contributed to changes in the image of the tree and that came out of the passage from monarchy to republic: in the eighteenth century, the image of the tree formed by the social elite changed as a result of Enlightenment conceptions of nature and Romanticism. An interpretation of this change has already been outlined[7] but can be clarified in light of some recent research: the eighteenth century effectively corresponds to a toppling of the learned elite's vision, "enlightened" by Enlightenment philosophy, with regard to nature and social relations. The link between society and nature is essential to an understanding of how the image of the tree is modified in the passage from the Classical to the Romantic age.

As some writers have already indicated,[8] a very clear association is formed during this period between the natural and the social, at a moment when the enlightened elite is engaged in a critique of absolutism and feudal power and in tracing in outline the functions of a democratic society founded on the legitimacy of political representation of the people and recognition of its demands. In fact, it is by the rejection of the old society's feudal system and the arbitrariness of political decisions when power is concentrated in the hands of only one man, by the obscurantism that characterizes feudal practices, and by this association of the social with the natural, that we can understand this change in the image of the tree in the consciousness of the elite.

While a desire for changes in the functioning of European societies manifested itself at this time, the learned elite was developing its own vision of the exploitation of space and land, a vision that connects a beautiful, healthy society with beautiful, healthy nature and, conversely, an ugly, unhealthy society with ugly, unhealthy nature.[9] A beautiful, healthy society is one that breaks its ties with absolutism and feudal relationships, in other words, with the routine social practices of exploitation of natural resources, and produces a beautiful, healthy environment. Conversely, feudal society, which is ugly and unhealthy in that its socially unjust order is opposed to individual liberty, submitting the individual to an absolute power, follows practices anchored in routines that produce ugly, unhealthy forms of exploitation of natural resources. Hence the profound reforms proposed by the agronomists of the eighteenth century to bring society from a state of shortage to one of abundance, reforms based on the institution of personal property and on a radical transformation of agrarian techniques that had fundamentally characterized rural feudal society (authorization to close off one's lands from another's, privatization of communal lands, cultivation of fodder, establishment of animal breeding as an activity independent from farming, abolition of fallowing land, the use of one field to grow two or more crops in succession, mechanization of production, etc.).

There is much testimony to this assimilation in technical and scholarly literature and in administrative records of the period stigmatizing the feudal practices of the rural population and advocating the rationalization of agricultural practices. We already know that the growing economy of the nineteenth century depended in large part on this technical, political, and economic revolution (including the institution of economic liberalism)— a revolution that certainly profits the bourgeoisie more than the peasant classes, but which, little by little, eliminated the food shortages and famines to which feudal society had so regularly been exposed. This testimony associates the destitution of the rural populations with the state of the natural resources they exploited, in particular in swampy or uncultivated regions (or those areas considered as such because they were under the authority of a feudal regime). This association thus combines several beliefs of the enlightened elite: rural societies find themselves in a poverty-stricken state because they are confined in an unhealthy environment (for example, fever is rampant in swampy areas), because they are kept in an uneducated state by the excesses of the feudal power structure, and because this lack of culture prevents them from gaining access to modernity and deprives them of the liberty to undertake projects or to change their practices.

Anything that can be seen by the elite to be symbolic of feudalism is suspected of belonging to a political regime that crushes populations and prevents them from emerging from their destitute condition. The visible manifestations of agrarian practices are therefore a part of what must be excluded from the new vision of a just, egalitarian society.

The aesthetics of tree trimming thus originates in various thoughts on the practice of trimming, which have been regarded as parallel to the elite's vision of the peasant as a greedy, uncouth character who demonstrates no sensitivity to any object and especially not to living things, be they plants or animals.[10] Behind the practice of trimming lies the knowledge of the profit that can be made from wood, although one might admit that this profit could be respectable if it is not linked to any barbaric practices.

To abolish these practices was therefore necessary in order to put the nation on a new track, pressing the peasantry into trade, liberal systems, individual ownership of land, and so forth. In this light, anything that could be seen as a fallback to the feudal system must be condemned—the practices of the peasant societies regarding nature[11] as well as their collective practices (i.e., communal lands). The practice of trimming thereby had an antiprogressive connotation in the French elite's vision of the role that the peasantry should play in the country's economic development.

There is still another aspect of the symbolism of the tree, one invented by the liberty tree of the Revolution. This tree obviously could not be trimmed! It had to be free to grow, to develop, to spread its branches without constraints, to bloom each spring following a rhythm that no aesthetically improper interference (according to the academic canons that were developed at this time) could hinder: a natural rhythm, established over many years, over a longer period than a man's lifetime; a rhythm tied to an internal biological process, corresponding to the concept of *natura naturans*, supported by the scholars and philosophers of the eighteenth century, rather than to the *natura naturata*, a previous notion implying that natural function was linked to an external intervention. The fine tree was and needed to be tall, strong, and free like the nation, because it was one of its symbols.

The shapes of trees trimmed by the peasants were not from the outset, however, seen as symbols of their social condition. It was in the Classical gardens and cities that the bourgeoisie first began to criticize the regular shapes given to trees, comparing these to the free, natural bearing of the Romantic tree. This is why, in this revolutionary era, the silhouette of the untrimmed tree became one of the symbols of the Republic. The choice of this symbol—the liberty tree—was never fully explained, though one explanation is that offered here. Incidentally, Henri Bernardin de Saint-Pierre once said that "L'arbre est une République" ("The tree is a Republic").[12] The Romantic tree is indeed one that is free to spread its branches with no opposition to disturb its growth, and certainly without the oppressive restriction it suffered at the hands of the peasantry under the unenlightened feudal regime. It is only later, in the first half of the nineteenth century, that the social elite would discover this opposition, once the travels of writers and scholars had permitted some observation of the shapes that Classical practices of trimming and pruning had given to trees in the countryside as well as in the cities.

A veritable ideology of the tree (barely studied by historians) was developed in the eighteenth and early nineteenth centuries, providing the Romantics with yet another opportunity to denounce the human race as a predator of nature and destructor of beauty.[13] Victor Hugo himself proclaimed, "Couper les branches d'un chêne, c'est couper les bras d'un homme" ("To cut the branches off an oak is to cut off a man's arms"),[14] and Stendhal attacked the mayor of Verrières-le-Buisson, who had had the trees of the town's main avenue trimmed for profit, thereby transforming the plane trees into vulgar plants grown for food.[15]

The same Romantic movement that had rediscovered medieval history and often reconstructed it, inflicting upon it numerous transformations designed to reinforce the ideology of fusion with nature, did not understand these forms of tree trimming in the context of their social rationality: it was above all the shape, which reflected the mutilation of the living being, that was stigmatized. The Romantic tree became a majestic tree, flaunting its branches in all their magnificence, as opposed to the *têtards* and *ragosses*, which were symbolic of the brutality of boors.

Even Elisée Reclus, who tries to understand relationships of modern society to nature,[16] sees the peasants' practice of cutting or mutilating trees with their axes as a reflection of ancient customs and the simple execution of a task necessary to survival, and does not place this practice in the context of a reasoned, civilized approach to nature. According to this view, the peasant simply obeys a sort of reflex that cannot be regarded as a manifestation of any aesthetic sentiment.

TREE SHAPES AND A REVOLUTION IN LANDSCAPING

This evolution in social relationships to both nature and society itself had profound consequences on garden art and on the use and treatment of plant species. In the Classical city, plant life was used to reinforce the structured, orderly appearance of urban figures, which reflected the political, moral, and religious order. As we know, in the gardens of this period, a regularity and geometricity of shapes were applied to plants. They give evidence of a veritable culture of tree shaping, developed by garden designers, who seem to have been inspired by peasant culture.[17]

This does not mean, however, that these gardeners sought to imitate the trimmed tree shapes created by peasants; rather, they interpreted, to an aesthetic end, the culture of plant trimming as it had flourished in rural societies. Obviously, it cannot be claimed that the Classical garden reproduced the tree shapes of the countryside, even if some analogies could encourage us to think in this manner. For example, in a canvas painted by Hubert Robert (1733–1808) at the time when the plantings at the château de Versailles were completely rethought and reorganized, the appearance of the few trees depicted (fig. 4) is quite troubling, and one could effectively see in them some similarities with trimmed trees in rural areas; but this is difficult to affirm. One could just as well suppose that the majority of gardeners employed in large gardens were of rural origin and brought with them the savoir-faire they acquired there.

The regularity of shape to which plant life was subjected in the city and the Classical garden is certainly a reflection of an aesthetics of order and perspective, which accompanied conceptions of urban spaces and nature and reflected the idea of a hierarchical, orderly society, as the representatives of the royal power wished to see it. The great majority of plantings in the Classical-era city did in fact consist of regular shapes, like the awnings along the

4. Hubert Robert, *Vue du bosquet des bains d'Apollon lors de l'abattage des arbres du parc de Versailles*, Versailles, Musée national du château.

avenues, the arches of greenery organizing space in public squares; in the garden there were conical, cylindrical, and rectangular shapes and the volutes of flower beds that could be broken down into elementary geometric shapes.

There was obviously nothing of this in the landscape garden that came into favor during the eighteenth century, evidently characterized by the English experiment and designed, as we know, to represent a sort of landscape revolution in opposition to the garden of regular shapes and figures, which was harshly criticized by designers of the era, such as René-Louis de Girardin and Jean-Marie Morel. In winding alleys, in the introduction of figures meant to evoke mountains, rocks, waterfalls, streams, and so on, a new aesthetic makes itself known, one that grows from a representation of unrestricted, freely developing nature—a representation that reflects the learned elite's vision of the ideal society. It is clear that these manifestations in the garden of the new mode of thought are only a simulation of nature, but they present themselves as a space reorganized according to new regulations, which are to be as influential in people's vision of nature as in their vision of society itself.

The idea of flow—in the circulation of natural elements, such as water or air—goes back to the idea of the development of communication and of the "flow" that, in the new society, should encourage the trade of goods and ideas, contrary to the feudal system, which had been characterized by immobility.[18] This idea is, incidentally, already present in the image of the tree, whose functioning is dependent upon the circulation of sap and the exchanges made between the roots and the leaves through its vessels. It becomes consolidated through its manifestation in gardens precisely because of the artificial streams and waterfalls. This reversal in the representation of nature does not, however, mean that nature, from now on more free in its development, is left to its own devices; on the contrary, it must still be controlled. This change may imply that control is even more easily maintained than before, in the sense that society is no longer afraid to give the garden a "natural" appearance, no longer restricting it to a narrow yoke of geometric shapes. This reasoning is just as valid with regard to society, governed by new political rules.

This question of control over the tree as a living thing raises several problems that confront urban society in its management of nature within the city. In order to grow freely, and to offer the spectacle of its spreading branches, a tree requires space. It

5. Fake tree composed of a dead trunk and geraniums, city of Ducey (Manche). Photo by Z. Gros.

had plenty in the large private parks of the late eighteenth century, which often consisted of collections of great native and exotic trees. In an urban public space, the situation is different: the narrowness of the roads, the rows of building façades, and all the spatial constraints of the city were opposed to the planting of tall trees, unless they were to be trimmed, contained within the amount of space available for them. That is what was done: the tradition of the trimmed tree was perpetuated in the cities in the nineteenth century and, in most cases, even today.

The creation of large public parks assured the liberty tree its freedom to grow: there it is no longer necessary to control the volume of the branches, and the tree can expand as it wishes. But, in fact, the designers of these new parks artfully manipulated the spectacle offered to visitor: cedars, oaks, sequoias, and so on were arranged with the intention of emphasizing their imposing silhouette and eliciting an emotional response from spectators. The public park was thus the ideal location for the growth of the tree imagined by the scholars of the eighteenth century.[19]

But representations of an object in nature do not generally last long. Many municipal leaders found that the temptation to abolish the barbaric practice of tree trimming led the gardeners who advised them to seek ways to allow trees to be planted in cities—especially as this became an electoral campaign issue—without trimming them. They therefore sought to plant species of smaller stature, such as certain varieties of maples and shrubs that were very popular during the period of reorganization and reconstruction in the municipal parks.

The type of tree production pursued subsequently is the result of the direction that objects of nature, both in the material and the symbolic sense, have taken since the Classical era. This is founded upon a practice that developed throughout Europe, perhaps not systematically in every country, but certainly in France. This practice of planting essentially consists in seeking a form of plant life that, as closely as possible, reproduces the shape of the tree, but that can thrive despite the constraints placed on it by humans who seek to control nature. In this newly developed form, the tree is no longer a living tree, in the psychological sense of the term: Bernardin de Saint-Pierre's image is quite distant and distinct. It is only an approximation of a tree, without roots, without expanding branches, without leaves that need collecting or that clog gutters; but it has the appearance of a tree, and besides, it is in bloom. An exemplary case, in the small community of Ducey (Manche), is a caricature that reflects a new relationship between society and nature, for this tree was pieced together from a dead tree trunk and a framework holding pots of geraniums (fig. 5); a drip watering system keeps the plants alive. When winter comes, the whole thing is removed, and in spring the town's park service again undertakes the ornamentation of plants, a new greenery. This example demonstrates an attitude profoundly anchored in human behavior, consisting in the rebuilding of objects in nature in order to assert our control over it, although this object is only a substitute for nature. Is this imitation tree natural?

This development of the tree as a natural object manipulated by mankind is not strictly limited to the garden. To extend the study of its forms beyond the garden, however, is fueled by a determination to transgress disciplinary limits and place this portion of history in a larger context; the example of trees in the countryside and in landscaping, be they the trimmed trees in rural areas, the canopies over the paths of public squares, or the tall trees of château parks, is an object of research that is not limited to an aesthetic analysis of plant life, but one that broadens our understanding of these forms into a research field approaching social history and the history of representations of nature. This does not, however, mean that specialists should not work on very specific aspects of the study of the garden. On the contrary, the methodological strengths of all disciplines are necessary to effect significant interdisciplinary syntheses.

However, the most important justification of these studies lies in research into contemporary societies. There is much to learn in what history teaches us about relations between mankind and nature, so that we might examine contemporary problems in a new light. Analysis of the history of the garden is therefore a veritable laboratory for our comprehension of the relationships of societies to nature and of their evolution over short or long periods of time. Moreover, the garden can serve as a laboratory for our comprehension of societies themselves, on one condition: it is precisely in resituating it in the field of social relationships to nature and in that of societies' relationships to themselves that it will have its optimum effect, that it will help us better to understand representations of nature and the ways in which societies have treated its materiality. It can be essential to our understanding of other processes that have come to be of global importance in contemporary societies.

Translated by Laura Lemay Nagle

Notes

1. *Ragosse* or *ragole*: a dialect form seemingly derived from the Galo, a regional language of central Brittany, that meant (and is still understood by older generations to mean) pollarded trees, whose branches were cut regularly for firewood and greenery for animal feed.

2. *Tassée*: idem, a local name given to the *cépée*, a bunch of saplings growing from a stump.

3. *Coupelle*: idem, term indicating a tree raised for its straight trunk, intending to provide wood for construction. This trunk is topped by rather tall, well-balanced branches.

4. The interdiction to plant a young tree is understood as the desire to avoid the possibility of assigning ownership of the future tree to the proprietor. This is why the trees growing along property lines were considered to be the products of spontaneous seeding and, as such, belonged to no one, except possibly God.

5. "Flippe" is the local name given to this day by some older residents of the Rennes basin (Ille-et-Vilaine) to an alcoholic drink, apparently made with an apple-based liquor. It is difficult to know more about it without an ethnological study. It seems, in any case, that younger generations have no knowledge of it.

6. If it is difficult to assimilate feudalism to absolute monarchy, it must be observed that local customs that remained in effect after the fall of feudalism and even after the Revolution had been formalized and become social rules during the Middle Ages; nevertheless, the monarchical regimes that followed only encouraged the continuation of these customs. The first attempts at suppression of communal lands took place, however, in the reign of Louis XV and in particular spurred on by Bertin, contrôleur général des finances, in 1759 and 1774, convinced that the path of individual landownership was in the best interest of agricultural development.

7. Yves Luginbühl, *Paysages: Représentations du paysage du siècle des Lumières à nos jours* (Lyon: La Manufacture, 1989).

8. M. C. Robic, ed., *Du milieu à l'environnement: Pratiques et représentations du rapport homme/nature depuis la Renaissance* (Paris: Economica, 1992).

9. Notable works on this subject include numerous publications from the first years of the French Revolution, now in the Archives Nationales (série F); also the works of Henri-Louis Duhamel Dumonceau (1700–1781), French engineer and horticulturist, who published many treatises on the cultivation of trees and notably proposed many new agricultural techniques. He was apparently inspired by English agronomists, who put in place in England a new agricultural system based on the cultivation of grasses (sainfoin, raygrass, alfalfa, etc.) and developed the practice of raising cattle and sheep; and A. J. Bourde's thesis, *Agronomie et agronomes en France au XVIIIème siècle, thèse de l'Ecole des Hautes Etudes* (Paris: Jean Touzot, 1967).

10. This elitist view of the peasant is found in the previously cited works. It continues throughout the nineteenth century, in particular in the works of writers such as Victor Hugo and of geographers such as Elisée Reclus, in "Du sentiment de la nature dans les sociétés modernes," *Revue des deux mondes* (15 May 1866): 381 ff.

11. In other words, the practices of social groups, such as peasants, using natural resources and transforming

them in order to gain benefits that assure the group's survival. Tree pruning falls into this category.

12. Henri Bernardin de Saint-Pierre, "Entretien sur les arbres, les fleurs et les fruits," in *Oeuvres complètes, mises en ordre et précédées de la vie de l'auteur*, ed. L. Aimé-Martin (Marnes: Maquigon, 1818).

13. Luginbühl, *Paysages*.

14. Victor Hugo, *Choses vues*, 4 vols. (Paris: Gallimard, Coll. Folio, 1972).

15. Stendhal [Henri Beyle], *Le Rouge et le Noir* (Bourges: Classiques Garnier, 1960).

16. Reclus, "Du sentiment de la nature."

17. The art of trimming trees had already been developed by the Romans; it consists of giving geometric shapes to the trees. But the agricultural practices of antiquity also included shaping other plants, such as elm and olive trees, in the context of the system of *cultura promiscua*, planting trees, shrubs, and grasses on the same plots of land. The traces of this practice remain in Italy and in central Europe, particularly in private gardens in Hungary and Slovakia.

18. [Editors' note] See Michel Baridon's essay in this volume for further discussion of this idea of "flow."

19. For more on this subject, see Luisa Limido, "Les pratiques paysagistes et l'usage de la nature sous le Second Empire: L'exemple et l'influence de Jean-Pierre Barillet Deschamps" (Diss., Université de Paris I, 1999).

6. Francesco Bettini and the Pedagogy of Garden Design in Late Eighteenth-Century France

DAVID L. HAYS

Francesco Bettini (ca. 1737–ca. 1815) was an unlikely yet important champion of irregular garden design in eighteenth-century France. A native of northern Italy, he spent twelve years of his middle age working abroad. While in Paris between 1778 and 1784, he immersed himself in the study of garden design, visiting dozens of recently developed sites and recording in sketches what he found there. Many of those drawings were eventually reproduced in the so-called *Détail des nouveaux jardins à la mode*, a monumental series of prints which contained an important visual record of developments in French garden design in the 1770s and 1780s.[1] Bettini also produced original designs, four of which were included in the *Détail*.[2] Beneath one of those, the publisher of the series, the cartographer Georges-Louis Le Rouge, added a note in which he called Bettini "truly full of genius."[3] As that remark proves, Bettini's work was esteemed by one of the chief arbiters of French taste in garden design. Even more, his drawings and original designs were thought worthy by Le Rouge to represent the state of that art in France.

Through Le Rouge, Bettini contributed in a significant way to the promotion of irregular garden design in France. In spite of that achievement, however, he was virtually ignored by historians until the mid-1970s, when Minna Heimbürger-Ravalli began to publish a series of scholarly texts concerning his life and work.[4] Drawing upon manuscripts and sketchbooks preserved in the Archivio Doria-Pamphilj, Rome, Ravalli portrayed Bettini as

an exemplary Enlightenment dilettante. Indeed, it would be hard to imagine a character more curious of mind and eager to experiment. The hundreds of surviving drawings in Bettini's hand depict subjects as diverse as a section through an artificial grotto; designs for rustic furniture; a view of the moon as seen through a telescope; sign language charts; Chinese characters; four drawings of a volcanic area before, during, and after an eruption; and—perhaps most peculiar of all—three stages of a rhinoceros erection ostensibly drawn from life in the Menagerie at Versailles (figs. 1–4).[5] The contents of Bettini's albums show that he was especially interested in mechanical devices; problems of translation, particularly between semiotic systems; and a host of concerns pertaining to the social and economic life of the Veneto (for example, table decoration, management of canals, gold). As frontispieces to two volumes of his sketches, Bettini drew self-portraits, in one of which he appears writing or sketching at a table with attributes of the arts and sciences displayed about him (fig. 5). Tacked to the wall next to Bettini are two sheets of paper, one showing a design for an irregular garden and the other, partly obscured, showing a section or elevation of a mechanical contraption, perhaps a pump. In the second frontispiece, Bettini is shown harvesting like fruits various attributes of music, drawing, reading, and writing (fig. 6).

The broad range of Bettini's interests suggested to Ravalli that he lacked an ability to focus and was thereby prevented from distinguishing himself in

1. Francesco Bettini, Section of an artificial grotto. Archivio Doria-Pamphilj, Rome, *Caos o Farraggine*, vol. 2, fol. 222.

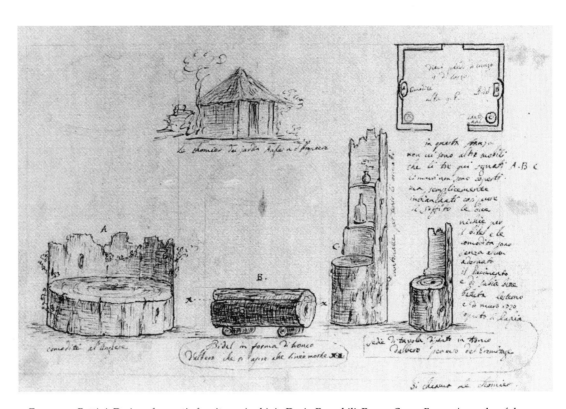

2. Francesco Bettini, Designs for rustic furniture. Archivio Doria-Pamphilj, Rome, *Caos o Farraggine*, vol. 2, fol. 219.

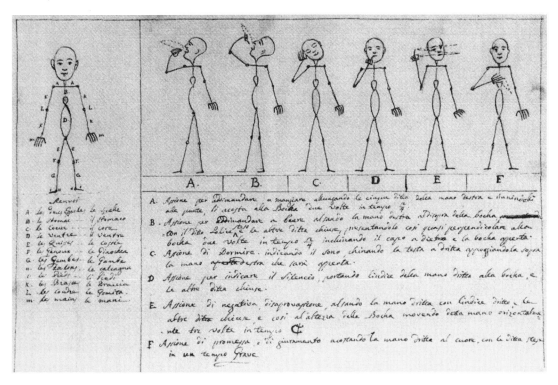

3. Francesco Bettini, Sign language chart. Archivio Doria-Pamphilj, Rome, *Caos o Farraggine*, vol. 1, fol. 16.

any one discipline. She noted that "without doubt, he was very loquacious. But as often occurs with people who talk too much, he had difficulty coordinating his own thoughts and concentrating on one thing at a time. His incongruent way of reasoning even manifested itself in his artistic work, in which he avoided concentrating on one specific field and choosing a determined artistic direction."[6] Ravalli believed that Bettini was "not inclined to get to the bottom of things in tackling a problem."[7] That criticism echoed Bettini's own claims about himself: "I had the disgrace of being of poor health, poor memory, and little patience, such that I never settled on a single thing. I took a fancy to wanting to learn that which I saw others doing. I began the undertaking but, in the middle, I abandoned it. Thus I remained still imperfect in my operations."[8] In taking Bettini's dubious remarks at face value, however, Ravalli seriously underestimated his intelligence and misunderstood the significance of his work. She supposed, for example, that he enjoyed the practical aspect of garden design without interest in, or ability to understand, its theoretical dimension: "He [i.e., Bettini] is not a theorist of architecture like Chambers, who expounds scientifically, nor a professor of philosophy like Hirschfeld, so precise and circumspect, nor the refined

poet and writer Pindemonte, in treating this topic of current interest, but a professional gardener, a garden designer who passionately defends his own trade and struggles to rouse the interest of his fellow countrymen to a subject which, for him, became a true and proper passion."[9]

Bettini was certainly passionate about garden design, and professionalism was one of his chief concerns, but Ravalli's interpretation of his intellectual disposition, repeated in subsequent scholarship, is contradicted by evidence that he had significant interests in the history and theory of garden design. In the late 1790s, he prepared several drafts of a treatise on garden design which, unfortunately, was never published. Besides their original content, those writings are filled with ideas lifted from contemporary theoretical texts, including crucial works like Thomas Whately's *Observations on Modern Gardening* (London, 1770; French edition, 1771) and C. C. L. Hirschfeld's *Théorie de l'art des jardins* (1779–85). Furthermore, Bettini's most important work as a designer, the so-called Agronomic and Anglo-Chinese Garden (also called the "Garden of Four Principal Characters") (1780), was conceived with theoretical questions in mind and was shaped by speculations on the historical origins of irregular design (fig. 7). That application of theory to prac-

4. Francesco Bettini, Chinese characters (top) and three phases of a rhinoceros erection drawn at the Menagerie at Versailles on 5 April 1779. Archivio Doria-Pamphilj, Rome, *Caos o Farraggine*, vol. 1, fol. 218.

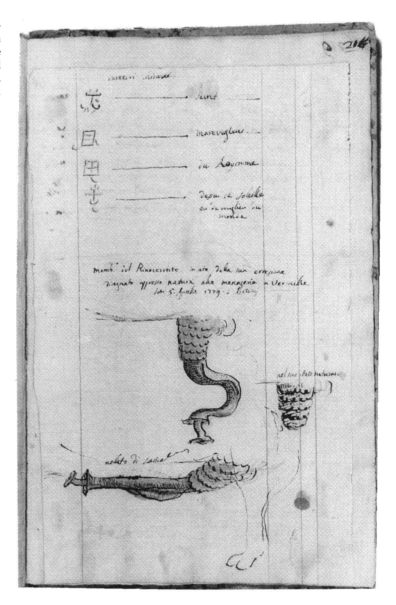

tice had roots in Bettini's own career as a student of garden design, the course of which offers valuable insights into how Bettini's approach was formulated and, more broadly, how the discipline was understood in late eighteenth-century France.

Bettini's accomplishments could hardly have been predicted from his unusual background. Born around 1737 in Maderno, a village on the west shore of the Lago di Garda, he spent the first half of his life migrating about the Veneto. While he was still a child, his family moved northeast to Rovereto, where his father continued his work as a manufacturer and merchant of paper.[10] The father was soon after charged with contraband trading, however, and so the family moved again, in 1746, this time to the fortress town of Palmanova on the east frontier

of the Venetian territory. There Francesco's father opened a coffeehouse and billiards hall, two potentially lucrative businesses in a fairly dull military town. In the meanwhile, young Francesco studied violin and hunting horn and eventually found employment as a musician in the military court of Luigi Pisano, the general of the city. That commitment was soon interrupted, however, after one of Pisano's valets told Bettini that he would easily find work in Venice if he could learn how to make wigs and comb hair. Following that cue, Bettini served an apprenticeship with a local wigmaker and then moved to Venice, where he worked for a year before taking a post as a valet to a young nobleman, Lunardo Foscari di S. Pantaleo.

About a year later, Bettini's career took an im-

5. Francesco Bettini, Self-portrait. Archivio Doria-Pamphilj, Rome, *Caos o Farraggine* [modernizing Bettini's spelling], vol. 1, frontispiece.

portant turn when he accepted a new position as a personal assistant to Giovanni Mocenigo, an ambitious scion of the contemporary ducal family of Venice.[11] For the next fifteen years, Bettini accompanied Mocenigo through political assignments in Udine and Verona and thereby gained firsthand experience in the three disciplines that eventually became staple preoccupations of his professional life: civil engineering, the coordination of entertainments, and garden design. In his journal, Bettini emphasized various feats of civil engineering that he performed for Mocenigo. For example, in Udine, Mocenigo's seat as lieutenant of the Venetian Republic in Friuli, Bettini supervised local engineers in the rebuilding of an old Roman road. At one of Mocenigo's properties outside of Legnago, near the Adige River, Bettini showed how a swamp could be drained and then carried out the work with great success. Bettini also concerned himself with the orchestration of social events. In Udine, he assisted Mocenigo by organizing festivals, stewarding, and providing musical entertainment at meals and social gatherings. In Verona, where Mocenigo was installed as *podestà* and general in 1770, Bettini organized a banquet in honor of local notables which Mocenigo hosted during the annual gnocchi festival.[12] At Carnival time, he accompanied the star of the opera with his hunting horn. Bettini also wrote plays for the Mocenigo family in which he himself often played a leading role, an activity very much like that performed by Carmontelle for the Orléans family in France.

Bettini's first known foray into garden design took place around 1771, when he developed a

6. Francesco Bettini, Self-portrait. Archivio Doria-Pamphilj, Rome, *Caos o Farraggine*, vol. 2, frontispiece.

scheme for a property belonging to Mocenigo at Abano Terme, south of Padua. The property evidently included a house and stable but lacked a garden. According to Bettini's account, his proposal was accepted by Mocenigo immediately. Unfortunately, however, no evidence of the project is known to survive except for a manuscript plan of the labyrinth preserved in Rome (fig. 8).[13] Bettini indicates that the garden also included a green theater, an amphitheater for dances, and a citrus grove.

In 1772 Mocenigo was named ambassador of Venice to France, and, on 15 October of that year, he and Bettini left for Paris. There and at Versailles, both men circulated freely within aristocratic circles and participated in court diversions, including royal hunts at Fontainebleau. Bettini also

made a point of learning all he could about the French lifestyle. In Paris, for example, he enjoyed studying the "arts of the table" (i.e., the arrangement of table settings and decorations) and worked in that capacity for several Parisian families. Given Bettini's freedom to circulate at Versailles and the interest in garden design he had already manifested in Italy, it seems likely that he would also have sought out Antoine Richard, *jardinier-botaniste* at the Petit Trianon since 1767.

Bettini enjoyed life in France so much that he decided to abandon his post with Mocenigo when the ambassador was recalled to Italy in 1774 following the coronation of Louis XVI. In the wake of the departure, Bettini began to frequent various academies of science and art and devoted him-

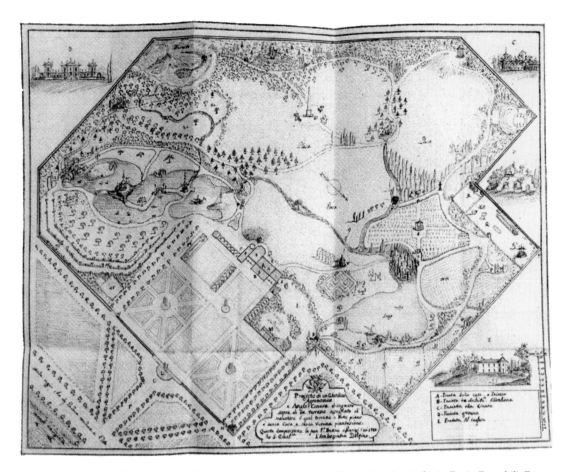

7. Francesco Bettini, "Progieto di un Giardino Agronomico e Anglo-Cinese," 1780. Archivio Doria-Pamphilj, Rome, Ms. 6, inserted between fols. 83 and 84.

self to reading, drawing, and playing the violin and viola. Music was the pretext for a strong personal friendship he developed with Adrienne-Catherine de Noailles, the comtesse de Tessé, in whose household he became something of a fixture. In 1776 Bettini made another foray into garden design when he transformed the garden of a friend, a certain M. Donival (or Denival), from a regular to an irregular arrangement.[14] Before describing that project in one of his manuscripts, Bettini offered a few general remarks in which he recommended that property owners convert entire holdings to the new style.[15] In the mid-1770s in France, that suggestion would have been fairly provocative since most patrons of irregular design at that time applied the style discretely to component areas of large gardens. That tendency to compartmentalize irregular design was one of the Scottish plantsman and garden designer Thomas Blaikie's chief complaints about working in France, even in the 1780s.[16] Bettini understood that some readers would think him

imprudent to suggest transforming whole properties, including practical gardens, to the new style: "I imagine that the reader wants to reproach me with being a madman, that my advice will not be followed except by madmen, for which he will say to me, 'And when I will have all of my property as a garden, where am I going to harvest the corn, the hay, the wine, and the vegetables? No, no, it is too absurd!'"[17] Nevertheless, he believed that irregular design could accommodate both practical and pleasure gardening and that produce gardens could be converted from regular to irregular form without long-term decrease in yield. Bettini idealized conversion as a practice of perfect translation in which the passage from regular to irregular form could be accomplished with no practical loss.

Donival's property was ostensibly situated in a rural setting within reach of Paris. The grounds were wholly occupied by a practical garden divided into rectangular beds with a water channel cut in a straight line across the middle (fig. 9,

Lamberinto efequito a Abano un Giardino contiguo la Cofa di Campagna di s. e.ª C.S. Mocenigo

8. Francesco Bettini, Labyrinth for the garden of Giovanni Mocenigo at Abano Terme. Archivio Doria-Pamphilj, Rome, *Caos o Farraggine*, vol. 1, 74 bis-75.

top). Bettini estimated that the garden could be converted to an irregular layout for only 30 louis, a paltry sum as far as such projects were generally concerned.[18] With the help of twelve workmen laboring in the dead of winter, he cut a new water channel in a gentle curve (fig. 9, bottom).[19] In one half of the garden, he divided the channel to form an island. A workman's hut that stood in the vicinity now stood on the island without having been moved. Bettini converted the building into a stable and used the island to hold animals without need of fencing. In the original layout, a circuit of rectilinear paths gave access to the different areas of the garden. Bettini reconfigured it as an undulating curve and added two shortcuts, one that crossed the island and one that ran along part of the canal. Lastly, the various beds of the garden were reshaped to fit the areas delimited by the canal and paths.

No evidence concerning M. Donival or his prop-erty is known save in Bettini's description. They may, in truth, have been purely fictional. In any event, Bettini's description and follow-up remarks made his scheme out to be both economical and a popular success. He indicates that the yield of the garden was low in the two years following its conversion but it reached a plentiful state by 1778, and neighbors came to express their admiration.[20] In 1780, as if to commemorate the accomplishment, Bettini supposedly erected a wood temple, painted to resemble marble, on a high point in the garden.[21] He also noted that Donival, who used to go to his rural property only to take care of business matters and who hardly ever stayed there overnight, now went for a month at a time.[22] "Now I ask you," Bettini quipped, referring back to his suggestion that produce gardens be transformed to irregular design, "are these the schemes of a madman? ruinous schemes without utility?"[23] Among those who answered no was the Baronet Jansen, for whom,

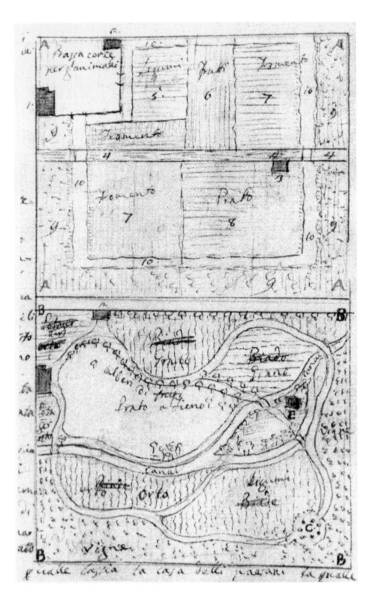

9. Francesco Bettini, Garden of M. Donival before and after conversion, Archivio Doria-Pamphilj, Rome, Ms. 143, fol. 26r.

around 1780, Bettini supposedly converted a regular parterre garden in Paris to an irregular scheme (fig. 10).

Bettini stayed on in Paris until August 1776, when he met an English nobleman, Lord Lucan, who offered him a post in London as a private music master to two of his daughters. Lured by the prospect of an easy life in the English capital, Bettini accepted the sinecure immediately. It helped, too, that he knew where he was going. Even before Mocenigo's departure from Paris, Bettini had made a brief trip to London and evidently enjoyed it enough to return for a longer stay. But Bettini never felt at home in England as much as he had in France. Each day, he gave lessons to Lucan's daugh-

ters in the morning and played chamber music in the afternoon with Lord Lucan and the queen's master of the viola da gamba, a certain Ebel. Bettini also practiced painting and occasionally decorated tables, but otherwise he had too much free time. He tried to design a perpetual motion machine.[24] He ate alone in his room and became very lonely. On top of everything, he was sometimes mocked on the street as a Frenchman, a scenario that made him uncomfortable.

Bettini's situation in London ultimately lacked the variety and excitement he had enjoyed in Paris. One of the few luxuries the position afforded was an opportunity to travel with Lord Lucan. In that way, he visited several important estates in south-

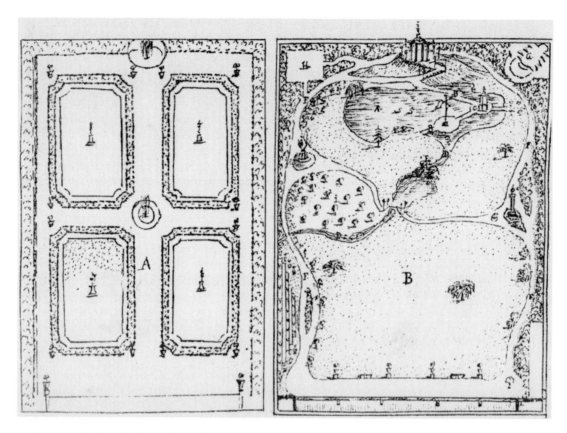

10. Francesco Bettini, Garden of Henry Jansen, Paris, before and after conversion. Archivio Doria-Pamphilj, Rome, Ms. 112, fol. 218.

ern England, at one of which his interest in garden design was significantly bolstered. On an excursion from late September to early December 1777, Lucan and Bettini stopped at Blenheim Palace (Oxfordshire), where Bettini first encountered the openness and pictorial richness of English garden design. Impressions recorded in his memoirs convey the intense excitement he came to feel while exploring the grounds: "Advancing along, I found at every step pictures that pleased me, delighted me, but I did not even know the reason why, since at first glance I prepared myself to be critical of them, but the more I advanced into those beautiful groves and that everywhere I found some beautiful decoration in marble or stucco, I went along always the more pleased, so that finally I became fanatical to such a degree that I would never have abandoned that magical site."[25] As that testimony makes clear, Bettini's revelatory experience at Blenheim introduced him to arrangements of prospects and ornaments on a scale he had not experienced before in irregular design. Unfortunately, however, he was unable to return to Blenheim or to visit other estate-scale gardens. His health began to fail to such a de-

gree that Lord Lucan's doctor told him he would be dead within two years if he did not leave the English climate. So Bettini returned to France in May 1778.

Back in Paris, Bettini had the great fortune not only of improved health but of immediately finding a position as a personal assistant to Giuseppe-Maria Doria-Pamphilj (1751–1816), papal nuncio to the French court since 1773. For Bettini, employment by Pamphilj meant an exciting return to the court life of Versailles and to liberties even beyond those he had enjoyed under Mocenigo. In the meanwhile, Pamphilj had a strong interest in the practices of irregular design then flourishing in and around the French capital and encouraged Bettini to learn all he could about them. The premise of the assignment was that Bettini would eventually create such a garden for Pamphilj in Rome.

Bettini's first step toward fulfilling Pamphilj's commission reveals much about his social situation in France. He began by approaching Antoine Richard (1735–1807), head gardener of the Petit Trianon at Versailles, whom he may have known already from his first stay in France. Bettini asked Richard how to go about learning to design in the new style, and the Frenchman responded by prescribing a rich program of study in six areas: botany, arboriculture, land surveying, water management, drawing, and theory.[26] Bettini records that he hesitated momentarily when faced with such an elaborate program, supposing that he would never be able to master all of the subjects. Nevertheless, he eventually embraced the challenge and, with Richard's guidance, made contact with individuals who could help him pursue each part of his education. In that way, he came to know many of the leading advocates and patrons of irregular design in and around Paris.

Bettini's adventurous approach to the study of irregular design and his freedom to consult its principal adherents were unique within his period. The ad hoc provisions for his education reflected the fact that no formal program for learning garden design existed yet in France, nor was that art recognized as a distinct profession. Bettini's course of study was thus a pioneering foray into the pedagogy of design and portended the development of that field as a professional discipline. Having been shaped by Antoine Richard, the program was also a unique interpretation of the prerequisites for irregular design in France.

Richard declared botany to be the cornerstone of garden design and arranged for Bettini to study the subject with none other than André Thouin (1747–1824), chief gardener and instructor at the Jardin du Roi (later renamed the Jardin des Plantes) in Paris.[27] Richard emphasized knowledge of plants in part because he, like his father and grandfather, was an accomplished botanist. It seems likely, however, that he also enlisted botany in an effort to delineate professional boundaries between garden design and architecture. As Richard well understood, garden design in France had long been associated not with plantsmen but with architects. Bettini noted in one of his own manuscripts that, in France, "every little architect is a garden designer."[28] Richard may also have harbored some personal bitterness on the subject since his proposal of 1774 for redeveloping the grounds of the Petit Trianon had been rejected in favor of a plan implemented by the queen's architect, Richard Mique.[29]

Bettini studied arboriculture with a certain Monsieur Jouette on a tree farm at Vitry-sur-Seine, about six miles southeast of Paris.[30] Of course, he must also have learned much about that subject from Thouin and Richard. For land surveying, Richard recommended Bettini to Georges-Louis Le Rouge, publisher of the celebrated garden design prints.[31] Le Rouge was a military surveyor (i.e., an *ingénieur-géographe militaire*) before becoming a cartographer and map dealer in Paris in the second half of the eighteenth century. Richard knew Le Rouge personally and had a professional connection with him. In 1777, the year before Bettini's return to Paris from London, Le Rouge had published a plan of Richard's design for the Petit Trianon along with details showing several of its architectural elements.[32]

Richard's suggestion that Bettini study land surveying is of great historical interest, though the exact motive behind the recommendation remains uncertain. He surely understood the utility of surveying as a tool of analysis but may also have recognized its more abstract value as a fund of inspiration for the generation of irregular forms. In either case, the inclusion of surveying in Bettini's program attests to Richard's appreciation of the plan as a format for conceiving and communicating design. In that way, his approach to irregular design was characteristically French. Devotion to the plan was a point of continuity between irregular design and its regular antecedent in France. It was also typical of designers working in and around Paris, the region where irregular design was first pursued in France.

The fourth element in Bettini's program was water management. Bettini wrote nothing about how he studied that subject in Paris. In fact, he may not have pursued it there at all since his work for Mocenigo in the Veneto had already given him a fair amount of practical experience.[33] Bettini's interest in the subject was nevertheless considerable. His notes and drawings include designs for a water elevation pump, a water screw, and a rolling water tank with a directional spray head, among other water-related devices.[34]

As for drawing, the fifth subject, Bettini needed little encouragement from Richard to practice his skills. The hundreds of sketches preserved today in the Archivio Doria-Pamphilj show that he drew readily as a way of recording ideas. Accordingly, it was perfectly natural that he would extend that practice to his investigation of garden design. Le Rouge took advantage of his student's enthusiasm for drawing as a way of collecting material for his garden prints. About half of the images in the eleventh installment of the *Détail* and a third of those in the twelfth, both published in 1784, were based on drawings by Bettini. Represented therein were well-known sites such as Rambouillet, Dampierre, Ermenonville, Bagatelle, and the Petit Trianon as well as properties that are now less well-known, such as comtesse de Tessé's garden at

11. Francesco Bettini, Views of the Rockery at the Petit Trianon; the Ruined Castle in the gardens of M. de Boulogne at La Chapelle; and the swing of the Redoute Chinoise at the Foire Saint-Laurent, Paris. Georges-Louis Le Rouge, *Détail*, cahier XI (1784), pl. 16.

Chaville, a few miles east of Versailles; M. de Boulogne's garden at La Chapelle, near Nogent-sur-Seine (L'Aube), about fifty miles southeast of Paris; and the duchesse de Tremoille's garden at Attichy (Oise), thirteen miles east of Compiègne, on the Aisne River (fig. 11).[35] Most of the sites were visited in 1781 and 1782, although the images of the Petit Trianon and Ermenonville were based on drawings made by Bettini in 1779. On most of the plates engraved after drawings by Bettini, his name appears at the bottom right corner. Sometimes the printed image was a reverse of Bettini's drawing, but other times the orientation was the same; Le Rouge was anything but consistent in such matters. Also, the quality of the printed image was occasionally much inferior to that of the drawing. Such was the case with the views of the grand canal at Dampierre, drawn on-site by Bettini in 1781 and published by Le Rouge in the eleventh *cahier* (1784).[36]

Le Rouge and Bettini seem to have made some garden visits together. That was surely true in the case of the duc de Chartres' garden at St.-Leu-Taverny, about fifteen miles north-northwest of Paris. The grounds were surveyed and drawn by Le Rouge, who also drew two views from a grotto in the garden.[37] Three other views in the *Détail* were drawn by Bettini: one of a bend in the stream with a bridge and the main house in the background,

one of the uppermost cascade, and one of another bend in the stream with a rockery and temple set in the background among some trees.[38] Several other images of St.-Leu were included in the *Détail* but are unsigned and remain unattributed.[39] None of those are represented among Bettini's papers in Rome, but, since the *Détail* contains a few images undoubtedly by Bettini for which originals are not found in Rome, that absence does not preclude the possiblity that he drew them.

Bettini also made many drawings which were not eventually included in the *Détail*. Some of those show sites otherwise published by Le Rouge (fig. 12). The rest indicate that, besides the places already mentioned, Bettini visited Monceau, Moulin Joli, the Désert de Retz, Romainville, Choisy, Bellevue, Pontchartrain, and Bonnelles.[40] A significant number of the drawings neglected by Le Rouge were published by Ravalli in the late 1970s and early 1980s. Nevertheless, other images, including a few of considerable historical interest, have remained unknown before now. In 1783, for example, Bettini drew a prospect of Mauperthuis, an estate about thirty-seven miles east of Paris belonging to the marquis de Montesquiou (fig. 13).[41] The view shows the regular and irregular gardens, the arrangements and relationships of which have been uncertain until now. It also shows the châ-

12. Francesco Bettini, View of the Hameau at the Petit Trianon. Archivio Doria-Pamphilj, Rome, *Caos o Farraggine*, vol. 3, fol. 26.

teau and seems to disprove the architect Claude-Nicolas Ledoux's claim that he rebuilt the old residence, at least as he represented that project in his *Architecture* (first published 1847) and at least as of 1783.[42]

Also of special interest among the unpublished drawings are a prospect of the Hameau at the Petit Trianon, a prospect of St.-Leu, and a plan and prospect of La Chapelle.[43] Le Rouge published a number of Bettini's views of La Chapelle but not his plan, the only surviving evidence of its arrangement. Bettini's prospect of that site includes an amusing detail. In the right foreground, a tiny sign posted on the grass says, "Defence de passer sour le tapi sur pene da mor" ("Do not walk on the grass, on pain of death").[44]

Bettini annotated some of his drawings, and the remarks occasionally offer interesting anecdotal information. On a drawing of the large swing at Rambouillet, for example, he indicated that the image was made in 1782, two years before it was published by Le Rouge, and that the woman on the swing was the princesse de Lamballe, daughter of the duc de Penthièvre (d. 1783), the man who then owned Rambouillet.[45] The anecdote shows that Bettini had access to people and places of the highest social echelon. That same point was expressed by two other, quite remarkable drawings in which Bettini included images of Marie-Antoinette. The

two may have met in the early 1770s when Bettini worked for Mocenigo and Marie-Antoinette was still dauphine. During his second stay in France, Bettini had access to the queen's circle through his patron, Pamphilj, but he had access to the queen herself through Antoine Richard. That connection is illustrated in a remarkable sketch by Bettini preserved in Rome and dated 1781 (fig. 14).[46] It shows the queen crossing a stone footbridge in the garden of the Petit Trianon with Richard walking behind her holding a parasol over her head. The Temple of Love is visible in the left background. The queen holds a small book in her right hand and is pointing with her left hand to something ahead. Off to the right, on the bank toward which the pair is moving, Bettini depicted himself, as he often did in his garden views, standing to one side and sketching the scene. In this case, he is framed by a dense clump of trees. In the right margin of the drawing, Bettini noted that the queen was making arrangements for the garden to be illuminated during a festival to be held there in honor of her brother, the emperor Joseph II, an event that took place on 3 August 1781. Beneath and to the right of the drawing, Bettini noted that the queen was pregnant with the dauphin at the time. The second drawing of interest is found in Bettini's first album and shows an astonishing design for a small, hand-powered paddle boat that he conceived for Marie-Antoinette, sup-

13. Francesco Bettini, Prospect of Mauperthuis. Archivio Doria-Pamphilj, Rome, *Caos o Farraggine*, vol. 3, fol. 57.

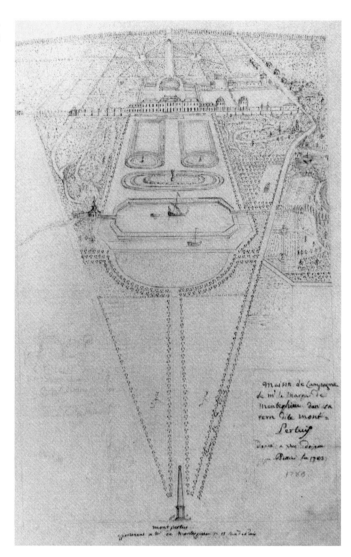

posing she might use it at the Petit Trianon (fig. 15). The drawing boldly includes a figure of the queen operating the vessel.[47]

Ironically, Richard had recommended in 1778 that Bettini copy the most interesting plates of Le Rouge's *Détail* in order to have a manual or pattern book to consult back in Rome.[48] Since Bettini and his patron could easily have afforded original installments of the *Détail*, Richard must have believed that drawing the images would help Bettini's hand and mind to master the formal vocabulary of irregular design. Bettini also indicated that he experimented with design itself, which he called "composissioni de Giardini," under the guidance of Richard at the Petit Trianon and the Scottish plantsman Thomas Blaikie at Bagatelle.[49] If that were true, it would mean that Bettini must have learned Blaikie's method of tracing forms directly on the ground.[50]

The last component of Richard's program was theory or, as Bettini put it, "to study the authors and philosophers who speak of this subject [i.e., gardens]."[51] Which specific works Richard had in mind remains unknown, but a sense of what Bettini might have read can be discerned from his notes and especially from the manuscript treatise on garden design he was compiling in Rome in the late 1790s.[52] In the earliest known version of that work (1798), Bettini recommended four texts: the French edition of Thomas Whately's *Observations on Modern Gardening* (1771; first English edition, 1770), the French edition of William Chambers's *Dissertation on Oriental Gardening* (1772), Jean-Marie Morel's *Théorie des jardins* (1776), and C. C. L. Hirschfeld's

14. Francesco Bettini, Marie-Antoin-ette and Antoine Richard in the gar-den of the Petit Trianon. Archivio Doria-Pamphilj, Rome, *Caos o Farraggine*, vol. 2, fol. 218 (detail).

Théorie de l'art des jardins (1779–85).[53] All of those were available in 1778, at the time of Bettini's meeting with Richard, except Hirschfeld's *Théorie*, the first volume of which appeared a year later. Bettini incorporated material from at least three of the works into his treatise in the late 1790s, and his familiarity with them is not disputed.[54] Their impact on his thinking is difficult to assess, however, because of the late date of his writings and because large portions of the treatise were lifted from source texts with little critical commentary. By his own testimony, Bettini considered Hirschfeld's *Théorie* the most important theoretical text, and he even referred to that author as his "master."[55] He also borrowed material liberally from François de Paule Latapie's rich preface to the French edition of Whately's *Observations*, though he could not praise the author by name since that essay was published anonymously.

In preparing his treatise, Bettini imitated Latapie and Hirschfeld by using history to frame discussions of the practical and theoretical aspects of garden design. Latapie enlisted history in a strikingly modern way to suggest that irregular design had universal, transhistorical significance. Specifically, he assembled excerpts and references from a wide range of ancient and modern literary sources in an effort to show that contemporary English design was essentially synonymous with that of ancient Rome and China. On the comparison of ancient Roman and English gardens, Latapie wrote, "Although the Romans did not totally banish regu-

larity from their country houses, they got much closer to nature than we do: their gardens had about the same extent and enclosed a large part of the elements that compose those of the English."[56] To show the links between English and Chinese design, Latapie turned, at one point, to William Chambers: "to furnish a complete proof of the perfect resemblance of English gardens to Chinese gardens, I will give here the entire chapter, *Of the Art of Laying out Gardens Among the Chinese*, extracted from a fairly rare book, entitled *Designs of Chinese Buildings, Furniture, Dresses, etc.*, by Mr. Chambers, architect, in folio, London, 1757."[57] Hirschfeld, on the other hand, was more skeptical about literary sources and took a radically different approach to legitimating irregular design. He pointed out that understanding of ancient Roman gardens was weak at best. Against the idea that French garden style, whether regular or irregular, had been inspired by ancient Roman practices, he complained, "Could one have taken as a model . . . these gardens of the ancients about which, after so much research and commentary, we do not know enough today to formulate a precise idea?"[58] Hirschfeld also questioned the veracity of contemporary accounts of gardens in China, particularly those reported by William Chambers: "And how would it be if this delirium, like almost all of those concerning fashion, had only an unsteady foundation? if these Chinese gardens with which one is so infatuated, which one tries so hard to imitate, never existed, or at least did not exist in the way one

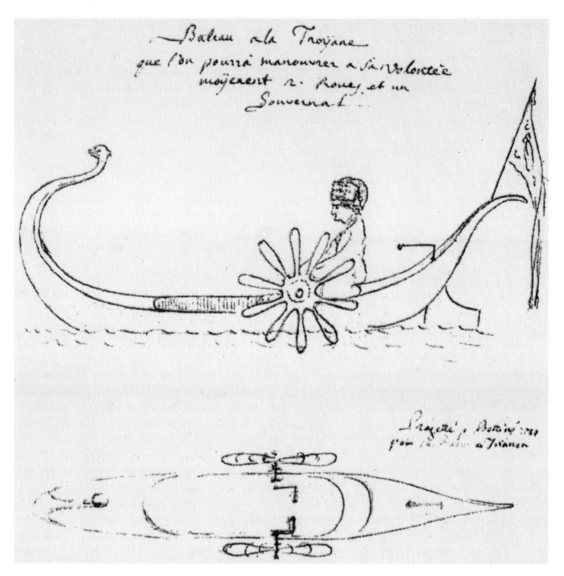

15. Francesco Bettini, Design for a "Trojan Boat which one can maneuver at will, comprising two wheels and a rudder." Archivio Doria-Pamphilj, Rome, *Caos o Farraggine*, vol. 1, fol. 7.

imagines? It would be quite remarkable, no doubt, and even more ridiculous to have chosen a model which, one can be convinced, never had reality."[59] Hirschfeld believed that China was an ancient but culturally primitive nation: "It has been proven that none of the fine arts achieved perfection among the Chinese."[60] In the first section of his *Théorie*, he presented a survey of western and Chinese gardens with the aim of showing that the emergence of irregular design in Britain was historically unprecedented.

Bettini began his own text by indicating, among other points, that irregular design required considerable intellectual preparation.[61] In order to create truly great works, a garden designer needed to

be, all at once, a philosopher, a naturalist, a poet, and a painter: "A philosopher in order to know completely the effects of the human heart. A naturalist in order to be able to choose the most beautiful things of nature. A painter and a poet in order to compose and assemble the most interesting scenes that nature offers to our eyes."[62] In other words, the designer needed to be what Bettini called an "artist-gardener," whose work united the useful and the pleasant.[63] The idea and the term were borrowed directly from Hirschfeld.[64] Bettini also believed that garden design ought to be a profession distinct from architecture. For comparison, he cited a passage from William Chambers' *Dissertation on Oriental Gardening*, one of the works held in contempt by Hirschfeld, where the Englishman indicated that garden design was a distinct profession in China and that Chinese designers were experts not only in botany but also in painting and philosophy.[65] Bettini strongly criticized architects for having usurped "the management of gardens" and for having, with their "habit of making forms symmetrical . . . transformed gardens into cities of greenery with the submission of trees to geometrical and architectonic figures."[66] Again following Hirschfeld, he argued that architecture had been a science, a daughter of necessity, before becoming an art.[67] Symmetry and balance were legacies of basic structural imperatives. But garden design did not hearken back to the same necessities. Accordingly, it was wrong to use architectural principles to make garden form: "how could the architect ever have confused that art with the design of gardens, which are founded—or should be founded—on the ingenious distributions [by] which Nature presents itself."[68] Furthermore, Bettini argued, "the greatest abuse which can be committed is undoubtedly that of wanting to force natural objects to submit to a law which does not agree with them in any sense."[69] The logic of the argument was completely modern.

Following those remarks, Bettini presented a condensed survey of the history of garden design, every part of which was excerpted from the first volume of Hirschfeld's *Théorie*.[70] He followed that section with a condensed version of Hirschfeld's statement on the origins of the "modern taste" in gardens, cycling through references to Addison, Bacon, Kent, Mason, Home, and others which ostensibly showed that the irregular design had first emerged in England.[71] Later in the treatise, however, Bettini incorporated Latapie's argument concerning the equivalence of ancient Roman, Chinese, and contemporary English approaches to garden design. To suggest that English and ancient Roman design were similar in many ways, he introduced a direct translation of Latapie's statement on that subject.[72] Elsewhere he asserted that English design was derived from that of the Chinese: "The English, however, cannot boast of being the inventors of such gardens as these but rather to a fair degree imitators of the Chinese."[73] Even more, he stated in no uncertain terms that the practices of irregular design then current in Europe were derived from Chinese precedents: "those [i.e., Chinese gardens] are the origin of the immense good taste of the modern gardens of Europe."[74]

Bettini's conflation of Hirschfeld and Latapie, two sources with opposing arguments concerning the origins of irregular design, was interpreted by Ravalli as evidence of his inability to think critically. Ravalli seems to have been particularly bothered by Bettini's endorsement of Latapie's syncretic viewpoint. Given Bettini's intelligence and interest in garden design, however, it is difficult to believe that he did not recognize the disparities between the two authors. Instead, he clearly remained unconvinced by Hirschfeld's argument that irregular design originated in England. He also surely understood that both Latapie and Hirschfeld used history for polemical reasons and that the true origins of irregular design remained uncertain. As a designer interested in theory not for the sake of argument but for its practical implications, Bettini preferred to view history as a fund of referents to be consulted for comparison and creative inspiration rather than as a polemical tool for nationalizing the new practices of irregular design.

Almost two decades before completing his treatise, Bettini manifested that exact approach to theory in one of his most important works as a designer, the so-called Agronomic and Anglo-Chinese Garden (see fig. 7). Conceived in 1780 after Bettini had been studying irregular design for about two years, that project was one of the great garden designs of the late eighteenth century, though it was never realized on the ground and has barely been discussed by historians before now.[75] A drawing of the scheme survives in the Archivio Doria-Pamphilj, Rome, where it was included in the third and final section of the large manuscript treatise on agriculture and garden design completed by Bettini in 1798.[76] The patron of the design, Andrea Dolfin (1748–98), had been named ambassador of Venice to France in September 1779 and met Bettini shortly thereafter.[77] Though conceived in Paris, the intended site was south of Padua along the Battaglia Canal. The Dolfin family owned a villa in that area which was being renovated while Andrea was abroad, and it has been suggested that Bettini's design was connected to that place.[78] As it happens, however, the villa being renovated was situated along the east bank of the canal at the hamlet of Carrara S. Giorgio while Bettini's site was along the west bank.[79] Accordingly, the tract in question may have been part of the Dolfin family's holdings in the vicinity, but it was not the core of their property. Bettini's claim that the site was "completely flat and without a house and without any plantings" was thus entirely plausible.[80]

The urban orientation of Bettini's training in France was apparent in the way he framed his design. First, he isolated the garden from the surrounding landscape. The wall enclosing the property, the form of which may have coincided with real property limits indicated by Dolfin, was broken only in the vicinity of the house. The description that Bettini attached to the plan never mentions views beyond the limits of the garden. Second, Bettini neutralized the space within the walls by insisting on the flatness and barrenness of the site. By circumscribing and leveling the field of design, he set up his work as a process of filling in an empty polygon. That approach duplicated the essential characteristics of designing in plan on paper. It was also typical of work in France, where the emergence and development of irregular design coincided with the rapid expansion of Paris after 1763, in the wake of the Seven Years' War. In that phase, irregular design tended to take place not on rural estates, as it had in Britain, but on urban and suburban properties which were often flat and usually enclosed by walls.

According to Bettini, Dolfin's main requirement for the design was that it be extraordinary: "the principal thing which the Ambassador wanted in this work was that, distancing myself from the commonplace and the usual, I was to follow both novelty and oddness [*bizzarria*] in shaping it."[81] Some historians have interpreted that statement as Bettini's own program for the design and have, along the way, deemed his work a success.[82] Yet nothing in Bettini's work itself suggests that his objective was to astonish. While he clearly wanted his design to be on the leading edge, and while revelation of the unexpected was an important part of his scheme, he was also fairly anxious that the result be germane to contemporary developments in France.

Having established an empty field for his design, Bettini divided the area of the garden into four principal zones: "regular," "agronomic" or "pastoral," "English," and "Chinese."[83] He also introduced three secondary zones: an Island of Tombs and Monuments, a Desert with a volcano fired by coal, and a verdant area called the Elysian Fields. Each of those components was meant to retain a distinct character so that visitors passing through the garden would experience a variety of contrasts. For example, Bettini inserted the Island of Tombs and Monuments between the Agronomic and English gardens "to make a contrast to the scene we [just] saw [i.e., the Agronomic Garden] and the ones we are going to pass through."[84] The Island was isolated from the adjacent areas by water, density of vegetation, and theme. Bettini's description of the Desert was highly theatrical and emphasized

its sublime character.[85] His account of the Elysian Fields focused on their singular plantings.[86]

To hold the design together, Bettini deployed a network of streams, "lakes," and fountains, all originating at a cascade near the top of the garden. Numerous prospects within the garden also contributed to a sense of interconnectedness among the component spaces. Bettini placed benches and chairs throughout the design to mark places from which views could be enjoyed. Most of those were situated within or around temples and open-air monuments. The Temple of Bacchus, composed of living pomegranate trees wrapped with vines and situated appropriately in the middle of the vineyard, opened onto "an entire country scene and [what] one can also call an Agronomic Garden."[87] The Temple of Momus, God of Ridicule, on a slope near the house, offered a panoramic vista over several areas of the garden, including "the pagodas of the Chinese Garden, the Great Obelisk, the Hermitage, and the cap of the Volcano; nearby passes the stream which crosses this flat area dividing the green meadow from the lawn in which lawn graze cows and sheep. This whole scene is decorated with plantings of rare trees and, behind the Temple, one sees the lake, and from there the Agronomic Garden and part of the Grotto (D), such that the whole forms a sublime and magical picture."[88] The prospect from the Temple of Apollo, in the upper part of the English garden, included "the totality of the English Garden and a large part of the Elysian Fields and the Chinese Garden."[89] The Rostral Column and the Great Obelisk marked viewpoints over more limited prospects. Because the garden was enclosed on all sides by a wall, each of the prospects was completely internal. That fact would not have been apparent to visitors, however, since Bettini masked the inner side of the wall with vegetation and massed earth, thereby creating an illusion of expansiveness which made the real limits of the garden difficult to discern.[90]

Another unifying element in the garden was a visual axis marked by the Temple of Apollo and the cascade-source. Those elements were placed in line with an axis defined on the other side of the property by the entry lane, the parterre garden, and the street façade of the house (see fig. 7). The extension of that axis through the English Garden implied that the latter had once been part of a regular scheme encompassing the whole property. While that was not, in fact, true, the axis marked the design with an aesthetic of transformation evocative of the "goût melangé" later recommended by Bettini's contemporary, the architect and garden designer Pierre Panseron (born ca. 1742). The arrangement was also a clever way of underscoring the absence of bilateral symmetry in the garden by marking the line about which such symmetry would have been constructed.

Yet another unifying theme in the design, and one that provides important insights into Bettini's program, was reading. The garden was, in a limited though very literal sense, a library.[91] Books were housed according to theme in four separate structures within the garden, and amenities for comfort were also included. At the Fisherman's House, set along the lake in the "agronomic" garden, books on fishing were kept in a room furnished with comfortable chairs, while tackle was stored on a porch outside.[92] Along the south edge of the "English" garden, the Hermitage featured a small library of so-called "moral" works, including Young's *Night Thoughts* (first edition, 1742; French edition, Paris: Lejay, 1769) and the works of St. Augustine.[93] The Hermitage also contained a second room "of an odd construction with a small armoire in which are found stacks of earthenware plates of the most ancient pottery works and the [provisions] for making hot chocolate and coffee. In a niche there is a sort of bed all of velvet."[94] The Temple of Pomona in the Elysian Fields contained a room that doubled as a coffeehouse ("Cafeaus") and a library of "decent but happy and fabulous tales."[95] In the Chinese garden, one of the two pagodas housed drawing supplies along with a collection of books and prints concerning astronomy and the Chinese empire.[96]

To explicate his design, Bettini wrote a description which he organized in the form of an imaginary tour. That format was deceptive insofar as it presented the design as a circuit garden, privileging a particular sequence of elements when the many forking and intersecting paths would, in fact, have offered visitors numerous choices about how to proceed. Yet the order of events in the tour was by no means arbitrary or insignificant. Instead, Bettini deliberately choreographed the visitor's experience in order to communicate basic lessons about irregular design drawn from contemporary garden theory. While Dolfin called for the garden to be compelling, Bettini's own intention was to educate. In this case, the objectives of the patron and the designer were related in the classical paradigm of "plaire et instruire."

The tour began just off the main road between Padua and Este where the entrance to the property was marked by a trident of tree-lined paths.[97] The center lane offered a fine prospect of the palatial house but, ironically, not the shortest route for at-

taining it since Bettini blocked the passage with a water channel placed between two walls. In other words, the shortest distance between two points was not, in this case, a straight line. An Italian visitor confronted with that situation would probably not have found it unusual, but a French visitor, for whom axial entries were conventional in rural properties, would have felt as if he were approaching the back side of the house (i.e., the traditional "garden" façade), particularly since one side of the water channel was in the form of a hemicycle, the arc of which projected away from the house. That arrangement was characteristic of the terminus of a classical French garden, not of an approach.

Between the front wall of the property and the house, Bettini laid out a parterre garden. According to Ravalli, the inclusion of regular elements in Bettini's designs stemmed from the fact that he learned garden design in France.[98] That was undoubtedly true, but Ravalli misunderstood the significance of her own observation, in part because she looked upon the French approach to irregular design as something only partially developed. In her opinion, regular and irregular were mixed in France because the French had difficulty disassociating architecture and regular design: "Reverent to tradition, the symmetrical garden was maintained around the house, assigning only the more distant zones to whimsical experiments with artificial landscape."[99] Similarly, the historian Osvald Sirèn considered Bettini's design "an excellent example of the eclectic method of composition that was developed on the Continent as a consequence of the encroachment of the new styles on the old domains. The combinations of old and new were varied in a number of ways, but as a rule without any attempts at an organic fusion of the different elements; they were coordinated as independent units rather than as parts of a homogenous composition."[100] Sirèn suspected the historical significance of Bettini's design but failed to pinpoint it because he, like Ravalli, neglected to consider the parterre garden in the context of the overall program for the design.

Bettini explained that he wanted visitors to have only a glimpse of the regular parterre garden in front of the house.[101] True to that intention, the space never appeared again on Bettini's imaginary tour. While some might perceive that incidental presentation as an oversight, it was surely purposeful and was probably intended to evoke a common complaint in late eighteenth-century theory that regular gardens were dull because their experience could be understood at a glance. Carmontelle, the designer of the Jardin de Monceau, expressed that idea when he wrote that the plan of an "ordinary garden" (i.e., a regular garden) "reveals everything it contains and when one has seen it [i.e., the plan], one can afterwards pass up visiting the garden."[102] In contrast, he suggested, the plan of a "natural garden" (i.e., an irregular garden) "is only an itinerary which does not reveal in advance a single picture."[103] By reducing the regular garden to a vignette to be viewed fleetingly even before entering the property, Bettini prefaced his design with a criticism of traditional forms and practices.

Bettini explained further that he hoped the limited perspective would deceive visitors into thinking that the whole garden within the walls was regular: "I did it to leave the traveler in the deception of believing that the remainder of the garden was in the old style."[104] In other words, he wanted to conceal the irregular aspect of the garden and to stage its discovery as a revelation. That scenario was probably meant to dramatize the historical novelty of irregular design on the Continent.

After glimpsing the parterre garden, visitors entered the property by passing through an iron gate to the right. A gate to the left also provided access, though it was far from the stable court and was therefore less convenient. From the gate to the right, a straight, tree-lined path led to an elongated arrival court where the house appeared once again, though this time in the unexpected form of a cottage perched on top of a cave. Framed by densely planted shrubs, which blocked views of other sides of the house, that prospect was the visitor's first proof that the arrangement of the property was not as it had initially appeared.[105] Bettini called the rustic façade "the first scene in the garden," a designation that played up the theatrical character of the design and inverted the traditional relationship between architecture and garden design by making the former dependent upon the imperatives of the latter.[106]

At the foot of the arrival court, a small gate marked the entrance to the previously unseen and unanticipated irregular portion of the design. Just beyond the gate, a broad prospect opened over several sections of the garden. Bettini placed a bench there to encourage visitors to stop and take in the scene. He also underscored the role of the house as a garden ornament by indicating that the rustic façade could be seen from the same spot.[107]

Bettini's tour led the visitor through the various components of the garden and ended by entering the house. Along the way, the visitor came to understand that the four façades of the house were mounted in different styles and that each of those corresponded to the type of garden it faced. Bettini drew tiny elevations of the four fronts in the margins of his plan (see fig. 7). The side facing the English Garden was configured as an English country house, while that overlooking the Chinese Garden was made to look like a Chinese palace. Bettini wrote that he developed the four-part scheme as a way of teaching designers how "to give to the garden the character which the main house demands."[108] According to that explanation, the forms of the garden were subordinate to those of the house, and the four themes were ostensibly collapsed together for reasons of economy, as a way of presenting several ideas on a single plate. The latter approach had numerous precedents in French garden design prints.[109] But Bettini's indication that the forms of the garden followed those of the house did not accurately represent the way in which his design was generated. It also failed to account for the inclusion of the secondary zones in the garden and for the function of the different sides of the house as backdrops for garden views. The particular variety of styles represented by both the faces of the house and the secondary areas of the garden pertained not to architecture but to garden theory. The themes presented in the scheme were clearly inspired by contemporary theoretical speculations on the possible sources of irregular design. The most commonly cited among those were English design, Chinese design, and rural landscape, while the less common included ancient Roman design, rugged or sublime landscapes, and imagery of Paradise.

In an era preoccupied with problems of historical origin, Bettini's idea to fashion a scheme based on speculations and uncertainties about the sources of irregular design was nothing short of brilliant. Contrary to what Ravalli proposed, he was led to that rich and intelligent design by his awareness of theory and of the polemical uses to which history had been put. Bettini's objective was to educate, not indoctrinate. On that note, he concluded his description of the design with a statement expressing his hope that the project would prove inspirational in a pedagogical sense. Specifically, he hoped that it "might suffice to lead the young student to open the way for deeper study through reading of that which many celebrated philosophers have written on the subject."[110]

How Bettini came up with the specific formula for the four-fronted house is not certain, but several possible sources merit consideration. In one sense, the house addressed the problem of visual crowding, a common complaint against irregular design in France, by cleverly collapsing four *fabriques* into a single structure. As a building immediately overlooking four discrete landscapes, however, the house bore a resemblance to the Petit Trianon at Versailles, the four sides of which faced strikingly different spaces: an entrance court, a regular garden with parterres and *bosquets*, a sloping lawn with a prospect of the Temple of Love, and a woodland hollow. Of course, Bettini spent a fair amount of time at the Petit Trianon and, according to his memoirs, experimented with design there.[111]

Ravalli suggested that the idea to have façades in different styles came from a house Bettini saw in England, the front and back of which were in French and English styles respectively.[112] That example was undoubtedly in Bettini's mind, but it does not explain how he arrived at four façades, a development that was not obvious and that Ravalli, in her own criticism, considered unfortunate: "While that combination of two classically inspired styles could produce an architectonic result with a certain harmony, the same could not be said of the building proposed by the artist."[113]

The idea of four façades in diverse styles may have been inspired by Alexander Pope's Temple of Fame, a structure imagined in his allegorical poem of 1711.[114] Bettini conceived a design for a Temple of Fame in 1776 and may have learned of Pope's idea at that time.[115] In Pope's structure, each façade corresponded in style to the part of the world it faced: Greek to the west, Gothic to the north, Asian to the east, and Egyptian to the south. By implication, the Temple of Fame was at the ancient center of the Christian world: Jerusalem. Bettini was certainly sympathetic to what Maynard Mack called a "characteristic Popian theme" expressed in the poem: "Particulars—ephemera—the flotsam and jetsam of experience: all are fascinating but have value for an artist only in so far as they can be organized in a patterned whole."[116] The Temple, like Bettini's house, was a central instrument of visual organization, an architectural metaphor for an eye and, as such, a figuration of the poet or designer. As in many of his drawings, Bettini appears to have introduced a representation of himself, though this time the figure was both central and abstract.

Bettini's tour ended inside the house in a room decorated in the Chinese style.[117] Linking the idea of central, organizing vision with irregular garden design and a Chinese vantage point, yet another possible source comes to mind: Jean-Denis Attiret's account of Yüan Ming Yüan, the imperial gardens near Peking. Attiret (1702–68) was a painter who, after studying in Rome, became a priest and joined the Jesuit mission in China. In Peking, he worked as a painter for the emperor and, in that capacity, gained special access to parts of the imperial residences and their gardens. In a letter of 1 November 1743 written to a friend in Paris, Attiret presented a lengthy account of Yüan Ming Yüan.[118] First published in Paris in 1749, the description had great influence on the development of irregular design in France. Bettini undoubtedly knew the text since it was reproduced in its entirety in Latapie's preface to the French edition of Whately's *Observations*.[119] One situation within the imperial enclosure that stood out in Attiret's description was a palace on a rock-platform in the middle of the artificial Great Lake. The island palace had four fronts, and, in panoptic fashion, it offered views over the whole of the garden. From any point but that of the island palace, the many elements of the garden appeared to be jumbled and confused. From the island palace, however, those spaces were visually resolved and appeared to rise up around the lake like the tiers of an amphitheater. The scenario evoked a principle described earlier by Sir William Temple in his essay *Upon the Gardens of Epicurus*. Temple suggested that irregular gardens of China "must owe it [i.e., their Beauty] to some extraordinary Dispositions of Nature in the Seat, or some great Race of Fancy or Judgment in the Contrivance, which may reduce many disagreeing Parts into some Figure, which shall yet upon the whole, be very agreeable." While the central prospect of Bettini's garden offered no such resolution in formal terms, the house was a point from which the eclectic variety of the scheme was most explicitly linked to the problem of design itself. In that sense, the interior of Bettini's house resolved the eclectic variety of the garden by reframing it as a resource for inspiration and invention.

In 1784, Le Rouge introduced the twelfth installment of his *Détail* with a version of Bettini's design for the "Agronomic and Anglo-Chinese Garden" (fig. 16).[120] While the axial orientation was shifted and many details were altered, the basic scheme remained the same. According to Bettini, Dolfin had circulated the design among "diverse intelligent, expert Professors" who recognized its novelty and recommended that it be published.[121] The identities of those "Professors" were not recorded. Also, it remains unknown whether Bettini was responsible for the modifications represented in the printed version of the design or whether those changes were introduced by someone in Paris. Bettini apparently learned of the publication only after the fact. Several years later, Le Rouge printed another

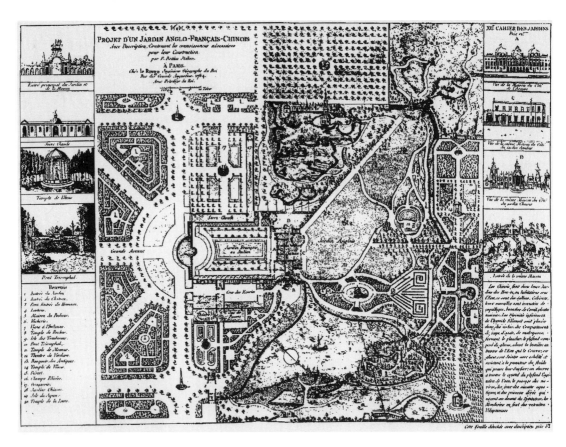

16. Francesco Bettini, Design for a "Jardin Anglo-Français-Chinois." Le Rouge, *Détail*, cahier XII (1784), pl. 1.

design by Bettini: the "Superbe Jardin Anglais" (fig. 17).[122] It was on that plate that Le Rouge called Bettini "truly full of genius." The design was much less elaborate than the "Agronomic and Anglo-Chinese Garden" and comprised a familiar assortment of *fabriques*—a few temples, a Chinese kiosk, an obelisk, and a belvedere—scattered over a gentle slope with a cascade and "river," several bridges, and an eclectic variety of trees. At least from one side, the garden was enclosed by a wall screened from the inside by trees and shrubs. The same was probably true of the other sides of the garden, although, as one might expect, the arrangement of the plantings did not allow the other boundaries to be perceived in Bettini's representation. Le Rouge noted at the bottom of the sheet that "M. the Nuncio took him [i.e., Bettini] away from us to make an English garden in Rome."[123] In fact, Pamphilj had been elected a cardinal in 1784, and he and Bettini left Paris together on 11 December of that year.[124] Le Rouge clearly regretted Bettini's departure. On a practical level, it meant a significant loss of source material for his garden prints.

On a more personal level, however, his praise for Bettini—the fact that he called him a genius—indicates that he recognized his intelligence, his judgment, and perhaps, too, his singular importance as a student who had become an acknowledged expert on irregular design in France.

The career of Francesco Bettini offers several valuable insights into the larger history of the French garden. First, the ad hoc nature of his education is a reminder that garden design had not yet been established as a distinct profession in France. The singularity of his experience also raises questions about how others in the same period learned to design in the new style. Second, the inclusion of land surveying in Bettini's program dramatizes the importance of the plan for irregular design in France and, through Le Rouge, hints at technical links with civil and military engineering. Historians before now have tended to emphasize the pictorial aspect of irregular design while ignoring issues of planning. Whereas views and prospects were important to Bettini and to many of his contemporaries, considerable evidence suggests that

17. Francesco Bettini, Design for a "Superbe Jardin Anglais." Le Rouge, *Détail*, cahier XX (1788), pl. 1.

French preoccupation with the plan as a format of design persisted across the shift from regular to irregular paradigms. Finally, Bettini's writings and his design for the "Agronomic and Anglo-Chinese Garden" epitomize contemporary uncertainty concerning the historical and conceptual provenance of irregular design. Unable to resolve that uncertainty by himself and unwilling to adopt one hypothesis for the sake of argument, Bettini embraced a syncretic approach which represented the general state of contemporary theory perhaps better than any other design of the period and which anticipated the pedagogical eclecticism of French garden design in the first half of the nineteenth century.

Notes

The author gratefully acknowledges the generous permission of S. E. Donna Orietta Doria-Pamphilj to consult and reproduce documents in the Archivio Doria-Pamphilj, Rome. Many thanks are also given to Cinzia Ammannato and Mirka Beneš for their assistance at the archive, to Paul Miller for his hospitality in Rome, to Polly Rubin for countless useful suggestions, and to the Department of History of Art, Yale University, for an Alumni Grant used to support research in Rome.

1. See Georges-Louis Le Rouge, *Détail des nouveaux jardins à la mode*, 21 vols. (Paris: ca. 1775–ca. 1788). The series is known variously as *Détail des nouveaux jardins à la mode* and *Jardins anglo-chinois*. The first title comes from a heading that appeared on plate 1 of the first installment. Later installments had different headings, however, most of which included the phrase *jardins anglo-chinois*, hence the alternative title.

2. See Le Rouge, *Détail*, cahier XII (1784), pl. 1: "Projet d'un Jardin Anglo-Français-Chinois"; pl. 14: "Labyrinthe d'Abano au Prince Mocenigo" and "Projet d'un Labyrinthe par Bettini"; cahier XX (1788), pl. 4: "Superbe Jardin Anglais Projetté par Bettini pour être executé dans les Environs de Paris Pour S. E. M. le C. de S."

3. Ibid., cahier XX (1788), pl. 4: "On peut dire que Bettini est réellement plein de Génie."

4. See Minna Heimbürger-Ravalli, "Francesco Bettini e l'introduzione del giardino romantico a Roma," in *Studia romana in honorem Petri Krarup* (Odense: Odense University Press, 1976), 213–25; idem, "Progetti e lavori di Francesco Bettini per il parco di villa Belrespiro," *Studi romani* 25 (1977): 27–37; idem, "Décors de fêtes françaises par l'italien Francesco Bettini," *Gazette des Beaux-Arts* 91 (1978): 83–92; idem, "Un décorateur de fêtes italien en France et son projet pour le feu d'artefice de Paris en 1782 à l'occasion de la naissance du Dauphin," ibid., 95 (1980): 1–4; idem, *Disegni di giardini e opere minori di un artista del '700, Francesco Bettini* (Florence: Leo S. Olschki Editore, 1981). See also Ravalli, "La genesi del giardino della regina Maria Carolina a Caserta," *Antologia di belle arti* 13 (1980): 38–40.

5. Francesco Bettini, *Caos o Faraggine* [*sic*], Archivio Doria-Pamphilj, Rome, vol. 2: 222, 2: 219, 2: 166, 1: 16, 2: 335–36, 3: 108–10; 1: 218.

6. Ravalli, *Disegni*, 164: "è fuor di dubbio che fosse molto loquace. Ma come spesso avviene con le persone che parlano troppo, gli riusciva difficile coordinare i pro-

pri pensieri e concentrarsi su di una cosa alla volta. Il suo modo incongruente di ragionare si manifestava anche nella sua attività artistica nella quale evitava di concentrarsi su di un campo specifico e di scegliere un indirizzo artistico determinato."

7. Ibid., 167: "Francesco Bettini non era incline di andare a fondo nell'affrontare un problema."

8. Francesco Bettini, "Viaggi et' Aventure di Francesco Bettini," Archivio Doria-Pamphilj, Archiviolo 343, interno (int.) 12: "Ebbi la disgrazia di essere di una salute debole, di poca memoria, e di poca pasienza, cosiche non mi fissai mai in una sol cosa. minvogliava facilmente di voler imparare cio che vedea fare agl'altri, cominciava l'impresa, ma alla metà labandonava. così rimasi ancora imperfeto nelle mie operasioni."

9. Ravalli, *Disegni*, 65: "Non è un teorico dell'architettura come Chambers, che disserta scientificamente, né un professore di filosofia come Hirschfeld, così preciso e ponderato, né il raffinato poeta e scrittore Pindemonte a trattare questo argomento di attualità, ma un giardiniere professionista, un compositore di giardini che difende appassionatamente il proprio mestiere e lotta per risvegliare l'interesse dei connzaionali a una materia che per lui è diventata una passione vera e propria." See also Ravalli, *Disegni*, 61–66.

10. For this and the following biographical information, including that on subseqent pages, unless otherwise cited, see Bettini, "Viaggi et' Aventure," Archivio Doria-Pamphilj, Rome, Archiviolo 343, int. 12, and Ravalli, *Disegni*, chap. 1: "La vita e le avventure di Francesco Bettini," 1–16. Ravalli's account is based strictly on Bettini's own memoirs.

11. Alvise IV Mocenigo (1710–78) was doge of Venice from 1763 until his death.

12. The "venerdì gnoccolare" is held each year in Verona during the Carnival.

13. Bettini, "Viaggi et' Aventure," fol. 73; Ravalli, *Disegni*, 45–46. Bettini's manuscript plan of the labyrinth is preserved in Bettini, *Caos*, vol. 1: 74bis–75: "Lamberinto eseguito a Albano [sic] nel Giardino contiguo a la Casa di Campagna di S: E.za H.la: G:ni Mocenigo. l'anno 1771 par F. Bettini." In 1784 Le Rouge published the plan of the labyrinth. See Le Rouge, *Détail*, cahier XII (1784), pl. 14 (detail).

14. See Francesco Bettini, Ms. 143, Archivio Doria Pamphilj, Rome, fol. 26r–26v.

15. Bettini, Ms. 143, fol. 26r: "io consigliarei tuti quelli che ano la fortuna di possedere de la terra di fare di tuta la sua tenuta un giardino al'inglese."

16. See, for example, Thomas Blaikie, *Diary of a Scotch Gardener at the French Court at the End of the Eighteenth Century*, ed. Francis Birrell (London: George Routledge and Sons, 1931), 20 September 1777: "This place [i.e., Maisons] is finely situated upon the banks of the River and might be made beautiful but there ideas seems so contracted that they only showed a piece of ground about 4 or 5 acres which they said they wanted to make an English garden of. I told them that was not what was meant by English gardens, that the whole ground round the house ought to correspond else they never could think of having anything beautiful but this they had no idea of. Mr Bellanger who had been in England understood beter than the others but he told me to have patience and to do as well as we could untill they saw something."

17. Bettini, Ms. 143, fol. 26r: "mi par che il lettore mi voglia rimporverare che sono un pazzo che il mio cosiglio non sara eseguitto che dalli pazzi parche mi dirà! e quando averò tuti li miei beni in giardino! dove andeno a coglier la Biada!, il Fieno, il Vino et i legumi! non non e tropo absurda!"

18. Ibid.: "e ben dissi io voi avette il sito che conviene, per far un bellissimo giardino al inglese, basta che voi sacrificiate 30. Luigi ed io ve lo fo nella vostra tenuta sensa che voi perdiate un soldo d'intrata."

19. For this and the following, see ibid., fols. 26r–26v: "tanti raggioni gli adessi [?] che l'amico mi lassio la libertà daggire nel crudo inverno diedi mano al'opera con una dozina di [b]iavi lavoratori e comincia per tornar il canalle nel modo che sta nel quatratto B.B.B.B. e formai un isola nella quale lassia la casa delli paesani la quale la converti in stalla e lisola che la lassiai a erba li servia di pascolo sensa aver bisogno di muro per chiuder, laqua li isolava."

20. Ibid., fol. 26v: "E vero che lamico perdette molti frutti il primo ano che nel 1776 che lo feci e nel 1777. la racolta de frutti non fu si abondante ma nel 1778. il total della racolta e si procuró una dilizia che tuti li vicini dimandano il permesso per andarvi a passeggiare."

21. Ibid.: "nel 1780. sopra una somita fece fare un tempio, in legno colorito a finti marmi che fa un bel effetto oltre che ofre un azilo grazioso, e una vista della bella guardate il sito C."

22. Ibid.: "cosi l'amico si trova contento a gendo, che non andava alla sua campagna che parche gl'interessi suoi lo portava una non restava quasi mai a dormire ora si passa de messi interri."

23. Ibid.: "ora dimando a voi, sono egli proggietti da pazzo? proggietti rovinossi sensa utilità?"

24. See Bettini, *Caos*, 1: 80: "Eseguito a Londra da Bettini 1777."

25. Bettini, "Viaggi et' Aventure," 232; Ravalli, *Disegni*, 47–48: "Inoltrandomi poi ogni passo trovai delli quadri che mi piacevano, mi dilettavano ma non sapevo ne pur la ragione, poiché a primo aspetto mi preparavo per farne la critica, ma più che mi inoltravo in quei belli boschetti e che da pertuto vi trovavo qualche bella decorazione o di marmo o di stucco, mi andava sempre più piacendo, che finalmente ne venni fanatico a grado che non mi sarei mai partito da quel sito magico."

26. Ibid., fols. 252–53: "per impare a comporli [i.e., giardini al'inglese] parlai con il Giardiniere della Regina Mons.r Richard, e li dimandai come avrei a fare per imparare a comporeere [sic] d[e] Giardini. Egli [i.e., Richard] mi sugierÿ in primo loco che bisognava sapere la Botanica, 2.d la coltura degl'alberi e piante Esotiche, terzo che era nessesario sapere misurare [i.e., to survey land] livelare le aqui, saper disegnare [i.e., to draw; Bettini used the verb "comporre" (to compose) to mean "to design"] e in fine studiare glautori e filosofi che parlano di tal materia etc."

27. Ibid., fol. 318. Ravalli's indication that Bettini studied with Gabriel Thouin is incorrect. Bettini identified his instructor as "Toin l'éné," a clear reference to André. (See Yvonne Letouzey, *Le Jardin des Plantes à la croisée des chemins avec André Thouin (1747–1824)* [Paris: Editions du Muséum, 1989].) Ravalli also suggested that Bettini studied botany with the comte de Buffon (1707–88), director of the Jardin du Roi since 1739, but this is doubtful. In his memoirs, Bettini noted that "monsieur de

Bugton" (i.e., Buffon) was director of the garden but did not state that the two worked together in any way.

28. Francesco Bettini, "Orto Agronomico o sia, li mezi piu Efficacci, per perfesionare l'Agricoltura e la coltura di ogni sorta di Piante. Con un tratatto de Giardini, e delle istrussioni necessarie per quelli che vogliono divenire compositori di Giardini Moderni e perfetti Agricoltori," Archivio Doria-Pamphilj, Rome, Ms. 6, fol. "24r" (i.e., fol. 28r): "ogni piciolo Architeto e Giardiner." Bettini added the following note in the left margin: "s'intende dire per giardiniere quelo cho li compore."

29. In turn, Mique consulted an amateur designer, the comte de Caraman, and the painter Hubert Robert.

30. Bettini, "Viaggi et' Aventure," fol. 318. Bettini called the place "Petit Vetrÿ."

31. Among Bettini's papers in the Archivio Doria-Pamphilj, Rome, is a tome (Ms. 30: "Suplimento alla Faraggine di Bettini. Trat. delle livelassioni e misure"), inside of which Bettini has written "Queste lessioni di Gieometria e misure di corpi e l'alture di le longietudini di [i.e., che?] mi furono date dal mio maestro mr. le Rouge ingenier del Re." The lessons are in Italian.

32. See Le Rouge, *Détail*, cahier VI (1777), pls. 19, 22, and 23. Two years later Le Rouge published Richard's five-sheet "Tableau de la plantation générale." See Le Rouge, *Détail*, cahier VII (1779), pls. 19–23.

33. See Ravalli, *Disegni*, 4 concerning the scheme conceived and realized by Bettini for draining a swamp on one of Mocenigo's properties near the Adige River.

34. See Bettini, *Caos*, 1: 1; 1: 3; and 1: 61.

35. See Le Rouge, cahier XI, pls. 1, 2, 12–18, and 20; cahier XII, pls. 13, 15, and 18–20.

36. Compare the two images of the canal at Dampierre in Le Rouge, cahier XI, pl. 20 with Bettini, *Caos*, vol. 2: fol. 29: "Le grand canal du jardin de Dampier dessine apre natture pr Bettinj 1781 a [M.] [le] D de Luines" and vol. 2: fol. 220 (top): "vue de la grand piece d'eau de Dampier a M. L. D. de Luines."

37. See Le Rouge, cahier XII, pls. 3–5.

38. See ibid., cahier XII, pls. 5 and 8.

39. See ibid., cahier XII, pls. 6–8.

40. See Bettini, *Caos*; Monceau: vol. 1: 102; vol. 2: 145; Moulin Joli: vol. 2: 112; Désert de Retz: vol. 2: 112, 113; Romainville: vol. 1: 39; vol. 2: 76 [copy of 1: 39], 77; Choisy: vol. 3: 182; Bellevue: vol. 1: 171; Pontchartrain: vol. 2: 39; and Bonnelles: vol. 2: 44, 51 (D).

41. Le Rouge published a few of Bettini's drawings of *fabriques* at Mauperthuis. See Le Rouge, cahier XII, pls. 14 and 15. Plate 14 corresponds to Bettini, *Caos*, vol. 2: fol. 147: "dan le jardin anglais de M. de Montesquieu a mont pertuj. / apre nature p Bettiny 1783." Plate 15 corresponds to Bettini, *Caos*, vol. 2: fol. 86 (top): "a mont pertui" and "Bettini 1783."

42. On the various controversies surrounding the history of Mauperthuis, see Robin Middleton, "The Château and Gardens of Mauperthuis: The Formal and the Informal," in *Garden History: Issues, Approaches, Methods*, ed. John Dixon Hunt (Washington, D.C.: Dumbarton Oaks, 1992), 219–41.

43. See Bettini, *Caos*; Hameau at the Petit Trianon: vol. 3: fol. 26; St. L'Eu: vol. 3: fol. 213; La Chapelle: vol. 2:, fols. 172v–173r.

44. Ibid., vol. 3: fol. 113.

45. Ibid., vol. 2: 33: "A Rambuÿer 1782 desiné apre natur pr Bettinj 178 / il ÿ avet la P. L'Abubal [i.e., the princesse de Lamballe, daughter of the duc de Penthièvre, widow of the prince de Lamballe and sister of Louise-Marie-Adélaïde de Bourbon, duchesse de Chartres, puis d'Orléans] que se ballaceana." The image was published by Le Rouge, cahier XI (1784), pl. 2.

46. Ibid., vol. 2: fol. 218.

47. Ibid., vol. 2: fol. 7. "Bateau à la Troÿane que l'on pourra manouvrer a sa volonté moÿenent 2 Roues et un Gouvernal. Progetté p. Bettini 1784 pour la Reine à Trianon."

48. Bettini, "Viaggi et' Aventure," fol. 255: "mi racomando che procurassi di disegnare li quadri piu interesanti delli Giardini moderni che io vedro per poterli poi Eseguire nel Giardino che farò in Roma."

49. See ibid., fol. 318.

50. See, for example, Blaikie, *Diary*, 30 December 1778: "Wednesday 30 December began the Gardens at Bagatelle upon the wood Opossite the Pavillion by cutting down the trees to open a Lawn along with Mr Briass enspecteur des Batiments; but how this surprized them to see me trace out this garden without line or toise was what non of them could emagin." Unfortunately, Bettini left no descriptions of his interactions with Blaikie, and Blaikie never mentioned Bettini in his own diary.

51. Bettini, "Viaggi et' Aventure," fol. 253: "studiare glautori e filosofi che parlano di tal materia etc."

52. Various drafts of the treatise are found in the Archivio Doria-Pamphilj, Rome: Ms. 6 (1798); Archiviolo 344, int. 17, part 2 (1799); Ms. 112 (1799).

53. Bettini, Ms. 6, fol. 28r (i.e., fol. 32r): "Nel numero di questi interesanti scriti non devessi trascurar di leggier li seguenti

1—Dissertation sur le jardinage de Lorient, par *Chambers*

2—Theorie de l'art des jardins par *C. C. L. Hirschfeld*

3—Theorie des jardins a Paris *1776*

4—L'art de former les jardins modernes, ou l'art des jardins anglois."

54. Bettini's use of Morel is less explicit than his other borrowings.

55. See Bettini, Ms. 6, fol. 89 r: "e particolarmente il mio maestro C. C. L. *Hirschfeld* nella sua Theoria de l'arte de giardini. opera in tre tomi tradota dal idioma Tedesco in lingua Francese a *Leizig* [sic] *1780* [sic]."

56. François de Paule Latapie, "Discours Préliminaire du Traducteur," in Thomas Whately, *L'Art de former les jardins modernes, ou l'art des jardins anglois* (Paris: Charles-Antoine Jombert, père, 1771; first English edition, 1770), xxxix–xl.

57. Ibid., ix: "pour fournir une preuve complete [sic] de la parfaite ressemblance des jardins Anglois avec les jardins Chinois, je donnerai ici le chapitre tout entier, *de l'art de distribuer les jardins, selon l'usage des Chinois*; extrait d'un livre assez rare, intitulé: *dessins des édifices, meubles, habits &c., des Chinois, gravés sur les originaux dessinés à la Chine par M. Chambers, architecte*, infolio, Londres, 1757."

58. Christian Cay Lorenz Hirschfeld, *Théorie de l'art des jardins* (Leipzig: Chez les Héritiers de M. G. Weidmann et Reich, 1779 [vol. 1]), 1: 135–36: "Auroit-on pu prendre . . . pour modele ces jardins des anciens, qu'après tant

de recherches & de commentaires nous ne connoissons pas même assez aujourd'hui pour en donner une idée précise?"

59. Ibid., 1: 93: "Et que seroit-ce si ce délire, ainsi que presque tous ceux de la mode, n'avoit qu'un fondement mal assuré? si ces jardins Chinois dont on est si engoué, qu'on s'efforce tant d'imiter, n'existoient point, ou du moins n'existoient pas tels qu'on se le figure? Il seroit bien singulier sans doute, & encore plus ridicule, d'avoir choisi un modele qu'on peut se convaincre n'avoir jamais eu de réalité."

60. Ibid., 1: 110: "Il est prouvé qu'aucun des beaux arts n'a atteint la perfection chez les Chinois."

61. Bettini, Ms. 6, fol. 24r (i.e., fol. 28r): "Per pervenir a saper formar una tal fata de Giardini che ora andro a descriver, ricerca che l'artista sia fornito di moltissime cognissioni."

62. Bettini, Ms. 112, fols. 158–159, quoted in Ravalli, *Disegni*, 61: "Filosofo per conoscere a fondo gl'efeti del cuore umano. Naturalista per poter fare la sielta delle cose le piu belle della natura. Pittore e Poeta per componere e mettere assieme le sene piu interessanti che Natura ofre agl'ochi nostri."

63. Bettini, Ms. 112, fols. 154–55.

64. See especially Hirschfeld, *Théorie*, 1: 158–63: "Remarques sur le goût ancien & moderne."

65. Bettini, Ms. 6, fol. 24r (i.e., fol. 28r): "Monsier *Chambers* nela sua disertassione deli Giardini del oriente, dice parlando deli giardini dela china, Li *loro* Giardiniere (1) [n. 1, in left margin: "sintende dire per giardiniere quelo che li compore] non solo sono Botanici ma essi sono anco Pitori e filosofi; loro ano una cognissione profonda del cuor umano, e sano l'arte con la quale ecitannono le piu vive sensassioni. nela china non e come in Francia e in italia, che ogni piciolo Architeto e Giardiner. ala china l'arte del Giardinaggio e una professione distinta che exiggie uno studio molto esteso e una cognissione perfetta della Natura aquistata con il Viaggiare." On Chambers' *Dissertation* and its reception in France, see Janine Barrier, "Chambers in France and Italy," in *Sir William Chambers, Architect to George III*, ed. John Harris and Michael Snodin (New Haven and London: Yale University Press, in assocation with the Courtauld Gallery, Courtauld Institute of Art, London, 1996), 32–33.

66. Bettini, Archivio Doria-Pamphilj, Archiviolo 344, int. 17, fols. 11–13, and Ms. 112, 151bis, quoted in Ravalli, *Disegni*, 62: "la condotta dei giardini"; "abitudine di simmetricare le forme . . . trasformato i giardini in città di verdure col assogietare gl'alberi alle figure geometriche e architetoniche."

67. Ravalli, *Desegni*, 62.

68. Ibid.: "come mai l'architetto a Egli potuto confondere quest'arte con la composissione delli Giardini, li quali sono fondati o devono essere fondati sopra la distribuissione ingieniose che si presenta Natura!"

69. Bettini, Ms. 6, fol. 33v (i.e., fol 37v): "il piu grande abuso che si possa cometere, e certamente quello di volere forzare li oggietti naturalli a sometersi ala legge che non li conviene in niun senso."

70. Cf. Bettini, Ms. 6, fol. 26r (i.e., fol. 30r) and passim with Hirschfeld, *Théorie*, 1: 7 and passim.

71. See Bettini, Ms. 6, fols. 39v (i.e., 43v)–41v (i.e., 45v): "Origine deli Giardini inglesi o anglo-cinesi," and Hirschfeld, *Théorie*, 1: 139–58: "Origine du goût moderne."

72. Cf. Latapie, "Discours préliminaire," xxxix–xl, quoted above, and Bettini, Ms. 6, fol. 158: "Benché li antichi Romani non avessero bandito totalmente la regolarità nelle loro case di campagna, si acostavano però molto più che noi ad'immitare la bella natura; li loro Giardini aveano quasi la medesima estensione e chiudevano in essi una grande parte di quegl'oggeieti che destinguono tanto ora li Giardini d'Ingilterra." This point and quotation are from Ravalli, *Disegni*, 60 n. 29.

73. Bettini, Ms. 112, fol. 6, quoted in Ravalli, *Disegni*, 60 n. 28: "Gli inglesi però non si pono vantare di essere gli inventori di tal fata di Giardini, ma bensì alquanto immitatori delli Cinesi."

74. Bettini, Ms. 6, fol. 34r (i.e., 38r): "sono essi [i.e., giardini cinese [*sic*]] la origine del buon gusto infinato delli Giardini moderni del Europa."

75. See Osvald Sirèn, *China and Gardens of Europe of the Eighteenth Century* (New York: Ronald Press, 1950; repr. Washington, D.C.: Dumbarton Oaks, 1990), 107–10; Ravalli, *Disegni*, 50–52; Iris Lauterbach, *Der französische Garten am Ende des Ancien Régime: "Schöne Ordnung" und geschmackvolles Ebenmaß"* (Worms: Wernersche Verlagsgesellschaft, 1987), 115–20; Margherita Azzi Visentini, "Giardino di Villa Dolfin a Mincana," chap. 10 in *Il giardino veneto tra sette e ottocento e le sue fonti* (Milan: Edizioni Il Polifilo, 1988), 178–86, 190–93.

76. Francesco Bettini, "Progieto di un Giardino Agronomico e Anglo-Cinese disegnato sopra di un terreno assegnato al'inventore il qual terreno e tutto piano e sensa casa, e sensa Veruna piantassione: Questa composissione la fece F. Bettini a Parigi l'an 1780. Per E. Eccel.za L'Ambassiatore Dolfino," in Archivio Doria-Pamphilj, Rome, Ms. 6, inserted between fols. 83 and 84. While this copy of the drawing may have been made in 1780, all that is certain is that it was made before 1798. In the text accompanying the drawing, Bettini referred to the project as "un giardino di quatro carateri principali" (see Ms. 6, fol. 84r).

77. Daniele Andrea Dolfin, called Andrea, belonged to the S. Pantalon branch of that prominent Venetian family. From 1775 to 1777 he served as *capitano* and *vice podestà* of Verona. He was named ambassador to France on 23 September 1779 and held that post until 17 May 1785. See N. H. Bortolo Giovanni Dolfin, *I Dolfin (Delfino) Patrizii Veneziani nella storia di Venezia dall'anno 452 al 1923*, 2nd ed. (Milan: Tipografia Ferdinando Parenti, 1924), 185. See also Bettini, "Viaggi et' Aventure," fol. 255: "dopo arivato avere delle suficienti cognissioni me fu ordinato dal Ambas.tre di Venezia Allora S. le . . . Dolfino un disegno di un Giardino Anglocinese."

78. See Azzi Visentini, "Giardino di Villa Dolfin a Mincana," 171–93, esp. 175–78. Correspondence between Dolfin in Paris and his family's managing agent Luigi Ballarini in Venice frequently mentions ongoing efforts to renovate the existing garden and waterworks at the villa. On the Villa Dolfin, see also Giuseppe Mazzotti, ed., *Le Ville Venete* (Treviso: Libreria Editrice Canova, 1954), 189; Ennio Concina, ed., *Ville, giardini, e paesaggi del Veneto nelle incisioni dell'opera di Johann Christoph Volkamer con la descrizione del lago di Garda e del monte Baldo* (Milan: Edizioni Il Polifilo, 1979), 114–15; Alessandro Baldan, *Ville venete in territorio padovano e nella Serenissima Repubblica* (Abano Terme [Padua]: Aldo Francisci Editore, 1986), 112–14.

79. Baldan, *Ville venete*, 112, situates the Villa Dolfin at

"Carrara S. Giorgio contra Mincana," a hamlet on the east side of the Battaglia Canal.

80. Bettini, Ms. 6, insert between fols. 83 and 84: "Progieto di un Giardino Agronomico e Anglo-Cinese disegnato sopra di un terreno assegnato al'inventore il qual terreno e tutto piano é sensa Casa, e sensa Veruna piantassione."

81. Francesco Bettini, "Descrizione d'un Giardino di delizia di nuova invenzione Fran-Cin-Angle," Archivio Doria-Pamphilj, Rome, Archiviolo 344, int. 18, fol. 1: "L'oggetto principale per altro che il S.o Ambasciatore desiderava in questa opera si era che io allontandomi dal comune, ed usuale, dovessi seguire e la novità, e la bizzarria insieme nel formarlo."

82. See, for example, Azzi Visentini, "Giardino di Villa Dolfin a Mincana," 180: "Il progetto punta sulla più assoluta e spregiudicata originalità: in breve vuole stupire, meravigliare." Also, ibid., 186: "L'intenzione [of Bettini] è quella di offrire novità, originalità e bizzarria in gran copia. Non ci sembra che nei diversi interventi promossi dal Dolfin, o anche solo fatti progettare, figurasse mai alcuno spunto ideologico, una qualche idea ci volesse trasmettere, un qualche ammonimento morale. Sembra invece di capire che suo vero, esclusivo obiettivo fosse quello di stupire i suoi ospiti. E nel Bettini l'ambasciatore aveva trovato un interprete che ben assecondava il suo desiderio."

83. Bettini used the terms "regolare," "agronomico," "Pastorale," "inglese," and "cinese." See Bettini's manuscript plan and Bettini, Ms. 6, fol. 84r.

84. Bettini, Ms. 6, fol. 86 r: "per fare un contrasto alla sena che abiamo veduta [i.e., the giardino agronomico] e a quelle che anderemo a percorere."

85. Ibid., 88r: "prendendo il camino a mano dritta questa via si va stringendo e entra in altro soteraneo tortuoso non piu lungo di quindici palmi, sortendo da questo sotterano si apre una sena oribille e romancesca. Questo e un Deserto nel quale non si vede alcuni pianta ne alberi verdi ma tuto e arido pieno di vulcani che gietano fumo e fiame, si vedono qualche ediffício destructo dal fuoco, si retrova in questo sito delli scheletti de serpi grossissimi e di'altri animalli Nocivi, si legono delle iscrissioni sopra a de sassi, che anunciano delli avenimenti toncici [?] arivati in quel sitto, ve poche aque e queste sono sensa corso paludose che dano un idea delle stiggi il camino e tuto imbarassato un solo sentiere stretto e incomodo resta a poter traversare questo deserto che per essir· conviene passare sotto il Vulcano per una grotta, nella quale si sente un mugitto di una specie di luono [?] sotteraneo, e il suolo trema come suol causare il teramotto, essiti da questo sottraneo si vede a mano dritta delle caverne profonde dali qualli esce parimenti del fumo p[u]ssolente di bettume e solfo. finalmenti si entra in col altro piciolo sotteraneo di linea curba." The description of the design published by Le Rouge in 1784 indicates that the volcano was powered by "charbon de terre." Bettini's volcano also predated the Stein at Wörlitz (constructed 1788–94).

86. Ibid., fols. 88r–88v: "essito da questa sena orbille, ad'un torto si apre una sena la piu amena e ridente dove tuto, ispira il piacere dove li fiori e fruti sono comuni. le aque limpide che percorano de verdi ponti seminati di anemoni giacinti e tulipani gl'alberi li piu rari come la trugnolia, le Linodendrum, le acacïa le Ridandine le

papaia le cephalantus le zengobiloba la Rubinéa rosa le Parchinsonia le Aralia li cedri le Rose mutabilis le Altec etc. etc. con un infinità d'alberi sono questi che dano li piu preciosi fruti sono questi che formano li ameni boschetti di questi campi deliciosi detti degl'ellisi."

87. Ibid., fol. 86r: "tutta una sena campestra e si puo anco chiamare Orto agronomico."

88. Ibid., fols. 86v–87r: "delle Pagode del giardino cinese la grande gulia l'eremitaggio, e la cima del vulcano, vicino vi passa il fiume il quale atraversa questa pianura dividendo il prato verde dalla Plusa nella qual plusa pasion le vacche e le peccore tutta questa sena e decorata di piantassioni di Alberi rari e dietro il Tempio si vede il lago, e di la del lago si vede l'orto Agronomic e prossione della grotta D che il tuto forma un Quadro sublime e magico." The Temple of Momus was surrounded by "ogna sorta di giochi campestri, con anco un gracioso lamberinto di Rose è gelsomini le fonte o spaliere del qualle non sorpassano l'altezza di cinque palmi cosiche ognuno si vegono. e da diletto il veder gl'atri perdutti etc. nel Tempio ve il gioco del Bigliardo, sotto il portico di questo Tempio vi sono due comodi canapè, e stando a sedere al'ombra si gode la vista del bel prato verde o sia del giardino inglese e la casa che si revede da questa parte e di un archittetura al gusto di quella nassione."

89. Ibid., fols. 87r–v: "la totalità del Giardino inglese e grande prossione delli Campi Elisi e del Giardino cinese." The Temple of Apollo was made up of eight columns supporting a cupola. In the middle of the temple stood a marble copy of the Apollo Belvedere.

90. That illusion evokes the well-known Jardin de Julie from Rousseau's *La Nouvelle Héloïse* (1761), though the practice of screening walls was quite common in French design in the 1770s and 1780s.

91. On the idea of gardens as libraries in the eighteenth century, see Monique Mosser, "La réunion des arts est dans le jardin," in *Le Progrès des arts réunies, 1763–1815*, ed. Daniel Rabreau and Bruno Tollon (Bordeaux: CERCAM, Université Michel de Montaigne; Toulouse: Université de Toulouse Le Mirail, 1992), 172–73, esp. "L'idée d'un petit jardin anglais, d'approximativement 3 ou uniquement 2 acres," Archives départementales du Haut Rhin, Colmar, 201 (117–19) (late eighteenth century, in German). See also Hirschfeld [German edition], *Théorie*, 4: 189, 211; 5: 142, 352 f, cited in Linda Parshall, "C. C. L. Hirschfeld's Concept of the Garden in the German Enlightenment," *Journal of Garden History* 13. 3 (Autumn 1993): 132 and 163 n. 29.

92. Bettini, Ms. 6, fol. 85v.

93. Ibid., fol. 87v. Tools for cultivating the back garden were kept under an awning outside the Hermitage.

94. Ibid., fols. 87v–88r: "di una costrussione bizarra, con un piciolo armario dove vi sono delle Pille e e [i.e., di] piatti di terra delle fabriche le piu antiche, e li cotersilli [?] per far la cioccolata e il caffé. in una nichia ve una specie di letto tuto di vilutelo."

95. Ibid., fol. 88v.

96. Ibid.

97. Bettini included a stretch of the "strada reggia che da Padova conduce a Este" in the bottom left (i.e., east) corner of his drawing and, beyond it, a fragment of a "canale navigabile" (i.e., the Battaglia Canal).

98. Ravalli, *Disegni*, 53.

99. Ibid.: "Si mantenne, riverenti alla tradizione, il giar-

dino simmetrico attorno all'abitazzione, destinando solo le zone piu lontane ad esperimenti estrosi di paesaggi imitati."

100. Sirèn, "Le Rouge's Publications: Illustrations of New Ideals," chap. 12 in *China and Gardens of Europe*, 110.

101. Bettini, Ms. 6, fol. 84v.

102. Carmontelle, *Jardin de Monceau, Près de Paris* (Paris: Delafosse, 1779), 6: "Le plan d'un Jardin ordinaire, fait voir tout ce qu'il contient et quand on l'a vu, on peut se passer d'après cela, de parcourir le jardin." Carmontelle's remarks represented a complete reversal of general opinion concerning a principle that earlier had recommended symmetry. See Werner Szambien, *Symétrie, goût, caractère: Théorie et terminologie de l'architecture à l'âge classique, 1550–1800* (Paris: Picard, 1986), 69.

103. Carmontelle, *Jardin de Monceau*, 6: "Mais dans un Jardin naturel, le plan n'est qu'un itinéraire, qui ne fait pas prévoir un seul tableau."

104. Bettini, Ms. 112, quoted in Ravalli, *Disegni*, 52: "Io feci per lasciar il viaggiatore nel inganno di credere che il restante del giardino esser del vecchio stile."

105. Bettini, Ms. 6, fol. 85r: "sopra la grotta ve eretta una rustica capana coperta di paglia, e al intorno di Essa vi sono delli arbusti abastanza elevati e folti che impediscono di vedere li muri della casa."

106. Ibid.: "La prima sena del Giardino e apunto questa Grotta."

107. Ibid.: "Entrati per il canceleto K si presenta un comodo seditore per godere nel suo vero punto di vista la sena che si e lasciata, cioe la casa sotto la figura di una grotta."

108. Ibid., fol. 84r: "Questo giardino potrà dare molti lumi, per gl'artisti giardinieri per sapersi rigolare nel fare li contrasti dele sene, e saper tirare partito dare al giardino il caratere che esigie la casa principale. percio lautor inventò una casa di quatro caratteri, cioè le quatro facciate, ognuno a un caratere d'architetura diferente e oposta l'una da lalter."

109. See, for example, "Quart de Parterre varié de quatre façons sur le même dessein," in Michel Le Bouteux, fils, *Plans et dessins nouveaux de jardinage du S.r le Bouteux fils* (Paris: I. Nolin, [ca. 1700]) and J.-F. Blondel, *Planches pour le Quatrième Volume du Cours d'Architecture* (Paris, 1773), pl. 1.

110. Bettini, Ms. 6, fol. 89r: "io mi protesto di non pretendere con questa mia opereta di dare lumi suficienti per un'arte cotanto dificile, solo mi lusingo che questo potra bastare per incaminare il giovane studiente ad'aprirsi la via per li studi piu profondi ricorendo alla lettura di quanto a scritto molti celebri filosofi sopra tal arte."

111. Bettini, "Viaggi et' Aventure," fol. 318.

112. Ravalli, *Disegni*, 52, n. 18: "L'idea di progettare una villa con le facciate in stili architettonici diversi, il Bettini la attinse probabilmente in Inghilterra, dove aveva visto una villa la cui facciata principale era costruita 'alla fran-

cese' e la facciata che dava sul giardino 'al gusto inglese'. (cfr. i disegni dell'artista in 'Caos o Faraggine,' vol. 1, pp. 86–87.)"

113. Ravalli, *Disegni*, 52 n.18: "Mentre questa combinazione di due stili di ispirazione classica poteva sortire un risultato architettonico di una certa armonia, lo stesso non si poteva dire dell'edificio proposto dall'artista."

114. For commentary on Pope's Temple of Fame in relation to garden history, see Jurgis Baltrusaitis, "Gardens and Lands of Illusion," in *Aberrations: An Essay on the Legend of Forms*, trans. Richard Miller (Cambridge, Mass.: MIT Press, 1989), 143.

115. Bettini, *Caos*, vol. 3: fol. 175, "Proggieto di un Tempio della Famo, da farsi nella Piazza del'Etoile a Parigi p. F. B. L. 1776 a di 6 Febraio."

116. Maynard Mack, *Alexander Pope: A Life* (New York and New Haven: W. W. Norton, in association with Yale University Press, 1985), 163.

117. Bettini, Ms. 6, fol. 89r: "e in fine per un bel cocchio d'agrumi si rientra in casa dove ve un bel apartamentino amobigliato ala cinese. Ecco terminato il giro di questo giardino Anglocinese, del qualle io ne o data una conflusa idea poiche volendolo bene detagliare sarebbe stata cosa troppo lunga."

118. Jean-Denis Attiret, "Lettre du Père Attiret à M. d'Assaut, le premier Novembre 1743," in *Lettres édifiantes et curieuses écrites des missions étrangères par quelques missionnaires de la Compagnie de Jésus*, vol. 30 (Paris: Chez les Frères Garnier, 1749), 8–10. The *Lettres édifiantes*, written by Jesuit missionaries, were published in Paris between 1717 and 1776.

119. See Latapie, "Discours préliminaire," xxiii–xxxvii.

120. Le Rouge, *Détail*, cahier XII (1784), pl. 1. A note at the bottom right corner of the plate indicated that it could be purchased separately. A description of Bettini's design was also printed separately: "Description du douzième cahier des jardins anglais, Du Sieur Le Rouge, Ingénieur-Géographe du Roi, rue des Grands-Augustins, 1784, Voyez la Planche première du 12.e cahier. Projet d'un Jardin Anglais-Français-Chinois, pour S. Exce M. le Chev.r Delphino, Ambassadeur de Venise à la Cour de France, par François Bettini, Italien" (Paris: L'imprimerie de Demonville, rue Christine, 1784). The rue Christine was just around the corner from Le Rouge's shop. Le Rouge could have printed the description himself but only if he engraved the text on copper plates, since he was not licensed to work with movable type.

121. Bettini, "Descrizione d'un Giardino di delizia di nuova invenzione Fran-Cin-Angle," fol. 2.

122. Le Rouge, *Détail*, cahier XX (1788), pl. 4: "Superbe Jardin Anglais Projetté par Bettini, pour être executé dans les Environs de Paris. Pour S. E. M. le C. de S."

123. Ibid.

124. Ravalli, *Disegni*, 13.

7. The Garden of the Perfectibilists

Méréville and the Désert de Retz

MICHEL BARIDON

In the last two decades of the ancien régime, the French garden went through a period of active creation and intense theorization. In a little less than twenty years were published François de Paule Latapie's translation of Thomas Whately's *Observations on Modern Gardening* (1771), Delarochette's translation of William Chambers's *Dissertation on Oriental Gardening* (1772), Louis Carrogis de Carmontelle's *Jardin de Monceau* (1779), Claude-Henri Watelet's *Essai sur les jardins* (1774), François-Henri d'Harcourt's *Traité de la décoration des dehors, des jardins et des parcs* (1775), Jean-Marie Morel's *Théorie des jardins* (1776), René-Louis de Girardin's *De la composition des paysages* (1777), the first volume of C. C. L. Hirschfeld's *Théorie de l'art des jardins* in the French version (1779–85), Pierre Panseron's *Recueil de jardinage* and his *Recueil de jardins anglais et chinois*, both in 1783, the duc de Nivernois's translation of Horace Walpole's *History of the Modern Taste in Gardening*, (1784) and the famous descriptions made by Georges-Louis Le Rouge in his *Jardins anglo-chinois à la mode* (1776–89), followed by Alexandre de Laborde's *Description générale et particulière de la France* (1781–84). In the same decades, Méréville, the Désert de Retz, Ermenonville, Bagatelle, Betz, Guiscard, and Mauperthuis were created, and Hubert Robert, François Boucher, Pierre Adrien Paris, Jean-Honoré Fragonard, the best painters of the age, were either employed in the creation of gardens or took them as subjects. Literature followed suit. In 1777, Dominique Vivant-Denon, who was

to distinguish himself as the creator of the Louvre during the Napoleonic period, wrote one of the most enchanting pieces of garden literature, *Point de Lendemain*.

This is a very impressive record indeed, and one likely to make us wonder whether there is anything in the intellectual life of the period that could account for those two memorable decades. One can think of physiocracy, a powerful intellectual movement that gave primary importance to agriculture and whose leaders were François Quesnay (1694–1774) and Anne-Robert-Jacques Turgot (1727–81); one can also think of the popularity of botany, so highly commended by Jean-Jacques Rousseau (1712–78) and Jacques Henri Bernardin de Saint-Pierre (1737–1814), or of the success of Georges-Louis Leclerc, comte de Buffon's *Histoire naturelle*, whose publication extended over more than twenty years and ended with his death in 1788. Certainly, physiocracy, botany, and natural history contributed to make gardens popular by creating an interest in nature. But this does not explain the intellectual atmosphere of Ermenonville, the strange charm of the Désert de Retz, and the enchanting round of landscapes created by Jean-Joseph de Laborde (1724–94) and Hubert Robert (1733–1808) at Méréville. When we look at these gardens we experience a feeling of intellectual exhilaration very aptly defined by Michel Conan as "l'expression d'un art majeur de l'Ancien Régime, le paysage idyllique, qui fut inventé en dehors de la cour et s'imposa à elle," to which he added: "L'art du paysage idyllique réalisa un enchantement du monde."[1]

The term *enchantement* is so apposite that one could almost wish to keep this enchantment inviolate by saying no more. But the garden historian knows that the enjoyment of gardens is not merely a matter of seeing them and strolling through them. He knows that literary descriptions, however vivid, cannot account for the beauties they present to our mental eye; and so, he is left with the hope that he alone can add a zest of intellectual pleasure to the many other pleasures they give us. The nature of this intellectual pleasure can best be discovered by reading the literature they inspired, and if Morel, Girardin, Carmontelle, or Hirschfeld have one thing in common, it is certainly the feeling that they all belong to an avant-garde. Like all avant-gardists, however, the garden designers of the time found it easier to proscribe the "old" style than to define the "new" one. They were unanimous in their rejection of André Le Nôtre as representing what they called an "architectural style." The duc d'Harcourt (1726–1802) considered that in the French formal style, "L'Art des jardins a été abandonné aux architectes."[2] Morel (1728–1810), always well informed and perceptive, also put the blame on his predecessors: "Toujours architectes quand il fallait être jardiniers, ils taillèrent un arbre comme une pierre, en voûte, en cube, en pyramide."[3] According to Girardin (1735–1808) "on a prétendu assujettir la nature à sa maison, au lieu d'assujettir sa maison à la nature,"[4] and Carmontelle felt that, "Si nous avons eu le désir d'imiter les jardins anglais, ce n'était que pour sortir de la monotonie des nôtres."[5]

So far, so good. But where were the positive values to be looked for? In England? In China? Valenciennes (1750–1819), the landscape painter, wrote: "Il parait convenu d'appeler anglais les jardins de ce nouveau genre: on devrait plutot les nommer chinois, car c'est d'après les dessins et les descriptions de la Chine qu'on a arrangé ceux qui jouissent de la plus grande réputation en Angleterre."[6]

But Hirschfeld (1742–92) thought otherwise: "[Chambers] thought that his ideas would be more favourably received if he presented a distant country as their place of origin. . . . In a word, he planted English ideas in a Chinese soil."[7] And Girardin agreed with neither of them. He warned the reader of his *De la composition des paysages*: "Il ne sera donc ici question ni de jardins antiques, ni de jardins modernes, ni de jardins anglais, chinois ou cochinchinois."[8]

Since the same controversy was taking place in England at the same time, one may safely assume that the issue was central to the development of the landscape garden in Europe. My view is that in the first phase of its development, the landscape garden allowed for a parallel development of the rococo, the Chinese style, and the Gothic revival, and that in the latter half of the eighteenth century the general trend of ideas made this ambiguous alliance impossible and caused a conflict among garden theorists in England, France, and Germany. But while the debate in England remained centered on the national origin of the picturesque, it involved much larger intellectual issues in France where the influence of Rousseau and the commotion created by the concept of *perfectibilité* made the relation of man to nature central to the intellectual scene. England had led the way, but the situation in France and the portents of great events to come caused a general fermentation of ideas in which *perfectibilité* took on political undertones and fostered utopias that are not unconnected to the *enchantement* described by Conan.

MAN'S RELATION TO NATURE AND THE CONCEPT OF PERFECTIBILITY

The French philosophes of the second half of the eighteenth century, the *Encyclopédistes*, as they were called, owed a great debt to England because their worldview had largely been created by the works of John Locke, Isaac Newton, and Robert Boyle. They criticized English politics and they sided with the Americans during the war of independence, but they knew that the works of these three men had effected a paradigm shift that had brought the life sciences to the fore while geometry suffered a decline. Newton's *Principia* (1687) and his *Opticks* (1704), Boyle's essential contribution to the early development of chemistry by the experimental method, and Locke's *Essay Concerning Human Understanding* (1690) had called into question the mechanistic philosophy prevalent in the seventeenth century. To take but one example, while René Descartes described the nervous system as a network of pipes in which animal spirits ran from the sense organs to the brain like water in a fountain, Locke, who was a medical doctor, considered sensations as the reactions of living tissues to the stimuli of the outside world. In his *Essay*, sensations are never divorced from the feelings of pain and pleasure provoked by a physical contact with the world. Locke had made a substantial contribution to Boyle's *History of the Air* (1692), because they were both interested in the nature of air, a gas on which life depended. Newton's *Opticks* stressed the fact that the universe was governed by two forces: gravitation and fermentation. His *Fluxions* (translated by Buffon) connected mathematics with the infinitely small variations which determined the growth, development, and decline of living organisms. The new school of thought, that the *Encyclopédistes* followed, considered bodies as fluid, elastic forms mutually penetrating and transforming each other, not as solids acting like cogwheels and pulleys.

The achievements of the "new science" had been brought to public attention by Joseph Addison and Alexander Pope who were widely read in France together with James Thomson, whose poem *The Seasons* (1726–30) had created a new climate of sensibility and new attitudes toward nature. All three praised the irregularity and freedom of the English garden. By the early 1760s, the interest in the life sciences so evidently linked with English empiricism had spread all over Europe and led to important advances in physiology and chemistry. Carl Linnaeus changed the nomenclature of botany (*Systema naturae*, 1735) and created a universal science of plants. Physiology led to the study of reflexes and experimental embryology. Caspar Friedrich Wolff refuted the idea that living beings preexisted in the organs of reproduction (*Theoria Generationis*, 1759) and showed that they developed freely from germs. Life was conceived as a process of growth, and the world was described as plastic and penetrated by fluids such as magnetism and electricity.

It is in this context that Turgot coined the term *perfectibilité* in 1748. He modeled it on *expansibilité*, another new word borrowed from the vocabulary of the chemists to define the nature of gases. In the same way as gases expand in space, Turgot thought, man always strives to improve his living conditions by increasing his knowledge; and since writing transmits knowledge from one generation to the next, he perfects himself by a process that transforms his very nature. Turgot, who was a chemist, a linguist, and an economist, thus combined many fields of research to present man's nature as plastic and capable of endless progress. This required the implementation of a long timescale because the progress of human societies from their origin to the present had been slow and gradual, and the long timescale was, so to speak, in the air, because Buffon's works had made it necessary to a true understanding of the development of species. His *Epoques de la Nature* was censured by the church for making the world ten times older than the Scriptures allowed it to be.

The first well-known man of letters who made use of the term *perfectibilité* was Rousseau. In his *Discourse on the Origin of Inequality* (1755), he gave it a twist that made it a key and paradoxical term in the late Enlightenment. Rousseau was ready to admit that man was engaged in an endless struggle to improve his condition, but since he was a sociable being, he was mentally fashioned by the laws under which he lived. Since the laws were part of the knowledge transmitted to him by former generations, and since they had been made by the mighty and the rich, he could only make them worse by perfecting their ruling principle. Try as he could, the progress he made was in the wrong direction until a providential figure, the *législateur*, intervened. In his *Contrat social* (1762), Rousseau explained that the *législateur* was a man of genius whose "sublime reason"[9] rose above circumstances and education. He alone could conceive a new system of laws which would regenerate man by making *perfectibilité* reverse the course of history. Such views created a shock because they ran against the facile optimism of the philosophes, who believed that progress would inevitably follow from their triumph over superstition. They also popularized a "whence and whither" problematic that spanned the whole history of mankind, over "des multitudes de siècles" ("a long succession of ages").[10] They presented man as endlessly on the march, moving away from the felicity and innocence of primitive times and heading for either greater corruption and misery or universal harmony.

The inquisitive minds of the period began to busy themselves with the origin of things (language, societies, architecture) and with the ultimate stage of perfection they might reach. Typical of this attitude is Jean-Antoine Nicolas de Caritat, marquis de Condorcet's *Esquisse d'une histoire des progrès de l'esprit humain* (1794) with its eulogy of *perfectibilité* represented as the discovery leading to the final stage of the history of man. When Condorcet wrote his *Esquisse*, the term *perfectibilité* had already been Anglicized and Germanized. We find it in the writings of Immanuel Kant, Richard Price, William Godwin and Joseph Priestley, a scientist who, like Turgot, was interested in human psychol-

1. Arc et Senans. Claude-Nicolas Ledoux's visual expression of the perfectibility of man. The geometry of the Doric portico symbolizes the perfection of ages to come, while the chaotic rocks evoke the bowels of the earth and the origin of the world.

ogy, chemistry, the nature of air, and that mysterious fluid, electricity. The Lunar Society of Birmingham, of which Priestley was a member, had sympathy with Rousseau, and its intellectual atmosphere is reflected in the paintings of Joseph Wright of Derby (1734–97), where chemistry, botany, geology, and physiology are assumed to be the leading sciences of the period.

Gardens, being the art form that offers the closest contact with nature, could not fail to interest the perfectibilists for they found in them direct evocations of the innocence of primeval times as well as intimations of the harmonious world yet to come. Moral regeneration began in the wilderness, as the Désert de Retz showed, and at Ermenonville Girardin announced that the landscape garden would contribute to an "agencement plus salutaire et plus humain dans les campagnes" ("a more humane, more beneficial organization in the countryside").[11] Meanwhile, the long timescale and concern for origins developed the interest in geology that had been awakened by Thomas Burnet's *Sacred Theory of the Earth*, a book praised by Buffon and influential in the vogue of mountain scenery. Big rocks representing the "entrailles de la terre" ("the bowels of the earth"), appeared in all the gardens of the 1770s. Jacques Montanier Delille's famous line, "Sa masse indestructible a fatigué le temps" ("its indestructible mass has tired out time") was inscribed on a huge rock at La Garenne Lemot near Clisson. Next to those big *rochers*, there were often grottoes, which, as in Méréville or in the parc Balbi, were made to look like Piranesian caverns in which primitive ages were revived. Similar effects were obtained by Claude-Nicolas Ledoux at the Salines (salt works) d'Arc et Senans, where he turned the traditional *rocaille* facing of the vaults into chaotic heaps of rocks (figs. 1, 2). The same

2. The salt works at Arc et Senans. The entrance gate, section. Illustration to Claude-Nicolas Ledoux, *L'Architecture considérée sous le rapport de l'art, des moeurs et de la legislation* (Paris, 1804).

interest in *rochers* existed at the Désert de Retz, where Laborde mentions that "des pins, des mélèzes et des hêtres couronnent et entourent ces rochers naturels et très bien rapportés qui ne sont pas sans rappeler la Grande Chartreuse."[12] Ermenonville also offered a wilderness and a philosopher's hut, a primitive habitation where the sage could meditate on the origins of mankind and the gradual improvement of human dwellings. This expansion of the historical imagination had its counterpart in geography: Monceau displayed a decoration worthy of a tour operator's shop window, the Désert had a *tente tartare* and a *maison chinoise*, Méréville had a monument to Captain James Cook.

We should remember, however, that while fabrics and literary reminiscences widen the overall significance of gardens by explicit allusions, they cannot give them a definite shape. One has to go deeper to study the connection which exists between the shape of gardens and the worldview that they implicitly convey.

PERFECTIBILITY AND THE CREATIVE IMAGINATION

In the present case, this problem can only be tackled by drawing parallels between the regular garden of the baroque age and the picturesque landscape of the following period. This makes it quite clear that, while gardens had geometrical shapes when the leading sciences were optics and geometry, they were degeometrized when the emergence of the life sciences changed the dominant world-picture. Alberti and Jacques Boyceau thought that regularity and symmetry provided a true image of nature because they existed in the human body and in the shape of a leaf. Addison and Pope held exactly opposite views. They wrote in praise of the asymmetrical, winding lines of the landscape which they presented as a true image of nature unmolested by scissors and by the tyranny of the central axis.

With perfectibility things changed again. Its basic assumptions, sumptuously expressed by the beauty of Rousseau's prose, conveyed images of the virtue and simplicity of primeval times. This

3. The ruined column in the Désert de Retz. Alexandre de Laborde, *Description des nouveaux jardins de la France*, 1808, Dijon, Bibliothèque municipale.

4. Rousseau raises his arms in admiration while he contemplates the Désert at Ermenonville. Alexandre de Laborde, *Description des nouveaux jardins de la France*, 1808, Dijon, Bibliothèque municipale.

implied an effort of the imagination which had to expand in order to conceive a huge span of time and an equally huge number of nations involved in a continuous process of self-transformation. Perfectibility was intrinsically colossal, and it partook of the rational sublimity of the mind of the legislator whose stupendous power could change the course of history. Time, like nature, must be embraced in its entirety. If the garden was to accommodate utopian visions, its ultimate limit must be the horizon on all sides. This implied a circular structure, which made geometry come into its own again.

The "genius of the place" was bound to lose part of its power in the process. At Méréville, the church spire is not part of the landscape, and the only tower you see in the distance is a Roman one. The same applies to the Désert de Retz, where the famous "colonne de ruines" suggests immensity in space and time (fig. 3). Girardin proscribed both the "jardin carré" and the "jardin contourné," both the axial perspective and contrived views. Much as he liked Shenstone's Leasowes, he saw Chaâlis with the eye of a landscape painter rather than that of an antiquarian. After having quoted Rousseau: "La Nature, dit un homme dont chaque mot est un sentiment, la nature fuit les lieux fréquentés; c'est au sommet des montagnes, au fond des forêts, dans les iles désertes qu'elle étale ses charmes les plus touchants; ceux qui l'aiment et ne peuvent la chercher si loin sont réduits à lui faire violence et à la forcer en quelque sorte à venir habiter parmi eux, et tout cela ne peut se faire sans un peu d'illusion,[13] he recommended: "Montez sur le haut de la maison."[14] From such a vantage point the entire landcape "le grand spectacle de la nature," appeared best (fig. 4). And prominent in the "grand spectacle de la nature" was "la voute azurée des cieux" ("the azure vault of the sky"), a direct echo of Rousseau's description of the primitive man "portant ses regards sur toute la nature, et mesurant des yeux la vaste étendue du Ciel."[15]

If "un peu d'illusion" ("un peu d'enchantement," Conan would say) must become part of the garden, the circular panorama viewed from the roof of the house must give a shape to the garden. M. de Monville's ruined tower had a salon whose sixteen oculi offered a completely circular view of the landscape (fig. 5). Méréville has a circular structure that looks like a plate (fig. 6). The Juine meanders in its flat part, and, as the visitor goes round it on his peripheral excursion, he sees a succession of landscapes forming a ring on the opposite side. He thus finds himself in a circular structure and discovers,

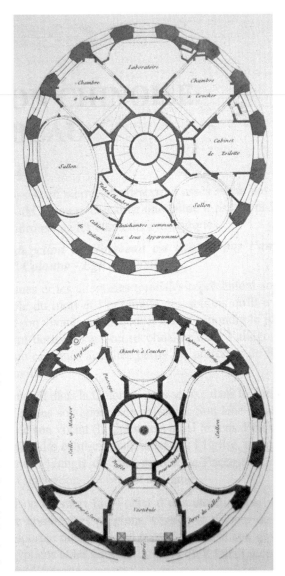

5. The Désert de Retz, the oculi of the ruined tower. "Coupe et plan de la colonne détruite," Alexandre de Laborde, *Description des nouveaux jardins de la France*, 1808, Dijon, Bibliothèque municipale.

as he moves on, a succession of picturesque landscapes reminding him of the origins of mankind, of Italy, of Cook, and of the daily life of the French peasants.

Such a structure made the circular form pregnant because the circle, being the symbol of perfection, could evoke both the "voute azurée des cieux" contemplated by the primitive man and the celestial visions of the harmony to come on the surface of the earth. It gave a truly cosmic dimension to the landscape and made it the home of the legislator by displaying the sublime spectacle of nature and in-

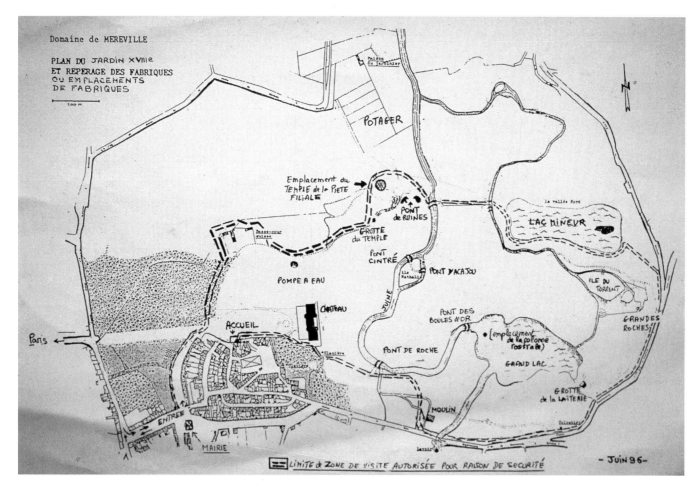

6. The circular structure of Méréville. With the kind permission of the Amis du jardin romantique XVIII siècle d'Hubert Robert à Méréville.

spiring his "great soul" with visions of the felicity to come. This was a complete break from the empiricism of the first half of the century because it made utopia, not experience, the true ruler of the world.

One finds here direct echoes of what Etienne-Louis Boullée and Ledoux were doing at the same time, both of them with an active interest in utopia and public buildings. It will be remembered that Ledoux's *Architecture considérée sous le rapport de l'art, des moeurs et de la législation* explicitly mentions the legislator's work. Both Boullée and Ledoux were familiar with the whence and whither problematic of perfectibility. In the introduction to his *Essai sur l'Art*, Boullée wrote: "Il faut concevoir pour effectuer; nos premiers pères n'ont bati leurs cabanes qu'après en avoir conçu l'image. C'est cette production de l'esprit; c'est cette création qui constitue l'architecture, que nous pouvons en conséqunce, définir l'art de produire et de porter à la perfection tout édifice quelconque."[16]

But what is perfection? Both Boullée and Ledoux considered that it was to be found in the simplest geometrical figures. Boullée said, "fatigué de l'image muette et stérile des corps irréguliers, je suis passé à l'examen des corps réguliers" ("having lost interest in the dumb, barren image of irregular objects, I started analyzing the regular ones"). He spoke of "la magnifique beauté de la forme sphérique."[17] Ledoux echoed this praise of regularity: "la forme est pure comme celle que décrit le soleil dans sa course" ("the shape is as pure as the path followed by the Sun"). This cosmic geometry could provide new aesthetic criteria. In 1800, Léon Dufourny declared: "Je suis d'avis que l'architecture doit se régénérer par la géométrie."[18] Combes, another architect, submitted to the National Assembly a project showing a huge hemispherical vault representing a map of the sky on 15 July 1789.[19] In fact, this general evolution, so obviously initiated by the perfectibilists, had started long be-

7. The circular shape of the saltworks at Arc et Senans. *L'Architecture considérée sous le rapport de l'art, des moeurs et de la législation* (1804).

fore the French Revolution. Boullée was already an old man when the Revolution broke out, and his aesthetic criteria concurred with those of Ledoux, who gave a circular shape to the Salines d'Arc et Senans (fig. 7) because he considered himself the legislator of the salt works. As such, he wished them to offer the very image of social harmony in a natural setting, and, had they been completed, they would have inscribed a perfect circle in the dark woods of the Jura.

PERFECTIBILITY AND GEOMETRIZATION: THE CIRCLE, THE PANORAMA, AND UNIVERSAL HARMONY

Perfectibility, however important its role seems to have been, cannot alone explain the emergence of regular forms and the restoration of geometry's position in the experience of the garden. Great movements and changes in aesthetics result from a conjunction of causes concurring in the emergence of new criteria. Some of these causes are technological, others philosophical, others still depend on a combination of science and aesthetics; such was the case with the renewed interest in mountain scenery which developed in the latter half of the eigteenth century, when even Samuel Johnson went to see the "protuberances" of Scotland long after Albrecht von Haller and Rousseau had published their famous descriptions of the Alps. It was there, near Chamonix, that Horace-Bénédict de Saussure went on his excursions, combining his love of natural sublimity with his interest in the virtuous life of the mountaineers. On one of these excursions, he climbed the glacier du Buet and then went to the top of the mountain; he discovered a unique view of the whole chain of Mont-Blanc and decided to keep a visual record of it by asking an artist he knew, Marc-Théodore Bourrit, to draw a "vue circulaire" of the whole panorama. His relation of this memo-

8. The Rotunda, Leicester Square, 1801. Aquatint by Robert Mitchell, National Film Archive; reproduced in *Panoramania*, an exhibition held at the Barbican Art Gallery, 1988, text by Ralph Hyde, p. 22.

rable event, as he published it in his *Voyages dans les Alpes* (1779–96), is as follows: "Le dessinateur peint les objets exactement comme il les voit en tournant son papier à mesure qu'il tourne lui-même."[20]

Saussure noted with satisfaction that this gave the picture "une exactitude presque géométrique." He thus reconciled the sublimity of the chaotic, gigantic forms of nature and the regularity of geometry—a combination we often find in the works of Ledoux, Boullée, and Clérisseau. The circular shape of "la voûte azurée des cieux," evoking the perfection of the cosmos, was now placed on a horizontal plane, as one could see it from an air balloon of the sort with which Joseph Montgolfier experimented in the 1780s. Boullée could not but be deeply sensitive to the beauty of a machine that was round in shape and had a direct relation to the scientific imagination of the age since it was the expansion of heated air that made it fly. He wrote a superb passage on the sublimity of the air balloon panorama: "Il en est de même d'un aérostat

qui, planant dans les airs et ayant perdu de vue les objets de la terre, n'aperçoit que le ciel dans toute la nature. Errant ainsi dans l'immensité, dans cet abîme d'étendue, l'homme est anéanti par le spectacle extraordinaire d'un espace inconcevable."[21] Johann Wolfgang von Goethe used similar terms to describe the panorama he discovered from the spire of the Strasbourg cathedral and compared it to the view from an air balloon.

The circular representation of the landscape was soon to achieve great popularity.[22] In the mid-1780s, Robert Barker, a portrait painter following (unknowingly?) in Saussure's footsteps, exhibited what he called a "total view" of Edinburgh from the top of Calton Hill. He had invented a process, he explained, which was to "fix a square frame at one spot, draw the scene presented in the frame, turn the frame to the area adjacent, and then continue to turn the frame and draw the scene until the complete 360 degree prospect was recorded."[23] Barker took out a patent for his invention (fig. 8). For he

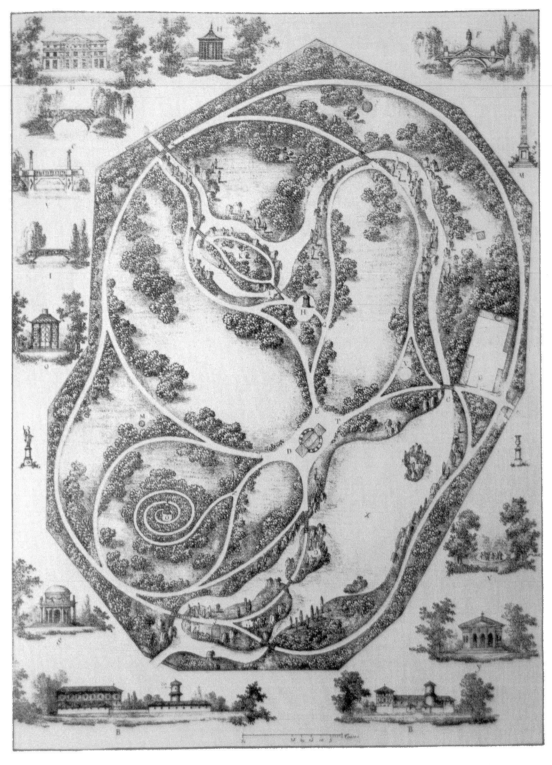

9. Gabriel Thouin, *Plans raisonnés de toutes les espèces de jardins* (Paris, 1820), no. 47, "Plan pour un jardin d'agrément."

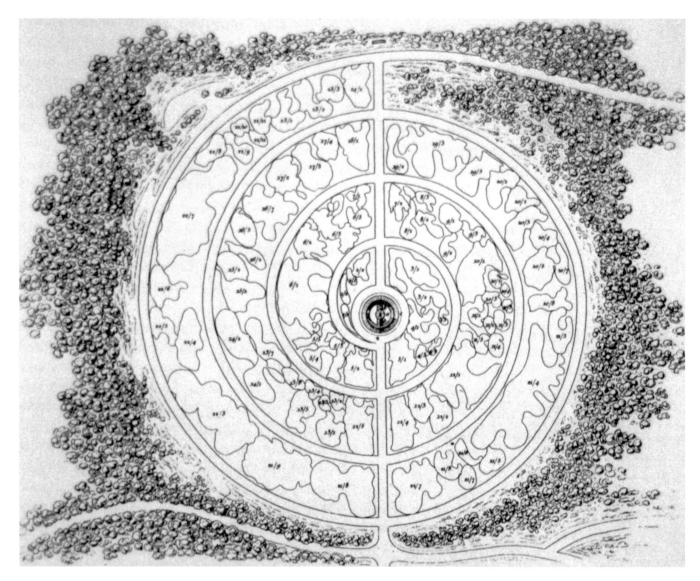

10. John Claudius Loudon, Design for a Botanic garden. *Hints for a National Garden* (London, 1811), illustration.

considered it as such, writing in the *Edinburgh Evening Courant* that it was "an improvement on painting, which relieves that sublime art from a restraint it has ever laboured under."[24] To him, the panoramic vision was the possibility of making landscape painting truly sublime. He had, he said, used "no deception of glasses," and relied only on "fair perspective, a proper point of view, and unlimiting the bounds of the art of painting." In other words, sublimity was attained by "perfecting" landscape painting and this implied that the artist should consider the horizon as a complete circle. This was probably what Girtin thought when he designed his *Eidometropolis* in 1797–98, showing the whole urban area of London from the top of a building

near Blackfriars Bridge. Meanwhile, in 1793, Barker opened a permanent establishment to present his panorama in Cranbourne Street, Leicester Square, and he replaced the terms "nobility and gentry" by "the public." This would have delighted Rousseau, who always gloried in the title of *Citoyen de Genève*. Circularity favored democracy.

In Paris, one of Barker's enthusiastic supporters was Dufourny, the architect who prophesied that geometry would regenerate architecture. He recommended the panorama to the Institute. In Germany, the greatest architect of the period, Karl Friedrich Schinkel, designed a huge panorama of Palermo in 1808. In 1834, when Eduard Gaertner painted a general view of Berlin from the Friedrich

Werdersche Kirche, he represented a group standing in the foreground on the roof of the church. Schinkel was there and next to him was Alexander von Humboldt with a telescope.[25] Quite clearly Gaertner saw the representation of a panorama as a manifestation of avant-garde thought in the sciences and in the arts, for Schinkel's name was associated with romantic sublimity in architecture, and Humboldt was the founder of modern geography. In his last book, *Cosmos*, Humboldt wrote that landscape painting was yet to reach its perfection. Only when young artists with "a soul fresh and pure" would paint "the immense variety of nature" in the wild expanses of America and Asia, only then, would art and knowledge be reconciled.[26] Once again the wilderness was associated with the virtue of primitive ages, and once again the primitive ages showed the way to the ultimate perfection the arts could reach.

One thinks here of Girardin surveying the whole extent of the landscape from the roof of his house, his brushes in hand. This brings us back to gardens, in which the perfectibilists introduced spiraling motifs in order to reconcile the free forms of nature with the geometrical regularity of circular structures. Such spirals can be seen in the gardens designed by Panseron, Alexandre Théodore Brongniart, and Gabriel Thouin at the turn of the century and in the 1810s (fig. 9); they can also be found in the ephemeral decorations built by the revolutionaries for their civic "fêtes" or for the decoration of the churches they had turned into "Temples de la raison." This can probably be explained by the fact that the spiral keeps expanding while following a circular motion. It thus provides an ideal, if elliptical, representation of perfectibility, for its gradual expansion is expressive of the growth of all living organisms, while its circular motion brings to mind the perfection of the social harmony to come.

In the history of the French garden, the late eighteenth century deserves particular attention. This contextual exploration has shed some light on the nature of the enchanting power with which gardens like the Désert de Retz and Méréville are rightly credited. The Désert was created before the Revolution. Méréville was not quite completed when Laborde was guillotined, but it would be a mistake to consider that their history came to an end with the ancien régime. In the same way as the term *perfectibilité* passed from Turgot to Rousseau and then to Kant and Hegel, echoes of the circular vision of the landscape and of the geometrization it implied could be found decades later in some of the great public parks of Europe and America.

The utopian visions of the eighteenth-century perfectibilists inspired John Claudius Loudon (fig. 10) and Frederick Law Olmsted. They may have lost their enchanting power by this change of scale, but utopias often do when they come true.

Notes

1. Michel Conan, postface to Girardin's *De la composition des paysages* (Paris: Champ Urbain, 1992), 183: "The expression of a major art form of the Ancien Régime, the idyllic landscape, in whose creation the court had no part though it soon adopted it . . . The art of the idyllic landscape created an enchanted world."

2. François Henri, duc d'Harcourt, *Traité de la décoration des dehors, des jardins, et des parcs*, no. 107 of *Art de Basse-Normandie* (1996), 27. "Garden art has been abandoned to architects."

3. Jean-Marie Morel, *Théorie des jardins* (Paris, 1776), 7. "They acted like architects when they were supposed to be gardeners, and they used trees as they would have done stone, cutting them into vaults, cubes, and pyramids."

4. René-Louis de Girardin, *De la composition des paysages* (1777), 7. "The house was made to lord it over nature, while the very reverse was the thing to do."

5. Louis Carrogis de Carmontelle, *Le Jardin de Monceau*, (Paris, 1779), 5. "We took our cue from England because we had grown tired of the monotony of our gardens."

6. Pierre-Henri de Valenciennes, *Elements de perspective pratique* (Paris, 1775), 347. "It seems to be accepted to call the gardens designed in the new style English; they should be called Chinese in fact, for those that enjoy the greatest reputation in England were designed according to drawings and descriptions from China."

7. C. C. L. Hirschfeld, *Theorie de l'art des jardins* (Paris, 1779–85), vol. 1: 113. "[Chambers] thought that his ideas would be more favorably received if he presented a distant country as their place of origin. In a word, he planted English ideas in a Chinese soil."

8. Girardin, *De la composition des paysages*, 6. "The gardens considered in my book are neither antique nor modern, neither English, Chinese nor Cochin-Chinese."

9. J. J. Rousseau, *Le Contrat social*, in *Oeuvres complètes* (Paris: La Pléiade, 1970), Gallimard, 3: 384. "La grande âme du législateur est le vrai miracle qui doit prouver sa mission" ("the great soul of the lawgiver is the true miracle which justifies his mission").

10. Idem, *Discours sur l'Origine de l'Inégalité*, in *Oeuvres complètes*, 3: 167.

11. *De la composition des paysages*, 136.

12. Quoted in *Jardins en France, 1760–1820: Pays d'Illusion, terre d'expériences* (Paris: Caisse National des Monuments Historiques et des Sites, 1977), 92: "this fine array of natural rocks is surrounded and crowned by pines, larches, and beeches which bring to mind the Grande Chartreuse."

13. *De la composition des paysages*, 23. "Nature, says a man who makes every word express a feeling, is not to be found where people congregate; it displays its most endearing charms on mountaintops, in the heart of forests, and on desert islands; those who love it and are unable to

go so far to find it are reduced to compelling it to come and dwell among them, and that can only be done by employing illusion."

14. Ibid., 26. "Climb to the top of the house."

15. *Discours sur l'Origine de l'Inégalité*, 134.

16. Etienne-Louis Boullée, *Essai sur l'art* (Paris: Hermann, 1968), 49: "Ideas precede creation. Our fathers had to conceive a mental image of their huts before they started building them. This image produced by the mind *is* Architecture, and this is why we may define it as the art of creating and bringing to perfection any edifice whatsoever."

17. Emil Kaufman, "Trois architectes révolutionnaires: Boullee, Ledoux, Lequeu," *Transactions of the American Philosophical Society* (1952): 431–564, French translation by G. Eruart and G. Teyssot (Paris: Editions de la S. A. D. G., 1978), 101.

18. J. P. Mouilleseaux and A. Jacques, *Les architctes de la Liberté* (Paris: Gallimard, 1988), 79. "I believe that architecture must be regenerated by geometry."

19. Ibid., 49.

20. Numa Broc, "Une découverte 'révolutionnaire': La haute montagne alpestre," in *Composer le paysage*, ed. Odile Marcel (Seyssel, 1989), 56. "The draftsman depicts objects exactly as he sees them while turning his paper as he himself turns around."

21. Boullée, *Essai sur l'art*, 85. "From an air balloon floating in the air, when one has lost sight of earthbound objects, one sees nothing but the sky. Drifting in this vast abyss, man dwindles into nothingness as he discovers the stupendous vastness of unfathomable space."

22. Whether this is related to Gaspard Monge's invention of projective geometry is a debatable point. In the 1770s, Monge invented a new system of describing objects by a simple geometrical device which implied the use of two perpendicular planes on which their elevation and their profile were projected. By rotating one of the planes, it was brought into conjunction with the other in order to obtain two side-by-side complementary views. Monge's system of representation is considered by René Taton as instrumental in the renewed interest in geometry that took place at the end of the eighteenth century, in the years when Quatremère de Quincy launched his attack on the English garden in the *Encyclopédie méthodique* (1788). The only problem is that it is difficult to assess the impact of his discovery before he published his treatise (1799). Monge felt certain that his invention would contribute to the "perfectionnement de l'espèce humaine," a remark typical of the impact of perfectibility on the scientific imagination of the age (Gaspard Monge, *Géométrie descriptive* [Paris, 1811], VIII–IX).

23. Ralph Hyde, *Panoramania! The Art and Entertainment of the "All-embracing" View*, introd. by Scott B. Wilcox (London: Trefoil Publications, Barbican Art Gallery, 1989), 57.

24. Quoted by Scott B. Wilcox, "Unlimiting the Bounds of Painting," *Panoramania!* 21.

25. Ibid., 60.

26. Alexander von Humboldt, *Cosmos, a Sketch of the Physical Description of the Universe*, trans. E. C. Otté (London: H. G. Bohn, 1848), 2: 452.

8. Jean-Marie Morel and the Invention of Landscape Architecture

JOSEPH DISPONZIO

When Jean-Marie Morel died on 7 October 1810 at the age of eighty-two, his death made national news. It was covered by Napoleon's daily, *Le Moniteur Universel*, after having first appeared on the front page of Morel's hometown newspaper, *Le Journal de Lyon*.[1] He was by then the most celebrated garden designer in France with a fifty-year career spanning the ancien régime, the Revolution, the Consulate, and the early years of the First Empire. No other French garden designer could claim such accomplishment, in either sheer longevity or —more important—in continuity. When he began his gardening career in the early 1760s, the style of garden he professed—the natural or picturesque style[2]—was still in its adolescence in France and had yet to be codified into a coherent theory and practice.[3] By the end of his life, however, the natural style of gardening had solidly entered the ranks of the liberal arts.

Morel was a central figure in the maturation of the natural style of gardening in France. Through his unprecedented career he established a rigorous theoretical framework for the new genre that helped direct and formulate its future practical course. Furthermore, his demonstrated command of the techniques for the new method of gardening was instrumental in effecting professional competence in the new design idiom; and his recognition of the newness of the genre led to his nomination of a new design professional, *architecte-paysagiste*, a term he coined in 1803. Just as significantly, his life and work coincided with the development of a new chapter in the history of gardening, that of the rise of a new discipline—landscape architecture, a consequence of the paradigmatic shifts that occurred in the wake of the Enlightenment. As both witness to and participant in the transformation of the garden in the eighteenth century, Morel was a major contributor.

While he was much appreciated in life, frequently referred to as "le Grand Morel" with his name often in the company of Humphry Repton and André Le Nôtre,[4] Morel entered an ill-deserved obscurity sometime during the latter half of the nineteenth century and remained there through most of the twentieth.[5] This has as much to do with those who have written the history of the natural style of gardening as it does with France's ambivalent reception of the tradition.[6]

If Morel is remembered at all today, it is for his book *Théorie des jardins*, which he published in 1776 and issued in a second edition in 1802. The work is perhaps the most comprehensive eighteenth-century garden treatise on the picturesque or natural style of gardening and the keystone to the corpus of eighteenth-century garden texts that can be considered the intellectual and theoretical foundations of landscape architecture. More so than any of his contemporaries, Morel demonstrated a command of the natural sciences commensurate with the complexity of landscape which enabled him to fashion his garden theory into proper intellectual form. The origins of the praxis of landscape architecture and of a modern environmental sensibility in landscape design can be situated in Morel's picturesque garden theory.[7]

MOREL'S LIFE AND CAREER

Jean-Marie Morel (fig. 1) was born in Lyon on 21 August 1728 and died on 7 October 1810 in the town of Ecully, a suburb of Lyon. However, he lived most of his life elsewhere. His family was of the well-to-do Lyonnaise bourgeoisie; his father, Pierre, was a *procureur*, somewhat similar to our district attorney. His mother, Françoise Ozinda, was the daughter of merchants. His older brother, Pierre, was a noted grammarian, and his younger brother, Bonaventure, became a lawyer like his father. The social origins are noteworthy if for no other reason than that they contributed to Morel's near execution, along with his two brothers, during the reign of terror that befell Lyon after its ill-fated coup against the Revolution.[8] For most of his adult life, Morel lived in Paris but frequently visited his native city, in particular in 1791, when he returned to marry a well-to-do woman who was some forty years his junior; Adelaide Morel bore him two daughters.

Before the Revolution, Morel's patron was Louis-François de Bourbon, prince de Conti (1717–76); after it, his client list was headed by Napoleon and Josephine. Of less renown, but of no lesser means, were clients drawn from the pre-Revolutionary aristocracy, including the comtesse de Pons-Saint-Maurice, the comtesse de Brionne, the duc d'Aumont, and the marquis de Montesquiou. In Burgundy he worked for two of the wealthiest families of the region: Chartraire de Montigny, mayor and member of the Parlement of Dijon, and the marquis d'Arcelot, whose family seat outside Dijon was the first neoclassical château built in Burgundy. During the Consulate and First Empire, Morel acted as a de facto designer to the circle of Napoleon, creating gardens for Queen Hortense, Josephine's daughter by her first marriage; Martin-Roch-Xavier, comte Estève, a financial backer of Napoleon; field marshal Trévise, as well as the Périer banking family of Grenoble. In all, over a five-decade career Morel designed or is associated with more than fifty gardens, of which only a handful survive.[9]

It is widely assumed that Morel was brought out of retirement by Josephine to work at La Malmaison (1802), but his career suggests otherwise. With the exception of a four-month period when he was imprisoned in Lyon (November 1793–February 1794), he appears to have led an exhausting life of work and travel. Indeed, a few months before his death he was tending to projects in the Mâconnais and Burgundy. Likewise, his reputation was not forgotten after his death—at least for a few decades—as his name appears on a poster, about 1840, for the sale of the château of Saint-Mury, outside of Grenoble. A selling point for the property featured ornamental gardens *"à l'anglaise"* by "MM. Maurel et Bertaud" (fig. 2).[10] Clearly, his name carried value.

Virtually nothing is known about Morel's early education and intellectual formation. He probably attended one of the Jesuit-run *collèges* of Lyon. However, in August 1754, at age twenty-six, he began an apprenticeship as an *ingénieur-géographe* (geographical engineer) for the *généralité*, or district, of Lyon, working under the chief engineer of the city, Nicolas-François De Ville (1712–70). Four years later he was sent to Paris to attend classes at the Ecole des Ponts et Chaussées, at which time he also studied architecture with Jacques-François Blondel (1705–74), France's most important teacher and theorist of architecture.[11] In 1760 a financial crisis forced the suspension of his yearly stipend of 600 livres, resulting in his termination as an *ingénieur-géographe* and his subsequent withdrawal from the school. Shortly after the Seven Years' War (1757–63) he secured a prestigious position with a prince of the blood, Louis-François de Bourbon, prince de Conti. Morel directed Conti's office of Bâtiments et Travaux, for which he was handsomely paid: he received 4,800 livres per annum, second only to the prince's Council chief, who received 6,000 livres. While the prince had vast landholdings and property throughout France, his financial affairs were in shambles, a situation that kept him at the brink of bankruptcy for much of his life. This might account for Morel's preoccupation with the maintenance and repair of the prince's buildings, rather than with the design of the nobleman's gardens. Indeed, there is no archival evidence (nor physical remains) of any garden design that Morel may have done for his illustrious patron.[12]

During his tenure with Conti, he designed gardens for the duc d'Aumont at Guiscard (fig. 3), Ermenonville for (and in collaboration with) the marquis de Girardin, and at the country seat for the princesse de Pons-Saint-Maurice, among others. After Conti's death in 1776, Morel is known to have traveled to England, and possibly Holland, Germany, and Italy as well.[13] Returning to France, he continued his unprecedented career, which

1. Jean-Marie Morel (1728–1810), anonymous engraving. Bibliothèque municipale de Lyon, Portrait Morel. Photo Bibliothèque municipale, Didier Nicole.

lasted through five decades, one Revolution, several coups, and general economic and political instability. With projects from the plains of Picardie in the north of France to the mountains of the Dauphiné in the southeast, Morel's career suggests a tireless professional, consumed with his work and, in the process, the creation of a profession in the early stages of becoming.

No doubt Morel's association with the court of the prince de Conti was advantageous for his career as a garden designer, as it positioned him for meeting future clients. Yet the measure of his professional success and the strength, rigor, and originality of his garden theory and practice cannot be accounted for by his favorable place in society alone. More significant is the congruence of his formal education and intellectual, academic, and professional development (as well as the beginning of his garden practice) with the rapid and tumultuous developments in intellectual history in mid-eighteenth-century France. These events, which taken as a whole constitute the achievement of the *siècle des lumières*, are beyond the scope of this discussion, yet themes central to Enlightenment science, epistemology, and metaphysics influenced, and are thus subsequently contained in, Morel's landscape theory.

MOREL'S EDUCATION, GARDEN THEORY, AND THE AGE OF ENLIGHTENMENT

Morel's academic formation and training as an *ingénieur-géographe* and his studies at the Ecole des Ponts et Chaussées must first be considered. It might immediately be noted that in an era when engineering was still the practice of manipulating the constituent parts of nature—earth, wood, water, and rock—it can be claimed that everything technical needed to practice landscape architecture is subsumed in the education and practice of the *ingénieur-géographe*. As such, Morel's training in the

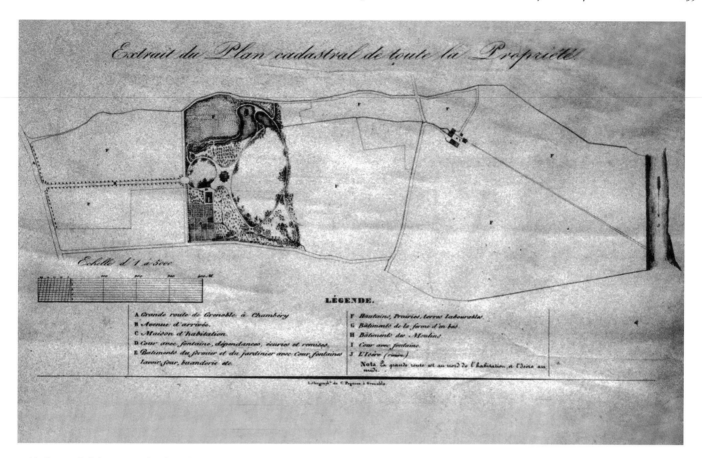

2. (*facing page*). Sales poster for the Château de Saint-Mury, outside of Grenoble. ca. 1840. (*above*) Detail. Private collection.

discipline was of considerable value for his future professional practice. Yet Morel's education and training had theoretical consequences that went well beyond the material and mechanical instruction he received.

The education of a geographical engineer in the eighteenth century was a field apprenticeship (*apprentissage sur le tas*) emphasizing practice over theory.[14] Instruction centered on identifying, interpreting, and recording the on-site components of landscape. This included natural landforms (surface and subsurface geology, topographic inclination, rock formations, etc.); hydrologic features including lakes, streams, springs, and groundwater tables; vegetative cover (forests, meadows, fields) and the knowledge of individual species of trees and plants; as well as a knowledge of the cultural landscape, including productive forests, cultivated fields, and arable land, and the constructed or inhabited landscape of cities, towns, and villages. In brief, one of the first requisites of the *ingénieur-géographe* was to learn how to *read* a landscape.

The second was the ability to analyze and synthesize the disparate elements of the landscape into a coherent whole and the skill to draw it. Such a process, otherwise known as cartography, is in essence the art of representing a landscape while not necessarily recording all its features.[15] Cartography was a major component of the education of an *ingénieur-géographe*. In learning how to read and represent a landscape from its constituent parts, Morel developed an understanding of how landscapes are formed, composed, and structured, all of which conformed to and was determined by natural law. That is, the process of map creation takes in the landscape tree by tree, rock by rock, stream by stream, spot elevation by spot elevation. When all the survey points are connected, the composite picture is not a unitary composition but a diverse field of fragments whose logic is revealed by the natural processes that determined them (an ignorance of which meant design failure). Landscapes revealed themselves not as something derived from an abstract aesthetic regulated by divine proportions, as can be claimed for architectural space, but as its antithesis, something seemingly chaotic yet natu-

3. View of the château of Guiscard. Alexandre de Laborde, *Les Nouveaux jardins de la France*. Paris, 1808. Francis Loeb Library, Harvard Graduate School of Design.

rally ordered. Beneath the infinite *accidents topographiques* of landscape lay the internal mechanisms that create them. Thus Morel's training with the *corps* led directly to an appreciation of the natural processes of landscape formation as well as the natural and nonnatural forces that alter them. He developed a critical understanding of the nature of landscape and an attendant sense of landscape process, which when coupled with the aesthetic imperatives of design, would inform his garden theory and practice. No doubt, his education at the Ecole put his field experience into proper intellectual form, allowing for the application of the techniques, practices, and methods used in recording and evaluating natural landscapes to the art of designing them.

Morel's education, apprenticeship, and early career coincided with a world consumed by the new spirit of natural inquiry, which is the essential hallmark of the Enlightenment. Indeed, Jean Le Rond D'Alembert (1717–83), one of the intellectual spokesmen for the age, wrote in his "Eléments de Philosophie" of 1759 that "a very remarkable change in our ideas is taking place, a change whose rapidity seems to promise an even greater transformation to come."[16] Denis Diderot (1713–84), the other intellectual expeditor of the age, put

it more dramatically: "A new order of things" was being born.[17] One of the most significant aspects of the "new order" that seized the Enlightenment was the methodology of empirical science: observation was the starting point of all inquiry to which principles were to be ascribed and from which natural laws identified. This Newtonian heritage cannot be underestimated as it pervades all intellectual occupation in the eighteenth century, from pure science to philosophy to garden theory.

The new methodological order is evident in one of the great intellectual enterprises of the age, Diderot and D'Alembert's *Encyclopédie*, which began publication in 1751. The encyclopedia's several dozen articles devoted to or related to gardening contribute little to the new genre other than signal that gardening in France died after Le Nôtre and that it is best to look to "our neighbors" across the Channel, that is, the English. More important are the dozens of entries devoted to the natural and physical sciences which are solidly grounded in the presuppositions of Newtonian science[18] and which accept that the observation of nature will reveal the universal laws and order of the material world. Noteworthy is the lengthy article by Nicolas Desmarest (1725–1815) on physical geography—required reading, one would wager, for an *ingénieur-géographe*—whose emphasis on direct observation of the natural world prior to formulating a coherent theory of the earth provided a methodological approach, if not raw material, for Morel's garden theory.[19] Earlier, the Abbé Noël-Antoine Pluche's *Le Spectacle de la Nature*, published between 1732 and 1750, did much to increase the interest and awareness of the physical sciences. Pluche (1688–1761) was not a scientist; however, he was an effective writer and skilled assimilator of knowledge, making it accessible to a general, and generally well-informed, audience. More authoritative and concomitantly more important than Pluche was Georges-Louis Leclerc, comte de Buffon's *Histoire naturelle*, which first appeared in 1749. Buffon (1707–88) continued to issue new volumes throughout the century. Thirty-six volumes appeared during his lifetime—there were forty-four in all—making it the only publishing venture of the eighteenth century to rival the *Encyclopédie* in importance and size.

These texts must be considered because they were widely distributed and the educated public would have acquired their knowledge and ideas of the general view of nature and the image of the natural world through them. In fact, the works by Buffon and Pluche were among the most popular books of the eighteenth century, surpassing Rousseau's *La Nouvelle Héloïse*, or the *Encyclopédie*.[20] Pluche's *Spectacle* had an astonishing fifty-seven French and seventeen English complete or abridged editions, while Buffon's *Histoire* went into reeditions almost from the appearance of volume one. It was translated in part or in its entirety into English, German, Spanish, Italian, Dutch, Portuguese, and Latin.[21] For the garden designers of the day, whose study embraced the natural world, these works would have been essential reading. The spirit, if not content, of these texts found their way into the era's garden theory, in particular that of Morel.

However, perhaps the more telling battleground in eighteenth-century science was not between Cartesian rationalism and Newtonian empiricism, but between the followers of a mechanical understanding of nature and the proponents of the life sciences. Diderot's exuberant declaration in his *De l'Interprétation de la nature* (1754) that geometry was dead was comically inappropriate,[22] but he correctly recognized a decisive turning point in the sciences. His philosophy found scientific voice in Buffon's powerful interpretation of nature in his *Histoire naturelle*. For Buffon, nature was a vital force—"une puissance vive"—that embraces and animates everything, a creative energy of perpetual change, which comes from within, not some static mechanical force measurable from without. Buffon directed his efforts to the newly emerging life and earth sciences. His achievement was to outline their structure independent of the authority of mathematics, a mathematics that could not meet the descriptive requirements of natural history.

Buffon was director of the Jardin des Plantes in Paris for some fifty years and in the process made it "the finest natural history museum in the world."[23] It is there that Antoine de Jussieu's qualitative approach to the natural world established an environmental classification method that included plant structure, behavior, and context, thus foreshadowing the development of ecological thought. It was there that Georges Cuvier and Jean-Baptiste de Lamarck conducted their seminal studies paving the way for the Darwinian revolution. It was in places such as the Jardin des Plantes that the exploration of the natural sciences revealed a complex world in continual transformation, a world understood as a system of organic interaction and mutability of natural phenomena.

The natural sciences were not the only realms of knowledge undergoing fundamental reevaluations. Empiricism infiltrated philosophy and changed the course of metaphysics and aesthetics forever, the greatest casualty being classicist reason yielding to sentiment and sensation. Through a tangled confluence of philosophical and aesthetic theories, linking and drawing from John Locke to the Abbé Condillac, from Roger de Piles and Abbé du Bos to Edmund Burke, the foundation was set for the assault on reason; by mid-century it was fully in place. Edmund Burke's *Philosophical Enquiry into the Origins of Our Ideas of the Sublime and the Beautiful* (1757; translated into French in 1765) is not about gardening, yet its influence on the aesthetics of sensibility was as nurturing for a new style as spring rain. His exploration of the senses and how they are produced, affected, and controlled released beauty from the hegemony of classical proportions, thus providing a theoretical structure for the new way of gardening. Burke's philosophy gave further authority to the privileging of emotion over reason, something Roger de Piles had voiced in his prescient *Cours de peinture* of 1708.

The development of an environmental scientific outlook on the natural world and a new sensationist metaphysics coincided with the rise of a new landscape gardening aesthetic. This cannot be a coincidence, as gardening, an art form so intrinsically tied to both culture and nature, cannot escape fundamental shifts in the intellectual environment that nurtures and sustains it. The Enlightenment legacy of changes in aesthetics, metaphysics, and especially in the idea of nature and the understanding of the natural world (not to mention social, political, and economic developments) almost by default insured that the art of landscape design would undergo dramatic change, and it certainly did. Yet it was not until the 1770s that the practice of the new garden style was given theoretical formulation. That decade, as Michel Baridon has noted in this volume, saw the remarkable publication of no less than eight texts devoted to the new genre. Henceforth garden theory would no longer be the same.

By the time Morel published his *Théorie des jardins* in 1776, at least four significant treatises on the new genre of gardening had been published. Thomas Whately inaugurated the fray with his *Observations on Modern Gardening*, first published in 1770, going into a second edition in the same year. It can rightfully be considered the first theoretical work on the natural style of gardening. François-de-Paule Latapie, a protégé of Montesquieu, quickly translated Whately into French the following year and included a lengthy introduction; in addition to providing large excerpts of William Chambers's 1757 text, "Art of Laying out Gardens Among the Chinese," he presented a historical perspective for the new gardening genre, or one might say he provided a French perspective on the genre.[24] It was not until 1774 with the appearance of Claude-Henri Watelet's *Essay sur les jardins* that a Frenchman published a treatise on the new gardening. Antoine-Nicolas Duchesne followed in 1775 with his *Sur la formation des jardins* (second edition, 1779). One year after Morel's treatise, René-Louis de Girardin published his *De la composition des paysages*. The first of five volumes of C. C. L. Hirschfeld's *Theorie der Gartenkunst* was published simultaneously in German and French in 1779 with the remaining volumes published by 1785.[25] Not to be excluded, and more closely aligned with each other than those texts just mentioned, were William Chambers's *Dissertation on Oriental Gardening* of 1772, published simultaneously in English and French, and Louis Carrogis de Carmontelle's *Jardin de Monceau*, published in 1779. Additionally, there was Georges-Louis Le Rouge's comprehensive, multivolume series, *Jardins anglo-chinois à la mode*, issued between 1776 and 1788. Le Rouge's series was not an original, theoretical work but is important for the numerous plates of gardens in the new genre

that it contained,[26] as well for reprinting the entire text of Chambers's essay on Chinese gardens of 1757.

The publication of these texts within ten years is suggestive of an important turning point in landscape history. Indeed, these texts constitute the theoretical foundations of the new discipline. While they are all tethered to some previous garden heritage, there is no mistaking the new, original, and wholly self-contained quality of the works. They incorporate to varying degrees the changes in aesthetics, philosophy, and natural science of the age. For the most part, they are devoid of plans, give few prescriptions, contain no plant lists, and are heavily weighted by pure landscape description in a direct appeal to the imagination. Perhaps most interesting, and unprecedented for garden theory literature, is that they look beyond the traditional garden wall and take in a view rich in pleasure, utility, industry, and ruin. We have arrived at a milestone in the history of garden theory, so much so that the garden is eclipsed by landscape, and gardening by a new entity—landscape architecture.

The works that had previously constituted garden theory—notably Antoine-Joseph Dézallier d'Argenville's *Théorie et pratique du jardinage* (first published in 1709 and reissued in enlarged editions throughout the century), Stephen Switzer's *Ichnographia Rustica* (1718), or Batty Langley's *New Principles of Gardening* (1725)—are now replaced by a succession of theoretically inclined texts that take nature and sentiment as their core; displacing horticulture or architectural design theory from their practice. What distinguishes the new texts as much as the new genre they explore is the sense of knowing that they are in utterly new theoretical territory. To stress the point, it is only worth noting that each author uses a different name to call the person who is to design the new garden genre. No author was satisfied with *jardinier*, but there was no consensus on a term to use. All the French authors used different terms, from Girardin's "artist" to Duchenes's "formateur." Morel was the most emphatic that *jardinier* was not the correct term, but offered no alternative. In his second edition (1802) he adds a footnote to lament that there was still no proper term for the person who designs in the new genre.[27] By 1804, however, he settled on *architecte-paysagiste*, a term with stronger design connotations than Humphry Repton's "landscape gardener."[28]

Most authors, and in particular Morel (and Chambers), agreed, however, that the architect—the traditional designer of gardens—was not ade-

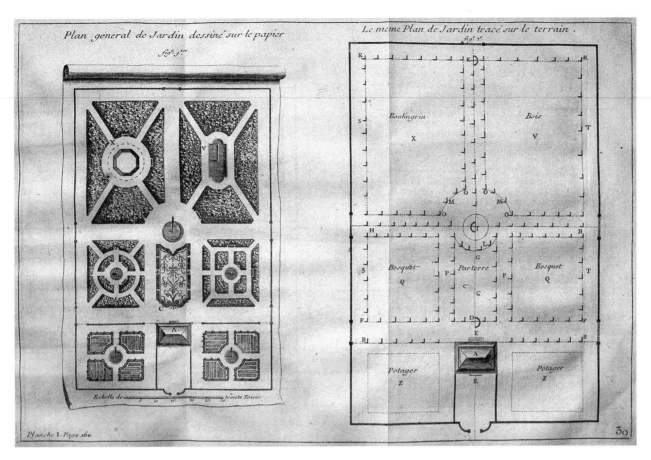

4. Designing on paper; implementation on the ground. Antoine-Joseph Dézallier d'Argenville, *La Théorie et la Pratique du Jardinage*. 4th ed. (Paris, 1749). Francis Loeb Library, Harvard Graduate School of Design.

quate for designing in the new genre. Garden design until the eighteenth century was predicated on the selected arrangement of regular geometries drawn on flat surfaces in accordance with the rules of proportion, perspective, and taste (fig. 4). Translating these designs into the field posed no problem as long as the ground was itself flat, whether a horizontal or inclined plane. Once the topography was to respect or emulate a "natural" condition, as required by the new gardening theory, designs of regular shapes were ill suited to the new site conditions. And once symmetry and formal arrangements were banned, as was also dictated by the new genre, garden designers faced a serious challenge. Architectural theory, such as found in Blondel's *Cours d'architecture*, that subsumed garden design was confounded by the requirements of the new genre.[29] Faced with a rapidly transforming gardening philosophy, architecture's inability to bend theory to practice resulted in its as yet unnamed replacement. The vacuum created by the flight—or expulsion—of the architect from

the garden was filled by an entirely new occupational entity still in the process of defining itself. Despite his architectural knowledge, it is not surprising that Morel would rely on his science and engineering training in charting the new course of garden theory.

The new garden theory immediately found resonance in related fields and was quickly recognized for its innovation. Ironically, it was enormously influential on architectural theory. Nicolas le Camus de Mézières dedicated his important book *Le génie de l'architecture; ou, L'analogie de cet art avec nos sensations* (The genius of architecture, or, The analogy of that art with our sensations) of 1780 to Watelet. Le Camus's thesis, that the materials of structure can be arranged and manipulated in certain ways to arouse the senses, owes much to Condillac, although the philosopher is nowhere mentioned in his book. Nor is Morel, who, more so than Watelet, is the more probable source of Le Camus's evocative description of how the light and shade of architecture can influence the senses.[30]

The environmental understanding of the new theory was given implicit recognition. Whately's *Observations* received a lengthy, two-issue review in Abbé Rozier's *Journal de physique*, the most prestigious scientific periodical of its day.[31] Whately's book, though groundbreaking, was not as rigorously scientific as Morel's *Théorie*, one review of which proclaimed that until then there had been the art of gardening, now there was its science.[32] The reviewer was indeed right, for of all the garden theory books, with the sole exception of Duchesne's opuscule, Morel alone deftly insinuates scientific knowledge and understanding of the natural world into his theory. One only need compare his treatment of landforms with that of his closest rival—Thomas Whately. The Englishman's book, good as it is (Morel modestly cites it as the best of the genre), states that landform is concave, convex, or flat—purely descriptive discussion straight out of painting theory. Morel's chapter on landform begins with the water cycle, stressing the perpetual rhythm of evapotranspiration. Rain, the liquid state of the cycle, is, short of catastrophic events, the primary agent in the modeling of natural topography. Morel's natural science lesson is lifted directly from Buffon's essay on the "Theory of the Earth" in volume one of his *Histoire naturelle*, yet his incorporation of this bit of natural understanding is entirely his own. Likewise, and less abstract, is Morel's discussion of islands—a subject hardly touched upon by Whately or any other writer. Morel admits two different types of islands for garden design: an island located within a lake and an island located in a river. Depending on location, each island will have a different shape resulting from the dynamic conditions that formed it. An island in a lake is the result of a valley being flooded; the island thus formed can take on any configuration. However, an island in a river is determined by the dynamics of the moving water; it must conform to the hydromechanics of the river's flow.[33] No other garden text of the eighteenth century included such a discussion.[34]

Morel's *Théorie* is not confined to principles of physical geography. Of great interest is his discussion concerning abandoned fields. If left to themselves, they will eventually become filled with grasses and trees in a distribution dictated by "the laws of nature." His discussion of the vegetative growth associations in mountain and valley landscapes is insightful and consistent with ecosystem succession distributions. Morel is close to formulating a system of plant community associations; what these passages suggest, in fact, is his careful observation of the vegetation at a given site and his understanding that plant distributions conform to natural law.

The incorporation of scientific principles and observations of nature drawn from texts on natural history of the mid-eighteenth century provides specific evidence of Morel's sources, but as such it does not, on its own, instance a broader theoretical framework grounded in the epistemology of the era. More telling is his calling landscape (*pays*) a "great machine," or his invocation of the Newtonian mantra "action and reaction." Such terminology is redolent of the mechanistic vocabulary of *lumières*. Yet, as much as Newtonian empiricism informs his methodology, it is from Buffon that he derives the sensibility of an organically driven, naturally organized universe. It is Buffon who puts into proper intellectual form the understanding of the natural landscape that Morel had experienced firsthand as an *ingénieur-géographe*. The visible chaos of the natural world is only apparent, not real. Rather, the apprehensible world is the result of natural processes, whose underlying principles conform to natural law.[35] Armed with such an understanding, Morel shaped his garden theory in conformance with the laws of nature.

Thus the foundation of Morel's theory is based on the notion that nature is a process the result of which is the landscape we see. He understood that the interrelation of natural forms was central to viewing the world as a dynamic environment of dependent systems. Landscapes were products of that system of dependencies, the understanding of whose internal laws must replace the normative characteristics of picturesque aesthetics as the object of landscape design. Utilizing the new methodological order that distinguishes eighteenth-century thought, Morel identified the formative constituents of landscape (hydrology, geology, soil science, and arboriculture) and maintained that an understanding of the dynamics of the natural world must guide, if not dictate, landscape design. To design a landscape effectively, one must know these laws and never circumvent them. Whately may describe a landscape feature, but Morel sees it as a product of natural process. Two centuries before it would become fashionable, Morel had adumbrated a method of designing with nature.

Morel puts his interpretation of nature's laws to the service of the four genres that he posits as the components of designed landscapes: *le pays, le parc, le Jardin proprement dit*, and *la ferme*.[36] He assigns each genre its own distinctive character: variety for the *pays*; nobility for the *parc*; elegance for the *Jardin proprement dit*; simplicity for the farm. Each has its own relative size, with the *pays* being the largest; and the *Jardin proprement dit* the smallest, and each has its own relative style. Morel admits to historical forces and social stratification of society as the determinants of the four genres; that is, the social rank and wealth of individuals will determine the kind of garden appropriate to their social status. The grand seigneur would have his château and *parc*; the lover of luxury, his *Jardin proprement dit*, while the man of taste would find his Elysium in the *pays*. The *ferme* is reserved for those seeking revenue.[37] Because of their differing size and scale, and their relation to society, taken successively the genres constitute, and indeed represent, the cultural (designed) landscape, in his case, the landscape of France. Once it is determined what the appropriate genre shall be, it is the designer's responsibility to create the requisite landscape character. This is not easily done if the site given does not itself have the potential for that particular genre, or, in other words, the desired effect cannot be achieved if the site is contrary to the genre's character. Character can be enhanced, never created. This implies that the designer must have a sufficient understanding of natural laws to recognize the constraints of individual sites in order to satisfy the requirements of the garden genre intended to be designed. The designer must assess the potential of the site to be altered and manipulated to the degree necessary for the desired design effects without destroying the essential character of the site. To do this one must know and understand the natural processes that created the landscape initially.

While the genres are a social as well as design imperative, Morel's treatment of them is much influenced by the natural philosophy of the day. He has defined them as individual components but implies that, taken as a whole, they constitute the entire cultural landscape. He writes that with the exception of the farm, the genres are not sufficiently distinct that they cannot merge ("se rapprocher"). They are flexible, proximate notions, not static. The *pays* and *parc* may resemble each other, especially at their extremities; likewise the *parc* and *Jardin*. The landscape he images locates the *Jardin proprement dit*, nearest to the house, with the *parc* following and the *pays* beyond that, and, still further, the natural landscape. The *ferme* is somewhere in the view.[38] With decreasing evidence of human intervention, the genres, when taken successively, form a seamless transition from house to horizon. This scenario is consistent with an essential problem of landscape architecture—how to design the zone between man and nature. In conformance with the scientific naturalism of Buffon and the era, Morel's answer is, apparently, "as naturally as possible, as progressively as possible in accordance with the laws of nature."[39]

MOREL'S GARDEN PRACTICE

While Morel's treatise remains the single most important source of his garden theory, a study of his practice faces severe limitations, as there are too few remaining documents and extant landscapes attributable to him for a comprehensive investigation.[40] Furthermore, those that do survive all date from the last decade of his life, thus limiting the source material to what must be considered mature work. Consequently, corroboration of his theory and practice can be investigated only cursorily, and a comparative study of his landscape approach through time is not possible. Nonetheless, what remains provides enough information for analysis and discussion in broad terms, and on occasion indicates solutions to site-specific problems. Together, they are suggestive of his theoretical intentions with respect to designing a garden around an existing structure, connecting the two and integrating both into a broader landscape, while at the same time adjusting each design to the site conditions. What the drawings unequivocally demonstrate, however, is his complete command of designing in the new genre. Each plan exhibits a mastery of spatial composition, a strong authority of execution, and a clear sense of intent.

Garden plans by Morel survive for the châteaus of Heudicourt (Eure), Arcelot (Côte d'Or), and Saint-Trys (Rhône), as do the gardens themselves.[41] Several similarities and differences distinguish each plan and property. All had a preexisting château and a history of landscape design interventions prior to Morel's engagement. Because of the centrality of the château at each site, and the respective size of each property, all of these gardens are of the *parc* genre.[42] Morel exploited site-specific constraints and opportunities distinct to each property and solved physical as well as design-related problems in each design. No two sites are similar in topography, and each has different climatic, hydrologic, and geologic circumstances. Although only four plans are available for scrutiny, they, along with secondary source material, such as cadastral plans, and visits to the remains of other garden sites,[43] allow for the identification of recurring design tropes. Some are clearly

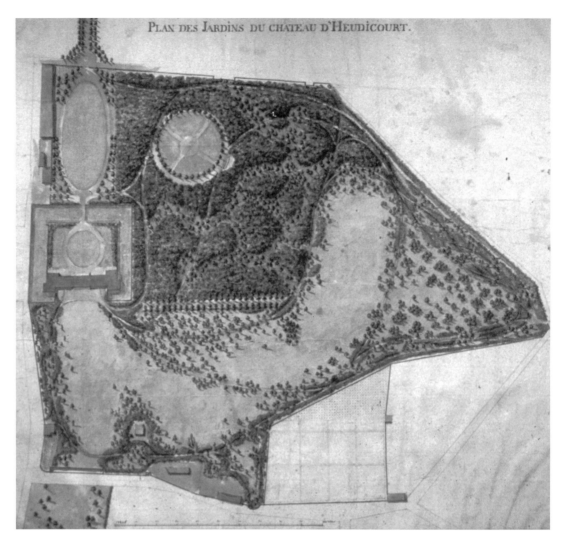

5. Château d'Heudicourt (Eure). Jean-Marie Morel, plan, ca. 1805. Reprinted with the permission of the Château d'Heudicourt.

consistent with the era's natural style of gardening, such as Brownian "clumps." Others are more personal and, significantly, are represented in his plans, in his book, as well as in the field. There is perhaps too little direct evidence to distinguish a Morel "signature," yet some identifiable characteristics can be noted in his landscape approach.

The château d'Heudicourt dates from the Renaissance. Martin-Roch-Xavier, comte Estève, *trésorier général* under Napoleon, bought the property in 1804 and shortly thereafter brought in Morel (fig. 5). Morel's design demonstrates a clear, strong, and unambiguous execution of spatial relationships, even while preserving some of the more regular garden elements, for example, the pinwheel motif. The broad sweep left of the open lawn (on the garden side of the *corps de logis*) is dictated by the site

restrictions, yet is an exceptionally well-executed spatial gesture that allows for transition and continuity to the rest of the park. To further enhance the communication of dwelling with garden, Morel filled in the château's moat on the garden side.[44] The treatment of the woods at Heudicourt exhibits an important feature of Morel's theory: it recalls an evocative passage from his book where he writes of the heightened sensations aroused when passing through the contrast of light and shade in a woodland.[45] At Heudicourt, he designed such a landscape event (fig. 6). The alternating thick, heavily planted areas with loose assemblages of trees allow for contrasting intensities of light to penetrate through the woodland canopy, thus providing for the effect Morel is seeking. He has combined this plantation with a path system for a less

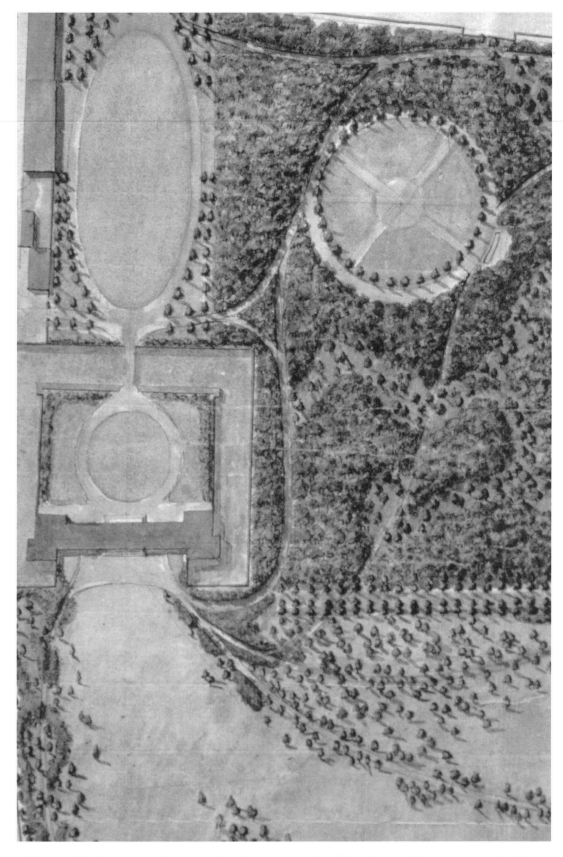

6. Château d'Heudicourt (Eure). Jean-Marie Morel, plan, ca. 1805 (detail). Reprinted with the permission of the Château d'Heudicourt.

7. Château d'Heudicourt. (Eure), existing cedar of Lebanon. Photo by J. Disponzio.

structured promenade through the property. The approach to the château displays another aspect of Morel's theory. Here the public façade of the residence demands a more formal design, which he has executed with an elongated oval forecourt followed by a circular entrance. Not visible in the plan but remaining in the garden are three mature specimen cedar of Lebanon trees.[46] Morel is known to have liked the species. One cedar is located just outside the *corps de logis*, on the garden side; the other two are found at the terminal points of site lines, as one progresses into the *parc*. Morel has used the trees to attract and subsequently draw the visitor into the garden (fig. 7).[47] Overall, Morel's plan for the

château d'Heudicourt demonstrates his mastery of the new genre with carefully designed sequencing of spaces that moves from approach and entry to the château proper, and on through it into the far reaches of the property. The unencumbered sweep of the horizontal plan is matched by Morel's eliminating vertical (architectural) obstacles to movement throughout the garden. The deft sweep of the design from the *corps de logis* into the depths of the property is as ingenious as it is stunning in its execution. The carefully modulated forest plantation not only provides the variety of a woodland experience, but functions as a design element separating the more formalized entrance sequence and

8. Château de Saint-Trys. (Rhône). Curten, plan, 1806. Copyright Château de Saint-Trys.

château forecourt from the remainder of the park. Overall, not only is Heudicourt well executed, but its logic is entirely legible, its coherence total, and its mastery of spatial forms complete.

The *parc* of the château of Saint-Trys, north of Lyon, is less well preserved, but it is the only property for which two plans by Morel exist. The residence, largely reconstructed in the nineteenth century, occupies a prominent position on a rise overlooking the Saône valley. Saint-Trys's early nineteenth-century owner, Jean-Baptiste Giraud de Saint-Trys, called upon the Lyonnais landscape gardener Curten to design a garden in the new genre (fig. 8). His plan, dated 1806, is a beautiful example of early nineteenth-century *anglois-chinois* style. For unknown reasons, Curten's plan was superseded by Morel's, who produced two similar plans for the property, both dating from 1807–8 (fig. 9). The distinguishing feature of Morel's plan is the lawn in front of the château. It works with the

rapidly descending topography to exploit the dramatic view of the Saône valley landscape. With no moat surrounding the château, Morel has brought the lawn directly to its garden façade, creating an on-grade link between the two. The unmistakable Morel treatment of the woods is even more legible at Saint-Trys, displaying the interplay of light and shade so integral to his garden theory. As at Heudicourt, Morel's design for the entrance to the château calls for regular geometrical elements—a design concession to the more formal aspects of entry to and arrival at a residence.

Perhaps the best-conserved Morel landscape is that of the château d'Arcelot near Dijon. It graces one of the more splendid eighteenth-century châteaus of Burgundy (fig. 10).[48] Morel was associated with Arcelot from as early as the 1790s, but his plan for the property dates from his more active participation with the park between 1800 and 1806 (fig. 11). His plan makes the most of a gently un-

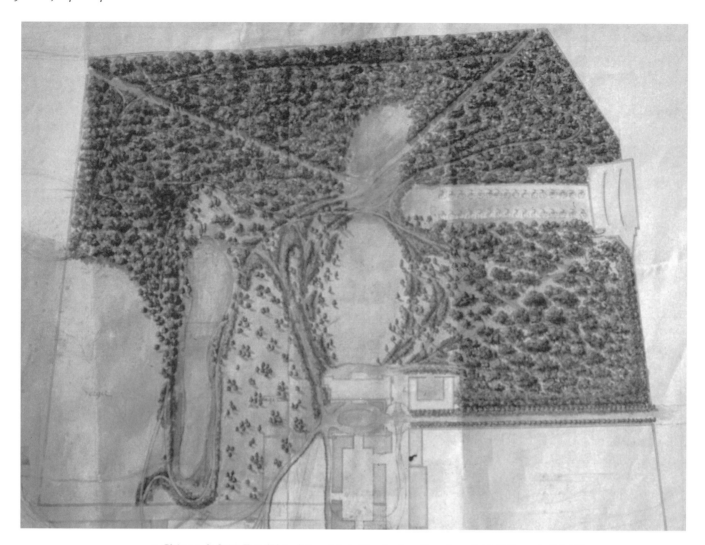

9. Château de Saint-Trys (Rhône). Jean-Marie Morel, plan, 1807. Copyright Château de Saint-Trys.

dulating site with a large wetland running through its middle. On the garden side, the design's leftward turn follows the natural contours of the property, placing the streambed roughly at its lowest point, thus making a drainage feature into a visually pleasing backbone of the design. The approach to the château displays the standard Morel treatment of public façades. While the plan for Arcelot is perhaps less dramatic than that for Heudicourt, it is no less accomplished. It makes advantageous use of the site and design constraints and demonstrates clear intentions.

The park at Arcelot still very much conserves the essence of a Morel landscape (fig. 12). It is simple yet majestic, neither tedious in detail nor boring in monotony. The sky is as important as the landscape. The lawn comes directly to the château; there is an effortless flow of space between house and nature.

No single element stands apart from the rest; all are equally important. It is a design that respects the natural landscape and works with it to suppress the hand of man; as such it is an image of a landscape true to the principles of Morel's theory.

TOWARD A LANDSCAPE ARCHITECTURE

In this essay I have introduced Jean-Marie Morel as a focus for a broader discussion of historical developments in eighteenth-century landscape history. Throughout that century, gardening underwent fundamental changes that resulted in its eclipse by a new discipline—landscape architecture. The origins of landscape architecture can be better appreciated by reviewing the set of events that consti-

10. Château d'Arcelot (Côte-d'Or). Thomas Dumorey, architect: garden façade, ca. 1760s. Photo by J. Disponzio.

tuted its professional development. Among these were the establishment of a new designed landscape typology and the creation of a new body of knowledge related to it; new developments in techniques and mechanical practices; recognition that the discipline and its practitioners are different from its predecessors; the consequent naming of the discipline and its practitioners (as well as having practitioners); and the rise of an economic class to sustain the discipline (of which little has been said in this essay).[49] All of these occurred or were put into place by the early nineteenth century.

Morel, as theorist and practitioner, was but the most convincing voice in the chorus of change. By grounding his theory in the laws of nature, he removed gardening from the realm of man and set it on a course from which, for better or worse, there was no turning back.[50]

But the lesson here, perhaps, is not about professional origins, landscape architecture, or even Jean-Marie Morel. Ernst Cassirer suggests that the legacy of the Enlightenment is its fascination with the activity and process of its new intellectual force, rather than with the creations brought forth by that activity.[51] Accordingly, one might submit that the natural style of gardening is less the achievement of the Enlightenment than a field in which the new way of thinking about and creating landscape unfolded. It was used, so to speak, in the service of a new theory. As all art forms, it would be eclipsed, yet in its wake neither gardening nor the gardener would ever be the same.

APPENDIX: NOTE ON *ARCHITECTE-PAYSAGISTE* AND LANDSCAPE ARCHITECTURE

The term *architecte-paysagiste* first appeared attached to Jean-Marie Morel's name in the *Almanach de Lyon* of 1804. In the previous year's *Almanach*, Morel was listed as *architecte et paysagiste*. Because

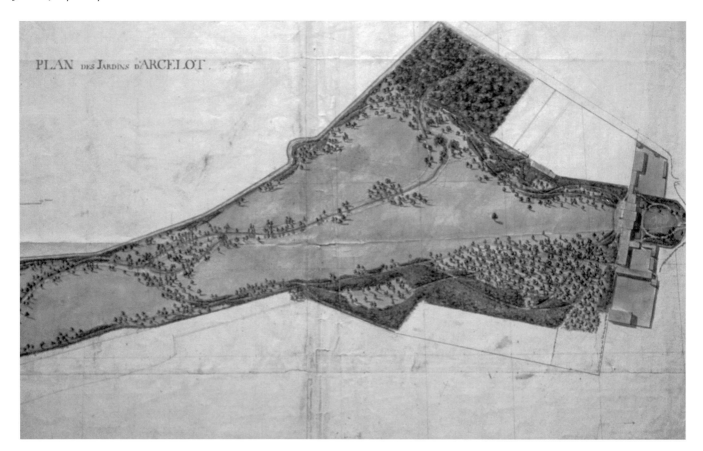

11. Château d'Arcelot (Côte-d'Or). Jean-Marie Morel, plan, ca. 1805. By permission of the Château d'Arcelot.

of his known preoccupation with the proper terminology for the new design professional there is sufficient reason to believe that Morel, not the editors of the *Almanach*, replaced the *et* with the hyphen. Further evidence of such a self-designation is found in the obituaries that announced Morel's death: he was referred to as an *architecte-paysagiste*, in both the *Journal de Lyon* and the *Moniteur Universel*, as well as in a book about Lyon and its notable citizens, *Lettres à ma fille*, by J. B. D. Madaze d'Avèze (Lyon, 1810). The Academy of Sciences, Belles-Lettres, and Arts of Lyon mourned their deceased member, "M. Morel, *architecte-paysagiste*" in its first meeting following his death. And some fifteen years later, a notice on his life and work published in the *Archives historiques et statistiques du département du Rhône* (Lyon, 1825) began by saying: "Suivant le jugement du chantre des jardins, J.-M. Morel est un architecte paysagiste." Such a consistent association of the term with Morel seems to indicate a self-identification that was clearly understood, as the term had little, if any, currency in the early nineteenth century. Yet even referring to him as an *architecte et paysagiste* seems curious. While

Morel was known as an architect, exclusively being referred to as such throughout his career, he was seldom, if at all, called a *paysagiste*, which at the beginning of the nineteenth century still meant a painter of landscapes. Morel himself used the term *paysagiste* only in its painterly connotation. (Two paintings by Morel survive, each a landscape scene of Mousseau at Evry. They are currently in the collection of the Musée de l'Ile-de-France.) Only through the course of the nineteenth century did the word take on the added meaning of landscape designer. Nonetheless, the coupling of *architecte* and *paysagiste* is unprecedented, and there is every reason to believe that the neologism is Morel's.

It is worth noting that at the time of Morel's death the nomenclature of natural gardening was, to say the least, still quite fluid, no doubt a reflection of the newness of the genre. To distinguish *jardinage* (gardening of yore) and *jardinier* (gardener of yore) from what is meant by the new genre and its practitioner, Vicomte de Viart in his *Le jardiniste moderne* of 1827 suggested *jardinique* for the art of gardening (the profession) and *jardiniste* for the artist (the professional). *Jardiniste* was not unknown at the time,

12. Château d'Arcelot (Côte-d'Or). General view of the park today. Photo by J. Disponzio.

but its provenance dates to Horace Walpole who had suggested it to the duc de Nivernois in a letter of 1785. Gabriel Thouin was identified as a "jardinier et architecte de jardins" in the *Almanach du bon jardinier* of 1808, while his preferred usage at the Jardins des Plantes was *jardins paysagistes* for the gardens and *jardiniers paysagistes* for garden designers. Meanwhile, Curten of Lyon, author of *Essai sur les jardins* (1807), liked neither *jardin*, for the new garden, nor *jardinier*, for the garden designer. Of particular note is his use of *architecte paysagiste* in a discussion of the similarities between the garden designer and the *peintre en paysage*. Curten's usage of *architecte paysagiste*—apparently for the first time in a text on gardening—without any discussion of its provenance suggests some familiarity with the term, possibly stemming from a personal acquaintanceship with Morel, as both were from Lyon, and Curten is known to have worked at two, if not more, gardens where Morel replaced him. Curiously, however, Curten referred to himself as *in-génieur des jardins* or *architecte de jardin* and sometimes both. While the French were still debating nomenclature, the English had settled on Humphry Repton's *landscape gardener* as early as 1790, and retained the usage. (Not without quarrel, however: Price never liked the term.)

The coupling of "landscape" with "architecture" in English first appeared in a book title, *On the Landscape Architecture of the Great Painters of Italy*, published by Gilbert L. Meason in 1828. The book had nothing to do with landscape architecture, but rather with the architecture in landscape paintings of Italy. J. C. Loudon used the two words together, with presumably more specific hortulan signification, in his edition of Repton's writings, under the title *The Landscape Gardening and Landscape Architecture of the Late Humphry Repton, Esq.* published in 1840, yet nowhere in the work is the expression discussed or indeed referred to again.

Landscape architect, as it is understood today, was coined by Frederick Law Olmsted and Calvert

Vaux sometime in the early 1860s, although neither man liked the term. However, Henry H. Elliott appears to have first used it as early as 1860 in a letter to Olmsted and Vaux, designating them as the "Landscape Architects & Designers" for the commission to lay out the parks of Manhattan's northernmost sector. Although the American term was not neglected (H. W. S. Cleveland added "Landscape Architect" to his name in his book, *A Few Hints on Landscape Gardening in the West* of 1871), by the end of the century a curious twist of garden history had occurred: the term had acquired French roots. Armand Péan's *L'Architecte-Paysagiste*, published in 1886, seems to be the first book title to use the coupling with its present professional meaning, although Edouard André identified himself as "*architecte-paysagiste*" on the title page of his book, *L'Art des jardins.* (1879). Perhaps because of these French works, Mrs. Schuyler van Rensselaer, in her book *Art Out-of-Doors* (1893), wrote of landscape architecture that "French usage supports this term." William Robinson was more characteristically blunt when he simply dismissed the professional title landscape architect as "a stupid term of French origin" in *The English Flower Garden* (tenth edition, 1906). Either Robinson was ignorant of the Olmsted-Vaux history, or he had information concerning French origins which has up to now escaped scrutiny.

Writing in 1911, Stephen Child, an early Fellow of the American Society of Landscape Architects (est. 1899), supported Olmsted's term and usage of landscape architect by noting that "French landscape designers had already adopted this term, their phrase, *architecte paysagiste*, meaning simply landscape architect." Not only does Child indicate a French origin, but he antedates it to that of Olmsted and Vaux (S. Child, *Landscape Architecture: A Definition and a Resume of Its Past and Present*, Chicago, 1911). Liberty Hyde Bailey's *Standard Cyclopedia of Horticulture* (1914–17 edition) succinctly labels landscape architecture "the French term for the profession," although he does give Olmsted and Vaux their due. Sometime between Bailey's work and *The Garden Dictionary* (1936, ed. Norman Taylor), the French connection was dropped. Without feeling the obligation for historical discussion, the *Dictionary* simply defines landscape architecture as "the art of design by which grounds are arranged for practical and aesthetic enjoyment," and merely notes that the term *landscape architect* "supplanted, in America, the older term Landscape Gardener." Thus, with this omission of origins or national as-

sociations, both the profession and the professional had come into their own.

Notes

1. *Gazette nationale ou Le Moniteur Universel*, no. 289, Tuesday, 16 October 1810; *Le Journal de Lyon et du Département du Rhône*, 11 October 1810.

2. The use of "natural or picturesque" is intended to distinguish the gardening style under discussion from the broader stylistic rubric of "English gardening style." This is in keeping with French garden historiography, as French writers of the eighteenth and early nineteenth centuries were at pains to refer to an "English" gardening style on their soil. Their use of *jardin anglais* or *jardin anglo-chinois* was more often than not pejorative and, in the case of the latter, meant to distance English origins from the style. Morel's preferred term was *jardins de la nature*. "Picturesque style" is an acceptable alternative, at least in France, as it did not risk being caught up in the Picturesque controversy of the late eighteenth century, which seems to have had little impact on the French.

3. The natural style of gardening had already infiltrated France by mid-century, but its position as the most widely preferred garden style was not solidified until some decades later. Furthermore, the early garden designs (in both France and England) demonstrate little mastery of the new genre with respect to the creation of coherent, spatially conscious designs. For reasons argued in the text, the 1770s might be considered the "decade" of the natural style in France, and as will be demonstrated, Morel was one of the most gifted designers of the new genre.

4. He was immortalized by Delille in his poem *Les jardins: Poëme*, praising his "éloquente voix" and calling his book *Théorie des jardins*, "charmante."

5. There is only one published work on Morel, Savalète de Fortair's *Discours sur la vie et des œuvres de Jean-Marie Morel* (Paris, 1813). It was first delivered as a eulogy at the Academy of Lyon in 1811. Little is known about Fortair; he was an architect from Charente-Inférieur (Charente-Maritime) and an aide-de-camp to the celebrated French general and noted expatriate Charles-François Dumouriez (1739–1823). The *Discours* is written with a sympathy for and sense of firsthand knowledge of Morel's life and work, but a direct link between Fortair and Morel is yet to be established. Caution must be taken with Fortair's *Discours*, as much of it is suspect, especially the dates. Of importance, however, is a list of gardens purportedly by Morel which Fortair included in the work. The *Discours* is hard to come by; the author thanks Professor Robin Middleton for permission to review his copy.

Elizabeth Cereghini recently published an article, "Jean-Marie Morel: 'Patriarch des jardins'" (*Revue de l'art*, 129 [2000–3]: 77–87) drawn from her unpublished dissertation on Morel, "Jean-Marie Morel: Un architetto paesaggista nella Francia del XVIII secolo" (Institute Universitaire d'Architecture de Venise, 1991). Catherine Berthoux in her unpublished M.A. thesis, "Jean-Marie Morel et les jardins de la nature" (Université de Bourgogne, Dijon, 1987), was the first to establish the essential facts of Morel's early life in Lyon. The information contained herein is based on the author's dissertation on Morel, "The Garden Theory and Landscape Practice of Jean-Marie Morel" (Columbia University, 2000).

6. There is still only one book in English devoted to the natural style of gardening in France, Dora Wiebenson's *The Picturesque Garden in France* (Princeton: Princeton University Press, 1978). Morel, Wiebenson writes: "adds no new material to our knowledge of French garden theory" (76). The French have not ignored the style, but have seldom given it serious scholastic attention until the important exhibition *Jardins en France* of 1977, which spurred interest in the heritage of the French picturesque. Ernest de Ganay is rightfully considered a major figure in the resurrection of the French picturesque, yet he was preceded at the beginning of the twentieth century by Albert Maumené, whose little-known series of articles on French garden history in his journal, *La Vie à la Campagne*, are still worth reading. See Y. Malecot, ed., *Jardins en France, 1720–1820* (Paris: Caisse Nationale des Monuments Historiques et des Sites, 1977). For de Ganay and Maumené see bibliography.

7. Morel published at least two other works: *Tableau dendrologique contenant la liste des plantes ligneuses, indigènes et exotiques acclimates* . . . [Lyon] an VIII (1800; 2nd ed., 1801), which was appended to the second edition of his *Théorie*; and "Mémoire sur la théorie des eaux fluentes, appliquée au cours du Rhône," *Archives histoiriques et statistiques du Rhône* (Lyon, 1825). Fortair attributes to him a *mémoire* on musical composition, and he is known to have left an unfinished treatise on rural architecture. Neither work has been located. It is very unlikely that he is the author of a work *L'Art de distribuer les jardins, suivant l'usage des Chinois* (London, 1757), a work attributed to him by Fortair. Unfortunately all subsequent biographical entries and notices of Morel's life include it. There is no evidence whatsoever that Morel is the author of such a work. Of note is its similarity to the essay by William Chambers, "Of the Art of Laying out Gardens Among the Chinese," which appeared in English and French in his *Designs of Chinese Buildings . . .*, published in 1757, but there is no evidence that Morel is responsible for the French translation.

8. Lyon's bourgeois *aristocratie mercantile* were, at best ambivalent toward the Revolution. In the spring of 1793 the city began a counterrevolution which was severely and savagely crushed by fall. The Morel brothers were accused of not showing sufficient republican convictions, as well as corruption, and summarily arrested, imprisoned and narrowly escaped death.

9. The author's catalogue of Morel's known works is published in *Studies in the History of Gardens and Designed Landscapes*, 21, nos. 3–4 (2001). Equally scarce are his archives. Only five garden drawings in his hand are known, all dating from the last decade of his life: one each for the château of Arcelot (Côte d'Or), the château of Champgrenon (Sadne-et-Loire), and the château of Heudicourt (Eure); two for the château of Saint-Trys (Rhône). Several of his *mémoires* delivered at Lyon's Academy of Science, Belles-Lettres, and Arts and the Society of Agriculture are preserved in manuscript form.

10. Morel's name is given a common misspelling; "Bertaud" refers to Louis-Martin Berthault (1771–1823), Napoleon's landscape architect who is often found in the shadow of Morel. Berthault succeeded Morel at St.-Leu–Taverny, residence of Queen Hortense.

11. Morel must have developed a close friendship with Blondel, as he was given the honor of being designated *parrain* (godfather) to Blondel's second son, Jean-Baptiste Blondel (1764–1825). Morel saw to the education and upbringing of Blondel *fils* after the death of his mother in 1776.

12. Fortair mentions that Conti put Morel to work immediately on transforming his gardens at the *châtellenie* of Isle-Adam, north of Paris, no doubt undoing the formal garden designed by Pierre Contant d'Ivry between 1740 and 1745.

13. Through an introduction from the Abbé Morellet, Morel was hosted by William Pette, the second earl of Shelburne (1737–1805) at Bowood in 1783. While in England, Morel visited Brown's work at Blenheim, as well as Kew, Stourhead, Wilton, and the Leasowes, among others. J.-M. Morel, *Théorie des jardins* (Paris: Chez Panckouke, 1802); preface to 2nd ed., pp. cxiv–cxxviii; Abbé André Morellet, *Lettres d'André Morellet*, ed. D. Medlin, Jean-Claude David, and Paul Leclerc, vol. 1 (Oxford: Oxford University Press, 1991).

14. For a concise discussion of the education of an *ingénieur-géographe* see François de Dainville, "Enseignement des 'géographes' et des 'géomètres'," in *Enseignement et diffusion des sciences en France au XVIIIè siècle*, ed. R. Taton (Paris: Harmann, 1964).

15. The mastery of landscape reconnaissance is a necessary prerequisite for the preparation of a landscape drawing in plan. However, the translation of the recorded visual field into a graphic representation requires different skills. Here the understanding of the conventions of mapmaking are paramount. Cartography is a distillation process, one where enormous amounts of detail are translated into two-dimensional images, whose aim is to maximize information while minimizing confusion. It is impossible, and not even desirable, to include all landscape detail in a map. Thus a map can be viewed as a set of essential landscape features, natural or otherwise, which are presented graphically. The mapmaker selects among the spectacle of a landscape what is important and what is not. It is a process of critical evaluation that requires ability in observation, analysis, and synthesis as well as conventions of rendering.

16. Jean Le Rond D'Alembert, "Eléments de Philosophie" in *Mélanges de Littérature, d'Histoire, et de Philosophie*, new ed., 6 vols. (Amsterdam, 1759), 6: 3. Quoted from E. Cassirer, *The Philosophy of the Enlightenment* (Princeton: Princeton University Press, 1968), 3–4.

17. "*Rerum novus nascitur ordo*": Denis Diderot, *Le Rêve d'Alembert*, in *Oeuvres philosophiques*, ed. P. Vernière (Paris, 1964), 300.

18. D'Alembert's "Discours préliminaire des éditeurs" in the first volume of the *Encyclopédie* (1751) is infused with a Newtonian epistemology.

19. Demarest's *Encyclopédie* article ran for some eleven pages. It was divided into two parts: the first, a discussion of methodology and observation; the second, a description of the mechanisms that form the physical features of the earth. He reduced physical geography to three general categories of study: "la première comprend ceux qui concernent l'observation des faits; la seconde ceux qui ont pour objet leur combinaison; la troisième enfin ceux qui ont rapport à la généralisation des résultats & à l'établissement de ces principes séconds, qui deviennent

entre les mains d'un observateur des instrumens qu'il appplique avec avantage à la découverte de nouveaux faits." Demarest would later publish a six-volume *Géographie physique*.

20. In his important study of some five hundred private eighteenth-century libraries in France, Daniel Mornet found 220 copies of Buffon and 206 of Pluche (second and third ranking, respectively). *La Nouvelle Héloïse* scored only 165; the *Encyclopédie* only 82. See D. Mornet, "Les Enseignements des bibliothèques privées, 1750–1780," *Révue d'histoire littéraire de la France*, 17 (1910): 248–49.

21. Buffon specifically aimed his book at an informed general audience, not to his colleagues in the *Académie*: "it was not at all for his colleagues, or what he called the 'common savant,' that he decided to write. Rather his intended audience was the large cultivated public, whose new philosophical tendencies he already knew or guessed, who would be more capable of accepting his ideas." Jacques Roger, *Buffon: A Life in Natural History*, trans. Sarah Lucille Bonnefoi (Ithaca, N.Y.: Cornell University Press, 1997), 75–76.

22. D. Diderot, *De l'Interprétation de la nature*, 1754, § IV, in *Oeuvres philosophiques de Diderot*.

23. Stephen Jay Gould, "The Man Who Invented Natural History," *New York Review*, 22 October 1998.

24. Latapie's introduction to his translation of Whately outlined the origins of the natural style. As with subsequent French writers on the subject, his account places the English contribution in the shadow of prior French origins. Latapie does credit the English with the first executed natural garden; he specifically cites Kent ("Kent . . . est le prémier en Angleterre qui ait osé s'écarter ver l'année 1720, des regles de le Nôtre," v), but notes that he wasn't the "inventor" ("mais il [Kent] n'en est pas l'inventeur; car, . . . il avait été prévenu en France par le célèbre Dufresny"). Dufresny, a contemporary of Le Nôtre, was reputed to have designed a garden in a non-regular style for Louis XIV, but it was never executed. Latapie's introduction thus informs the reader that while the English may have been the first to *execute* a picturesque garden, the French were the first to *think* about doing it.

25. Hirschfeld had already published *Anmerkungen über die Landhäuser und die Gartenkunst* in 1773 and *Theorie der Gartenkunst*, in 1775. Neither work was translated into French or English.

26. With the exception of Carmontelle's *Monceau* and Latapie's translation of Whately, none of the treatises mentioned contained designs of the style of garden under discussion.

27. "La langue n'a pas encore adopté de mot pour désigner l'artiste qui professe cet art tout nouveau": Morel, *Théorie des jardins*, 2nd ed. (Paris, 1802), 34 n. 5. Morel also adds that there is no proper name for the new style of garden either.

28. A discussion of the origins of *architecte-paysagiste* and its English equivalent, landscape architect, is in the Appendix to this essay.

29. The same can be claimed for A. J. Dézallier d'Argenville and Stephen Switzer, as the garden designs and methods presented in their respective works essentially rely on bona fide architectural theory and proportional systems, no matter how different the interiors of the de-

signed spaces might appear. Indeed there is not one plate in either Dézallier or Switzer that can be considered of the new genre.

30. See Robin Middleton's introduction to Nicolas Le Camus de Mézière, *The Genius of Architecture; or the Analogy of that Art with Our Sensations*, trans. David Britt (Santa Monica, Calif.: Getty Center for the History of Art and the Humanities, 1992).

31. Abbé Rozier, *Journal de physique ou Observations sur la physique, sur l'histoire naturelle et sur les arts*, 4 (October 1771); 5 (November 1771). On the importance of Rozier's journal, see James E. McClellan, III, "The Scientific Press in Transition: Rozier's *Journal* and the Scientific Societies of the 1770s," *Annals of Science*, 36 (1979): 425–49.

32. *Affiches, annonces et avis divers*, 29 (July 1776): 113.

33. We might recall here that Morel wrote a *mémoire* on the hydromechanics of the Rhône River, delivered at the Lyon Academy of Science, Belles-Lettres, and Arts. See note 7 above.

34. Morel's use of scientific principle and accompanying vocabulary was often criticized, if not entirely misunderstood, as not being appropriate for a gardening treatise. Carmontelle, who differed so dramatically from Morel in his own garden theory, found Morel's science tedious. He sarcastically wrote that all Morel seems to have shown is that water runs downhill (*Correspondance Littéraire* [November 1776]). La Harpe, writing in *Mercure* (September 1776) in an otherwise favorable review of Morel's work, made specific reference to offending words, such as "réfrangibilité" (used with reference to the light spectrum) and "angles saillans et rentrans" (salient and receding angles). This last couplet was used by Morel in a discussion of mountain valleys whose facing slopes have corresponding angles, a bit of geomorphology also lifted from Buffon.

35. "The true goal of the *Natural History* [of Buffon] . . . was the order of the 'operations' of nature, an order of the processes that give rise to life and its perpetual renewal, an order of the forces that animate the living world and the laws that govern them." Roger, *Buffon*, 218.

36. Morel's division into four *genres* is both historical and French. French, because the English were less inclined to discuss landscape in terms of genre, although Thomas Whately did give four categories of landscape types (he refers to them as "subjects"): the garden, the park, the riding, and the farm. While they resemble Morel's four genres, and Morel cites Whately as evidence of the strength of his theory, Whately does not place as much emphasis on them as does Morel. (Whately introduces them well into his book; Morel discusses them almost from the start.) Of more interest is the strong resemblance Morel's genres have to the historical "three natures" of landscape, traditionally given as garden, cultivated landscape and natural landscape. No doubt Morel saw his genres as a means of structuring a solution to the essential problem of landscape architecture: fitting the garden to the house and surrounding landscape. Yet, as discussed later in the text, Morel's genres constitute a landscape continuum, not a discontinuity among the three natures. For a discussion of the "three natures" see John Dixon Hunt, *L'art du jardin et son histoire* (Paris: Editions Odile Jacob, 1996), 26–34.

37. See discussion in Morel, *Théorie des jardins*, chap. 3, "Division des Jardins."

38. After noting that a "Jardin" must surround a château, Morel adds, with respect to the other genres: "le *parc* doit ressembler au *pays* par les extrémités & au *Jardin* par le centre; c'est par cette association, qu'il réunira les agrémens de l'un aux beaux effets de l'autre, & qu'il alliera la noblesse du style aux graces de la Nature." Morel, *Théorie des jardins*, 112.

39. Any designed landscape must resemble as much as possible the product of the natural laws that create landscapes in general. For most of the inhabited landscape, especially of France, the natural order excludes abrupt, cataclysmic changes. Rather, disparate landscapes merge into one another via intermediate landscapes, which on their extremities blend in with those flanking them. Morel would have gotten such an understanding of landscapes from his field experience, reinforced by Buffon, among others.

Whately includes a discussion of the contiguity of the landscape genres, but allows for their "intermixing," something not sanctioned by Morel. Missing from Whately, however, is the sense of seamless connection so apparent in Morel's theory. Such a distinction was not missed on William Gilpin: "Nature . . . seldom passes abruptly from one mode of scenery to another, but generally connects different species of landscape by some third species, which participates of both." William Gilpin, *Forest Scenery* (London, 1791), 295.

40. For none of Morel's gardens do we have a plan, plants list, or description of design intentions—a trio of documents necessary for any investigation of a landscape garden.

41. One plan each for Arcelot and Heudicourt; two for Saint-Trys. The garden at Arcelot is the best preserved of the three. The survival of these landscapes is credited to their private ownership from the creation of the gardens; yet, owing to the ephemeral nature of gardens, all extant Morel landscapes have necessarily been altered over the last two centuries. There is no record of historic preservation, or restoration undertaken at any of these gardens. Indeed, the importance of a Morel landscape has only recently been recognized. A plan for Champgrenon also survives, but the garden does not.

42. One of the features of the *parc* is that the château be central; such is the case with each of the gardens discussed herein. As for size, Morel does not give a specific figure; it is relatively large, yet not very large by eighteenth-century standards. The approximate sizes of the *parcs* under discussion are: Heudicourt, 15 hectares; Saint-Trys, 53 hectares; Arcelot, 59 hectares (1 hectare = 2.471 acres). The categorization given here is the author's, as Morel left no written statement as such.

43. The author visited the sites of all known locations of Morel's gardens. Sites that have not been obliterated by development survive in varying states of ruin. A well-designed landscape still leaves traces of its design intentions even after year of neglect. It was very important was to view the site's topographic and hydrologic conditions in order to assess Morel's specific design solution.

44. As discussed in his *Théorie des jardins*, Morel held that moats are obstacles to the direct linkage of building and garden and should be filled in. He proposed this for the *parc* of the château of Savigny-lès-Beaune in Burgundy.

45. A fundamental tenet of sensationist philosophy is that the inanimate elements of nature can arouse the senses. Morel's treatise is infused with such sentiment: "Les objets dont ils se composent, quoiqu'insensible & inanimés, en agissant sur la faculté intellectuelle, parviennent à élever notre esprit jusqu'aux plus sublimes contemplations." *Théorie des jardins*, 157. For his discussion of the effects and treatment of vegetation see ibid., chap. 9.

46. "Specimen" here implies the type of plantation of the cedars. They are planted individually, not crowded in a forest plantation. This allows the tree's canopy to reach its maximum spread and the bole its maximum caliper.

47. There is no archival evidence that Morel planted these trees; however, the age of one cedar has been confirmed at some two hundred years (personal communication, comte Estève).

48. Arcelot was built by Thomas Dumorey (1717–72) for Philibert II Verchère, a member of the parliament of Burgundy, in the 1760s. It is believed to be the first château in Burgundy in the neoclassical style. Initial gardens for the château, also dating from the 1760s, by Pierre-Joseph Antoine were designed in the style of mid-century French, with elaborate regularity and detail.

49. "Professional," as opposed to "craftsman" or "tradesman," implies the transfer of a body of experience into a body of knowledge, codified by theory and practice, and administered or taught by a school or institution with a self-regulatory capacity that oversees the education, qualifications, and conduct of its members. It implies that work done is for wages, not remunerated in a patronage system. It requires an economic class able to sustain the profession. At the beginning of the nineteenth century, most of these factors were in place. However, the education of a landscape architect would not become institutionalized until the establishment of the first program in landscape architecture at Harvard University in the spring of 1900. For more on professions and professionalism in eighteenth-century France, see Charles C. Gillispie, *Science and Polity in France at the End of the Old Regime* (Princeton: Princeton University Press, 1980), and Gerald Geison, ed., *Professions and the French State, 1700–1900* (Philadelphia: University of Pennsylvania Press, 1984).

50. The events discussed throughout this essay may be framed in a Foucauldian shift of episteme, from classical to modern, as, no doubt the events of the Enlightenment were instrumental in the modern episteme's "reordering of reality" and its "reconceptualization of representation." Such a broader discussion is not undertaken here because my emphasis throughout is on securing a place for Morel and his theory within garden history; to have discussed him in the larger context of the history of thought, as is Michel Foucault's project, as important as it is, is beyond the intentions of this essay. Nonetheless, such a discussion would be bracketed by Morel's "new way of regarding things and their interrelationships" and the consequent "decline" or "failure" of representation implied by his theory. With reference to the decline of representation in the modern garden (natural style of gardening), John Dixon Hunt has often noted that the Brownian landscape "provided the mind with no precoded messages, no language of idea or feeling." Morel, a French Brown, offered as much (or as little). Where Hunt laments that the modern garden only represented *la belle nature*, where "the perfect forms of natural things

were the material of Brown's parks," thus resulting in the confusion between the imitation and the real, Morel, one might wager, would have no quarrel. For a discussion of Foucault, see his *The Order of Things. An Archaeology of the Human Sciences* (New York: Pantheon, 1970); and Gary Gutting, *Michel Foucault's Archaeology of Scientific Reason* (Cambridge: Cambridge University Press, 1989), esp. chap. 5. For Hunt's views on representation and the decline thereof in the modern garden, see *Garden and Grove: The Italian Renaissance Garden in the English Imagination, 1600–1750* (Philadelphia: University of Pennsylvania Press, 1996), and *Gardens and the Picturesque* (Cambridge, Mass.: MIT Press, 1992).

51. Cassirer, *Philosophy of the Enlightenment*, 5.

BIBLIOGRAPHY

PUBLISHED WORKS BY JEAN-MARIE MOREL

Théorie des jardins. Paris: Chez Pissot. 1776. [Reprinted by Minkoff Press (Geneva, 1973) with erroneous inclusion of eleven leaves of plates which do not appear in Morel's original. The plates are form Louis Le Berryais's *Traité des Jardins, ou le nouveau De La Quintinye*, Paris, 1775.]

Théorie des jardins, 2nd ed. 2 vols. Paris: Chez Panckoucke, an XI-1802. [Includes a new "Préface" and dedication to Josephine.]

Théorie des jardins. Paris: Chez L. Colas. 1818. ["Syracuse University edition." The Syracuse edition, in the F. Franklin Moon Library, is the same as the 1802 second edition, with the following changes: the title page is reset; the dedication to Josephine is omitted. The errata of the second edition have not been corrected. The date is uncertain. The Syracuse copy has a publication label, with the 1818 date, appended to the text; that is, it is pasted onto the title page, whose date and publication underneath read: "D. Colas, 1806." The Syracuse copy is a mystery. It is from the library of Fletcher Steele, but is nowhere listed in any of the major library catalogues, including the Bibliothèque Nationale, the New York Public Library, the British Library, or the Widener Library, Harvard University. The publisher, Colas, is the same as Fortair's *Discours* on Morel's life.]

Tableau dendrologique contenant la liste des plantes ligneuses, indigènes et exotiques acclimates . . . [Lyon], an VIII (1800); 2nd ed., 1801.

"Mémoire sur la théorie des eaux fluentes, appliquée au cours du Rhône." *Archives historiques et statistiques du Rhône*. Lyon, 1825.

Work attributed to Morel by Fortair, but almost certainly not by him: *L'Art de distribuer les jardins suivant l'usage des Chinois*. London, 1757.

The Bibliothèque Nationale catalogue attributes the following book to Morel, but it is more likely the work of the botanist Dr. Jacques-François-Nicolas Morel, founder of the Botanical Garden of Besançon. The BN attribution dates to Antoine-Alexandre Barbier: *Tableau de l'école de botanique du Jardin des plantes de Paris, ou Catalogue general des plantes qui y sont cultivées et rangées* . . . Paris, an VIII-1800.

PRIMARY SOURCES

PERIODICALS

Affiches, annonces et avis divers (July 1776)

Almanach de bon jardinier (1808)

Almanach de Lyon (1803–1810)

Correspondance Littéraire (November 1776)

Gazette Nationale ou Le Moniteur Universel (16 October 1810)

Le Journal de Lyon et du Département du Rhône (11 October 1810)

Journal de physique ou Observations sur la physique, sur l'histoire naturelle et sur les arts (October-November 1771)

Mercure de France (September 1776)

BOOKS

Buffon, George Le Clerc, Comte de. *Histoire naturelle, générale et particulière*. 15 vols. Paris, 1749–67. [The remaining 29 volumes, forming the complete *Histoire*, were published from 1770 to 1804.]

Burke, Edmund. *Philosophical Enquiry into the Origins of Our Ideas of the Sublime and the Beautiful*. London, 1757.

Carmontelle, Louis Carrogis de. *Jardin de Monceau*. Paris, 1779.

Chambers, William. *Design of Chinese Buildings, Furniture, Dresses, etc.* London, 1757. [Published simultaneously in French as *Dessins des édifices meubles, habits, machines et ustensiles des Chinois* . . .]

———. *Dissertation on Oriental Gardening*. London, 1772. [Published simultaneously in French as *Dissertation sur le jardinage de l'Orient*.] 2nd English ed., 1773.

Curten, M. *Essai sur les jardins*. Lyon, 1807.

D'Alembert, Jean Le Rond. "Discours préliminaire des éditeurs," *Encyclopédie*. Paris, 1751.

"Eléments de Philosophie." In *Mélanges de Littérature, d'Histoire, et de Philosophie*. 6 vols. Amsterdam, 1759.

Delille, Jacques. *Les jardins, ou l'art d'embellir les paysages: Poëme*. Paris, 1782. [Multiple editions into the nineteenth century.]

Dézallier d'Argenville, Antoine-Joseph. *La Théorie et pratique du jardinage où l'on traite à fond des beaux jardins* . . . Paris, 1709. [Multiple editions throughout the century.]

Diderot, Denis. *De l'Interprétation de la nature*. Paris, 1754. [Reprinted in *Oeuvres philosophiques de Diderot*, ed. P. Vernière. Paris, 1964.]

———. *Le Rêve d'Alembert*. [Reprinted in *Oeuvres philosophiques de Diderot*, ed. P. Vernière. Paris, 1964.]

Diderot, Denis, and Jean Le Rond D'Alembert,. *Encyclopédie ou Dictionnaire raisonné des sciences, des arts et des métier* . . . 35 vols. Paris, 1751–80.

Duchesne, Antoine Nicolas. *Considérations sur le jardinage*. Paris, 1775.

———. *Sur la formation des jardins par l'auteur des Considerations sur le jardinage*. Paris, 1775; 2nd ed., 1779.

Dumas, M. "Biographie Lyonnaise. Notice sur Jean-Marie Morel . . ." *Archives historiques et statistiques du département du Rhône*, 2 (Lyon, 1825): 49–53.

Fortair, Savalète de. *Discours sur la vie et des œuvres de Jean-Marie Morel*. Paris: Colas, 1813.

Gilpin, William. *Forest Scenery*. London, 1791.

Girardin, René L. de. *De la composition des paysages* . . . Paris, 1777. [Multiple editions thereafter.]

Hirschfeld, C. C. L. *Anmerkungen über die Landhäuser und die Gartenkunst*. Leipzig, 1773.

———. *Theorie der Gartenkunst.* Leipzig, 1775.

———. *Théorie de l'art des jardins.* 5 vols. Leipzig, 1779–1785.

Langley, Batty. *New Principles of Gardening.* London, 1728.

Le Rouge, Georges-Louis. *Jardins anglo-chinois à la mode ou Détail des nouveaux jardins à la mode.* Paris, 1776–89.

Locke, John. *An Essay on Human Understanding.* London, 1689.

Madaze d'Avèze. *Lettres à ma fille.* Lyon, 1810.

Piles, Roger de. *Cours de peniture par principes.* Paris, 1708.

Pluche, Noël-Antoine. *Le Spectacle de la Nature.* 8 vols. Paris, 1732–1750.

Switzer, Stephen. *Ichnographia Rustica.* 3 vols. London, 1718.

Watelet, Claude-Henri. *Essai sur les jardins.* Paris, 1774.

Whately, Thomas. *Observations on Modern Gardening.* London, 1770. [Trans. François-de-Paule Latapie as *L'Art de former les jardins modernes ou l'art des jardins anglais.* Paris, 1771.]

SECONDARY SOURCES

Bailey, Liberty Hyde. *Standard Cyclopedia of Horticulture.* 6 vols. New York: Macmillan, 1914–1917.

Berthoux, Catherine. "Jean-Marie Morel et les jardins de la nature." M. A. thesis, Université de Bourgogne, Dijon, 1987.

Capon, G., and Yve-Plessis, R. *Vie privée du prince de Conty. Louis-François de Bourbon (1717–1776).* Paris: Jean Schemit, 1907.

Carlton, D. G. *New Images of the Natural in France.* Cambridge: Cambridge University Press, 1984.

Cassirer, Ernst. *The Philosophy of the Enlightenment.* Princeton: Princeton University Press, 1968.

Chase, Isabel Wakelin Urban. *Horace Walpole: Gardenist.* Princeton: Princeton University Press, 1943.

Child, Stephen. *Landscape Architecture: A Definition and a Resume of Its Past and Present.* Chicago: R. J. Haight, 1911.

Cleveland, H. W. S. *A Few Hints on Landscape Gardening in the West.* Chicago: Hazlitt & Reed, 1871.

Dainville, François de. "Enseignement des 'géographes' et des 'géomètres.'" In *Enseignement et diffusion des sciences en France au XVIIIe siècle,* ed. R. Taton. Paris: Hermann, 1964.

Edmonds, W. D. *Jacobinism and the Revolt of Lyon. 1789–1793.* Oxford: Clarendon Press, 1990.

Fleming, John, Hugh Honour, and Nikolaus Pevsner. *The Penguin Dictionary of Architecture and Landscape Architecture.* 5th ed. London: Penguin, 1998.

Foucault, Michel. *The Order of Things: An Archaeology of the Human Sciences.* New York: Pantheon Books, 1970.

Ganay, Ernest de. *Bibliographie de l'Art des Jardins.* Ed. M. Mosser. Paris: Bibliothèque des Arts Décoratifs, 1989.

Geison, Gerald, ed. *Professions and the French State, 1700–1900.* Philadelphia: University of Pennsylvania Press, 1984.

Gillispie, Charles Coulston. *Science and Polity in France at the End of the Old Regime.* Princeton: Princeton University Press, 1980.

Gould, Stephen J. "The Man who Invented Natural History." *New York Review,* 22 October 1998.

Gutting, Gary. *Michel Foucault's Archaeology of the Sciences.* Cambridge: Cambridge University Press, 1989.

Hunt, John Dixon. *Garden and Grove: The Italian Renaissance Garden in the English Imagination, 1600–1750.* Philadelphia: University of Pennsylvania Press, 1986.

———. *Gardens and the Picturesque: Studies in the History of Landscape Architecture.* Cambridge, Mass.: MIT Press, 1992.

———. *L'art du jardin et son histoire.* Paris: Editions Odile Jacob, 1996.

Joudiou, Gabrielle. "Contant d'Ivry et les jardins classiques du XVIIIe siècle." *Jardins en Val d'Oise.* Conseil Général du Val d'Oise, 1993.

Knight, Isabel F. *The Geometric Spirit. The Abbé de Condillac and the French Enlightenment.* New Haven: Yale University Press, 1968.

Loudon, John C. *The Landscape Gardening and Landscape Architecture of the Late Humphry Repton, Esq.* London, 1840.

Malecot, Y., ed. *Jardins en France, 1720–1820.* Caisse Nationale des Monuments Historiques et des Sites, Paris. 1977.

Maumené, Albert. "Deux siècles des jardins à l'anglaise." *La Vie à la Campagne,* 9, no. 108 (Paris, 15 March 1911): 151–87.

Maumené, Albert, and Pierre-M. Lambert. "La décoration des jardins à l'anglaise." *La Vie à la Campagne,* 13, no. 156 (Paris, 15 March 1913): 153–200.

McClellan, James E. III. "The Scientific Press in Transition: Rozier's *Journal* and the Scientific Societies of the 1770s." *Annals of Science* 36 (London, 1979): 425–49.

Meason, Gilbert L. *On the Landscape Architecture of the Great Painters of Italy.* London, 1828.

Middleton, Robin. Introduction to Nicolas Le Camus de Mézières, *The Genius of Architecture; or the Analogy of That Art with Our Sensations,* trans. David Britt. Santa Monica, Calif.: Getty Center for the History of Art and the Humanities, 1992.

Mornet, Daniel. "Les enseignements des bibliothèques privées, 1750–1780." *Révue d'histoire littéraire de la France,* 17 (Paris, 1910): 248–49.

Olmsted, Frederick Law. *The Papers of Frederick Law Olmsted.* Vol. 3, *Creating Central Park,* ed. Charles Beveridge and David Schuyler. Vol. 5, *The California Frontier,* ed. Virginia Post Ranney. Baltimore: Johns Hopkins University Press, 1983, 1990.

O'Neal, John C. *The Authority of Experience: Sensationist Theory in the French Enlightenment.* University Park: Pennsylvania State University Press, 1996.

Péan, Armand. *L'Architecte Paysagiste.* Paris, 1886.

Puttfarken, Thomas. *Roger de Piles' Theory of Art.* New Haven: Yale University Press, 1985.

Robinson, William. *The English Flower Garden.* 10th ed. London: J. Murray, 1906.

Roger, Jacques. *Buffon: A Life in Natural History,* trans. Sarah Lucille Bonnefoi. Ithaca: Cornell University Press, 1997.

Taylor, Norman. *Garden Dictionary.* Boston: Houghton Mifflin, 1936.

van Rensselaer, Schuyler, Mrs. *Art Out-of-Doors.* New York: Charles Scribner's Sons, 1893.

Vartanian, Aram. *Diderot and Descartes: A Study of Scientific Naturalism in the Enlightenment.* Princeton: Princeton University Press, 1953.

Wiebenson, Dora. *The Picturesque Garden in France.* Princeton: Princeton University Press, 1978.

9. The Coming of Age of the Bourgeois Garden

MICHEL CONAN

In 1819, at age sixty-five, Gabriel Thouin published his only book with a dedication to his brother André, a professor at the National Museum of Natural History in Paris: *Les Plans Raisonnés de toutes les espèces de jardins*, a general classification of all sorts of gardens. This book is in several ways a late example of the new bourgeois culture that came to the fore in all sorts of domains with the advent of the French Revolution. It became a source of inspiration for later developments of bourgeois gardens in France. It was meant from the start as a source book for the largest possible number of rural owners starting with the humblest countrymen, up to the most wealthy owners, as well as for pleasure gardens built around townhouses where bourgeois citizens could walk, and take a rest from the filthy and foul air of the streets. It was also meant to be useful in all climates from the north to the south and the center of Europe. To achieve such a universal project, Thouin chose to offer a system, a reasoned description as he calls it, of all possible kinds of gardens, in order to posit clearly the models he wanted to offer for pleasure gardens, within the larger realm of garden-making (fig. 1).

Instead of considering that each garden expresses the singular essence of a particular place, and that the task of the landscape gardener consists in discovering the hidden geometries of the countryside as the classical school did, or in "consulting the Genius of the Place in all" as the English landscape school did, he attempted to subsume all possible individual garden places under a finite number of positions within a system of classification. It is the more telling of the bour-

geois passion for classifying, describing, conserving, and managing because it failed. We all know that the Revolution substituted decimal systems for measurements of distance, weight, surface, volume, and prices, replacing a huge variety of existing measures, but we cannot imagine how unsystematic these measures had been because the idea of a coherent system of physical measures is an integral part of our culture. However, the idea of system introduced radical changes in ways of thinking of form in a general sense.

François Dagognet has studied the emergence of this new idea of form during the eighteenth century in France. Instead of taking form to be always the expression of a particular essence, a way of making a mere thing into a singular being, he has shown that a new idea of form came into existence: form could be conceived as a position in a typology, a type comprising any number of instances. It allowed the reduction of any particular object to a few variables, and eventually to their measures.[1] This idea of form allowed any particular being to be made into a thing. It was almost the reverse of the previous idea of form. This radical move allowed the creation of a fiscal system, a penal system, and a free market system on the same models that had been used to create a general classification of plants —the Linnaean system and the Tournefort classification scheme—and that had allowed the creation of the first accounting systems for a nation, the *tableau économique de Quesnay*.

The general system of gardens by Thouin emulates a botanical system but fails to establish itself upon a hierarchical set of principles. Thouin was not a successful structuralist. His system attempts a hierarchical description of all gardens into *sections principales, séries principales*, and *sections ou caractères*. The vocabulary itself is confusing. The first *sections principales* correspond to functional differences. This is a rather clear distinction. It starts from a central concern of bourgeois society with use-value, which had already, at that time, been instrumental in reframing ideas about architecture. Thouin distinguishes gardens that fulfill an economic role by providing vegetables and those that produce fruits, then he defines the pleasure gardens which contribute to the joys of private life. Thus the *section principale* expresses an economy of the consumption of natural goods: vegetables, fruits, health (science as a means to health), pleasure. Difficulties begin with the *série principale* because there is no general system of further division that applies. Instead Thouin has to introduce different principles for each *section principale*—public or private consumption for vegetables, pruned or growing untouched for fruit trees—and the same inconvenience repeats itself for the third subdivision. Pleasure gardens are of special interest since the whole classification was meant to allocate them to a definite place in a formal space. Thouin mentions that their variety can be infinite, and yet his book seems to deny this very explicitly in two ways: first, he subdivides them into three *séries principales*—symmetrical, mannerist, and natural gardens—and then each of them is further subdivided. Thus he is successful in reducing the infinite variety of pleasure gardens to only eleven garden characters. Mannerist gardens, for instance, comprise gardens in the Chinese manner, the English manner, and the Fanciful manner.

Moreover, a rapid glance at the plates for pleasure gardens reveals an apparent unity of all the garden compositions that are presented: they all seem to emanate from the same aesthetic of landscape design, whatever the character they are supposed to represent. Of course we must be careful when looking at these designs. The impression of visual uniformity may be created by the drawing technique, which is very elegant and personal, and by our failure to explore the internal structure of the figures, reacting in a sense in the same way as we do when thumbing through a book in an ideographic language. Yet a systematic analysis of these figures and of the explanations given by Thouin in a very few pages of commentary confirm that there are very few design features of the landscaped countryside that may account for strict differences between the eleven different characters of

pleasure gardens. In the introduction to his book, Thouin gave four general rules that should apply to all pleasure gardens. The house should offer pleasant prospects onto the gardens to invite visitors to walk through them, and the same should be true for each monument in the garden; the closest trees to the house should be of a dark green, and the trees further away should be lighter; a path should allow walking, riding, or driving all around the property and should be made as long as possible while remaining pleasant; all garden paths must reach a place of interest and be lined with a variety of trees, either in mass or isolated; and finally, he advises against strong color tone contrasts between contiguous trees and recommends that clumps of trees be scattered in the meadows.

There are, however, a number of features of garden design that should contribute to iconographical differences in character. A "rustic landscape garden" retains many features of a rural countryside and is very similar to a *ferme ornée*; a "pastoral landscape garden" retains features of pastoral economy. But the rustic landscape garden no. 40 has none of the fields, orchards, and rural buildings that would suit its character according to Thouin; moreover, the rustic landscape garden no. 21 (fig. 2) and the pastoral landscape garden no. 23 (fig. 3) seem to be very alike with fields, vineyards, orchards, vegetable gardens, clumps of poplars, rural buildings, hedges, and coppices. Yet a closer look at the description shows the difference: the rural buildings in the pastoral landscape garden no. 23 are sheep-pens, the trees are poplars, weeping willows, and osiers, all of them belonging to a classical representation of Arcadia since Honoré D'Urfé's celebrated novel *L'Astrée*. However there is a water mill and a hermitage with vineyards and orchards, and beyond another sheep-pen that houses sheep, horses, and cows. There are also fields of wheat and a temple of Ceres as well as an isle of Cytherea. Thus the iconography of this pastoral landscape is highly idiosyncratic. It is constructed from pieces of traditional pastoral iconography onto which are grafted other symbolic *topoi*; some of which, such as the temple of Ceres, the orchards, and the wheat fields, could stand as rural emblems, while others, such as the hermitage or the isle of Cytherea, would belong to still other mythical or symbolic worlds. This observation can be repeated for almost all of Thouin's landscape gardens. Even when an iconographical theme is clearly dominant, as in some sylvan or Chinese gardens, one must be ready to discover symbolic elements, follies, bridges, and place-names that are foreign to

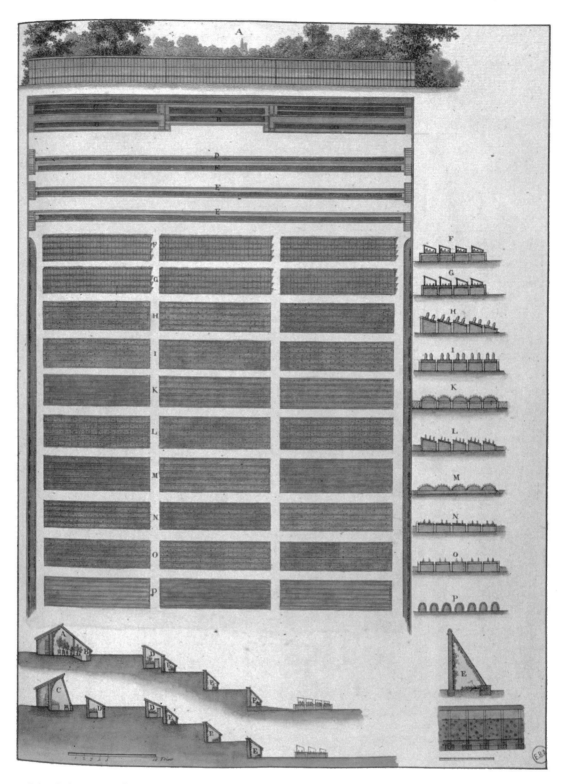

1. Gabriel Thouin, *Les Plans Raisonnés de toutes les espèces de jardins* (1819), no. 4, "Jardin grand potager."

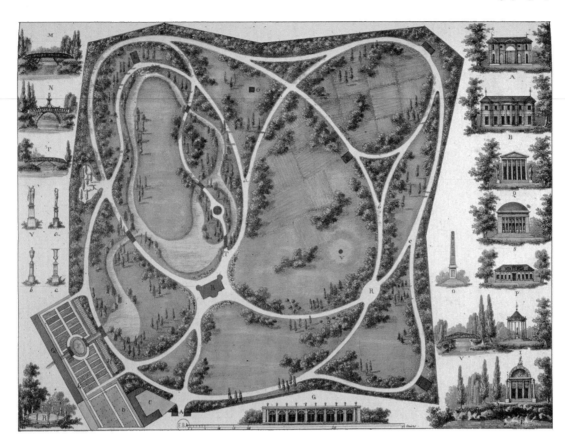

2. Thouin, no. 21, "Jardin champêtre."

it. All of this seems very incoherent and undeserving of careful scrutiny.

Nevertheless when looking at all these *topoi*, as they are mentioned throughout the book, one is led to two conclusions: first, most of these places show stereotypes belonging to a very small number of cultural universes, the world of Greco-Roman myths, Egypt, Turkey, China, the Netherlands, or to a few lyrical themes such as love, friendship, religious faith, or heroic warfare; and second, a few of them seem to result from a search for arcane characters of the fable in antiquity. I suggest that these *topoi* were used as symbolic material in order to produce a statement in spatial terms slightly akin to a personal or a family-centered myth. Each garden may be read as an expression of the anchoring of personality in a place.

These interpretations suggest that these gardens offer a symbolic solution to a fundamental dilemma of bourgeois egalitarianism: how to insure that all members of society can be equal as citizens and all different as individuals? Thouin proposes a universal system of rules that can be used for all classes of society alike and ways of using the resulting lan-

guage of forms in order to derive pleasure out of putting a personal stamp on a transformation of nature into art. The classification of gardens proceeds from the vision of a bourgeois social order, all functionally equal but each with a spirit of its own.

GABRIEL THOUIN
AND HIS PREDECESSORS

Gabriel Thouin was the grandson of Jean André Thouin, a master gardener at Stors (near L'Ile Adam, Oise), and the son of Jean Thouin, head gardener at the Jardin du Roi since 1745.[2] Gabriel was born there in 1754.[3] He became, at the end of the eighteenth and the beginning of the nineteenth century, according to Pierre Denis Pépin and Stéphanie Robinet, "one of the most skillful garden architects, and a successful teacher of landscape architecture whose precepts had been followed by many distinguished practitioners among his students" (fig. 4).[4] Louis Bouchard, one of the most critical readers of the garden and agricultural literature of the mid-nineteenth century, devoted a special notice in his

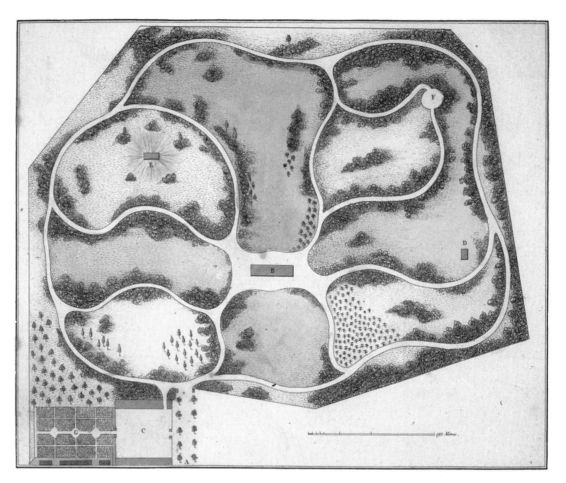

3. Thouin, no. 23, "Jardin pastoral."

bibliography on garden design of 1860 (the first one in France as far as I know) to the book published by Gabriel Thouin. Bouchard mentions three printings of the book, in 1820, 1823, and 1828, and adds: "This is the most beautiful work that has ever been published in France on pleasure gardens; almost all the plans that the author presents have been executed on site under his direction. The characteristic features of Gabriel Thouin's work are a choice of elegant curves for the alleys, a skillful choice of points of view in order to achieve picturesque effects, and varied uses of clumps and coppices in order to enhance these effects. He has been copied, in a rather awkward way by many landscape architects."[5] This passing remark must be taken seriously. Louis Bouchard was very critical of plagiarism and of all sorts of imitations that authors failed to acknowledge. An interesting illustration can be found in the comparison between plates 43 and 45 of Thouin's *Plans Raisonnés*, and the last two plates for a book published anonymously in Brussels in

1829, the *Aperçu et Nouveaux Modèles sur l'Art de Composer et Décorer toute espèce de jardins*. One may see how the plans are simplified. The general form of the curves of the allées is kept, while many of them are deleted, so that the same drawing could be adapted to a smaller estate. It looks like a very crude imitation even if there is an attempt at transforming the second plate by introducing a body of water to replace what was a hilly site in Thouin's garden (figs. 5, 6). Surprisingly enough, this alteration led to allowing a temple to stand in the middle of the waters! It shows that some imitators were looking at these plans as mere drawings without any attention to the landscape they were meant to represent. One may also notice that Bouchard praises Thouin for the form he has given to landscape ideas, and not for the ideas themselves. Five years before Bouchard, in 1855, Paul de Wint had already noted in his "Essai Historique sur les Jardins" the importance of Thouin's contribution to garden design in France in the nineteenth century.

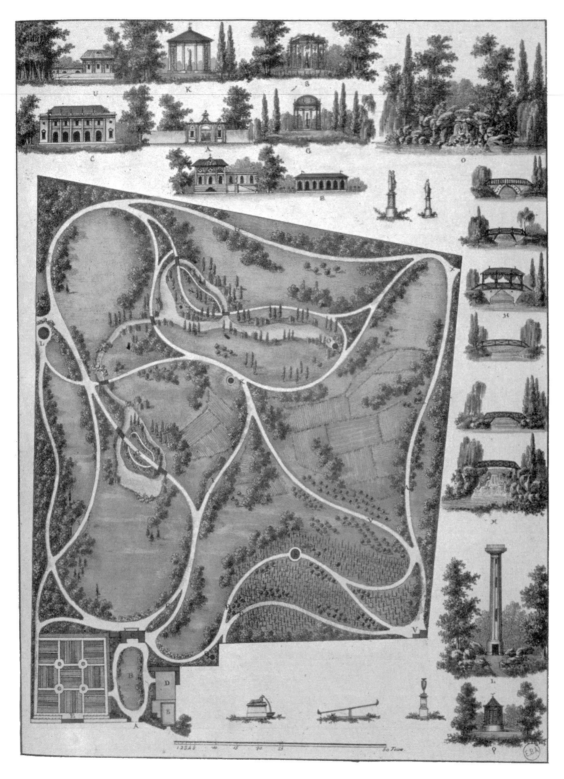

4. Thouin, no. 49, "Jardin champêtre."

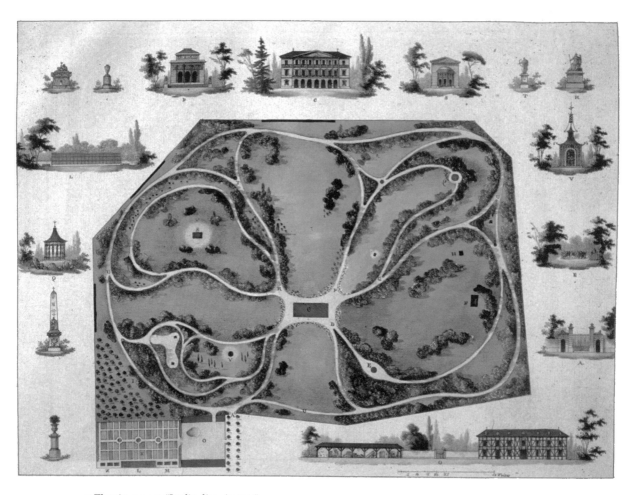

5. Thouin, no. 45, "Jardin d'agrément."

However, very little is known about Gabriel Thouin. He was born in 1754, the fourth child of a family of six, four boys and two girls. His father died in 1764, when his elder brother André was seventeen years old; the youngest child, Marie, was born after their father's death. This was a tragic situation for the family. Geoffroy Saint-Hilaire accounted for the events in the following words: "Bernard de Jussieu pays a visit to Buffon to whom the rights attached to his position (as director of the museum) conferred the charge of appointing personnel. 'These orphans, he said, become our children: I shall take care of matters of gardening; I take hold of the eldest; I shall teach him myself in the mornings and the evenings; we are short of time; I shall cram him up with knowledge.' Buffon shares this affectionate interest: the position remained vacant."[6] Four years later, in 1768, André Thouin was appointed head gardener. Eighteen years later he was elected to the Académie des Sciences at the initiative of Buffon. In 1793 he be-

came the first professor of culture as well as one of the trustees of the Museum of Natural History. This energetic man had raised his younger siblings with the help of his eldest sister. He never married and remained the head of the family: all of them, except Gabriel, lived with him in the garden of the museum after the first years of the Revolution. This may explain why we have so little information about Gabriel and so much about André, and to a lesser extent about the other members of the family. In fact, several authors have confused Gabriel and André, probably because André was known for the development he gave to the gardens of the museum in 1784. He mentions at this time, in a letter to Buffon, that his brother "has made several projects for the embellishment of the mount and in order to link this ancient part of the garden with the new ones, during the leisure hours that the inspection of terraces leaves to him."[7] This brother must be Gabriel, who was already practicing landscape gardening at the same time that he

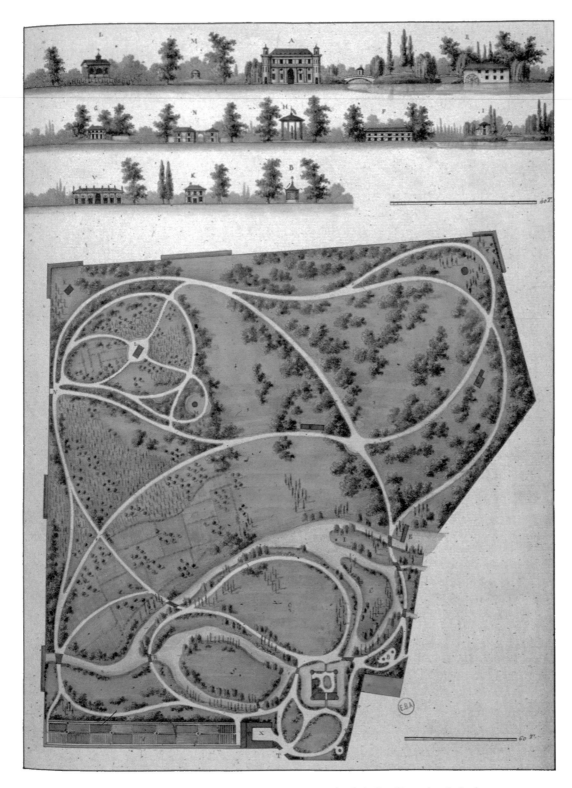

6. *Aperçu et Nouveaux Modèles sur l'Art de Composer et Décorer toute espèce de jardins* (Brussels, 1829), pl. 45.

fulfilled a public office. Like all the other members of his family, he engaged himself in the Revolution. According to Pépin and Robinet, "He became an officer of the National Guard when it was created (1789). He showed great fortitude and devotion to the fatherland, in particular in 1814. And upon his retirement from the National Guard in 1818, he received from his fellow officers marks of their greatest esteem and deepest regrets at his departure."[8] Gabriel Thouin died in Paris on 9 March 1829. We do not know in which circumstances he designed gardens after he had entered the National Guard. We may assume that he pursued this activity during his leisure hours, as had been suggested earlier by André.

However we know that in 1796 (28 Messsidor an IV), the maintenance of the Champ-de-Mars, the Esplanade des Invalides, and the Champs-Elysées were taken out of the hands of the local administration of Paris and entrusted to the Ministry of Interior to which the National Guard belonged. This may explain why, in 1812 during the Empire, Thouin was made inspector of the Champs-Elysées, the Avenues of the Invalides, and the Champ-de-Mars, and four years later, after the Restoration, the first inspector for the gardens of the archbishop.[9] This seems to suggest that his activity at the Ministry of the Interior was linked to his skill as a landscape architect. He actually included in his *Plans Raisonnés* a plan for the improvement of the Champs-Elysées.

Thouin's book shows mostly pleasure gardens, which he introduces "not as the result of bright theories [but as] the result of more than forty years of research and experiments."[10] However, the book had the broadest ambition of presenting models for all kinds of possible gardens and for all kinds of landowners. This was not, by any means, the first book meant to be a guidebook for the new bourgeoisie and, in particular, for the small and middle bourgeoisie who might have a garden of one to sixty acres. Two authors whose works were successful enough to be republished many times preceded Thouin: J. Lalos, with his *De la composition des parcs et jardins pittoresques*, first published in 1817, which went through five editions; and Charles Bailly, with his *Manuel complet théorique et pratique du jardinage*,[11] which went through four editions. They are very different books. Lalos was an architect, and his first fifteen chapters were almost entirely lifted from René Louis Girardin's "De la composition des paysages," to which a few extracts from Morel and Delille were added in the fifth edition. Each edition also included very short

and vague descriptions of places that Lalos had designed himself. This was clearly a book of aesthetic theory aimed at potential patrons. In this respect, the fact that it was republished five times may be taken as an indication of garden tastes among landowners from 1817 to 1832, many of whom belonged to the bourgeoisie. The book by Bailly, in two very small and dense volumes, was a far more ambitions undertaking. It was aimed at gardeners engaged in maintenance as well as design of gardens. Bailly was a former student of André Thouin at the Museum of Natural History and dedicated his book to him. The first volume deals with cultivation techniques and includes a large section on grafting. The second volume offers a broad presentation of garden design history, theory, and ideas. It is a compendium of all kinds of knowledge useful for creating and maintaining a garden; the larger part of the volume is devoted to describing the flowers, shrubs, and trees that could be used.

Both books include a few plates showing examples of plans for gardens. However, they fail to provide varied and stimulating images of gardens, as did the much earlier book by J. Ch. Krafft, the *Recueil d'Architecture Civile de Paris*, published in 1812 with 293 plates in folio. Yet Krafft's book was never reprinted — a sign of the growing distaste for the contrivances that had been associated with the landscape garden style at the end of the eighteenth century in France which were illustrated in various books by Krafft. Lalos echoed these criticisms in the introduction to his own book, distancing his style from the "so-called jardin Anglais": "The gardens of the fastidious man who accumulates in a garden of several square rods several mausoleums, bridges, pavilions, huts, an hermitage, kiosks, rocks, that is gardens where one finds everything except a view, shade and walks as well as good sense in the overall design."

However, neither Lalos nor Bailly were offering beautifully crafted overall garden designs. This is where the major contribution by Gabriel Thouin can be located. He provided an already well received aesthetic doctrine with typical forms that captured many ideals of rural retirement at the time of its publication. These three authors were all trying to attract the attention of the new classes of landowners. Lalos is the most explicit: "It is my aim to make the science of gardening more familiar, and . . . more widespread more . . . popular, by putting it within the reach of everyone."[12] These works appeared at a time when things were changing rapidly in France. The division of large estates into smaller domains that resulted from the abolition of primogeniture made it almost impossible for rural owners to remove a large part of their lands from agricultural use in order to create huge gardens such as Ermenonville or Méréville. This had initiated a long trend of change in garden scale. Despite the large number of landscape gardens that had been created just before the French Revolution, very few survived the events of 1793. The "Black Gang" turned many of those that escaped destruction into farmland. The military defeat in 1815 had crushed French imperialism, but it had not ruined the bourgeoisie. Landowners wanted peace and were ready to live under a parliamentary monarchy. In his comprehensive analysis of French industry, Jean-Antoine-Claude Chaptal, comte de Chanteloup, the former interior minister and member of the Academy of Sciences, noted, "Everything is changed; there is not a single landowner, who out of need or taste, would not attend in the greatest earnest to progress of agriculture and would not seek to improve his domains. The events that took place during the last thirty years have doubled the number of landowners as well as allowed the larger number of former landowners to increase their own lands." He further commented that this had led to economic improvements and to a more stable society "because only a landowner can become a good citizen."[13] In fact, a strong movement of agricultural and horticultural improvement had swept the country before the fashion for pleasure gardens took a new start. From 1815 until the Congress of Aachen in 1818, France was occupied by approximately 1.2 million foreign soldiers. As soon as they left the country, landowners felt relieved and started making pleasure gardens. These gardens were designed in a picturesque style but were far smaller than the modern garden of the 1780s that had been celebrated by Alexandre de Laborde in his magnificent volume published in 1808. They also expressed a different view of rural retirement.

THE ANTIBOURGEOIS CRITIQUE OF THE TASTE FOR LANDSCAPE GARDENS

The aesthetic ideas advocated in the early nineteenth century by landscape gardeners in France originated in the practice and aesthetic ideas of eighteenth-century aristocrats, but they were put to use in design according to formal principles and social practices that emanated from bourgeois landowners. However, it is worth noting that the English fashion for garden landscaping was de-nounced as smacking of bourgeois impudence as early as 1775.

On 11 October, an anonymous writer, Mr. L.L.G.D.M., published an open letter on the English garden addressed to the authors of an imaginary "Journal de XXX." It was obviously an excuse. The booklet was directed at the patrons of Moutard, bookseller to the queen, madame the king's sister, and the Countess d'Artois, the wife of the king's brother. Each of these prominent members of the French aristocracy was known to have created much-admired English gardens. The fifteen-page letter with an elegant neoclassical frontispiece is written tongue-in-cheek in a slightly affected style. The author claims that he has just inherited from his father a hundred-year-old castle built by François Mansart surrounded by magnificent gardens designed by André Le Nôtre on a domain of 785 acres (Versailles has a total area of 1,100 acres). He tells how, upon advice received from friends who had come to visit the gardens, he has decided to replace them altogether by English gardens. This project met with hostility and lack of understanding from his head gardener: "Milord, said he, is it true that you intend to spoil all your gardens to make them into meadows? How many hands shall I fire?" But the aristocrat felt comforted when his plan met with the approval of his steward. The lord knew this bourgeois to be a well-educated person and was rather pleased to learn that the steward could boast that he had read the best available books on landscape gardening, which the reader would recognize as the recent translation of Thomas Whately by François-de-Paule Latapie, and that he had developed two landscape designs of great beauty. In a perfectly ironical passage, the fastidious bourgeois teaches principles of the art of landscape gardening to the gullible aristocrat, invoking the authority of Horace's "Poetical Art" in order to prove that unity is a requirement for any piece of art as if speaking to a totally uneducated person!

The steward's first design took stock of the existing house and its gardens. It substituted, by degrees, rural features for formal decoration leading from artificial parterres to a bountiful nature in the English landscape manner. His second design was far more radical: it was a purely rural domain. Castle and gardens had been replaced by a hamlet of twenty thatched huts, each with its own vegetable garden and an orchard, in a rural countryside. These simple retreats for rural happiness were not far from a temple to Comus, the god of revelry, which would house a kitchen, dining room, and large drawing room with four gambling cabinets. This hilarious description, which builds on the usual features of aristocratic caricatures of bourgeois life under the monarchy, is supposed to show how the bourgeois ideal of rural happiness would bring about a great improvement in English gardening. The steward spells it out very bluntly: "because flowers, fruits, vegetables all find their own place, whereas in your English gardens they are pitilessly excluded. One might come to the conclusion that in the making of English gardens man has forgotten about himself and has given all his care to mowing and chewing animals." Of course you may understand that a sensible bourgeois would never forget about himself! In order to press the caricature even further, the bourgeois designer is made to extol the charms added to such a delightful place by the "songs of cocks and hens." The letter ends with a rhetorical question by the author, claiming that he was enchanted by both designs invented by his steward, and called for help from the authors writing in the journal in making a choice between these two alluring garden improvements.

This letter is completely unfair to the English garden and to new landscape gardens that had been finished at the time of publication, but it makes a point that could not escape aristocratic readers: this garden art allows one more piece of bourgeois impudence, since now they even feel entitled to educate the taste of noblemen. This is an ironical warning, and yet a serious one: such art derives from bourgeois ideas that have no relationship to familiarity with nature (the head gardener rejected them) and that are seducing aristocrats, such as the friends and the author himself, to forego the greatest inheritance from their forefathers, such as a Mansart house in a Le Nôtre garden. The new style is a threat to aristocratic tradition and the leading role of aristocrats on matters of taste, as well as a perfect expression of bourgeois mediocrity compounded with vulgar imitations of noble pleasures.

THE QUESTION OF ORIGINS

Many garden owners of the time would have disagreed with a view linking class and garden style. Many aristocrats indulged in the new English garden styles as much as bourgeois landowners did. Yet there was a big difference among aristocrats between those who clung to past claims of political legitimacy anchored in the principles of absolutist rule and those who looked for a new system of government, some kind of parliamentary system legitimized by its pursuit of the common good, and who

pleaded for a renewed interest on the part of the nobility for agricultural and social improvement. These ideas were translated by Jacques Delille into a new ideal of rural retirement that ignored differences between bourgeois and aristocratic landowners. Delille was certainly, in France, the major reference on gardens from 1782, when he published his poem "The Gardens," until well into the middle of the nineteenth century. This poem seems immediately to have been an undisputed source of authority that all authors writing on gardening felt compelled to invoke.

Delille was born out of wedlock on 22 June 1738. His father, M. Montanier, a lawyer in the parliament of Toulouse, died a few years later, leaving him barely enough money to go to school. However, he succeeded in becoming a schoolteacher in 1765 and worked at a translation of the *Georgics* by Virgil which made him immediately famous upon its publication in 1769. Three years later he was elected to the Académie Française, and in 1775 he was offered a professorship in Latin poetry at the Collège de France. He was thirty-seven years old. Five years later he published his own Virgilian poem, *Les Jardins*, under the aegis of the count of Artois, who was so pleased that he gave him the privileges and benefits of the abbey Saint-Severin, which did not require that he take religious orders but provided him an income. This new fortune allowed him to befriend many aristocrats who enjoyed his conversation. During the dark years of the Revolution he lost his fortune and many of his friends. Summoned to the Revolutionary courts, he was saved from the guillotine by a man who exclaimed at his trial: "we should not kill all the poets, but spare a few to celebrate our victories." When ordered by Robespierre to write a hymn for the Feast of the Supreme Being, he refused and went into exile in 1794. He became a citizen of l'île Saint-Pierre near Berne, where he wrote the poem *L'Homme des Champs (The Country Man)*, first published in 1800, which may be his best. He was recalled to Paris by his friends from the former Académie and returned in 1802. Reinstated in his chair at the Collège de France, Delille resisted the honors offered by the imperial court as he had resisted the Revolutionary government. He died a blind and highly celebrated poet in 1813.

Delille was considered the greatest living French author after the death of Voltaire in 1778, and his writings went through a large number of reprintings. A Mr. Dubois even took the pains to translate *The Country Man* into Latin; this was not wholly inappropriate since Delille had called this poem "The

French *Georgics*." Delille's translation of Virgil's *Georgics* had come at a time when there was a large public interested in discussing agriculture and new ideas about country life. It had been published in 1769, and republished in 1782, 1785, and 1809, as well as in his complete works in 1816 and 1824.[14] The French *Georgics* by Delille developed new themes. It described in four books, or *chants*, how one may lead a happy life in the countryside and give happiness to others, how to make agricultural innovations, how to learn from the observation of nature, and how to disseminate the taste for the pleasures of the countryside by depicting them skillfully. Thus Delille conjured up four figures of the happy man in a rural estate: the wise man, the agricultural improver, the naturalist, and the artist.

According to Delille, the wise man is a more sensitive kind than commoners; he enjoys the variety of the rich fabric of the countryside and augments his pleasures by searching for an increase in the number of sensations this may give him. Thus he chooses the times of the day and of the year when he will delight in the scenery. He may go hunting for deer or birds, or choose to angle silently for fish with a line and rod, gazing intently at a dancing float. In short, he will take special delight in pursuing with skill and dedication any activity that is possible in the countryside and only there. Besides, being a happy man in his rural abode, he makes other people happy by his goodwill, following the model of nature, which is "an endless chain of exchanges and a concert of mutual services."[15] But he may also take pleasure in entertaining the memory of artists who have celebrated nature—painters or poets. Finally, he will indulge in being the "benefactor" of rural villagers who live nearby, bringing help to old people, education and work to the young, and pleasures to all.

The second figure is the agricultural improver. This is an important figure of the *Encyclopédie* and of physiocratic thinking, the foremost figure of progress in society. He is called to practice an experimental and scientific attitude in his efforts to improve the amount and worth of his crops and in introducing new techniques and new plants, in producing hybrids of indigenous and exotic plants on his estate. Adopting foreign species of trees is bound to procure him a special aesthetic enjoyment since:

Your plants are as many lands, your thoughts as
    many voyages,
And you will move in your garden through one
    hundred climates and places.[16]

He should not hesitate to change the course of brooks, to introduce artificial irrigation, to drain marshes, to create artificial meadows. Dutch civil engineering offers a much-praised example of land improvement:

And in this happy soil, thanks to great toil,
Nature is nothing but Art, Art nothing but
    delight.[17]

The third figure that Delille depicts is the naturalist, the man of science dedicated to the knowledge of nature. His interests may start with the study of the history of the earth, retracing his own way in the steps of Buffon. It may lead him to the study of botany and to all sorts of ways of applying it in horticulture and in grafting of trees. He may also develop for his own enjoyment collections of natural history as a way of discovering the hand of God in all aspects of Nature. However, these collections should be correctly classified, and they may comprise a collection of stuffed animals.

The last figure is probably the most surprising. He is called the "Paysagiste," the "landscape artist." This is a man who is able to express his love of nature in such a way that he may enable people around him to share his appreciation and develop their own. The landscape artist is a poet, not a painter! He is able to disseminate by his poems a greater awareness of the beauties of nature around him.

BOURGEOIS WAYS OF LIFE
IN THE PLEASURE GARDEN

These lofty ideals were published in 1800 and cannot be mistaken for descriptions of actual ways of life in bourgeois pleasure gardens of the 1820s designed along models by Lalos, Bailly, or Thouin. Fortunately, Louis Eustache Audot, a publisher who had established his business as a purveyor of specialized books aimed at the new landowners, discovered that they lacked a comprehensive description of the pleasures of country life. He commissioned one of his collaborators, a specialist of trellis construction, A.-O. Paulin Desormeaux, to conduct a survey of pleasurable practices in rural estates and publish the results of his investigation. He published the results in 1826. The description of the book by its publisher states its purpose most clearly: "Man travels to the countryside in order to breathe its pure air, and does so less to increase his instruction than to relax from his serious activities in the cities. Hence the content of our book had to be limited to rural pleasures and contain all of them inasmuch as possible." This is a seminal book for our understanding of life in rural domains because it emulates the encyclopedia, proceeding from empirical observations and aiming at a complete description. It resulted in a set of four volumes which described in great detail all sorts of possible pleasures to be found in a rural estate and the necessary steps that any reader would have to go through in order to achieve them. Rather than attend to all its detailed proposals, we may read it with an eye on the pleasure gardens designed by Thouin in order to discover some characteristics of the bourgeois ways of life that were experimented with during these years. It is quite remarkable that some of the themes of the happy husbandman proposed by Delille are still echoed, some have disappeared, and new themes are appearing. Let us examine four characteristics of life in the pleasure garden of a rural estate: profitable pleasures, patterns of family life, patriarchal sovereignty, and change of bourgeois ideals from the heroic to the entrepreneurial bourgeois.

PROFITABLE PLEASURES

In a way that is slightly surprising to present-day readers, the very first chapters describe the pleasures of managing and improving the poultry yard, the vegetable garden, the orchard, and the breeds of cattle. It can be noticed that a large number of the gardens by Thouin have a vegetable garden, an orchard, or a poultry yard, a few have a herd or a flock of sheep, but this did not imply that they were more than a feature contributing to the economy of the estate. In fact, they are never very conspicuous and could very well be overlooked in a study of these gardens. However, Paulin Desormeaux helps us understand that bourgeois landowners could take delight in the "improvements" of their own fortune. He spells out the difference between labor and pleasure in these words: "Daily care demanded by the poultry yard is hardly a pleasure; it can even be thought of as labor, even rather painful at times. Hence we shall not entertain the reader with their description, but rather with the management of activities, with race-breeding, cross-fertilization, artificial incubation and a few other unusual and interesting matters."[18] But lest we would too quickly divorce the economies of labor and leisure, he notes immediately that when planning for a poultry yard or dovecotes, feed-

ing of different fowls, and daily care of the birds, "all the small details are quite necessary to derive all the profits they may yield, and such profits are large."[19] In the second chapter he pays special attention to methods of grafting, describing three of them in some detail, and then invites the reader to attempt the newly discovered grafting of herbaceous plants, a technique invented by André Thouin, whom he does not mention, or to try to cultivate several different fruit species on the same tree. Throughout the books one may read that the use of knowledge and of thoughtful experimentation is one of the great sources of pleasure to be enjoyed in a rural domain.

PATTERNS OF FAMILY LIFE

These texts echo rather faintly the ideal figure of the agricultural improver that Delille was celebrating. They share his enthusiasm for agricultural innovation; however, Delille was thinking of agricultural improvers who would work at a general economy beyond their own interest, whereas here improvements of the economy are sought for the sake of the owner's family. The importance of family life is found throughout the four volumes. Here I will single out five aspects of life on the domain: the education of children, making boys into men, allowing for a sentimental education, the relationships between flowers and femininity, and fostering family intimacy.

The education of children is a typical concern of bourgeois families. Paulin Desormeaux expresses great interest in the education of children and insists on the opportunities given to any father for a better upbringing of his children in the countryside. In a rather poetical evocation of the family sitting on the belvedere in the garden and admiring the starry skies by a beautiful night in the fall, Paulin Desormeaux explains why a father should study astronomy: "Let his son, sitting at his side, ask for some explanation, he has no choice but to answer, I do not know, or to change the course of an unpleasant conversation. How much more pleasant, on the contrary, the delight of the family father who has acquired for himself the ability to explain to his children the course of the stars, the order of seasons, the measure of time, the phenomena of nature!"[20] The responsibility of the father in providing for physical exercises for his children is also seen as a consequence of his duty to help them develop their minds. In the introduction to a long section devoted to a description of all sorts of sports outfits and their uses, Paulin Desormeaux states: "It would be easy if it were the purpose of this book to prove beyond any doubt that physical education, while developing and even producing physical strength, helps at the same time the development of intellectual capacities."[21] The same reason led to the recommendation that children, boys and girls alike, should learn how to ride a horse.

Even though he advises that girls should wear trousers like boys and should be taught to ride in the same way, most educational attention seems aimed at making boys into men. Boys receive most of the attention in his books. The question is how can they be taught the intellectual skills that will make them into independent individuals able to engage in new and daring enterprises as adults. I give only one example: the importance of teaching children how to swim. He certainly recommends that young maidens should learn how to swim without being afraid that "their roses would wither," since they might simply avoid standing in the sun with their faces wet with water, but most of his advice and the reasons that he gives for learning how to swim are directed to the development of independence and virility: "Young men who can swim will be more virile, more assured of their own strength, more courageous in difficult circumstances."[22]

Almost all the large pleasure gardens by Thouin have a river or a lake where it would have been possible to go swimming or boating. Such activities were very uncommon at the time, and Paulin Desormeaux goes into great detail on the techniques of swimming, ways of learning how to swim, and methods for making a buoy for preventing beginners from drowning. He pleads in favor of swimming: "The art of swimming is not simply a source of great pleasures, but also a means to keep good health, and even to improve health when it has been weakened by too much indulgence in city pleasures."[23] He explains that cold baths are to be much preferred to warm baths, which may make young men effeminate, and that swimming in the open air is likely to strengthen their fortitude. The argument that he develops concludes that learning how to swim is a way to "learn how to be independent of any outside rescuer, [to] emancipate yourself from the tutelage of society."[24] Being able to swim gives one the freedom to go boating and to experience the delight of a boat ride on one's own. Actually the boat ride appears as a metaphor of independence in life and entrepreneurship. "He who sits on a boat seat to be taken on a ride does not share any more feelings than a traveler in a horse-drawn cart. He finds the chill of water un-comfortable, the fog unfavorable, the sun scorching. He cannot indulge in the pleasure of being alone, giving a free rein to his sweet dreams. . . . He must satisfy himself with the pleasures of sight, remaining idle; a ride upon the waters does not give him this hearty appetite that makes the most rustic meal taste absolutely delicious."[25] Being able to row by oneself gives access to the "joy of perfect freedom."

Paulin Desormeaux remarks in passing that rowing a boat by oneself is a necessary condition for a young man to be allowed the privilege of some sentimental privacy with a young lady. Of course this would require that waterways offer secluded passages and hidden beaches where one may land unheeded. The same remark would be true about routes throughout the garden. Shady paths may be more conducive to sentimental experiences than others open to view at a distance. A look at pleasure gardens by Thouin may convince us that they offered such desirable places for personal development. Paulin Desormeaux does not dwell upon this aspect of sentimental walks. However, he is very direct in his advocacy of dancing grounds to be made in the garden for the pleasures of youth in the house. He explains that this will stimulate young men to take exercise since they would do anything to have the opportunity of social encounters with young ladies. The same argument leads to recommending in a contorted vocabulary all sorts of games allowing young men to show their skills in front of young maids: "Man prefers exercises that can be shared with the part of the human species that seems to have been created for the happiness of the other one."[26] Even though sentimental education is never introduced explicitly, there is a lingering eroticism in several descriptions of games, which expresses a concern with encouraging and controlling sexual impulses. Several gardens by Thouin show dancing rooms and, of course, that most frivolous of games, the swing, which has been an infinite source of erotic delights until the beginning of the twentieth century.

Many of these dancing rooms were surrounded by benches and shrubs where fragrant flowers dispensed their sweet smells. Alain Corbin has shown that a new attitude toward femininity and to sweet scents developed during the first decades of the nineteenth century.[27] Women, and young maidens in particular, were supposed to need very sweet scents around them in order to enjoy good health. The gardens of Thouin testify to this in at least three ways: first, flowery meadows are to be found in almost each garden, dotted with small wildflowers, and beds of flowers were placed near the house, as can be seen in a detail of plate 24 showing the beds of flowers at the edge of the lawns surrounding the house (fig. 7); second, a few sitting places were decorated with flowers in the garden, such as the green room decorated with orange trees that is shown in garden no. 32, which also had another open lawn for rest (left), planted with shrubberies and all sorts of roses with a small basin at the head and a small hermitage close by; and third, flowering trees and shrubs were clustered along one or several sections of the allées. Flora, the ancient goddess of flowers, is honored with a temple on an island where rare flowering trees and shrubs are planted as in garden 24 (right).

Paulin Desormeaux devotes special attention to the language of flowers. It consists in creating flower arrangements in a bouquet or a bed of flowers in the garden that convey a symbolic message. He goes into great detail on this subject, giving a very long list of meanings that can be conveyed by the use of special flowers, and describing as well an allegorical language of colors that can be used to deliver subtle messages when displaying flowers in a vase. The vocabulary of the flower language that he proposes is entirely directed to the expression of feelings and amorous intrigues. However, he points out that since this is only worthy as a secret language it has to be reinvented by each of its users: "Hence it is necessary, shall we repeat again, for those who want to communicate privately without unnecessary witnesses to create a more discreet love cipher."[28] This seems to be one of the few domains of pleasurable initiative he leaves for women.

The last vignette of family life pictures family intimacy. A well-chosen company is a wonderful way of enjoying family life. Children, parents, uncles and aunts, grandparents form the first members of such a company, but friends and their families can be a pleasant addition to it. "It is during the best season, when the weather is so hot, that a voyage on the waters is the most pleasant . . . [the boatman may then] . . . in the evenings without a breath of wind, together with a well-chosen company, give a concert in the boat as it glides on the smooth mirror of the stream."[29] Besides boating on the rivers, or touring the garden, the most common way of enjoying the shared pleasures of family life was to organize a ball game. Of course, you had to make the ball yourself with the bladder of a pig, but this was easy: Paulin Desormeaux provided directions. The ball should be hung by a string in the middle of a rope attached high in the air to the branches of two trees, and the company should form a circle around it. The game consisted in trying to throw the ball into the face of someone who failed to pay attention. "This game that excites a boisterous joy is the more amusing for the pleasing postures that a few ladies may adopt, and by their shouts and cries of surprise that can be heard from a distance."[30]

A PATRIARCHAL SOVEREIGNTY

As these last remarks indicate, this book is written by a man addressing other men and advising them on the way of exercising their responsibilities as the head of a family. Its insistence on the family head's capacity to be independent, as where he is vehemently encouraged to learn how to swim so that "you may learn how to avoid calling upon the help of foreigners, you may become emancipated from the tutelage of society,"[31] and on his capacity to make his own furniture, buildings and improvements in his poultry yard, trellised follies in the garden, snares for hunting, fireworks for large celebrations, or even paper for his herbal, build up an ideal picture of independence from the rest of society. Boys and men should strive for autonomy; women should be cared for. When discussing skating, Paulin Desormeaux demands that fathers encourage their boys to learn how to skate because this will give them a sense of achievement and will make them into objects of admiration, while he notes simply, "The sledge is the asylum of ladies and crippled individuals; thanks to its help they may share in the pleasures of the crowds."[32] Self-sufficiency of the family under the enlightened guidance of a fatherly figure seems to be one of the new ideals of rural retirement. The rural pleasure garden offers a kingdom for the imagination of the bourgeois family father. Of course, the manual written by Paulin Desormeaux is very impractical, but it has the power of myth. It may also be an inspiration for many actual situations, such as the garden walk.

Paulin Desormeaux, in his introduction to the game of ball mentioned earlier, remarks: "This game is the more pleasant for not involving any specific expenditure and for being amenable to immediate implementation when, during a nice evening after dinner, the company has visited and revisited all the nooks of the garden and starts looking at one another asking: what shall we do now?"[33] The garden was the proper place for family strolls, and we should pay attention to the constraints that this kind of use put upon its de-

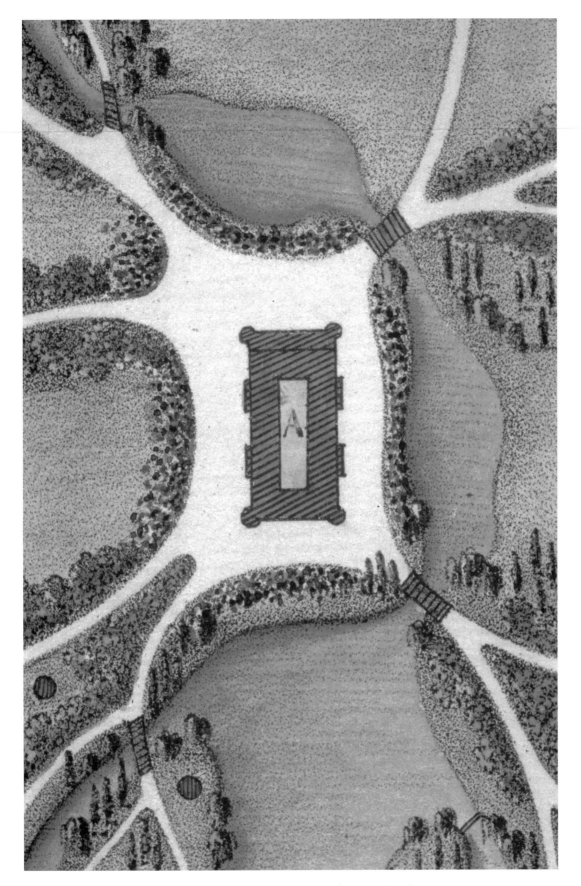

7. Thouin, detail of flower parterres around the house in no. 24, "Jardin romantique."

sign. However, all promenades would obviously not take place on foot; riding a horse or riding in a carriage were just as likely in large gardens. The gardens by Thouin were designed so as to allow all of these activities. They display great attention given to the smoothness of the paths, introducing only long, elegant curves that allow several long different tours of the same garden. One notices very quickly that the paths, to a large extent, guide the choice of tour that one can make, and that they lead to different discoveries. There was a risk that such paths would be very tedious and monotonous, which was the main reproach that had been leveled at allées in baroque gardens. In order to circumvent such an inconvenience, Thouin follows many uses of picturesque garden design in a systematic fashion: when roads are very long he varies the experience of the visitor as much as possible, and he builds as much as he can a sense of bewilderment during the stroll (fig. 8).

To that effect he creates a sense of hesitation at each fork in the road by preventing the traveler from seeing where the two branches that offer themselves to him would lead, he varies the slopes of the road, he creates a succession of shady, open stretches with variety in the types of landscape experience that one goes through in the open stretches, so that they would not seem to repeat one another. One should insist on this idea of landscape experience, because there is an obvious difference between the kind of visual experience of the landscape that Thouin builds up from the house, where the landscape is looked at as a picture, that is, from a fixed point, and the kind of multisensory experience of landscape that he prepares along garden tours. The first one is constructed along the precepts of R. L. Girardin and uses masses of trees to create the wings that frame usually two or three eye-catchers or open perspectives toward the horizon (fig. 9). It allows those sitting in the house to look at the garden and the surrounding countryside upon which it eventually opens by means of a ha-ha, as if it were a classical picture or an opera decor. These landscapes offer a pictorial space rather than an experienced one. The second one is much more inventive. The motion along the road on a tour offers a succession of different experiences of space (fig. 10). When going on a tour of the garden, one may feel constricted between the edges of a wood that totally encloses the path, or experience an asymmetrical space, closed on one side and rather open on the other, or even go through a stretch that is very open in both directions, but the road leads

very rarely directly into the landscape that opens itself in front of the stroller.

Instead, landscapes are discovered sideways. In fact, most spaces that paths go through are asymmetrical, and from time to time traveling along on the road offers a glimpse into a much deeper landscape. Yet it is only a glimpse, and even if the visitor pauses to look at it, the view is so narrowly framed that he will not have much to explore. This may give him a vague idea of the extent of a broad and variegated landscape through which the path is taking him. Furthermore he is invited to establish an equivalence between the landscape outside the estate that he discovers over a ha-ha and the landscape inside the estate, because he is usually exposed to both kinds of views at the same time, his attention being attracted to the right and to the left sides in quick succession. However, when traveling another route, on some other occasion, he may recognize that he is going through a part of the landscape of which he had had a glimpse when making a long tour of the estate. Going through different tours will enable the visitor to build up a comprehensive image of the landscape, integrating into a whole the surrounding landscape and the estate. This introduces an image of the landscape totally different from the ones that can be gained from the house, with their almost two-dimensional appearance. It is a mental image that affords olfactory, kinesthetic, and tactile differences to be located in a three-dimensional space. Ritual exchanges during family tours reinforce the symbolic bonds between a family and its landscape. The images from the house only contribute in a very limited way to the formation of this multisensory experience of space because they are not integrated into the same bodily exploration of space. The gardens designed by Gabriel Thouin seem to fit perfectly the bourgeois dream of self-sufficiency on the family estate, precisely because they invite touring through their roads, and because each tour reinforces the richness of the image of nature that can be appropriated.

Aesthetic enjoyment of tours through the gardens creates a personal sense of acquaintanceship and familiarity with the whole countryside. Sharing this experience in the exclusive company of the family group makes this experience of landscape into a symbolic bond between all family members around the figure of the family father. Since touring the garden is an important social activity, and an important part of family life, we may see the aesthetic of garden design that Thouin

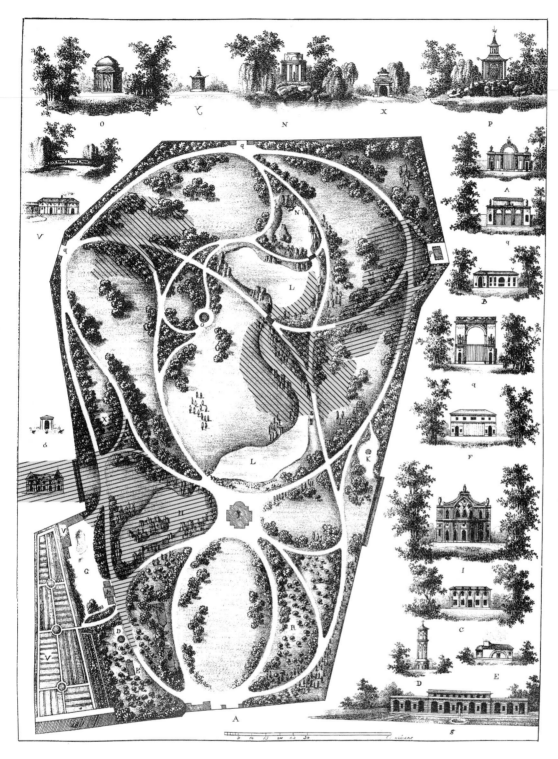

8. Thouin, no. 41, "Jardin d'agrément," details shaded by the author and digitally rendered by Lisa Switkin.

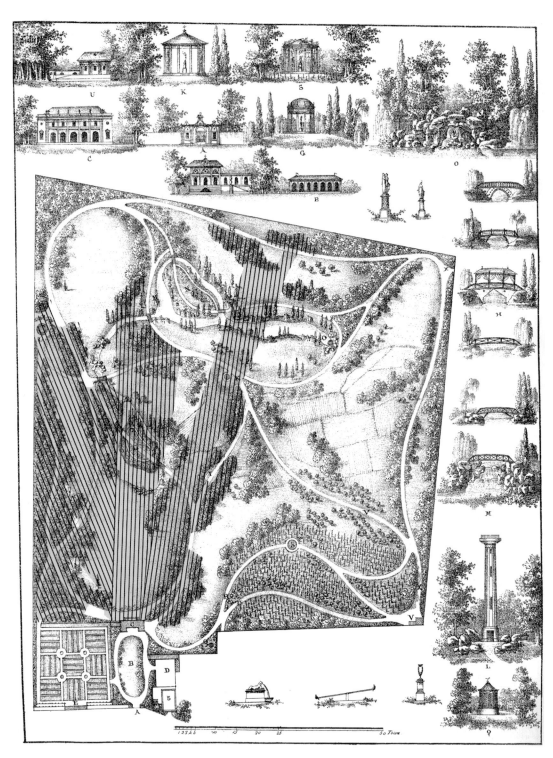

9. Thouin, no. 49, "Jardin champêtre," the framing of views from the house, details shaded by the author and digitally rendered by Lisa Switkin.

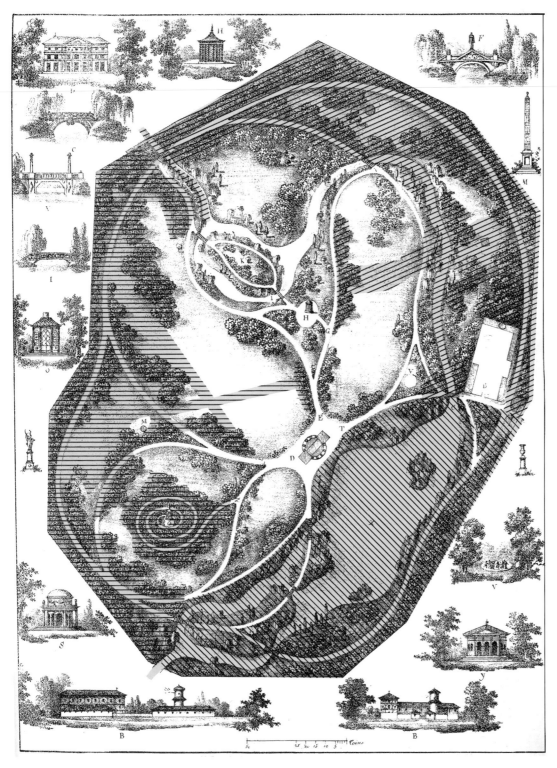

10. Thouin, no. 47, "Jardin d'agrément," the different fields of view along a tour, details shaded by the author and digitally rendered by Lisa Switkin.

culled from half a century of experimentation as a definite contribution to the coming of age of the bourgeois mind.

FROM THE HEROIC TO THE ENTREPRENEURIAL BOURGEOIS

This does not mean that the gardens by Thouin exhibit a perfect fit with the ideology of rural retirement that is expressed by Paulin Desormeaux; there is, in particular, one huge difference between them. The plates by Thouin are surrounded by a series of vignettes showing the elevation of small follies meant to decorate the gardens. These buildings, bridges, and monuments are usually dedicated to a deity, a mythological character, or a country. They point to common interests among wealthy Frenchmen at the turn of the century: China and the Netherlands were two countries that had paved the way toward a society governed by manmade laws rather than by kings. Moreover, the Netherlands was a perfect example of a country where man's endeavor had curbed the hostility of nature; Egyptian monuments seemed to recall the great enthusiasm for Egyptian antiquities in the wake of Napoleon's campaigns in Egypt; and the large number of allusions to the Greek or Roman gods of war, hunting, love, and crops seemed to express common sources of interest. However, one must acknowledge that each garden seems to be made out of some choice between these symbols of common concerns, and to add to them a few idiosyncratic ones, usually borrowed form obscure sources in fables as if the owners had been keen to create in their garden a strictly personal or family pantheon claiming heroic relations. This concern is present in every garden designed by Thouin, even the ones that he introduces as inventions that he had not realized. It seems to show that Thouin perceived the importance for his patrons of anchoring their family identities in a mythical description of some sort. Such a concern is totally absent from the books by Paulin Desormeaux. In fact, one would not find in the very large collection of publications by Audot a single book that could have been of help to a landowner trying to invent a mythological description of his real or imaginary feats or ancestors. Even if we do not know clearly what was the meaning of the strange system of signs made of follies, monuments, and place-names which is present in the plans for the gardens of Thouin, such a difference is obvious. Instead, the bourgeois ideals seem to lay in the mastery of knowledge and the know-how that would make them into self-sufficient stewards of their family estate.

Now we may understand how Thouin's classification of all sorts of gardens failed. It illustrated his intention to distinguish between different "characters" of pleasure gardens, each offering its own mode of enjoyment, as one might distinguish theater plays into comedy and tragedy (figs. 11, 12). Each of his eleven "characters" would enable a landowner to personalize his estate by dotting it with signs of his choice. This probably had some relevance for bourgeois who had lived through the Revolution, who had been active in the Freemasons or in the armies of the Republic or the Empire. Yet bourgeois mores were moving in a different direction, and Thouin's classificatory system became anachronistic. However, the forms of his garden designs offered all the amenities that allowed generalization of new forms of bourgeois family life. He actually created only one design form instead of eleven "characters." In this respect I should stress that his work was successful even though his intentions failed. Did the invention of these forms play a role in the development of the sphere of intimacy in bourgeois family life?

CONCLUSION

Even if the volume by Gabriel Thouin could be considered by Louis Bouchard-Huzard in his 1860 bibliography of French garden writings to be the most beautiful book for the design of bourgeois garden for forty years after its publication, we have to take a slightly more moderate view. We have seen how the designs by Thouin are part of a process of cultural change whereby a new form and a new culture of pleasurable life in a rural estate came into being. How could such a process be characterized, and why should we call it bourgeois rather than anything else? Let me suggest briefly the broad assumptions to which this work is leading me.

Habermas, leaning upon his reading of Kant, sees the French Revolution as the historical process of emergence of a public sphere differentiated from a private sphere of communication. In the public sphere, individuals freely debate all issues according to their capacity for reasoned judgment, whereas in the private sphere they speak and act according to some role to which they are committed in society. Thus the workplace, the trade union, the school are all parts of the private sphere. This view identifies society with a *Gesellschaft*, a group of humans tied together by manmade contracts.

11. Thouin, no. 49, "Jardin champêtre" (detail), the "Island of Love, with a temple of the same name. This island is planted with all sorts of rose bushes, and flowers of all seasons." Thouin, p. 51.

12. Thouin, no. 49, "Jardin champêtre" (detail), the "Rock of Neptune. Double-flower blackberry bushes have been planted between the rocks as well as jessamines, honeysuckles, birthwort, cornus." Thouin, p. 52.

The public and the private spheres allow discussion of different domains of interest structured by reason. However, bourgeois societies also raised issues about the development of self, questions of identity, that were structured by emotions rather than reason. These questions had been more or less under the control of the church during the monarchy. The weakening of the church seems to have allowed the development of a strengthening of emotional expectations vested in family life. It led to the development of family bonds as the locus of intimate relationships. In the rural pleasure gardens of the early nineteenth century, we are probably observing the development of some aspects of this intimate sphere, which so strongly distinguishes the bourgeois family from both the aristocratic family and the peasant's or worker's family. It may be of some interest for students of garden history to discover to what extent these new forms of family life and identity have found support and emotional moorings in the invention of pleasure gardens. One may wonder, then, how did changes in landscape garden forms contribute to the construction of the sphere of intimacy in the bourgeois families of the first half of the nineteenth century?

Notes

1. François Dagognet, *Pour une théorie générale des formes* (Paris, 1975).

2. Trouvé, Cuvier and Cordier, *Notice nécrologique de André Thouin par Trouvé, Cuvier et Cordier de l'Académie Royale des Sciences* (Paris, 1824).

3. Pierre Denis Pépin and Stéphane Robinet, *Notice historique sur Jean Thouin, chef des cultures au Muséum* (Paris, 1859).

4. Ibid.

5. Louis Bouchard, *Ouvrages publiés jusqu'à ce jour sur les Constructions Rurales et sur la disposition des jardins* (Paris: Chez Madame Vve Bouchard-Huzard, 1860).

6. Etienne Geoffroy Saint-Hilaire, "Notice Nécrolo-

gique sue André Thouin par M. Geoffroy Saint-Hilaire," *Révie encyclopédique* (November 1824).

7. Yvonne Letouzey, "Le jardin des Plantes à la croisée des chemins avec André Thouin, 1747–1824." MS 882, Muséum d'Histoire Naturelle, Paris, 1989, p. 90.

8. Pépin and Robinet, *Notice historique sur Jean Thouin*.

9. Letouzey, "Le jardin des Plantes," 29.

10. Prospectus for the *Plans Raisonnés de toutes le espèces de Jardins; ouvrage proposé par souscription* by Gabriel Thouin, cultivateur et architecte de jardins, in *Annales de l'Agriculture Française*, rédigées par MM Tessier et Cros, à Paris dans la librairie de Mme Huzard, imprimeur de la société royale et centrale d'agriculture, 1819.

11. Charles Francois Bailly de Merlieux, *Manuel Complet Theorique et Pratique du Jardinage*, 4th ed. (Paris, 1829).

12. J. Lalos, *De la composition des parcs et jardins pittoresques* (Paris, 1817), introduction.

13. Comte Chaptal, *L'Industrie Française*, 2 vols. (Paris, 1819).

14. I am using the sixth edition of Jacques Delille's complete works, published with scholarly notes by many authors, at Firmin Didot, in 1860.

15. Delille, *L'Homme des Champs*, preface.

16. Ibid., 205.

17. Ibid.

18. Paulin Desormeaux, *Les Amusemens de la campagne*, "Recuillis par plusieurs amateurs et publiés par M. A. Paulin Desormeaux" (Paris: Audot, 1826).

19. Ibid., chap. 13, "Recreations Astronomiques," 137–38.

20. Ibid.

21. Ibid., chap. 23, "Amusements gymnastiques," 254.

22. Ibid., chap. 11, "La natation," 78–79.

23. Ibid.

24. Ibid., 59.

25. Ibid., chap. 12, "Navigation d'agrément sur les lacs et rivières," 80.

26. Ibid.

27. Alain Corbain, *The Foul and the Fragrant: Odor and the French Social Imagination* (Cambridge, Mass.: Harvard University Press, 1986), 186–94.

28. Paulin Desormeaux, chap. 3, "Le langage des fleurs," 146.

29. Ibid., chap. 12, "Navigation d'agrément sur les lacs et rivières," 81.

30. Ibid., chap. 22, "Jeux dans un jardin particulier," 225.

31. Ibid., chap. 11, "La natation," 60.

32. Ibid., chap. 24, "Le patin," 289.

33. Ibid., chap. 22, "Jeux dans un jardin particulier," 224.

10. Freedom from the Garden

Gabriel Guévrékian and a New Territory of Experience

GEORGE DODDS

My learned friend Martial Canteral had invited me . . . to visit the huge park surrounding his beautiful villa. . . . The Professor had chosen as his objective a kind of gigantic diamond . . . which had often attracted our attention already from afar by its prodigious brilliance. This monstrous jewel . . . gave out, under the full radiance of the sun, an almost unbearable luster, flashing in all directions. . . . In reality . . . the diamond was simply an enormous container filled with water. There could be no doubt but that some unusual element had entered into the imprisoned liquid's composition.

Raymond Roussel, *Locus Solus* (1914)

The gardens that Gabriel Guévrékian designed during the 1920s in France have long been considered peripheral to the history of landscape architecture.[1] The reasons for this marginalization are clear: they were too decorative for such major polemicists as Sigfried Giedion and too bourgeois for the Congrès International d'Architecture Moderne (CIAM).[2] Even their designer rejected these gardens, suggesting that one neither take them too seriously nor measure his worth by these works alone.[3] No sooner than Guévrékian had completed them, he began the process of distancing himself from the entire project of the modern garden. Yet in recent reappraisals of both Guévrékian and the early "modernist" garden in France, his works have become de facto icons of the garden art of this period.[4] Largely because Guévrékian's gardens no longer exist, these analyses often privilege their representations, in drawing and photographs, over the physical sites themselves. These recent valuations characterize Guévrékian's gardens as among the earliest attempts to translate the lessons learned in cubist painting into garden design. They tend to be judged, consequently, not by their intrinsic qualities as physical landscapes, but by how well they simulate and stimulate associations with analytical cubist paintings. Contemporary newspaper articles in which Guévrékian's garden for the 1925 Paris exposition was called "cubist" are typically cited to bolster this reading of his work.[5] Yet references are rare. Moreover, the precise meaning of the term *cubist* as it was used in the popular press during this period carried a wide range of associations from "communist" to simply foreign (i.e., German) or strange.[6] More commonly, Guévrékian's gardens were described during the interwar years in such general terms as "modern," "modernistic," and "original." Firsthand descriptions of Guévrékian's gardens typically focused on the physical experience of them. More recent discussions of Guévrékian's gardens have marked them as direct translations of drawings or models[7] or as elaborately constructed full-scale maquettes meant to be seen through the medium of photography rather than experienced directly.[8]

Many of these recent assessments can be traced to a single article on Guévrékian that Richard Wesley published in 1980. This was the first scholarly treatment of Guévrékian's gardens, and it did much to stimulate interest in his work. Using a conceptual apparatus developed by Colin Rowe and Robert Slutzky in their seminal essay "Transparency: Literal and Phenomenal," Wesley asserts that Guévrékian was attempting to copy the effects of cubist painting in his gardens.[9] Wesley echoes Rowe and Slutzky's lamentation that one of the problems of developing cubist ideas in the medium of architecture is that buildings cannot suppress the third dimension.[10] Wesley asks, "How could Guévrékian translate the implied spatial conception of a Cubist painting into a three-dimensional art which itself deals essentially with the articulation of a two-dimensional opaque plane? . . . [A]s long as the perceiver moved horizontally along the ground plane it appeared that it was impossible to create the essential experience of spatial layering expressed in a Cubist painting."[11] Thus Wesley discounts Guévrékian's "cubist" gardens because they lack the spatial sophistication and nuance of the paintings that they ostensibly mimicked.[12]

To reach this conclusion, Wesley compares gardens designed by Guévrékian between 1925 and 1928 and paintings made by Picasso during the period retroactively known as analytical cubism.[13] Beyond the problem of judging the efficacy of a work of art by the standards of another medium, this comparison raises other doubts. By the time Guévrékian relocated to Paris in 1921, the cultural forces out of which analytical cubism emerged in the decade before World War I had substantially changed.

The gardens of Guévrékian, along with those of his contemporaries Paul and André Vera, Jean-Charles Moreux, and Le Corbusier, exhibit numerous influences such as surrealism, purism, and, in the case of Guévrékian, *simultanéisme* and Persian Paradise gardens. Through reconsidering these gardens as complex cultural artifacts we can better understand the gardens Guévrékian designed during this period, the rich panoply of ideas upon which they were based, and why he felt the need to escape from them.

Author, educator, industrial designer, polemicist, and architect, Guévrékian is principally remembered today for the three small gardens he designed between 1925 and 1928. They are the temporary garden for the 1925 Exposition Internationale des Arts Décoratifs et Industriels Modernes in Paris, often called "The Garden of Water and Light" (fig. 1), the small triangular garden for the Villa Noailles at Hyères (1926–27) (fig. 2), and the terraced gardens of the Villa Heim (Neuilly, 1928) (fig. 3). The Paris and Hyères gardens, largely because they are similar formally and conceptually, are central to understanding the received view of Guévrékian's work.

J. C. N. Forestier, the chief designer of the grounds for the Paris exposition, commissioned Guévrékian to design a small garden with the intention of creating something that was at once "Persian" and "modern." Forestier explained: "As part of this Exposition, I very much wanted to have a garden conceived in a modern spirit with some elements of Persian décor. Unfortunately the imitations of Arabian gardens and Spanish patios one typically encounters tend to be as banal as they are ubiquitous. Because there is so little room in an exposition such as this one, I stipulated that there must also be a modern spirit to this garden."[14]

The garden was triangular in shape, largely consisting of tiered triangular reflecting pools and planting beds. At the center of the ensemble was an electrically propelled and internally illuminated sphere of stained glass. Fletcher Steele observed: "The mirror globe turning slowly to reflect lights is rather a night-club trick than a serious attempt at garden decoration. But it is completely successful in focusing the interest and relieving, by its unexpected location, what would otherwise be an altogether stiff pattern."[15]

A single water jet issuing from a small pylon fed the basin from a position located midway between the sphere and the apex of the enclosure along the garden's central axis. The metalworker Louis Barillet designed both the sphere and the pylon, the latter suggesting the influence of Vladimir Tatlin's project for the *Monument to the Third International* (1919–20), exhibited in the Russian Pavilion. Triangular-shaped planting beds of blue ageratum, white pyrethrum, red begonia, and green lawn bordered the pools and sphere on two sides.[16] The walls and floors of the basins were painted with colors and concentric patterns designed by Robert Delaunay. Two large stone blocks punctuated the point of connection between the planting beds and the water basin, visually anchoring the composition. The entire ensemble was contained on two sides by low, diaphanous partitions made of small triangles of colored glass in white and various hues of pink. Although the garden was visually open on the side facing the Esplanade des Invalides, the garden was designed as a tableau that one looked at but did not enter.

Shortly after seeing Guévrékian's temporary garden at the Paris exposition in 1925, Vicomte Charles de Noailles wrote to Robert Mallet-Stevens suggesting that Guévrékian be retained to make a garden for his villa that Mallet-Stevens was then

1. Temporary garden designed by Gabriel Guévrékian, Exposition Internationale des Arts Décoratifs et Industriels Modernes, Paris, 1925.

2. Guévrékian garden, Villa Noailles, Hyères, 1926–27.

3. Villa Heim, Neuilly, Gabriel Guévrékian, 1928.

designing for the Noailles at Hyères; Guévrékian, who had joined Mallet-Stevens's office in 1922, was still working there.[17] The villa was to be an artistic and architectural tour de force, exemplifying Charles and Marie-Laure Noailles's patronage of avant-garde art. In addition to Mallet-Stevens and Guévrékian, Pierre Chareau, Theo van Doesburg, Eileen Gray, Henri Laurens, Jacques Lipchitz, and Jan and Joël Martel contributed to the villa. A model of Guévrékian's project for the Hyères garden was exhibited at the 1927 Salon d'automne and was

widely reviewed in the press (fig. 4).[18] Georges Rémon published a construction drawing of the garden that same year in *Jardins et Cottages* (fig. 5).[19]

The Paris and Hyères gardens are similar in a number of key areas. Each was bilaterally symmetrical and triangular and had as its focal point a rotating sculptural element. In the Paris garden, the Barillet sphere occupied the center of the ensemble; the focus of the Hyères garden was Jacques Lipchitz's bronze *Joie de Vivre*, which hovered and rotated above the apex of the garden. Beyond the

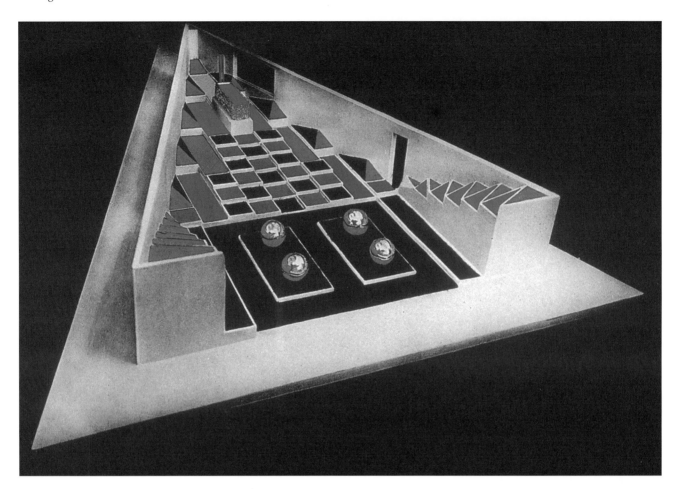

4. Model, Villa Noailles, Hyères, Gabriel Guévrékian, from Salon d'automne, 1927.

formal similarities of the Paris and Hyères gardens, they share key ideas and thematic devices. One of the most critical of these is the theme of reflection, indicated by the manner in which Guévrékian represented his designs in drawings, by the materials out of which they were built, and, in part, by how one experienced them.

Mirrored surfaces were an important element in surrealist, cubist, and dada art and literature in Paris since World War I.[20] In *Locus Solus* (1914), Raymond Roussel describes a proto-surrealist garden of his protagonist, Professor Canteral. Like Guévrékian's garden in Paris, the center of Canteral's garden was dominated by a gigantic crystal that "gave out, under the full radiance of the sun, an almost unbearable luster, flashing in all directions."[21] While Roussel filled the faceted crystal in Canteral's garden with water (*aqua micans*), the internally illuminated crystal in Guévrékian's Paris garden was surrounded by facets of water.

Fernand Léger produced similar effects in his short film *Ballet mécanique* (1924), in which he used "mirrors to complicate images."[22] This general theme is mirrored in André Breton's novel *Nadja* (1928), in which one encounters images of glass beds covered with glass sheets in glass houses, "where who I am will sooner or later appear etched by a diamond."[23]

During the 1920s and early 1930s, Guévrékian and his colleagues explored the theme of reflection, both as an iconic device and as a way of altering one's experience, in the gardens and buildings they designed.[24] Mirrors have long been a part of both the design and experience of architectural interiors and landscapes. In his famous grotto at Twickenham (ca. 1719), Alexander Pope imbedded modest-sized pieces of silvered glass within the recesses of the grotto's walls, affecting an "enlarged aquatic imagery," in a grotto too small to accommodate such an effect physically.[25] Like Pope's mirrors, the reflective surfaces in the gardens of Guévrékian,

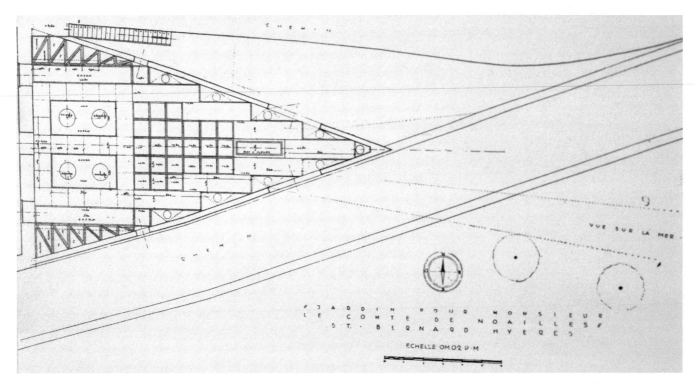

5. Villa Noailles, Hyères. Construction drawing, Gabriel Guévrékian, from Georges Rémon, *Jardins et Cottages*, 1927.

the Veras, Jean-Charles Moreux, and Le Corbusier often augmented or displaced conventional physical elements.

In the triangular front garden for the Hôtel de Noailles (1926) in Paris, garden designers Paul and André Vera and Jean-Charles Moreux clad one of the garden walls facing a wide street and tall buildings with a continuous row of mirrors. The other major wall, a composite of low shrubs and open wrought iron fencing, fronted a large urban square and side street. The ground plane of this Noailles garden largely consisted of alternating textures of colored pebbles, paved walkways, and beds of low-growing plants, arranged in triangular motifs. In Man Ray's photograph of the garden, taken from above, the mirrors reflect the triangular patterns of the pebbled garden's multi-textured paved parterres (fig. 6). Another photograph of the garden from the 1920s illustrates how the mirrors, when viewed from ground level, principally reflected the other walls of the garden, one of which is the hôtel's entry façade (fig. 7). The long horizontal band of mirrors served a dual role in the garden; it reflected the interior surfaces of the garden and its surroundings while, at the same time, it deflected the vision of onlookers and the residents of the tall

buildings directly across the street.[26] After visiting the Hôtel de Noailles, Fletcher Steele commented on the effect of the mirrors: "One quite loses consciousness of the definite boundaries of the place." He continued, "In this case one's sense of immediate dimension is lost in a thoroughly justifiable illusion."[27]

Mirrors were an important part of a number of other gardens from this period. Among these are the *côté-jardin* for Jacques Rouché (ca. 1931) by Paul Vera and Jean-Charles Moreux and the Besteigui garden (1929) by Le Corbusier. Mirrors were installed in the end wall of the *côté-jardin*, obfuscating the limits of the enclosure (fig. 8). An artificial fountain occupied the center of this ensemble. Glass ribbons created the illusion of water jets suspended in time. Below the glass fountain, actual water jets issued from the pylon into a basin, setting up a tension between the real and the imagined. In Le Corbusier's rooftop garden for the Besteigui apartment, which included such devices as movable shrubs and roofless rooms with floors of green lawn, horizontal sheets of polished black glass simulated the effects of reflecting pools. In these gardens, mirrors function as devices of illusion and allusion, defamiliarizing nature and desta-

6. Front garden, Hôtel de Noailles, Paris, 1926. Designed by Paul and André Vera and Jean-Charles Moreux; photo by Man Ray.

7. Front garden, Hôtel de Noailles, Paris, 1926. Designed by Paul and André Vera and Jean-Charles Moreux, ca. 1927.

8. *Côté-jardin*, Jacques Rouché, ca. 1931. Designed by Paul and André Vera and Jean-Charles Moreux.

bilizing one's understanding of volume, space, and surface.

In Guévrékian's garden for the 1925 Paris exposition, there is a more subtle reflection at work (beyond the obvious one of reflective surfaces) that returns us to the idea of the Paradise garden and to Guévrékian's gouache drawing. This drawing is often cited as a direct translation of an "overscaled Cubist painting in which the depth of field was frontally compressed" (fig. 9). Yet it is more accurately identified as a ninety-degree or "straight-up" axonometric.[28] The ninety-degree axonometric was a popular drawing type of the period, used in both architectural drawings and in purist paintings. The palette of colors that Guévrékian used in the drawing is neither cubist nor purist, but an extension of color schemes of *simultanéisme* developed by Robert and Sonia Delaunay. Both Le Corbusier and Guévrékian used axonometric projections to represent many of their architectural projects of the 1920s and early 1930s. In a draw-

ing published in André Lucrat's *Terrasses et jardins* (ca. 1929), the Veras represent the Noailles garden in Paris using a ninety-degree axonometric. Paul Vera also used a "straight-up" axonometric to represent an early version of the *côté-cour* garden (ca. 1930) for Jacques Rouché. Unlike perspectival representations where one's perception of an object or space is deformed by diminishing ratios and parallax, in an axonometric all measurements remain true. The axonometric, therefore, represents an idealized image of an object, privileging part-to-part relationships and the general morphology of the object. In Guévrékian's section-axonometric of the Alban studio (1925)—a project on which he was working while designing the garden for the Paris exposition—there is a clear sense of a volume having been cut to reveal the volume and objects within (fig. 10).

Guévrékian's axonometric drawing of the Paris garden directly relates to the formal and conceptual programs of a Paradise garden. Forestier ob-

9. Temporary garden designed by Gabriel Guévrékian, Exposition Internationale des Arts Décoratifs et Industriels Modernes, Paris, 1925. Gouache drawing, from Marrast, *Jardins*, 1925.

served of it: "Here Guévrékian sought to retrieve his memories of Persia."[29] The fundamental model of Persian gardens is the Paradise garden.[30] Paradise gardens are isolated and idealized enclaves in which a water element ostensibly representing the four rivers of Paradise divides the space into four equal precincts. The water element typically occupies the center of this walled garden type in which the mystical significance of trees and mountains are also key tropes.[31] The inherently closed-off and private nature of these precincts, however, is not at all consistent with the realities of an esplanade in an international exposition. One does not promenade past a Paradise garden in a state of distraction, to paraphrase Walter Benjamin, any more than one promenades past a sacred space. In Persian culture, the garden "is not a place where [one] wants to stroll; it is a place where [one] wants to sit and entertain [one's] friends with conversation, music, philosophical discourse, and poetry."[32] Perhaps because of the incongruity of the site for the task at hand, perhaps in response to the geometric

and spatial limitations of the site that Forestier described as "a very cramped triangle,"[33] Guévrékian built only half of a Paradise garden. Standing on one of the two paths that symmetrically flanked the central esplanade of the exposition grounds, one did not look at a "cubist" *tableau jardin*, rather one stood on a virtual cut-line—the idealized plane of reflection of a virtual garden (fig. 11). By cutting the garden diagonally rather than axially, Guévrékian may have been invoking another trope of ancient Near Eastern gardens: "[T]he early Mesopotamian settlers conceived of the sky as a triangle and depicted it as a mountain. The moon, which brought relief from the relentless sun, was depicted as a tree atop the mountain of the sky. As trees mark an oasis and the moon is a life-giver, so the sap of the moon tree must be water—the elixir of life."[34] In a Paradise garden, therefore, it is not the garden that feeds the tree; rather, it is the tree that nocturnally waters the garden through the intercession of the radiant moon. The central tree in Guévrékian's partial paradise is an illuminated sphere that, like

10. Section-axonometric, Alban studio (1925), Gabriel Guévrékian.

the moon tree, feeds the triangular pools below and is flanked on two sides by faceted planting beds, suggesting a mounding-up of earth. In his gouache drawing, Guévrékian used the purist technique of a "straight-up" axonometric to represent half of a Paradise garden filtered through the reflective lens of surrealism and formally structured, not by the asymmetrical fragments and multiple viewpoints of analytical cubism, but by the faceted forms and balanced arrangement of synthetic cubism.

Many of these themes reappear more vividly in Guévrékian's garden for the Noailles at Hyères.

11. Montage (2001, by author) from gouache drawing, Gabriel Guévrékian, Temporary Garden, Exposition Internationale des Arts Décoratifs et Industriels Modernes, Paris, 1925.

12. Villa Noailles, Hyères, Gabriel Guévrékian, 1926–27, view north from villa doorway.

There are important differences among the model Guévrékian exhibited at the 1927 Salon d'automne in Paris, the construction drawing published by Rémon in *Jardins et Cottages*,[35] and photographs and descriptions of the original garden. These discrepancies help illuminate the role of reflection and the tradition of the Paradise garden in the project (see figs. 4, 5). In the built garden, the enclosing wall lowers abruptly at the apex of the triangle, opening onto an unobstructed view of the surrounding countryside. Yet the model demonstrates an opposing intention, for the surrounding wall is continuous with a horizontal opening in the south wall near the apex of the triangle; the window is not repeated in the north wall. The sense of enclosure and interiority apparent in the model is consistent with Guévrékian's desire to block out the

view of the adjacent countryside and sea—a ubiquitous sight from the villa and its gardens.[36] Also present in the model and missing in the garden as built are an elevated rectilinear trough of water covered in a reflective material and a red pylon, both of which occupied the garden's central axis. Lipchitz's sculpture *Joie de Vivre* is another critical element that is not present in either the maquette or the Rémon drawing.[37] A series of spheres or discs in the raised triangular planting beds are also visible in the Rémon drawing, but do not appear in either the realized garden or the model.

The most critical difference between the maquette and the realized garden, one that returns us to the theme of reflection, is found at the base of the triangle nearest the villa, which is contiguous with a series of rooms at the villa's lowest level

13. Villa Noailles, Hyères, Gabriel Guévrékian, 1926–27, view south from apex.

(figs. 12, 13). The door from these rooms is located on axis with the garden. In Guévrékian's model, four large reflective spheres form a forecourt to the ascending checkerboard pattern of planting beds and tile terraces. Guévrékian placed the spheres on a pair of rectangular raised platforms that he colored green in the model, ostensibly representing ground cover. The planting beds float on a surface of black glass. It is unclear whether Guévrékian intended this material to denote a reflective glass surface or real water. Alternately, he may have envisioned a shallow pool lined with black glass, creating the kind of water terraces found in Persian gardens. Both Le Corbusier and Mies van der Rohe used this technique of black-glass-for-water: Le Corbusier in the rooftop garden he designed in 1929 for the Besteigui apartment in Paris. Perhaps the most published photograph of Mies van der Rohe's Barcelona Pavilion (1929–30) is the shallow pool lined in black glass reflecting the image of Kolbe's sculpture of a standing female nude hiding her eyes from the sun. The terrace of black glass—the water notwithstanding—in the Noailles garden at Hyères and four chromed spheres would have created a powerful tableau lit by the morning sun and framed in the doorway leading to the villa. No less spectacular, however, would have been the view of this tableau at night, particularly if Guévrékian intended the reflective chromed globes to be internally illuminated and made of glass similar to the Paris garden. Either as polished chrome or as radiant glass, the spheres would have hovered ghostlike above the reflective surface of the terrace, evoking associations of the life-giving moon trees of Persian tradition and key surrealist themes. As a water terrace, framed by the doorway to the villa, the reflective black platform and spheres also evoke a number of specifically surrealist associations: Raymond Roussel's suspended crystals in *Locus Solus*, the general theme of the useless so important to surrealist imagery, as well as the watery dreamscapes later published in Max Ernst's collage novels *Femme 100 têtes* (1929) and *Une Semaine de bonté* (1934).[38] The surrealist program of the Villa Noailles is more explicitly documented in a short film commissioned by the Noailles and directed by Man Ray (who photographed the garden at the Hôtel de Noailles in Paris). *Les mystères du château du dé* (1928) depicts a kind of idealized vision of everyday life at the villa with dreamlike sequences, many of which take place at the large indoor pool that opens onto a terrace garden.[39] Much of the film involves the acting-out of games with hidden meanings. Whether the idea of creating a set-

ting for mystery-laden games may have influenced Guévrékian's design—particularly in terms of its large checkerboard pattern—remains one of the unanswered questions regarding the design of the garden.

It has been suggested that both the Paris and the Hyères gardens were designed anticipating their translation into photographs—that they were, in effect, full-size maquettes for the expressed purpose of creating a photographic image. The three extant photographs of the Hyères garden are used to support this argument, indicating the three principal station points from which the garden was to be viewed.[40] As represented in the maquette, however, Guévrékian's design requires more than three points of view to appreciate the experience he intended. Unlike Guévrékian's half-garden at Paris, the Hyères garden was designed with physical occupation in mind. This is evidenced by the diagonal path Guévrékian creates leading from the door of the villa, ascending the checkerboard pattern of tile platforms and tulip beds, to the window facing south. In the drawing of the Hyères garden published by Rémon, a notation indicates that from this location there was a "vue sur la mer." The unearthly forecourt of the four globes/moon trees was the beginning of a series of orchestrated physical movements that were, perhaps, best understood, like the Paradise gardens, on a moonlit night. Passing through the glowing and reflective spheres and ascending the walkway, one would have been bracketed between the converging planes of the stark white perimeter walls turned silver in the reflected moonlight. Passing the water basin and the red pylon/sculpture, one would have arrived at the uppermost yellow tile platform. The highest platform in the iconographic landscape of this garden is yellow, suggesting a solar or lunar association. From this analogously planetary prospect, one's vision was to be directed through the single window, to a framed view of the distant and moonlit Mediterranean below.

When Guévrékian's gardens are reduced to the weak image of a cubist painting or enlarged to nothing more than full-size maquettes for the production of elaborately staged photographs, their power is diminished and their meaning obscured. Only *in situ* can one successfully experience the oscillating perception of space, material, and symbol prompted by these or, indeed, any gardens. Attempting to access the program of these sites via photography alone will always prove to be insufficient. To appreciate these gardens, absent the original sites, one must invent one's own experiences, or vicariously recall the experiences of others, projecting oneself into the "continuous message"[41] of the photographs and drawings of Guévrékian's gardens.

Having made such a substantial and original contribution to the emerging idea of a "modern" garden, why did Guévrékian subsequently work to distance himself from these gardens and the ideas they represent? Guévrékian's work with CIAM may hold some of the answers to this question. Guévrékian was one of the founding members of CIAM, serving as its first secretary general.[42] In his opening comments to the first CIAM meeting at the Château de la Sarraz (1928), Guévrékian outlined the criterion of what he calls a "truly universal architecture. The forty-three architects united have in succession limited the goal of the Congress by eliminating the questions of pure aesthetics. The question of taste does not enter into the discussion."[43] Shortly after the CIAM conference, Guévrékian further distanced himself polemically from his gardens in Paris and Hyères. Having just completed the Villa Heim at Neuilly (1928) he explained: "[D]ecoration that concerns the embellishment of objects of utility is antithetical to the work of art. In my judgment, wanting to decorate all manners of utilitarian objects is an inferior idea. . . . [M]odern architecture is marked by a new organization of plan that is logical and necessary in response to the differing conditions of life."[44]

The series of simple, undecorated, and "functional" terraces Guévrékian designed for the Villa Heim at Neuilly reiterated his shift away from the ornamental and metaphorical toward that which is "logical and necessary in response to the differing conditions of life."[45] A year later Guévrékian admonished Fletcher Steele in an interview that he not read too much into his garden at Hyères. It was not expressive of his general point of view, he claimed, but rather a singular work for a singular condition.[46] The Hyères garden was not unique, of course, but one of two such projects that Guévrékian designed in as many years. Yet by the time Steele interviewed Guévrékian he had already retreated from individual garden design in favor of the CIAM project of open, neutral landscapes in the service of collective living. His work in Paris after 1928 resembled what Christopher Tunnard later characterized as the proper model for the designer of modern landscapes: "orchards, . . . truck gardens and experimental grounds, where plants are grown scientifically."[47]

Guévrékian's pre-CIAM work is highlighted by a desire to reinvent the Persian Paradise garden in the crucible of Parisian avant-garde culture using the devices of surrealism (displacement and reflection), purism (axonometric representation), and synthetic cubism (symmetrically composed faceted surfaces). After the first CIAM conference (1928) any notion of the garden is absent from his work. One finds this quite explicitly in his "orchard" landscape for the Villa Lejeune in St.-Tropez (1929) (fig. 14) and by the vast industrial and institutional "truck gardens" illustrated in his monographs *Bâtiments Industriels* (1930) and *Hôtels et Sanatoria* (1931).[48] The final two plates in *Hôtels et Sanatoria* depict a hospital ship on the open sea. Hygienic, technologically advanced, and unencumbered by conventional boundaries of place, these images recall the photographs of cruise ships from Le Corbusier's *Vers une architecture* (1923).

Guévrékian left behind no record of his thinking on the matter of the modern garden; yet his actions are clear. In the wake of the 1928 CIAM conference and Le Corbusier's "Virgilian dream," where houses on stilts rose "above the long grass of the meadow where cattle will continue to graze," Guévrékian never made another garden like that for the Villa Noailles at Hyères.[49] There was no place for this kind of bourgeois paradise in CIAM's collective vision of a utopian tabula rasa.

In a lecture delivered to the International Federation of Landscape Architects in 1962, Bruno Zevi seems to speak for Guévrékian when he argues:

Too many books and essays on landscape architecture are concerned mainly with gardens. Is this right, or does it demonstrate that the philosophy of landscape architecture has to be brought up to date? The transition from city-design to town-planning took place a long time ago: the same cannot be stated of the transition from the architecture of gardens to the architecture of landscapes. . . . Do you feel, that the time has come to establish a distinction . . . between garden design and landscape design?[50]

For Gabriel Guévrékian, Le Corbusier, Sigfried Giedion, Christopher Tunnard, Bruno Zevi, and many others of this generation of architects, landscape architects, and polemicists, freedom from the garden meant freedom to imagine a new mode of living in which landscape and architecture were different in degree rather than kind. In this new mode, the structure of both landscape and architecture is spatially open, unencumbered by delimiting garden walls and typically unbisected by idealized planes-of-reflection. In the Paradise gardens Guévrékian designed for Paris and Hyères he used idealized planes-of-reflection and actual reflective surfaces to destabilize the concrete and to provoke new associations, a new territory of experience in

14. Project for Villa Lejeune, St.-Tropez, Gabriel Guévrékian, 1929.

garden art. Surrealism informed the design of these gardens. Michel Carrouges has called surrealism "a movement of revolt," born out of the "tragic conflict between the powers of the spirit and the conditions of life."[51] Yet if the gardens that Guévrékian and his colleagues designed during the interwar years in Paris represented a revolution of sorts, it was short-lived. At the close of *Vers une architecture*, Le Corbusier had cautioned: "Society is filled with a violent desire for something which it may obtain or may not. Everything lies in that: everything depends on the effort made and the attention paid to these alarming symptoms. Architecture or Revolution. Revolution can be avoided."[52] If revolution could be avoided, so too could revolutionary gardens.

Freedom from the garden also meant a freedom from thinking about landscape in painterly or, at least, pictorial terms. Zevi is critical, for example, of Isamu Noguchi and Roberto Burle Marx for making garden landscapes "unrelated to architecture," that seem more like "beautiful paintings done with greenery and exotic plants."[53] Zevi proposes an alternative path, theorizing a new kind of town planning that looks to the "action-paintings" of Jackson Pollock rather than the dreamscapes of Jean Arp, Joan Miró, and Giorgio de Chirico. Recognizing that because of "suburban sprawl, build-

ing[s] [were] already in the landscape," Zevi proposes an "action-city" and an "action-architecture" that together create a kind of *action-landscape* and "offer the third dimension to the new image of the territory."[54]

We are situated today between the certain patrimony of Le Corbusier's dream typified by the CIAM project of open and unarticulated "green spaces" where "cattle will continue to graze" and the uncertain trajectory toward which these gardens might have led had the little revolution that Guévrékian's gardens represented been sustained.[55] Guévrékian's gardens are not part of the histories written by Sigfried Giedion, Norman T. Newton, or, more recently, Philip Pregill and Nancy Volkman, because they do not support the narrative these histories document, which for Newton and Giedion lead to city planning,[56] parkways and highways, and "open-space systems."[57] What do we see when we look at the photographs and drawings of Guévrékian's gardens: a revolution long passed or the possibility of another territory of experience? While this kind of question may lie outside the normative parameters of historical discourse, it may be the question that has prompted so many architects, landscape architects, and historians to return to this work, as they rethink the way history is written and the forces about which they write.

Notes

The following individuals and institutions assisted in the production of this essay: French Institute for Culture and Technology, University of Pennsylvania, Barry Cooperman, director; Hammons School of Architecture, Drury University, Bruce Moore, acting director; Jori Erdman, Alcibiades P. Tsolakis, and Caroline B. Constant, the latter of whom read and corrected many versions of this essay. In particular I would like to thank the University of Illinois Archives, Urbana, Illinois, for access to the Guévrékian archival collection and for permission to reproduce images from Gabriel Guévrékian's personal portfolio: figures 1, 2, 3, 10, 12, 13, and 14.

1. Among the basic texts in garden history that have overlooked Guévrékian's gardens are Norman T. Newton, *Design on the Land: The Development of Landscape Architecture* (Cambridge, Mass.: Harvard University Press, 1971); Charles W. Moore et al., *The Poetics of Gardens* (Cambridge, Mass.: MIT Press, 1988); and Philip Pregill and Nancy Volkman, *Landscapes in History: Design and Planning in the Western Tradition* (New York: Van Nostrand Reinhold, 1993).

2. Sigfried Giedion, *Deutsche Kunst* (1932), cited in Elisabeth Vitou, Dominique Deshoulières, and Hubert Jeanneau, *Gabriel Guévrékian: Une autre architecture moderne* (Paris: Connivences, 1987), 36.

3. Fletcher Steele, "New Pioneering in Garden Design," *Landscape Architecture* (October 1930), cited in *Modern Landscape Architecture: A Critical Review*, ed. Marc Treib (Cambridge, Mass.: MIT Press, 1993), 111.

4. See Dorothée Imbert, "Gabriel Guévrékian: The Modern Paradise Garden," in *The Modernist Garden in France* (New Haven: Yale University Press, 1993), 125–46; and Imbert, "Unnatural Acts: Propositions for a New French Garden, 1920–1930," in *Architecture and Cubism*, ed. Eve Blau and Nancy J. Troy (Montreal: Canadian Centre for Architecture, 1997), 167–85. Half of the new essays in Marc Treib's *Modern Landscape Architecture* cite Guévrékian's gardens. Also see Marc Treib and Dorothée Imbert, *Garrett Eckbo: Modern Landscapes for Living* (Berkeley: University of California Press, 1997); Robin Karson, "Spheres, Cones, and Other Least Common Denominators: Modern French Gardens through the Eyes of Fletcher Steele," in *Masters of American Garden Design III: The Modern Garden in Europe and the United States*, ed. Robin Karson (Cold Springs, N.Y.: The Garden Conservancy, 1994), 7–16; Kenneth Frampton, "In Search of the Modern Landscape," in *Denatured Visions: Landscape and Culture in the Twentieth Century*, ed. Stuart Wrede and William Howard Adams (New York: Museum of Modern Art, 1991), 51; Michel Racine, "Gardens of the Côte d'Azure," in *The Architecture of Western Gardens*, ed. Monique Mosser and Georges Teyssot (Cambridge, Mass.: MIT Press, 1991), 457–59; Catherine Royer, "Art Deco Gardens in France," ibid., 460–62; Vitou et al., *Gabriel Guévrékian*; Cécile Briolle and Agnès Fuzibet, "Une pièce rare: Le jardin cubiste de Gabriel Guévrékian à Hyères (1926)," *Monuments Historiques* 143 (February–March 1986), 38–41; and Richard Wesley, "Gabriel Guévrékian e il giardino cubista," *Rassegna* 8 (October 1981), 17–24.

5. See "Le jardin de Garbriel Guévrékian . . . inspiré des théories cubistes," *La Liberté* (5 March 1930), cited in Vitou et al., *Gabriel Guévrékian*, 144 n. 32. Elisabeth Vitou summarizes much of the popular opinion of the day regarding Guévrékian's garden for the 1925 exposition in Paris: "His success in the press and with the public was immense. One qualified it as 'the prettiest garden of the exhibition,' 'cubist garden,' indeed a 'Persian garden,' the perceptible reference which substantiated the origin of its author beyond any precise allusion" (34). (All translations are by the author unless otherwise noted.)

6. On Picasso's latent "Germanic" influences, see Kenneth Silver, *Esprit de Corps: The Art of the Parisian Avant-Garde and the First World War, 1914–1925* (Princeton: Princeton University Press, 1989), 144–45. See, for example, "An Example of Garden Design in the Modernist Manner at St. Cloud, France—Cubistic Landscape on the Outskirts of Paris; Mme. Tachard, Owner," *House and Garden* (August 1924), 62–63. On the problem of terminology, see Yve-Alain Bois, "Cubistic, Cubic and Cubist," in Blau and Troy, *Architecture and Cubism*, 188–94.

7. See Imbert, "Unnatural Acts: Propositions for a New French Garden," 172.

8. Ibid., 180. *Marked* terms are inherently dependent upon *unmarked* terms. In this context the marked terms are Guévrékian's gardens; the unmarked terms are the models and drawings from which the gardens are ostensibly copied. See Roland Barthes, *Elements of Semiology*, trans. Annette Lavers and Colin Smith (New York: Hill and Wang, 1984), 76–78.

9. Written in 1955–56, the essay did not appear in print until 1963. See Colin Rowe (with Robert Slutzky) "Transparency: Literal and Phenomenal," *Perspecta* 8 (1963), cited in Colin Rowe (with Robert Slutzky), "Transparency: Literal and Phenomenal," in *Mathematics of the Ideal Villa and Other Essays* (Cambridge, Mass.: MIT Press, 1976). The conceptual apparatus used by Rowe and Slutzky is largely based on Sigfried Giedion's *Space, Time, and Architecture* and Alfred Barr's catalogue from the 1936 exhibition *Cubism and Abstract Art*. In *Space, Time, and Architecture*, Giedion formulates a direct parallel between the space/time implications of analytical cubism and that of international style architecture. See Sigfried Giedion, *Space, Time and Architecture: The Growth of a New Tradition* (1941; Cambridge, Mass.: Harvard University Press, 1956), 433 and 490–91. Giedion's reading of cubism is largely based on Alfred Barr's now famous codification of analytical and synthetic cubism. See Alfred H. Barr, Jr., *Cubism and Abstract Art* (1936; New York: The Museum of Modern Art, 1964).

10. Rowe (with Slutzky), "Transparency: Literal and Phenomenal," 166.

11. Wesley, "Gabriel Guévrékian," 20–24.

12. Imbert concludes, "Wesley was justly reserved in accepting the successful application of cubist principles to the garden." Imbert, *The Modernist Garden in France*, 144.

13. Wesley ("Gabriel Guévrékian," 18) tests the efficacy of the "cubist" paradigm in Guévrékian's garden for the 1925 Paris exposition by comparing it to Picasso's *Man with a Mandolin* (1912). He concludes his essay (ibid., 24) by comparing Guévrékian's gardens for the Villa Heim in Neuilly with yet another cubist painting, Picasso's *Glass Pipe and Lemon* (1914). Moreover, the interpretations of Guévrékian's work invariably fail to consider how the profound cultural changes in France after World War I affected cubism in general and Guévrékian's work in particular. In the wake of the physical and psychological

devastation of the war, the public turned away from the fragmented, asymmetrical, and highly abstracted work of the prewar "analytical" cubists. Picasso and many of the artists included under the "cubist" umbrella responded to this cultural shift by producing works retroactively called "synthetic cubism" and "neoclassicism" which were largely based on complete and recognizable tropes, often symmetrically arranged.

14. J. C. N. Forestier, "Les jardins à l'exposition des arts décoratifs," *L'Agriculture Nouvelle* 1450 (12 September 1925): 526.

15. Steele, "New Pioneering in Garden Design," 165.

16. A. Loizeau, "Le Jardin Persan," *Le Petit Jardin* (10 November 1925).

17. Letter from Charles de Noailles to Robert Mallet-Stevens, November 1925, cited in Briolle and Fuzibet, "Une pièce rare," 38–39. Vicomte Charles de Noailles commissioned Mallet-Stevens to redesign and rebuild his villa in Hyères in 1924, when Guévrékian was still working in Mallet-Stevens's office.

18. See Vitou et al., *Gabriel Guévrékian*, 127–32.

19. Georges Rémon, "Les jardins de l'Antiquité à nos jours," *Jardins et Cottages* (Paris 1927): 106–7.

20. See Dalibor Vesely, "Surrealism, Myth and Modernity," *Architectural Design Profiles* 11 (2/3/1978): 86–95.

21. Raymond Roussel, *Locus Solus* (1914; Paris: Gallimard, 1963).

22. See Christopher Green, *Cubism and Its Enemies* (New Haven: Yale University Press, 1987), 112.

23. André Breton, *Nadja*, (1928: Paris: NRF, 1963), 18; translation in Vesely, "Surrealism," 92.

24. Imbert (*The Modernist Garden in France*, 63) argues: "Symbolism and iconographic references played no part in [the design of the gardens of Guévrékian, Moreux, and the Veras]. Materials were chosen for their physical characteristics rather than for their semantic associations, and meaning derived from the contemporaneity of the form and the intrigue of the textures." My analysis offers an opposing interpretation.

25. John Dixon Hunt, *Gardens and the Picturesque: Studies in the History of Landscape Architecture* (Cambridge, Mass.: MIT Press, 1992), 94. Nicolas Le Camus de Mézières argued for the necessity of a restrained use of the "looking glass" in *Le génie de l'architecture; ou, L'analogie de cet art avec nos sensations* (1780). See Nicolas Le Camus de Mézières, *The Genius of Architecture; or the Analogy of that Art with our Sensations*, trans. David Britt (Santa Monica, Calif.: Getty Center for the History of Art and the Humanities, 1992), 111. Sir John Soane, who translated the first fifth of *Le génie de l'architecture* as part of his lectures at the Royal Academy (1808), strategically placed mirrors to enliven the analogous landscape of the ruin-filled interior of his house at No. 13 Lincoln's Inn Fields. See Robin Middleton, "Introduction," ibid., 62.

26. The mature trees that canopied the garden along its periphery enhanced the sense of privacy and enclosure provided by the mirror-wall.

27. Steele, "New Pioneering in Garden Design," 165.

28. Axonometric drawing was first popularized in late nineteenth-century France by Auguste Choisy to demonstrate structural systems and methods of construction.

29. Forestier, "Les jardins," 526.

30. Paradise gardens are the oldest surviving example of a garden tradition. See Elizabeth B. Moynihan, *Paradise as a Garden in Persia and Mughal India* (New York: Braziller, 1979), 12.

31. "The reverence for water, the mystical feeling for trees, the symbolic division of the earth into quarters by the four rivers of life and the significance of a mountain are among the most ancient and enduring traditions of the Near East" (ibid., 2).

32. Victoria Sackville-West, "Persian Gardens," in *Legacy of Persia*, ed. A. J. Arberry (Oxford: Oxford University Press, 1953), 287, cited in Moynihan, *Paradise as a Garden*, 18. See also James L. Wescoat, Jr., and Joachim Wolschke-Bulmahn, "Sources, Places, Representations, and Prospects: A Perspective of Mughal Gardens," in *Mughal Gardens: Sources, Places, Representations, and Prospects* (Washington, D.C.: Dumbarton Oaks, 1996), 25.

33. Forestier, "Les jardins," 526.

34. Moynihan, *Paradise as a Garden*, 6–7.

35. Rémon, "Les jardins de l'Antiquité à nos jours," 106–7.

36. Steele, "New Pioneering in Garden Design," cited in Treib, *Modern Landscape Architecture*, 111.

37. The only comment Lipchitz made about the relation of the garden to his sculpture was regarding how the work would be viewed. "Because of the location and the problem of seeing the sculpture in the round, I suggested installing a machine so that it could rotate. . . . It is a culmination of all my findings in cubism but at the same time an escape from cubism." Jacques Lipchitz, *My Life in Sculpture*, with H. H. Arnason (New York: Viking Press, 1972), 96. Guévrékian never commented on the sculpture in print. It is unclear how the red pylon relates to the Lipchitz sculpture. The location of the sculpture in the garden as built does not coincide with the location of the pylon in the model. Imbert (*The Modernist Garden in France*, 135) suggests that the pylon represents, not the Lipchitz sculpture, but a vertical jet of water.

38. Dalibor Vesely ("Surrealism," 88) explains, "The fluidity of water, which is also the fluidity of desire opposing the solidity of matter, remains a permanent obsession of the Surrealists." The theme of the useless extends to include even the garden's primary botanical feature. In that the tulip produces no scent, within the floral history of the French garden it has been characterized as a "useless flower." See Elizabeth Hyde's essay in this volume.

39. See Michel Louis, "Mallet-Stevens and the Cinema, 1919–29," in *Rob Mallet-Stevens, Architecte*, ed. Dominique Deshoulières and Hubert Jeanneau (Brussels: Archives d'Architecture Moderne, 1980), 123–59.

40. Imbert, "Propositions for a New French Garden," 175.

41. "The photographic message is a continuous message." Roland Barthes, "The Photographic Message," *Image—Music—Text*, trans. Stephen Heath (New York: Hill and Wang, 1977), 17.

42. See "Au Château de La Sarraz: Le congrès international d'architecture moderne," *Gazette Lausannne* (28 June 1928). Also see Gabriel Guévrékian, "Un congrès international d'architecture moderne au Château de la Sarraz," *La Patrie* (31 July 1928).

43. Guévrékian, "Un congrès international d'architecture moderne."

44. "Propos de Guévrékian sur l'art moderne," *La Liberté* (18 December 1929).

45. Ibid.

46. Steele, "New Pioneering in Garden Design," cited in Treib, *Modern Landscape Architecture*, 111.

47. Christopher Tunnard, "Modern Gardens for Modern Houses: Reflections on Current Trends in Landscape Design," *Landscape Architecture* (January 1942). After leaving Paris in 1933 and becoming the chief architect of Tehran (1933–37), Guévrékian designed a number of villas and private gardens that were unrelated to either his Paris and Hyères gardens or his CIAM-based work.

48. Gabriel Guévrékian, *Bâtiments Industriels* (Paris: Editions d'Art Charles Moreau, 1930), and *Hôtels et Sanatoria* (Paris: Libraire Nouvelle de l'Architecture et des Beaux-Arts, 1931).

49. Le Corbusier, "Poésie, lyrisme apportés par les techniques," in *Précisions sur un état présent de l'architecture et de l'urbanisme* (1930: Paris: Vincent Fréal, 1960), 138; translation from Tunnard, *Gardens in the Modern Landscape*, 79.

50. Bruno Zevi, "The Modern Dimensions of Landscape Architecture," in *Shaping Tomorrow's Landscape*, ed. Sylvia Crowe and Zvi Miller (Amsterdam: Djambatan, 1964), 18.

51. Michel Carrouges, *André Breton and the Basic Concepts of Surrealism*, trans. Maura Prendergast (Tuscaloosa: University of Alabama Press, 1974), 1.

52. Le Corbusier, *Vers une architecture* (Paris: Editions G. Crès, 1923): citation from *Towards a New Architecture*, trans. Frederick Etchells (New York: Dover, 1986), 288–89.

53. Zevi, "Modern Dimensions," 18.

54. Ibid., 19. It is ironic that in light of his criticism of pictorial determinism in landscape design, Zevi should look to painting as a possible model for this new vision of landscape.

55. In the first edition of *Modern Gardens and the Landscape*, Elizabeth B. Kassler tacitly asserts a continuity between Guévrékian's garden art and more recent works by grouping Guévrékian's garden at the Villa Noailles (dated 1925) with three other gardens with a similar pattern: a roof garden by Lawrence Halprin (1952), a terrace by Roberto Burle Marx (1957), and a patio by Alexander Girard (1954). See Elizabeth B. Kassler, *Modern Gardens and the Landscape* (New York: Museum of Modern Art, 1964), 52–53.

56. See Giedion, *Space, Time, and Architecture*, 727–58.

57. See Newton, *Design on the Land*, 586–639.

11. Reinventing the Parisian Park

JOHN DIXON HUNT

PREAMBLE

There has been a flurry of park-making in Paris—Parc André-Citroën, Parc Bercy, the Jardin Atlantique, the Jardin Diderot, the Promenade Plantée—to name the main examples discussed here. All of them seem to have been created in dialogue with the Parc de la Villette, which from 1983 came to symbolize for many the glorious reinvention of the Parisian park. Yet this recent focus on providing the French capital city with a repertoire of green, open spaces must be considered within a longer duration of landscape history. That perspective includes at least the greening of Paris that Baron Haussmann had undertaken a century earlier under Napoleon III; this political and civic enterprise, like no other nation's or city's at that time, had been sustained and institutionalized by the creation of the Office of Promenades of Paris.[1] But the provision of prime new designs as part of a political agenda—the Grands Projets under President François Mitterand to celebrate the bicentennial of the Revolution—has roots also in the invention of new symbolic public spaces at the time of the Revolution itself. The new parks constitute, like those earlier moments of revolutionary urbanism, green sites where a new order is both inscribed and advertised, a new order that overwrites but does not completely obliterate the old.[2]

Despite a rather single-minded focus on the modernity of these new Parisian parks, which the example of La Villette has encouraged among commentators and designers alike, there are other topics that need to be addressed, not least being the new parks' dialogue with their past, an embarrassing topic for landscape architects or architects eager to secure a niche in the modernist pantheon. My concern in this essay (and in the context of this volume) is with one aspect of that historical dialogue: what this cluster of twentieth-century works may tell us *en revanche* about the French garden art that is treated in other contributions here.

Gardens and parks have a triple regard upon their place in time (a temporal responsibility that is often neglected for their attempts at innovative spatial treatment). Parks and gardens address past, present, and future. They are first and foremost atavistic, involving above all our individual and collective memories, so that their references to the past are therefore inevitable.[3] They must also be timely, because they spring from current concerns and are addressed to current use. Not least, they need to be timeless (or untimely) because they are always designed for a future that cannot be known and can only be predicted, if at all, by being predicated on our experience of the past.

MODERN PARK DEBATES

The Parisian parks of recent creation are all very self-consciously concerned with the role, scope, and form that the park might take in the modern city. They have contributed, sometimes explicitly through the publications of their designers and critics, to a voluminous discourse on modern park design.[4] The agenda of these discussions is varied, but its items all focus, as already noted, on the modern garden's dialogue with its past. This is often a dialogue either repressed or severely distorted by designers and critics alike, a refusal of history in favor of what George Dodds in this volume calls "the project of modernity." Yet this obsession with an independence from previous work distracts discussion from other essential design questions. For instance, it privileges models over types: this means, first, that design issues tend to be set out simply in formal terms of style; second, such stylistic concentration neglects in particular any consideration of the long-standing invocation of the idea of the garden in the making of parks.[5]

An emphasis on formal matters inevitably privileges the designer and his agenda over the inhabitant and visitor and their concerns; these latter play a far more important role in the park than its original creator, not least because of the long-term nature of their involvement, and they probably put stylistic criteria low on their list of requirements. In this respect—namely, what users might legitimately require of their park experience—recent discussions of modern park design are astonishingly neglectful of the need to provide meaningful experience, what Louis Aragon in *Le Paysan de Paris*, writing of course about an earlier piece of Parisian place-making, Les Buttes-Chaumont, termed "la liaison intime . . . entre l'activité figurative et l'activité métaphysique."[6]

Perhaps this need to consider what meaningful experiences the modern park can provide is taken up by the concern of both *concours* promoters and designers to carve out some role for the public park in the ideological theater of the city, to give it a distinctive urban objective. This ambition, as understandable as it has also been excessive, manages to sideline a more complex ambition of all gardens and parks, to refer outward to other worlds (rural, "natural," exotic, faraway). For Carmontelle, another tutelary French garden commentator, his creation of the Jardin Monceau in the eighteenth century (to be transformed into a public park in the nineteenth) was an opportunity to provide, in his now famous phrase, a "pays d'illusions," zones of virtual realities to be surfed or promenaded at will by the visitor.[7]

PARKS AND GARDENS

As the official program for the La Villette *concours* made starkly clear, the repertoire of needs and functions for the modern park is extremely varied, not to say complex and contradictory. The perceived obligations of a park as a "multifunctional social condenser" (in the nasty jargon of Andreu Arriola, one of the contestants)[8] require a designer's attention to a whole roster of social needs that are extremely various even within the same culture, city, or period. Perhaps this sheer spatial and social versatility of the park explains why many designers work energetically to reduce the idea of the park to manageable proportions. But when a "new" formula and form for the park are claimed, it is worth noticing that people do not desert the old parks for the new one; it is not simply the lure of Parisian locality, of established *quartier*, that explains why Parc Monceau and Buttes-Chaumont are not emptied of people rushing to La Villette or Bercy.

The effort to delimit the notion of park is, of course, part of a modernist reaction against the eclecticism of landscape architectural design by the end of the nineteenth century. In this process history is distorted into unnecessary generalizations that the designers themselves have no stake in refuting.[9] At a 1992 conference in Rotterdam on modern park design, Adriaan Greuze offered the half-truths that an eighteenth-century park was constituted of idealized images of contemporary traveling—an encyclopedia of times and places, whereas the nineteenth-century version compensated with a green oasis for the monstrous city adjacent or around it;[10] he went on to ask for both ideas to be rejected. Parks were defined in Rotterdam, as they were during the La Villette *concours*, with sectarian fervor: greenery in parks is a "worn-out cliché";[11] no symbolism or ornament is required any longer.[12] Beth Meyer can claim that mass culture and production and a pervasive technology have now been substituted for nature as "the basis of park design."[13] And so on and so forth.

Two related factors, however, should make one skeptical of these reductive agendas. One is the topographical distribution of, the other is the variety within, Parisian parks. We need only look at where literally on the urban map Parisian parks (old and new) are established (fig. 1) to appreciate their versatility in scope, scale, use, and form and that their success is predicated upon that variety. Whether they are central, suburban, inside, or beyond the *périphérique*; whether in working-class, middle-class, or elite neighborhoods; whether pocket parks or *squares* or urban *places*,[14] or in the form of promenades like the Champs-Elysées or the newly established Promenade Plantée; whether in proximity to housing, offices, or cultural or recreational facilities—it is clear that there is room

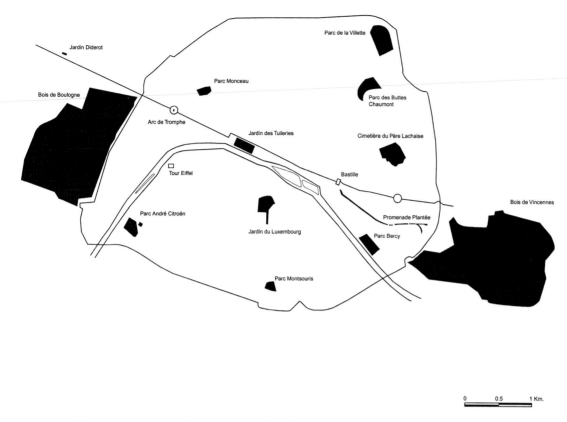

Parc de la Villette

Jardin Diderot

Parc Monceau

Bois de Boulogne

Parc des Buttes
Chaumont

Arc de Tromphe

Jardin des Tuileries

Cimetière du Père Lachaise

Tour Eiffel

Bastille

Bois de Vincennes

Parc André Citroën

Promenade Plantée

Jardin du Luxembourg

Parc Bercy

Parc Montsouris

0   0.5   1 Km.

1. A map of the parks and gardens of Paris. Drawing by Philippe Coignet.

for parks of all sorts. Just as Paris always had its contrasting social worlds of the two Bois (of Vincennes and Boulogne),[15] its different landscape images at Parc Monceau and Les Buttes-Chaumont, the different functions of the Tuileries and the Champs de Mars, the different opportunities of the Luxembourg gardens and Père Lachaise, so contemporary Paris has rightly scattered its new work around different social areas, (to some extent) in different formats, and certainly in different scales, everything in fact from La Villette and Citroën through Bercy and Atlantique to Diderot and two new *squares* inaugurated in 1997.[16]

And all these new designs suggest that the idea of the park seems in practice to suffer no diminution. Even Bernard Tschumi's La Villette acknowledged in theory that a diversity of modes was necessary; this was translated into the double strategy of a ribbon of sunken gardens set below the open surface of the parkland. Later creations seem to capitalize on this diversity and invoke some of it even within their own, singular spaces. The design of Parc Bercy brings together three strikingly different zones (see figs. 2–4).[17] First, there is an open space of mixed gravel and grassland (with some

rather odd bus shelter-like pavilions—are they an ironic allusion to the grid of follies at La Villette or simply meant as refuges from sudden showers, not usually available in gardens like the Luxembourg?); then comes a checkerboard of different and highly cultivated garden types; and finally, what is offered as a separate, romantic landscape (though its play with geometrical forms somewhat belies that claim). The Jardin Atlantique, within a much more limited area than Bercy, also indulges a variety of scenes—indeed, its scenographic inventiveness is one of its successes. The Promenade Plantée, by its very nature, traverses a series of different *quartiers*, and along the route of this former elevated railway line are installed a series of gardens, about which my only reservation is that they do not exploit the potential for different modes fully enough and that the identification of historical garden sites in its vicinity is rather ineffective. What the Promenade Plantée does literally *in extensio* across different social areas Bernard Lassus's unrealized design for the Tuileries proposed vertically in historical palimpsest: different gardens laid bare, stacked one above the other and culminating in a contemporary layer along the Seine.[18]

2. Parc Bercy, a view from the Palais Omnisports through the open zone.

The group of Parisian sites on which this essay focuses includes parks and gardens, a deliberate choice because the two forms or types are intricately linked. Indeed, Parc Bercy contains within itself—as do many other earlier parks as different as Regent's Park in London or Bagatelle outside Paris—actual gardens. The modern urban park, of course, evolved from smaller and more concentrated aristocratic domains of the late seventeenth century onward. And these domains—whether Tuileries, Luxembourg, Monceau—were all gardens, which gave a distinctly gardenist flavor to the emerging concept of the public park. When brand new public parks *per se* were later established, especially under the Second Empire, it was again a variety of gardenist models and strategies that prevailed: whether in London-type squares, avenues of trees along boulevards, the picturesque scenes of Buttes-Chaumont, or the extended shrubbery or wilderness walks of the new Bois de Boulogne. The idea of the garden, therefore, quite properly haunts

the Parisian park and cannot be gainsaid in considering its modern designs.

Yet this very mode has been most often attacked by the modern park designer. The German Peter Latz seems happy enough to invoke the garden.[19] But Bernard Tschumi, of course, despairing of what he termed the "obligation" to provide gardens, repressed them quite literally, burying them in a serpentine meander below eye level at La Villette. The resurgence of the garden in other new parks —Bercy, above all, with its patchwork of different garden types, the sunken gardens at Citroën, the wonderful bravura appearance of the Diderot gardens in the labyrinthine fastness of La Défense (see fig. 10)—all these suggest that the garden has not only its advocates but also has telling contributions to make to the park scene.

What are these gardenist contributions that may be realized in parks without necessarily establishing a garden *tout court*? There is, of course, above all the contribution made by planting, especially

3. Parc Bercy, a view inside the zone of different garden parterres.

flowers; though rejected by many designers,[20] this effect obviously provides many opportunities: fragrance, color, strong seasonal emphases, close-up encounters with natural material (even if it has come from municipal greenhouses). In the large scale at which plant materials were introduced by Haussmann's associates, they also add strong architectural elements in large, open areas as well as equally eloquent reminders of new horticultural technology (this was realized and applauded by William Robinson).[21] Here we have to note that, to judge by the current conditions of both the "obligatory" sunken gardens at La Villette and parts of Parc Citroën, horticultural maintenance is not as accomplished as it was under Adolphe Alphand and Pierre Barillet-Deschamps.[22] Perhaps the Promenade Plantée, the garden parts of Bercy, and the Jardin Diderot will give the lie to that inefficacy at other parks.

Further, the idea of the garden offers to the park the solicitations of intimacy and protection that come with the overall enclosure that is always implied in garden worlds, and their inevitable subdivisions, compartments that provide seclusions within the larger open spaces. This is especially achieved at Parc André-Citroën, both in the series of terraced and sunken gardens and around the smaller greenhouses; whereas La Villette largely eschews such sheltered and private spaces.

Gardens have also always implied completeness: partly by their being self-contained and so seemingly self-sufficient, partly because horticultural gardens have always equally implied the recovery of the plenitude of lost Eden through their conspectus of as many available materials and formulations as possible. It is as if the idea of the Jardin des Plantes, long a conservatory and laboratory of horticultural species, were spreading itself around the French capital; since the Jardin des Plantes had from the seventeenth century always elicited admiration also for its variety of formal zones (a diversity of habitats), its claims to be a model of com-

4. Parc Bercy, a view in the third, romantic sector.

pleteness were further urged. Both Parc Citroën, with its range of different habitats (inside and outside), and Parc Bercy, with its deliberate anthology of garden types, emphasize this effort at completeness or (at least) broad diversity. The Promenade Plantée, as its name implies, makes a feature of this gardenesque element in the surprising situation of an elevated walk (fig. 5) through the Twelfth Arrondissement. The idea of the garden is therefore, by virtue of its richness and variety, an important element in these modern parkscapes, even endorsing in its own way the versatility of the park idea itself.

"NI FRANÇAIS, NI ANGLAIS"

The poster that announced the opening of Parc André-Citroën in the early 1990s claimed it was neither French nor English.[23] This was a trifle disingenuous and misleading, the municipality sporting a modernist heart upon its sleeve. But it none-

theless acknowledged the need and the desire to get beyond a habitual and long-standing historical and historiographical cliché, that garden designs just came in two modes (French formal and English informal). In the early nineteenth century Gabriel Thouin had provided one of the more dramatic statements of this choice when he grafted onto the familiar ground plan of Versailles a virtuoso display of various picturesque, or *à l'anglaise*, modes.[24] The persistence of this view, even when claiming to be rejected in the Citroën poster, is tenacious and hugely limiting. For example, Christophe Girot in Rotterdam spoke of "the fundamental and age-old rift between the Latin tradition and what we would call the Nordic tradition . . . between the Anglo-Chinese style and the baroque or rationalist style."[25] Beyond observing once again how extraordinarily maladroit some designers can be with historical pronouncements, there is an urgent need to recognize that the styles of Le Nôtre (so-called formal) and Lancelot Brown (so-called informal)

5. Looking along the Promenade Plantée.

are not antithetical, nor do they constitute what Girot calls a "rift." Nor is one more "natural" than another; both present or represent nature in certain distinctive ways. Both are culturally determined forms that serve different purposes at different times, places, and localities, and these can be endlessly adapted for new occasions. The transformation of the Bois de Boulogne under Baron Haussmann, which effected a radical change from a grid of straight lines to a whirligig of paths and carriage drives, may have played upon the opposition of the two styles, which is certainly the meager narrative into which many historians choose to fit them; we would do better to see them as alternatives aimed at different social and political agendas.

At several of the new Parisian parks, the invocation of different forms is more than a recognition of historical possibilities. Anthony Vidler has noted that La Villette recalls—in fact rather starkly—the old historical opposition between a French grid of fixed points played off against a me-

andering ribbon of sunken gardens where sometimes, though not always, irregular planting is adopted.[26] Rather than mingling its modes, Parc Bercy opts for a clear triadic demarcation: open, modern urban spaces; regular and profuse garden plots largely in vernacular style; and a supposedly romantic, nineteenth-century zone. But these gestures toward historical precedent would merely be obvious, if that was all they achieved. In fact, the historicist diversity reveals a new resourcefulness in representing the natural world for cultural consumption, which is after all one of the essential roles of park-making and park use. Whatever the ostensible or unconscious attraction of people to parks and gardens in the city, their time in such sites presents them with intimations or an epitome of larger worlds beyond the park pale, including the whole organic and inorganic universe along with old and new cultural takes or perspectives on it.

Parc André-Citroën, despite its poster's claim,

marries a regular ground plan *à la française* to plantings that reflect both modern municipal horticultural traditions (including the technology of greenhouses) and an ecologist's dreamworld of random pioneer growth on abandoned industrial sites (of the sort that Peter Latz has encouraged for the abandoned steelworks at Duisburg in the Ruhr.[27] We must surely be skeptical of disclaimers of precedence here: the ground plan of Citroën (fig. 6), in fact, bears an uncanny resemblance to Louis XIV's Marly, with the lateral lines of greenhouses or *serres* on the north and the southern sequence of nymphaea replacing Marly's guesthouses and the two large conservatories, Louis XIV's central mansion.[28]

The Garden of Movement by another Citroën designer, Gilles Clément, explores a different tradition. It establishes one end of a scale of representing plant life ("natural") that at the other end involves the technology of the greenhouses and in between the studied planting of the black and white gardens and the hanging gardens of another sector. Of the Garden of Movement, notionally the most radical element of the Citroën park, Clément claims that it is unique, "ne figurant dans aucune tradition parisienne."[29] Maybe. Yet we must note that what is involved is the transposition of random plant growth on urban wasteland into a designed site, where visitors are invited to see its cultural significance in a brave new context of ecological sensitivity.

NATURE AND CULTURE

Garden history should ideally chronicle and explain endless permutations of a dialogue between what we economically term nature and culture. Maybe the Citroën poster wanted to gesture toward that possibility. Such a history would set out the story of a whole matrix of social, economic, and political motives and techniques working to shape for a given time and place an acceptable, even idealized, version of that particular world view (we have after all learned effectively to tell such a story for Versailles). It's an approach that fleshes out in detailed analyses what Dean Joseph Hudnut of Harvard's Graduate School of Design only suggested of garden-makers in his *Architecture and the Spirit of Man*, that "they looked into the heart of their time and made it visible."[30]

The rhetoric of the Citroën poster may have smacked too much of the old historiography. Yet the park itself (fig. 7) used different dispositions of material and space, not for their own formal sakes, but so as to highlight a series of collaborations between natural materials—plants, water, earth (considered especially as platform), sky (reflected in pools)—and human technology (computerized fountain play; greenhouses; habitat creation; color coding and other taxonomies). Nature was offered "en mouvement"—as constantly changing,[31] in process, and of course moved or blown by the winds, lit by the changing lights of hour, day, and season: haptic as well as optic.

Parc Bercy also offers, in its central section especially, a series of nine different "parterres" or dialogues between art and nature—not just in formal terms either (they are largely "formal" in the old, bad sense of geometrical), but in use and application: a children's garden, an orchard, a rose garden, "one for so on and so on."[32] Bercy also offers a succession of spaces handled in different ways so that one form (those French parterres) is not privileged over the next, which its designer calls "romantic, because you find all the elements of a romantic garden: the island, the canal, the lake, the hill, etc."[33]

In contrast, La Villette does not succeed in communicating any real dialogue between different treatments of the natural world (this is due in part to the absurdly small energies, cash, and apparently interest that went into the planting of the park). Nor, in fact, does their juxtaposition work on the ground as much as it does in plan. Tschumi was egregiously cavalier with trying to communicate his ideas in gardenist or landscape architectural forms, wishing to "[unsettle . . .] both memory and context"; as Anthony Vidler has argued, Tschumi's references to earlier modes of representing the "Nature and Art" dialogue are simply "reused as empty signs of their patrimony."[34] We might compare that emptiness with the fullness of reference in the proposal for the reconstitution of the Tuileries site, submitted by Bernard Lassus: he reused the different historical versions of the "nature-art" dialogue in a palimpsestial scheme that would have revealed the changing circumstances of the event that constitutes the Tuileries today.[35]

THE REINVENTION OF LOCALITY

The failure of that dialogue or dialogues between nature and culture at La Villette has various explanations. One is that it is clearly not something that interested the modernist agenda of the designer. As Beth Meyer cogently demonstrated, Tschumi chose to be willfully ignorant of "French park traditions" and his proposal suffered accordingly "from

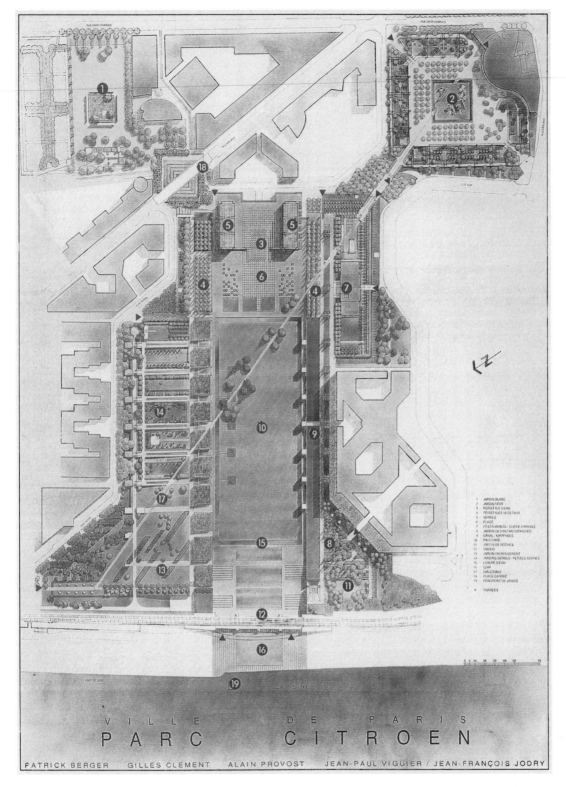

6. Plan of Parc André-Citroën. (1) the White Garden; (2) the Black Garden; (5) the two big conservatories with the fountain plaza (3) between them; (14) the serial gardens with the small greenhouses above; (9) the sequence of nymphaea; (13) the Jardin en Mouvement.

7. Parc André-Citroën, a view past the small greenhouses.

the burden of premature historicity."[36] And among those "park traditions" we should include the Revolutionary invention of symbolic public spaces, including the neutralization of potent icons of the ancien régime, overwriting without obliterating them; the Revolutionary creation, for instance, of Festivals of Federation, where large spaces, decorated with admonitory monuments and architectural fabriques, were left open for crowds to assemble, bears a striking resemblance to both the rhetoric and the spatial intentions of La Villette.[37]

A less historical explanation of why, in particular, the nature-art dialogue fails to take off at La Villette is that nothing locally determined the form, structure, and outcome of that dialogue: it is wholly decontextualized (as Tschumi himself proudly declares).[38] The international modernism of the proposal works effectively and endemically to preempt any localization of the design; like its grid of red follies, it extends everywhere and anywhere, literally and necessarily grounded by the specific site, but in effect oblivious of context or of any con-

stituent elements of the place and its topography. Yet at La Villette, we are surrounded by a conglomeration of large specialist buildings, the remains of a fine iron hall, and other relics of the abattoir on which Tschumi essentially turns his back or to which he simply attaches a fragment of a folly (figs. 8, 9). Meanwhile, the noise and sight of the *périphérique* are oppressively insistent around the perimeter of the park. The splendid opportunities of the Canal de l'Ourcq that runs directly through La Villette and that was a contribution of Napoleon I to Parisian infrastructure are again simply not seized and made part of the parkscape experience.[39]

Landscape architecture is, however, above all else grounded. Its sites are rooted and located, and that locality—either in itself or in the reinventions of it by a designer—must feature in the experience of the place. Contemporary landscape architecture, heaven knows, is not afraid of invention; the problem is that its skills and creativity with invention are not focused on locality, on what used

8. Looking across Parc de la Villette.

to be called "genius of place." All of the new Paris parks, for instance, have reoccupied former industrial sites, with varying degrees of success in acknowledging their vestigial histories: La Villette retains at least the iron halls of the former abattoirs: Bercy, the old streets and trolley lines of the Dépôts de Vin; the Promenade Plantée, perched on its viaduct, recalls constantly the former railway line; the Jardin Atlantique is suspended above the platforms and tracks of Gare Montparnasse. Perhaps Citroën alone neglects to absorb and reflect its urban past; only its name, along with a bust of the eponymous industrialist, recall the former car factory on the site.

Now Augustin Berque has argued in *Être humains sur la terre* that "en lui-même, le génie du lieu n'existe pas."[40] He means that *genius loci* does not exist or adhere endemically in the physical elements of a given place; actually he is quite wrong, since GIS (Geographic Information Systems) mapping of the various physical elements of a site establishes a repertoire of facts of a given place

that constitute beyond a doubt part of its "genius" or "special character and quality."[41] So, too, do any archaeological remains, like the industrial vestiges—trolley lines at Bercy, the iron hall at La Villette—that still feature in Parisian sites. But, as Berque's own wider discussion demonstrates, genius of place can exist, drawn out of that trajective energy by which a person or subject experiences and responds to place or object. In this "trajective enterprise" (as Berque terms it),[42] the reinvention of locality first by the designer and then by its inhabitant or visitors plays a major role.

As I have already hinted, location has its own, at least inert, function in Parisian park-making. On the green map of Paris (see fig. 1), the parks of Citroën and La Villette carefully respond to the historical circumstances of their location: one provides for a newly established lower middle-class residential district in the west of Paris, and is clearly very appealing to that audience; the other serving, in the first place, visitors to a cluster of invented events (music conservatory, science and in-

9. Parc de la Villette, one of the series of sunken gardens.

dustry museum, a village of "happenings") as well perhaps as local inhabitants, if fewer and poorer, and far less responsive to the opportunities which the park offers. These two parks may be read in their demographic appeal and siting as latter-day equivalents—within the *périphérique*—of the Bois de Boulogne to the west and the Bois de Vincennes to the east beyond it. As such they participate in locality and topography largely through the determination of the planning authorities rather than via their designers.

Citroën responds better to its immediate locality than La Villette. The views out of Citroën are of apartments and Seine riverscape, the banks of which—as the final phase of construction—are being joined underneath the railway to the park meadow; the edges of the park penetrate the surrounding housing areas by the geometrical protrusions of its ground plan; at least in one corner near the White Garden, elements of *quartier* life, includ-

ing bar and bistro, mingle with the designed spaces of the gardens.

Parc Bercy, as analyzed by one of its designers, Bernard Huet, responds to its site in at least two ways. Unlike the Palais Omnisport on which it is aligned but which is itself sited diagonally to the prevailing street pattern, Parc Bercy honors the former pattern of streets as well as the remaining old treescape in a double grid of space (city) and time (tree growth): "We wanted to keep the memory of the past activity. This is very interesting because it is a base, a piece of urban archaeology, and the idea of the park was archaeology. Archaeology made a grid, a reference grid."[43] Yet these gestures are timid, even slight, and curiously insufficient, inadequately creative in the way that Lassus "invented" patrimony and opportunities for us to apprehend it at both the Tuileries and, more emphatically, Jardin des Retours at Rochefort-sur-Mer.[44]

Both Provost's terraced garden near La Défense

10. Looking up the Jardin Diderot at La Défense, sector 3.

(fig. 10) and the Jardin Atlantique at Montparnasse respond to locality more energetically and more creatively. The former does this simply enough, with its urban site, centered among the ponderous highrise buildings, and its consequent play with scale and ground, including a roller-coaster formatting of the descents—aquatic, vegetative, and pedestrian—which recall with some wit the escalator-served, multileveled complex of La Défense itself. The Atlantique reinvents a locality that certainly acknowledges its modern site above the platforms of the Gare Montparnasse (equivalent, perhaps, to the deliberate inclusion, because of their modernity, of the railway lines at the Buttes-Chaumont in the nineteenth century). But it also invents a "locality" for itself, which is not of that place but rather belongs to the destination of those who take trains from the station below to the Atlantic Coast.

PAYS D'ILLUSIONS ONCE AGAIN

The Jardin Atlantique (figs. 11, 12) makes a strong case not just for a sufficient attention to locality, but for the reinvention of locality by the designer.[45] It urges some renewed attention to how contemporary Parisian parks recapitulate and renew an important tradition of French garden and park-making, namely, of making their sites a theater of pastimes, a *pays d'illusions*.

It might be argued that Carmontelle's famous justification or explanation of the Jardin Monceau in 1779, with its invocation of theatrical scenery for the promotion of make-believe in gardens, was *sui generis* and is hardly applicable to later public parks. Yet we do not have to buy into Carmontelle's design details and effects to see that all works of landscape architecture can be territories of illusion,[46] and that their success should be judged precisely in terms of their achievement of sufficient

11. Jardin Atlantique, the "waves" breaking on the "shore."

illusions to satisfy a given clientele (at a given time and place). After all, a landscape architect is—as Denise Levertov has defined the poet—somebody "with a genius for lying and an adoration of the truth."[47]

The Jardin Monceau apparently mixed its truths and its feigning to the satisfaction of the pre-Revolutionary elite; its later, democratic, yet still somewhat elitist public version, Parc Monceau, lovingly celebrated as a successful public enclave by the Impressionists, clearly discovered a fresh balance between its illusions and truths. So did yet another, nineteenth-century park, the Buttes-Chaumont, where Barillet-Deschamps and Adolphe Alphand produced a wonderful illusionist playground of romantic scenery and modern imagery, a virtual reality which Louis Aragon in 1926 made the setting for his meditation on "le bizarre de l'homme." Les Buttes-Chaumont provoked him to ask, "pourait-il [le bizarre] tenir dans ces deux syllabes: jardin?"[48] Admittedly, we have no adequate evidence of how Carmontelle's

Jardin Monceau really worked its magic upon visitors—we desperately need a reception history of garden art, of how gardens and parks have been experienced (we have more materials for the Buttes-Chaumont, but even here its "reception," as opposed to its design intentions, has been insufficiently explored).

The full potential of modern parks needs to draw upon and refurbish the traditions of *pays d'illusions* and *terrain du bizarre*. And it is not as if these modern parks entirely eschew the repertoire of effects —follies, fountains, promenades—that sustained these traditions in earlier landscape architecture. Indeed, some contemporary parks seem to have their eye, albeit warily, upon the possibility of illusionary spaces. Bercy's own version of a magic land in the third segment of the park is not yet ripe for proper assessment. At Citroën, the ambition to create what Carmontelle called "tous les temps et tous les lieux" for plants and water effects is at once adventurous and clumsy. Its computer-operated fountain slope at Citroën is fun and constantly in-

12. Jardin Atlantique, a sideways view (behind the scenes) of some of the "cliffs."

triguing, the series of nymphaea along the southern side of the meadow are damp and desolate, an opportunity missed to set out some further commentary on the diversities of water throughout the park. This aquatic schemata is apparently meant to connect with a repertoire of horticultural effects that present (or re-present), like any Jardin des Plantes, the riches of the natural world—as its plant designer puts it in the subtitle of his book, "de la vallée au parc."[49] To start with, the greenhouses are a big disappointment—ill-stocked and neglecting the real opportunities of the conservatory world of illusion, which the late nineteenth century so wonderfully exploited. The sectors of the so-called serial gardens are elaborately labeled for daytime and nighttime reading (the daylight ones almost illegible). The whole of botanical creation, with special focus on plants growing in industrial wasteland sites, is classified in a taxonomy at once elaborate, ingenious, and mostly inaccessible without the elaborate commentary that Clément has provided. His explanations are frequently presented "d'un point de vue conceptual,"[50] with links between different metals, colors, senses, planets, days of the week, and "nombres atomiques," which his book (but not the garden) sets out in tabular format as well as descriptive prose. It claims to be an enriching matrix. Certainly on many visits before I read Clément's book, the significance of its intricacies escaped me; moreover, the maintenance—specifically and very interestingly claimed as innovative and experimental—was clearly not responding to the challenges posed. Should the scheme and system indeed prove accessible, it promises at least a means of annexing (as Aragon proposed) the physical examination of plantings to a visitor's metaphysical pleasures. But Michel Racine in his guidebook to French gardens is surely right to be skeptical about the need to master the complex lessons of the gardens, commenting rather dryly that "Il ne parait pas indispensable d'en approfondir les thèmes 'pédagogiques.' "[51]

The follies and sunken ribbon of gardens at La Villette should in theory be a true *pays d'illusions*, a world where the bizarre greets any ascent or descent from the green sward of the park surface, smooth and uneventful except where, as on some unexplored archaeological site, protrudes the tricycle wheel of some giant race long since vanished from the earth. But the follies (with occasional exceptions) do not function, their emptiness ironically a commentary on the deliberate voiding of park typology. Apart from the *chambre sonore*, the sunken spaces or what Tschumi called "obligatory gardens" where cultural invention, not just natural re-creation, could be encouraged, are ill-maintained. Only the mirror garden, perhaps, detains one for long, and yet its invention flags because of the insufficient natural growth that would make its fictive spaces more of a mystery.

It is the design of the Jardin Atlantique that recalls us best to the traditional idea of gardens as sites of representation, presenting over again in gardenist terms their creators' understanding of both its specific locality and worlds beyond it (maybe visually glimpsed—the city that surrounds it, for example—or recovered only in the wider and more generous spaces of the imagination, the distant seaside). The Jardin Atlantique succeeds, in part, because it does not fight shy of making the most of its proposed moves. Its self-consciousness (as, for that matter, that of the Jardin Diderot) directs visitors' attention to its invented locality: the curving, zanily tilted boardwalk, with the "waves" moving across the open spaces of the lawn toward it; the whole repertoire of play in all the senses of that word—from the games of children's corner to the sea-blue tennis courts; from the meandering walks "behind the cliffs," with opportunities to look down onto the "beaches" below, to the two very scenographic, stagelike presentations of cliffs and cavelike entrances. It recalls perhaps a fantasy seaside for Jacques Tati's Monsieur Hulot, slightly tilted toward the absurd as he was himself, eccentric and peeked by curiosity. Yet if it were all just a fantasyland, it would pall fairly quickly (maybe just in time to catch a train below and reach the real thing); but in fact, with its stolid perimeter of housing, its arenas for sports, its references in the names of allées to the liberation of Paris in 1945, and above all its meteorological station in the center, it locates us strongly enough in a real world— where the rain it raineth everyday, where the wind blows, and the barometer goes up and down. This is a modern, technologically sophisticated locale, a match for the TGV bullet trains in the station beneath, sounds from whose depths percolate up-

ward through the numerous vents accommodated in the floor of these hanging gardens.

Michel Pena and François Brun reinvented this space by contriving in the capital an epitome of the Brittany coast. In the process they have drawn upon many earlier types of Parisian park. Allusions to other places (and to the travel by which they are reached); the provision of a zone of some seclusion within, even suspended above, the busy city; an invented repertoire of seaside planting; homage to technology and our enduring human submission to weather, even if it can now be better predicted; the inherent love of play, of acting, and the need for sufficient stages on which to play out our fantasies or dreamworlds. The Jardin Atlantique is likely to be, for some people, too busy, too inventive, while for others it will hold out the possibility of many exchanges or what Aragon termed "liaisons intimes." If it does indeed succeed, in ways that elements of the parks elsewhere fail to do, this is perhaps because the Jardin Atlantique takes more seriously than they do landscape architecture's dual commitment to both truth and lies.

Notes

1. See Antoine Grumbach, "The Promenades of Paris," *Oppositions* 10 (1977): 51–67; also David H. Pinkney, *Napoleon III and the Rebuilding of Paris* (Princeton: Princeton University Press, 1958).

2. I am indebted for this additional perspective and for relevant reading suggestions (see note 37 below) to Michael Lannutti, a graduate student in my seminar on modern landscape architecture at the University of Pennsylvania. On the grand projects themselves see Jean-François Poirier, "The Grand Projets in Paris," *Daidalos* 49 (1993): 130–37, and Emile J. Biasini, "Les Grands Projets: An Overview," *RSA Journal* (1991): 561–70.

3. I have addressed this atavistic motive in landscape architecture more fully in *Greater Perfections: The Practice of Garden Theory* (Philadelphia: University of Pennsylvania Press, 2000).

4. Two works in particular should be noted at the start: Lodewijk Baljon, *Designing Parks* (Amsterdam: Architechura e Natura Press, 1992) is focused on the various entries for the Concours Prix International: Parc de la Villette of 1982–83; the second is the publication in 1993 of a symposium held in 1992 at Thoth, Rotterdam, *Modern Park Design*, 2nd ed. (Bussum, The Netherlands, 1995). I have relied mainly upon these in establishing the agenda for discussion here.

5. It was Proudhon in *Du principe de l'art* who wrote that "we must transform France into a vast garden," cited by Maria Luisa Marceca, "Reservoir, Circulation, Residue: J. C. A. Alphand, Technological Beauty and the Green City," *Lotus International* 30 (1981): 57–66; see also Michel Vernes, "Genèse et avatars du jardin public," *Monuments*

Historiques (Dec.–Jan. 1987–88), 4–10. On the role of the garden as inspiration or "engine" of contemporary landscape architecture, see also my *Greater Perfections*.

6. "Le sentiment de la nature aux Buttes-Chaumont," *Le Paysan de Paris* (1926: new ed., Paris, 1953). I take Aragon to be insisting upon the need to connect what one sees and what one thinks.

7. *Le Jardin Monceau* (Paris, 1779), 4. And see in this connection my essay on "The Garden as Virtual Reality," in *Das Kunstliche Paradies* (special issue of *Gartenkunst*), ed. Marcus Kohler (1997), 5–14.

8. *Modern Park Design*, 59.

9. Elizabeth K. Meyer criticizes Tschumi's La Villette along such lines, in particular offering the example of the Parc des Buttes-Chaumont as a precedent that Tschumi wholly ignores: see "The Public Park as Avant-Garde (Landscape) Architecture . . . ," *Landscape Journal* 10, no. 1 (1991): 16–26.

10. *Modern Park Design*, 37.

11. Ibid., 38.

12. Ibid., 74.

13. Meyer, "The Public Park," 16.

14. However awkwardly I use the French word *place* to designate square or piazza, and the French adoption of the English word *square* for the feature that Adolphe Alphand made especially his own, small urban segments contrived out of the spaces between the larger geometrical reformulation of Parisian boulevards: see Alphand's *Promenades de Paris* (Paris, 1867; reprinted Princeton: Princeton Architectural Press, 1984), 211–28.

15. See Jean-Michel Derex, *Histoire du Bois de Boulogne: Le bois du roi et la promenade mondaine de Paris* (Paris and Montreal: Harmettan, 1997) and *Histoire du Bois de Vincennes: La foret du roi et les bois du people de Paris* (Paris and Montreal: Harmettan, 1997).

16. They were the Square Dorian (designed by Bernard Lassus) in the XIè Arrondissement and Mail Michel-de-Bourges in the XXè. See Eric Biethy-Rivierre, "Deux petits jardins de plus," *Le Figaro*, 17 July 1997.

17. A plan of this park is illustrated in my *Greater Perfections*, pl. 71.

18. See *The Landscape Approach* of Bernard Lassus (Philadelphia: University of Pennsylvania Press, 1998), 143–49.

19. *Modern Park Design*, 97.

20. See ibid., 66.

21. See my remarks on this in "French Impressionist Gardens and the Ecological Picturesque," *Gardens and the Picturesque* (Cambridge, Mass.: MIT Press, 1992), 276–80, where Robinson's comments are invoked.

22. On this rather neglected figure see Jean-Pierre and Denise LeDantec, *Reading the French Garden* (Cambridge, Mass.: MIT Press, 1990), 153–87.

23. This was reproduced in my *Greater Perfections*, pl. 72.

24. Thouin identifies the various "irregular" forms in this plate (25) as "un Jardin Sylvestre," "un Jardin Champetre," "un Jardin Romantique Chinois," and "un Jardin Romantique Français," thereby showing some determination to categorize the newer forms with some subtlety: see Thouin, *Plans Raisonnés de toutes les espèces de jardins* 3rd ed. (Paris, 1828). But another, less nuanced version of this choice is contained in the ironic and slippery text, to which Michel Conan first directed my attention in the Garden Library at Dumbarton Oaks, namely, the anonymous *Lettre sur les jardins anglais* (Paris, 1775).

25. *Modern Park Design*, 68 (my italics).

26. Anthony Vidler, "Trick/Track," *The Architectural Uncanny* (Cambridge, Mass.: MIT Press, 1994), 101–16.

27. Udo Weilacher, *Between Landscape Architecture and Land Art* (Boston: Birkhauser, 1996), 121–33.

28. One of the Citroën designers, Alain Provost, denied this energetically when I put it to him a few years ago; methinks he did protest too much, but it is not in the interest of designers to gainsay their creativity by acknowledging precedent! For a comparative plan of Marly, see *Views of the Gardens at Marly*, ed. Emmanuel Ducamp (Paris, 1998), pl. 1.

29. See his *Le Jardin en Mouvement de la vallée au parc André Citroën* (Paris, 1994), 66; also for his recent developments of that idea the novel, *Thomas et le voyageur, esquisse du jardin planétaire* (Paris, 1997); also *Le Jardin Planétaire* (Paris: Albin Michel, 1999).

30. *Architecture and the Spirit of Man* (Cambridge, Mass.: Harvard University Press, 1949), 135.

31. Alas, also subject to inadequate planting and maintenance: much of the northern site had to be restored after only a few years, while the bamboo garden at La Villette was also dying at my last visit (1998). So much for process!

32. Bernard Huet, its designer, in *Modern Park Design*, 26–27.

33. Ibid., 27. This third zone at Bercy will perhaps need time for its planting to flourish and become suitably romantic and dense; when last seen (January 2001), the geometry—especially a circular lake and the emphatic grid of paths—works against what is apparently the desired "romantic" effect.

34. On these see Vidler, *Architectual Uncanny*. For Tschumi's remark, see *Cinegram Follie: Le Parc de la Villette* (1987), VII. Tschumi has of course argued that his design invokes signifiers that have no connection with the things signified (ibid., p. VI). The literature on La Villette is, of course, considerable; but see in particular three pieces by Bernard Tschumi, "The La Villette Park Competition," *Princeton Journal of Architecture* 2 (1984): 200–210; *Le Case Vide—La Villette* (London: Architectural Association, 1985); and "Parc de la Villette, Paris," *Architectural Design* 58 (1988): 33–39.

35. Lassus, *The Landscape Approach*, 143–49.

36. See above, note 9.

37. See James A. Leith, *Space and Revolution: Projects for Monuments, Squares and Public Buildings in France, 1789–1799* (Montreal: McGill-Queen's University Press, 1991); also Michel Vernes, "Genèse et avatars du jardin public."

38. *Cinegram Follie*, VII.

39. We might compare the responsive handling of this same canal further along from La Villette where it arrives at the Place Stalingrad, another design by Bernard Huet: see *Modern Park Design*, 21–26.

40. Augustin Berque, *Être humains sur la terre* (Paris, 1997), 187. See my *Greater Perfections* for further discussion of this topic.

41. See Raymond Williams, *Keywords* (New York, 1976), 143.

42. Berque, *Être humains sur la terre*, 26.

43. *Modern Park Design*, 26.

44. For both designs see Lassus, *The Landscape Approach*, 143–49, 131–40.

45. See Dianne Firth, "Jardin Atlantique," *Landscape Australia* 2 (1997): 160–63; and Melissa Maldonado, "Le

Jardin Atlantique," *Studies in the History of Gardens and Designed Landscapes* 20 (2000): 297–312.

46. The invocation of this phrase for the title of a groundbreaking exhibition in Paris in 1977, *Jardins en France, 1760–1820: Pays d'illusion, Terre d'expériences*, devoted largely to the eighteenth-century French garden, has rather obscured its relevance to garden-making of other periods.

47. This is an old *topos*: cf. Touchstone in Shakespeare's *As You Like It*, who volunteers that "the truest poetry is the most feigning [i.e., pretending]."

48. *Le Paysan de Paris* (note 6), 147.

49. Clément, *Le Jardin en Mouvement*.

50. Ibid., 71.

51. Michel Racine, *Guide sur les jardins de France* (Arles: Actes Sud, 1997), 201–2.

12. Stories for Tomorrow

BERNARD LASSUS

The need to invent, which manifested itself clearly at the beginning of the twentieth century and is just as imperative today, led the self-described Modernists to advocate a break with the past in order to create something new. This distantly echoes the famous expression of Maximilien Robespierre: "To fulfill your mission, you must do precisely the opposite of what existed before you."[1] Only this perilous rupture would allow the necessary leap to true innovation. Thus it was that Adolf Loos (1870–1933), considered by Henry-Russell Hitchcook to be one of the four most important architects of the first Modernist generation (along with Perret, Frank Lloyd Wright, and Peter Behrens), wrote in "Ornement et crime": "We have vanquished ornament, we have learned to do without it; soon the city roads will be radiant like great white walls, the city of the twentieth century will be dazzling and naked like Sion, the Holy City, capital of Heaven."[2]

Some years later, Fernand Léger suggested that the Modernist architects who had advocated "architecture for the masses" deprived the inhabitants of a sensory presence through the absence of art, as they did not simultaneously use all of the plastic arts, such as drawing, color, contour, and representation, and so on.[3] He himself, on all too rare occasions, intervened in building designs with splashes of solid color. Le Corbusier, who was influenced by him, examined color collections for paint manufacturers,[4] who, owing to the introduction of industrial techniques in their production and the absence of demand, and to facilitate the rotation of their stock, reduced their inventories of paint for construction to less than a dozen colors.

Loos further explained in "Ornement et crime" that "Modern man is, in our society, still an isolated individual, a maverick, an aristocrat. He respects the ornaments often produced in previous eras. He respects individuals' tastes as well as those of peoples who have not yet attained our degree of culture. But, for his part, he no longer needs ornaments and knows that a man of our times cannot create any that are practicable."[5] Before considering why the rejection of ornamentation calls into question the direction of landscape architecture, it must be noted how much Loos's remarks distance themselves from the discipline of history and above all from those for whom he is supposed to work and who might, in his own words, not yet have attained his degree of culture.

In the 1960s André Hermant explained the absence of ornamentation, namely, an appearance mobilized in the formal expression of the function: "One of the essential characteristics of the 'natural architectural act' is what one might call the 'self-conditioning' of the shape: a plant, a stalk of wheat for example, organizes itself while growing, so that at each moment its shape and its structure correspond to the fundamental demands of strength, functioning, and economy. Objects and buildings do not evolve through growth but from the outset, they have a similar equilibrium between their function, structure, and shape that precisely suits the fundamental demands of functioning and economy."[6] This similarity between the object and the building, which confirms the isolation of the latter, recalls an interview with Pierre Dreyfus, president of the Renault factories, who told me that they had called upon Le Corbusier to study the production of houses compared with that of automobiles, but that nothing came of this since the substantial investment required could not be absorbed owing to the flexibility of the international labor market. Since then, mobile homes and caravans have multiplied by the hundreds, gathered at the periphery of large cities, where they are making new, permanent homes. In order to be well settled, their inhabitants decorate them and surround them with embellishments, creating gardens of varying sizes.

Attempts to compare a building to an object, identified with the astonishing trend brought about by the establishment of industrial mass production of objects, which makes them available and thus international in nature, seem to offer a useful hypothesis about the absence of garden and landscape art at this point in the Modernist movement. Despite some bold attempts, gardens remained under the direct influence of what was taking place at the same time in architecture, painting, or sculpture; they ran against the very foundation of an art based on emergence, cross-influences, adaptability, and transformation.

Ornamental embellishment allows us to address the problematic of appearance. This can effectively reinforce the shape of the object in the expression of its proper function, so that it can be the same in Rio de Janeiro as in Moscow, simply by changing the air conditioner setting from cool to hot. Conversely, and this is clearly the option that I am exploring, one can use aesthetic devices to open an object to different social and physical contexts, as well as to support the history of places and people's collective imagination. When an object becomes an element of concrete space, it constitutes, along with that place, a reinvented call for new landscapes. One particularly symbolic illustration of this is the camouflaged battleship, anchored amid the forest of masts and cranes of a Swedish port, for many years undiscovered despite its massiveness, because it was covered with a filmy coat of paint with intertwined patterns in black, brown and green, in imitation of a paratrooper's uniform.[7]

Several decades later, the repercussions of the modernist "rejection of embellishment" made it possible to consider as empty the beet fields in the Parisian region on which would then be constructed large urban clusters and then new cities. Little by little, here and there, critics emerged to denounce the completed projects as having little relation to what was commonly called "a city," since they did not even have any "antique monuments."

One of the last major competitions, that of the new town of L'Isle d'Abeau, involved the creation of an urban center with several thousand homes along with several thousand square meters of office space and a park. For this, I proposed the idea that the "monument" of this new urban center be, precisely, the park. This garden would effectively be both a representation and a symbol of what had been there before: the age-old traditions of the peasants' daily life. After having argued, not without difficulty, against plans for apartment buildings on the banks of the pond located on the site, I managed to make the pond one of its principal poles, surrounded by a few meadows framed by hedges and in particular by a large wooded area with freely growing oaks.[8]

Many places appear on old maps with evocative names such as "Hanged man's tree," "Tower of the beautiful German," "Wolf of Virieux," and "Drowned or buried village." In conversations with the townspeople, we learned that very often these names corresponded closely with stories that used to be told at evening gatherings in each of the villages. Therefore, I proposed representations of these stories, each one separate from the others, as the principal theme of the garden and thus suggested that this park, called Garden of the Anterior, become the town's memory—in other words, the "antique monument" of this new urban center (fig. 1). After all, wasn't this oral, poetical rural culture, founded on these lands and extended from generation to generation, its most authentic monument? Although this proposition was selected by the local members of the prize committee, it was challenged by the urbanists of the Ville Nouvelle and was never realized. In 1975 it was premature. As it was in all probability during consultations for the reconstitution of the Tuileries Gardens.[9]

From studies of realizations and the realizations of studies, the approach initiated for the purposes of this competition developed into an inventive analysis. Today I can phrase it thus: this approach consists of moving beyond initial ignorance with the goal of approaching the site in its uniqueness, its history, its possibilities.

First, in order to become immersed, over the course of long visits at varying hours of the day and in all sorts of weather, in the site and its environs, and to absorb, spongelike, everything from the ground to the sky, almost to the point of boredom, I adopted a "floating attention." Little by little seeking preferential points of view, discovering mini-landscapes, the perspectives that connect them, picking out and testing the visual and tac-

1. Bernard Lassus, Garden of the Anterior, L'Isle d'Abeau, 1975.

tile scales, all while plunging into the archives to uncover these hamlets, these tales, these histories; then analyzing the existing traits and discovering in the uses of the spaces what had been covered up by everyday wear and tear, what was in the process of disappearing, and whether it was worthwhile to recall it. We must render visible the traces of new and as yet unidentified practices, making the invisible first visible and then obvious.

Each case is unique and requires specific approaches. Those selected, once clarified and adapted to the situation, can point in new directions.

Isn't the inventive analysis already a rough sketch of the "project"?[10]

The intervention of a landscape designer is no longer aimed at a "bringing to," which was the habitual approach in the era of conquests, from the times of Captain Cook to the Modernists. This era ended with Neil Armstrong's and Buzz Aldrin's first steps on the moon, for in July 1969 we moved, in an instant, from visual conquest to tactile management. Our world is a garden only from the distance of the moon; down here we know that it is more garbage dump or wasteland than garden. Inventive analysis is part of the transformation of approaches to design, stemming from this fundamental change.

Once horizontal conquest becomes outdated, such analysis encourages the emergence of strata of human activity, in other words, of the depth of places. Perpetuated, brought to light, the various elements that create the process are modified in the directions suggested by the analysis. The new elements are progressively woven in, in a nonrepetitive fashion. This approach to landscape architecture leads to a shift in the ordinary evolutionary process of the place.

Isn't it also an introduction to an art of transformation? Today, planting a tree, here, makes it possible for someone, someday, in this space to rest in its fifty-year-old shadow, a cool and dense shadow, haunted by the singing of birds. Of course, one cannot be sure that the tree will still be there, as any number of possible occurrences could lead to its disappearance; but if I do not plant it there, at this moment, then in fifty years no one surely will be able to enjoy its fifty-year-old shadow. If in its first several years, this tree figures in the mind of the passerby in some plan, some conception of the landscape, some perspective, and is identified with that plan, then when it is one hundred years old this same tree will be a world unto itself, while the landscape gardener has been forgotten. That is very satisfying.

In order to stress that this approach to landscape design involves a shift in the process (*inflexion du processus*), I would suggest that a new term, *inflexus*, replace the word "plan," which too often today has the connotation of fixedness and of a "bringing to," linked to the notion of conquest.

This progression prompts me to mention two other formal interventions that might be encountered. The first, which is not usually deemed to be formal, may be summed up, using the example of a highway route, in the question, "Will it cross through this valley or not?" considered as much for the presence of the road as for the digging, the creation of embankments, and the occasional works of art added. The decision to be made will evidently carry the consequence of the valley being formally changed or not. The second (if it has been decided that the route will cross through this valley) question will be, "How will it cross through?" Both the decision to cross and the treatment of the crossing in the end carry important formal implications to the landscape design. But one must not think, as it is all too common, that a decision to impose the route through the valley simply eliminates the impossibility of doing so.

Now, from this high panoramic viewpoint, looking about, recalling the scent of the sunwarmed grass, I recognize this sloping meadow in the cold light that surprised me as I left the soft shadow of the woods, refined by numerous reflections of light from leaf to leaf.

Divided up by these memories, the landscape becomes intertwined with the already surveyed gardens.

Returning for a moment to the measurable, it is necessary to pay attention to the water, the narrow stream that runs between the meadow and the edge of the wood, which must be drinkable and refreshing to the visitor breathless from his or her walk.

Let us return for a moment to those first steps of Armstrong and Aldrin on the moon and recall that Aldrin is unsure of having really been there, as he writes in his memoirs, because it was not his foot that touched the moon, but only his shoe. For the first time, his discovery of that land was made real only by his fragile tactile tie to the lunar surface. This abrupt return to the garden erased the few remaining blank spaces on our maps.

THE GARDEN OF RETURNS

The execution, year by year and step by step since 1982, of the planned Garden of Returns (Corderie Royale, Rochefort-sur-Mer),[11] heralds an uncommon sort of professional intervention corresponding to the wishes of the municipality, consistent with the means of a city of 28,000, which implies that the realization of the project, spread out over several phases, developed little by little over time. For that matter, it is still not finished. Only in 2001, we completed the entrance to the tourist port. After that, I hope, a greenhouse, with plants brought from other lands to Rochefort-sur-Mer that were unable to acclimatize to conditions in the botanical garden. Still to be constructed are the ships in the completed Naval Battles Labyrinth, the marine garden (figs. 2–5).

Let us retrace our steps. In order to formulate my entry to the competition, I obviously went to the city in question, settled in the hotel, and spent three days wandering about the city and the space to be transformed, soaking in the surroundings. Separately, I sent my collaborators and advisers to the spot. I say separately because I wanted each one, whether engineer, landscape artist, ecologist, or architect, to make his own impression of the places and people he encountered, and because, after their various trips, I would come into possession of many

2. The Garden of Returns, Rochefort-sur-Mer, from 1982 onward.

3. The Garden of Returns, the ramp leading into the town planted with tulip trees from Virginia.

4. The Garden of Returns, the rigging area and the river.

5. The Garden of Returns, the "tontines" for transporting plants.

separate pieces of information and many impressions that gave rise to questions leading some collaborators to the Musée de la Marine, others to the archives of the Museum of Natural History, and still others, back to the area in question.

What we learned from these excursions led me to propose the transformation of this military arsenal into a botanical arsenal. After all, if the ships built in Rochefort in the eighteenth century sailed away full of immigrants and provisions, their holds were empty upon return, except for pebbles from the St. Lawrence, to prevent the ships from foundering in storms. Even today, they punctuate the marshes around the city. But after botanists obtained permission from Louis XIV to fill the ships with plants on the return trips, many plants were unloaded and brought to the botanical garden, no longer in existence, to attempt to acclimate them.

One of these plants became quite famous. Brought by the botanist Charles Plumier, it was named by Admiral de la Galissonnière, admiral of the fleet, for his grandfather, the governor of Rochefort, Monsieur Bégon: and thus was born the begonia. Around this plant and what it symbolically represents (hence the name Garden of Returns), our proposition included a plan not only to redesign the surface of the site, but also to direct the city toward a horticultural policy. Today, between Charente and the city, a horticultural production not only of begonias but also of geraniums and fuchsias is growing, which will provide more than a hundred stable jobs.

From the history of the site, I kept the following in the plan:

· the initial state of the land, in other words, the marshes upon which the arsenal and the city were built in the seventeenth century;
· the industrial period when, in front of the Corderie Royale building (which measures 400 meters), the ships' armament was prepared on compacted earth, on which six-ton rolls of rope were transported; and
· the repossession of the land by the typical vegetation of marshes: willow, ash, and other local trees.

The land around the Corderie that had successfully hosted numerous maritime armament activities would now have to support new activities, and so we required a large meadow around the Corderie, which also facilitated a perspective on the whole project and allowed the assembly of anywhere from twenty to thirty thousand people. To have put only a meadow there, such as is often seen about patrimonial buildings in order to pro-

vide a viewpoint for them to be admired, would have amounted to fabricating an old-style unified composition bringing together the various surfaces of riverbanks, meadow, and the building, which would at the same time have suppressed the impressive range of dualities present on the site.

In order to preserve these differences, it seemed to me necessary that the qualities unique to each of the cultural and landscape fragments present on the land—the marshes, the history of industrial naval construction, the exoticism, the freedom—be allowed to function for themselves, that variety be our deliberate choice for the present, as opposed to the homogeneity of a composition.

As there were, for example, clusters of willows, a local tree, along the river, it was necessary then that one might imagine the entire site reconquered by these willows, in order to retrieve the marshes of the past. Similarly, the fact that the marsh reaches right up to the Corderie effectively brings the building into the marsh and thus into the sea. But it was also important to be able to imagine the space covered entirely with compacted, dug-up earth, as was the case during the industrial era under Louis XIV. However, if all of these elements—meadow, willow, marshland, battered earth—had been deliberately adjusted to accommodate one another and associated in a whole, a composition, it would have been impossible to imagine them dissociated, each one independently exhibited.

All of these flaws or faults, introduced deliberately, contribute to as many beginnings of stratifications, each one having a presence, a limitation, some remarkable characteristic in its constituent parts. They correspond either to the concrete surface of the land or to spaces somewhat distanced from it, for example, the sea, the marshes, the exoticism of the plants. Because of this, the visitor is perfectly free to imagine that the entire surface between the Corderie and the Charente was an industrial space, along the lines of the idea we were now considering, or not at all a surface made of compacted earth, but rather paved in an old-fashioned style, which is more likely, in such a way that it would be possible for him to think, based on the paved surfaces we put in place, that the pavement runs even under the meadow. This makes the meadow seem like a carpet that one is tempted to roll up in order to find the rest of the pavement. The inconsistency between two strata is introduced by an overhang that stops the grass with a concrete border, in imitation of the land. Inclined on a slant in relation to the meadow, it produces a dark shadow above the pavement, hiding the end of the paved surface; because it is in this way undefined, the "industrial" surface can extend indefinitely, beneath the meadow.

Another factor was the activity of the royal navy, represented on the one hand in the flag grounds and on the other in the labyrinth of naval battles. The latter, already complete in terms of setup and plant structure, will soon acquire models of the ships built at Rochefort, depicted in France's great naval combats. The former, or pennant ground, consists of two groups of masts raised over a paved surface. One group is shaped like a diamond, in a naval strategic arrangement, and carries the flags that identified the various ships of a squadron, in a hierarchy of blues and whites; the other masts bear the large flags of the naval powers of the seventeenth century, including that of the king of France, magnificently hand-embroidered with gold thread by the students of the Rochefort technical school. From that space, naval communication games may be organized for the public with the rigging area being another part of the garden in which a display of colors could also be exhibited.

At the northernmost part of the Corderie, near the rigging area, lies a landing stage. Stuck in the bank, a concrete block remaining from the last war and now covered over by a wooden construction upon which was heaped about half of the rigging of an old ship, with a faithful reconstruction of its masts (two structures, 26 and 24 meters tall, one beside the other so as not to too closely resemble a ship) and ropes manufactured here: a precise reconstruction of the past, and at the same time, an entertainment for children.

Near these riggings, the plants discovered long ago are exhibited on a wooden binnacle and in concrete *tontines* with conical caps molded after a wicker model, similar to those in which the plants—*Gaultheria procumbens, Mahonia aquifolium, Choisya ternata*, the Canadian *amelanchier, Rhododendron catawbiense, Buddleia globosa, Ampelopsis quinquefolia, Campsis radicans, Lonicera sempervirens, Fuchsia triphyllia*, varieties of begonias— were shipped. Displayed in a precious manner, in other words, their originality restored to them, the plants reveal their present value, reinvented to invite the visitor to imagine the lands from which they were brought to France. For example, among the plants on display is a *Chaemerops humilis* discovered in Japan by the Swedish naturalist Carl Thunberg in the eighteenth century, later learned to have been brought to Japan from northern China.

The reinvention of a place is not restricted to the land surface subject to intervention; if this can sometimes be the case, it is only by chance. The place as created by the inventive analysis is more precisely the site of a crisscrossing and superimposition of entities, the nature and extent of which are extremely variable and which, on the land surface in question, will appear only in parts, their significance impossible to measure only by the area they occupy. In Rochefort, the ocean and overseas lands extend into the port, because of the presence in the city's gardens of the plants brought from those lands by navigators.

THE GARDEN OF OPTICAL BUSHES

If the Garden of Returns begun in 1982 will probably not be "completed" until around 2006, conversely, the execution of the Garden of Optical Bushes created in 1993 for the Niort trade fair was carried out in only a week.[12]

This was an opportunity, not now to enter into a space, but to present a question and a theme of experimentation in the form of an attempt to emphasize the colors and outlines of flowers arranged according to the color spectrum; following the laws of simultaneous color contrast established by Eugène Chevreul, the flowers were juxtaposed with surfaces painted in various shades.

The project was based on the natural spectrum of colors, represented either by a series of painted bands or by bunches of flowers. These were separated by double lines of colors emphasizing the color of the band through their complementary colors, so that these double lines give value to each term of continuity through their discontinuity. Thus I obtained the following series:

red/ yellow+blue / *orange*/ blue+blue violet / *yellow-orange*/ green+red / *light yellow*/ red+violet / *light blue*/ ultramarine+green / *blue*/orange+light blue / *ultramarine* / yellow+red / *violet*

Thus the yellow line reinforces the density of the red by its contrasting value, and the blue line reinforces the intensity of the orange by its complementary contrast. Contrasts of lines (painted boards) and of bunches of flowers, contrasts in the colors of the flowers themselves, contrasts in the painted colors themselves, contrast of material (between paint and flowers), contrasts of natural and painted colors; all of this allowed me to assure that the boards of painted color would set off the colors of the flowers to their advantage.

It was possible to carry out the project in two ways: on the one hand, to use the same type of flowers throughout, for instance tulips; or, and this is the option that I chose, to use flowers of different species for each color. Indeed, it was impossible to find enough flowers of any one species to make bunches of flowers in all of the planned colors. This new variation in the flower species added another contrast, in the shapes of the flowers—the outline of the corolla providing mini-variations of the same shape in a single floral species. However, this softening of the initial constraints still did not allow for the completion of certain color bands with adequate flowers, especially in the range of blues, and so finally the painted strips had to play this role. This added inconvenience turned out to provide a supplementary contrast.

The initial plan was to arrange all of this on a flat surface, which would put the viewer at liberty to observe the contrasts. The introduction of two planes at different heights raised the additional question of the discontinuity between these two levels. I therefore needed to provide a passage from one to the other.

A garden normally makes use of bushes for such passages. Couldn't one imagine that, in its infinity, horizontality could transform into verticality through a simple turning over, since, from a given perspective, parallel horizontal lines do not simply meet horizontally, they climb to the horizon. So I used a slanting mirror that moved the gaze from the first horizontal plane to the second, using the continuity of the geometric lines. I called the obliqueness of the reflected flowers, very striking when one observed the garden without moving, *optical bushes* to call attention to its natural aspect.

The continuity of the three planes was so efficient that visitors did not notice the difference between the real and reflected flowers unless they moved and bent down to try to understand what they were seeing, destroying by their movement the logic of this visual continuity. The ambiguity among the real flowers, real colors, reflected flowers, and reflected colors effectively created a continuity between natural elements and painting, but more than that: by the contrast of the painted lines, the naturalness of the color spectrum effected by the flowers, which could have come into opposition with the naturalness of the flowers, in fact enhanced their colors and the outlines of the corollas.

The ephemeral nature of this garden thus provided an opportunity to demonstrate to an informed public how the use of scientific knowledge allowed the flowers to become even more truly flowers, the colors even more pure, and to break down a taboo: that of combining painted colors with those of flowers.

THE QUARRIES AT CRAZANNES

One of my most recent interventions revealed to me the unexpected role that drawing can play in the course of a project. In southwestern France, on the Atlantic coast, highway A837 connects the city of Saintes to Rochefort-sur-Mer. The Highway Company of Southern France (Autoroutes du Sud de la France, ASF) put me in charge[13] of choosing the locations and then designing two rest areas along this route (figs. 6–8).

For the past ten years, the landscape policy of the national Highway Authority has been to encourage travelers to take rest stops by constructing areas for this purpose. There were two reasons for this: safety of drivers, who stop only rarely and do not generally rest for a long time, and to encourage an interest in seeing the surrounding region, so that visitors will not only stop longer in the rest area, but may also be intrigued by information gathered there and venture further, as tourists, by visiting the region.

The ASF firm gave me an opportunity to demonstrate the role that rest areas can play in a traveler's stop. For example, I proposed that one of the rest areas be located not far from Saintes, near some ancient abandoned quarries overrun with vegetation. They are made up of parallel faults, connected here and there by underground rooms. These successions of dark hallways, deep underground, overrun with trees and numerous hart's-tongues, create a romanticized space that calls to mind *Paul et Virginie* as much as a Steven Spielberg film or the engravings of Hubert Robert.[14]

Initially, the administrators, while the layout of the highway was being worked out, avoided having it cross over the quarries but had it pass along the border of this area, which was popular with local residents, especially children. The establishment of a rest area between the highway and the quarries would theoretically allow drivers to visit them during their stop. But what no one had predicted was that during the construction of the highway, which at this point was sunk about six or seven meters, some rock debris would emerge from the

6. The Crazannes Quarries, Saintes-Rochefort rest area, 1995.

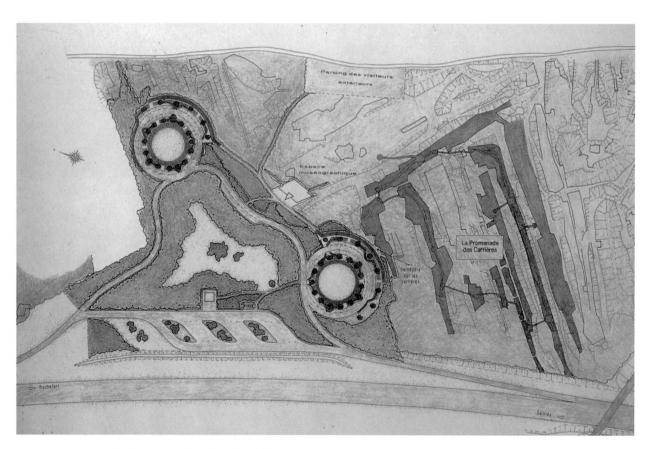

7. The Crazannes Quarries, plan of the rest areas, 1996.

8. The Crazannes Quarries, viewing the pergola way to the quarries, 1996.

rock slopes. The president and several other members of the ASF administration were, therefore, entrusting me with the mission of exploring a mysterious area.

Until now we have tended a bit too much, I believe, to treat landscape improvements along the highways as accompaniments to the route, not unlike the trees lining urban boulevards. As it happens, it seemed necessary to me not to accompany the route with landscape improvements but, conversely, to add some intersections to the latter, so that drivers might come upon a succession of lateral spaces of different characters. Breaking into the rock slopes perpendicularly to the highway, guided by some visible rocks, required the use of dynamiters and large machines, excavators or trucks. We did not know what we would discover; I even considered that we could be led to construct some fake rocks, and, with the help of local quarrymen, we even made one that is still on the site. But no others were furnished, because in the course of our work we brought to light a significant number

of rocks that turned out to be the remains of forgotten old quarries, filled in long ago and covered over with sparse vegetation.

Once this worksite had appeared, the engineers in charge of it asked me to draw the projected end result, so that they could make an estimate of the intervention. It was only grudgingly that I agreed to make these drawings because, not knowing what we would find, I would have preferred to work on a day-to-day basis. Their insistence obliged me, on the basis of the few elements already discovered, to imagine what the site could become.

I drew two elevations, each one concerning more than 500 meters of the side of the road, with advances and retreats. But, and this is why I am recounting all of this, these drawings proved very useful. Indeed, during each of my weekly visits, I needed to indicate to the engineers, project heads, and machine operators if it were necessary to blow up a certain rock, to free up a view, to scrape a certain area of the ground to expose the rock and, in general, if they should continue or stop, and if so how. At that moment, the drawing of the whole project—its principles, its character—entered half-consciously into my mind and allowed me to say, here we must continue to scrape, here we must stop, and so on. The rhythm of the succession of progress, depths, light, dark shadows, the whole plan drawn to scale facilitated each regular contribution; decisions were made without a direct reference to the drawings, but keeping in mind the scales of the different elements represented.

Although not initially anticipated, the execution of this project became at once an announcement of the rest area and of the quarries to be visited. The rest area itself consists of a parking lot for trucks and two round dining areas with latticework which allow travelers to park their cars, then go to dine under the pergola while within sight of their children playing on the grass in the round central area. This setup aims to prevent children from crossing the road and allows them to play within sight of their parents, who can also keep an eye on their car while they eat. Between the two round dining areas, a small museographic space presents a film on the "vegetal" quarries, for the benefit of visitors who cannot spare the time to visit them. In any case, visits to the quarry are quite limited for the time being, because of the fragility of the vegetation that decades ago overran the depths of the faults, in particular of the splendid hart's-tongues that would be destroyed by a large number of visitors.

So I proposed a tour in which the faults to be seen are separated from the ones to be walked in; in other words, one cannot enter into the most fascinating places, but it is possible to walk in the less remarkable sections. This dissociation of the visual and the tactile allows in particular the preservation of the hart's-tongues that cover the ground from the footsteps of visitors. The path further progresses to a wooden footbridge that leads from one panoramic viewpoint to another, inviting visitors to walk hidden from the rock face, to skim and look upon the more remarkable landscapes without being able to crowd around, touch, and possibly ruin them.

The prodigious increase of audiovisual techniques has eliminated the visual primacy of the countryside, stemming from the time of its conquest and since perpetuated by academic discourse. This development of the visual makes it absolutely necessary that we renew and reinvent sensory relationships with the real. I shall not concern myself here with the current debate between those who oppose real, in the sense of tangible, to

virtual and those who think of the virtual as not opposed to concrete but as a vector of the creation of reality.

The landscape required today by the representatives of local interests is surely a substitute for "tomorrow's songs," for a loss of territorial sense in various forms. This may have come about through the abandonment of the countryside or via the dizziness of virtuality, which involves no longer being content with being "from there," which certain people today passionately proclaim, but with being "really there," whether that is the old "from there" or the new "being there." The fresh emergence of place that this implies can be recovered in the concerns of local interest groups with the word "landscape": this represents a balanced interaction among the tactile, sonorous, olfactory, and the visual that in fact corresponds much better to the notion of ambiance or even of successive ambiances. Rather a new concrete reality than a virtual empire.

(Weren't we thrilled, as children, to sit on our grandmother's knee to hear her terrible stories of children eaten by wolves, or these days by Godzilla, and to feel fear in perfect safety?)

The landscape architect who works for the public at large has, above all, the responsibility to facilitate not only the public's grand gestures but also its everyday life. A mother can push her pram of children in peace in a subtly shaded atmosphere; but at the same time, certain elements, seemingly or at first glance useless, can lead her to wonder, to pass from daydream to imagination, for which the environment provides a medium. This interaction between ambiance and prompts for the imagination, in a concrete space where the facilitation of daily actions is combined with calls to the imagination, requires a name: "proper space" (*l'espace propre*).

Translated by Laura Lemay Nagle
and John Dixon Hunt

Notes

1. "Discourse on the Constitution," 10 May 1793.

2. *L'Esprit nouveau*, 2 (1908), 159–68.

3. Opinions expressed to his students in his studio.

4. Le Corbusier collection, Stic B.

5. *L'Esprit nouveau*.

6. *Découvrir l'architecture*. Conseil de l'Europe S.D.87.

7. See "Stockholm, the Landscape," in Bernard Lassus, *The Landscape Approach* (Philadelphia: University of Pennsylvania Press, 1998), 24.

8. "The Garden of the Anterior," in *The Landscape Ap-*

proach, 110–16. See *Le Jardin de l'Antérieur* (Paris, 1975), edition limited to 300 copies.

9. See *Le Jardin des Tuileries de Bernard Lassus* (London: Coracle Press, 1991).

10. See *The Landscape Approach*, 37–38. See also "Mouvence," in *Cinquante mots pour le paysage* (Paris: Editions la Villette, 1999).

11. See *The Landscape Approach*, 131–41.

12. See ibid., 171–73, especially for color reproductions of this exhibit.

13. Together with M. Jacques Houlet, council member of the ASF.

14. See *The Landscape Approach*, 176–81.

Contributors

MICHEL BARIDON is emeritus professor at the University of Burgundy. His main line of studies is the interrelation between ideas and forms in literature and in the visual arts, with particular emphasis on epistemology and the scientific movement. His publications include *Gibbon et le mythe de Rome: Histoire et idéologie au siècle des Lumières* (1977), *Le Gothique des Lumières* (1991), and *Les Jardins: Paysagistes, jardiniers, poètes* (1998), which won the Essai France Television prize in 1999.

RICHARD CLEARY teaches architectural history in the School of Architecture at the University of Texas at Austin. He is the author of *The Place Royale and Urban Design in the Ancien Régime* (1999) and *Merchant Prince and Master Builder: Edgar J. Kaufmann and Frank Lloyd Wright* (1990).

MICHEL CONAN, director of Studies in Landscape Architecture at Dumbarton Oaks, is a sociologist interested in the cultural history of garden design. He contributed to a renewal of garden history in France during the 1970s with the publication of several reprints of seminal works. He recently published the *Dictionnaire historique de l'art des jardins* (1997), edited two Dumbarton Oaks symposia, *Perspectives on Garden History* (1999) and *Environmentalism and Landscape Architecture* (2000), and contributed to the catalogue of the 2000 exhibition at the National Gallery, Washington, D.C., *The Triumph of the Baroque*.

JOSEPH DISPONZIO teaches landscape architecture in the Harvard Graduate School of Design. Formerly he worked for the New York City Department of Parks and Recreation. A registered landscape architect in New York and Connecticut, he holds an M.L.A. from the University of

Virginia and a Ph.D. from Columbia University. His research interests include eighteenth- and nineteenth-century garden theory, the intellectual origins of landscape architecture as a distinct profession, and contemporary European landscape practice and thought.

GEORGE DODDS is a professor of the history and theory of architecture at the University of Tennessee, having obtained his B.Arch. and B.S. degrees from the University of Detroit and his M.Arch. and Ph.D. in architecture from the University of Pennsylvania. He has practiced as an architect in Detroit, Washington, D.C., and Philadelphia and taught at various schools including Temple University, where he founded and directed its Summer Program for Architectural Studies. He is currently preparing a monograph on the Philadelphia-based architectural firm of Kieran Timberlake Associates for Princeton Architectural Press and a collection of essays, jointly edited with Robert Tavernor, on *Body and Building* for MIT Press.

CLAIRE GOLDSTEIN received her doctorate in Romance languages from the University of Pennsylvania for a dissertation entitled "Building the *Grand Siècle*: The Context of Literary Transformations from Vaux-le-Vicomte to Versailles (1665–1715)," an interdisciplinary study examining the emergence of French classicism by situating court literature in its historical, material, and cultural context. Her work has appeared in *Romance Review* and *Word & Image*. She teaches French at Miami University of Ohio.

DAVID L. HAYS completed his doctorate in 2000 in the Department of the History of Art, Yale University, with a dissertation on "The Irregular Garden in Late Eighteenth-Century France," which is currently being prepared for publication. He also holds an M.Arch. degree from Princeton University. He was a junior fellow in landscape studies at Dumbarton Oaks in 1997–98, and is now an Assistant Professor of Landscape Architecture at the University of Illinois at Champaign-Urbana. He has published in *Eighteenth-Century Studies*.

F. Hamilton Hazlehurst is emeritus professor of the history of art at Vanderbilt University, where for many years he was chairman of the Department of Fine Arts. He received his Ph.D. from Princeton University and taught at Princeton and the University of Georgia before Vanderbilt. He is the author of monographs on Jacques Boyceau and André Le Nôtre, including *Gardens of Illusion: The Genius of Andre Le Nostre* (1980), which was awarded the Alice Davis Hitchcock award of the Society of Architectural Historians in 1982.

John Dixon Hunt is a professor at the University of Pennsylvania, where he chaired the Department of Landscape Architecture and Regional Planning from 1994 to 2000. He is editor of *Studies in the History of Gardens and Designed Landscapes* and author of many books and articles, including *L'Art du jardin et son histoire* (1992) and most recently *The Picturesque Garden in Europe* (2002), where the French contribution to this phase of garden art is explored. He was director of Studies in Landscape Architecture at Dumbarton Oaks from 1988 to 1991.

Elizabeth Hyde received her Ph.D. in history from Harvard University in 1998. She is the author of several articles on the political culture of flowers, and her book, *Cultivated Power: Flowers, Culture, and Politics in Early Modern France*, is to be published in the Penn Studies in Landscape Architecture series by the University of Pennsylvania Press.

Bernard Lassus, professor at the Ecole Nationale Supérieure des Beaux-Arts, is a distinguished landscape architect whose design work has appeared in various journals and has been collected in *The Landscape Approach* (University of Pennsylvania Press, 1998) and published in other volumes such as *Jardins imaginaires* (1977), *Jeux* (1977), and *Autoroutes et Paysages* (1994). He was an adjunct professor of landscape architecture, teaching elective studios, at the University of Pennsylvania from 1996 to 2000. He directed the doctoral program DEA Jardins, Paysages, Territoires at the Ecole de La Villette, Paris, and was a founding member of the Ecole Nationale Supérieure du Paysage, Versailles.

Yves Luginbühl succeeded Bernard Lassus as the director of the doctoral program DEA Jardins, Paysages, Territoires at the Ecole de la Villette, Paris. He is the author of, among other studies, *Paysages*, and he edited the catalogue *Paysages mediterranéen* (1992), for the World Exhibition at Seville.

Chandra Mukerji is professor of communication, sociology, and science studies at the University of California, San Diego. She is the author of *From Graven Images: Patterns of Modern Materialism* (1983); *A Fragile Power: Science and the State* (1989), which won the Robert K. Merton Award in 1991; and *Territorial Ambitions and the Gardens of Versailles* (1997), which won the 1998 Culture book prize from the American Sociological Association. She coauthored *Rethinking Popular Culture* (1991) with Michael Schudson.

Index

Page references to illustrations appear in italics.